COLORBLIND

Stanford Studies in Middle Eastern and
Islamic Societies and Cultures

COLORBLIND

*Racial Thinking and Cultural Production
in Modern Iran and the Diaspora*

Amy Motlagh

STANFORD UNIVERSITY PRESS
Stanford, California

Stanford University Press
Stanford, California

© 2026 by Amy Motlagh. All rights reserved.

No part of this book may be reproduced or transmitted in any form or by any means, electronic or mechanical, including photocopying and recording, or in any information storage or retrieval system, without the prior written permission of Stanford University Press.

Library of Congress Cataloging-in-Publication Data
Names: Motlagh, Amy, 1976- author
Title: Colorblind : racial thinking and cultural production in modern Iran and the diaspora / Amy Motlagh.
Other titles: Stanford studies in Middle Eastern and Islamic societies and cultures
Description: Stanford, California : Stanford University Press, [2026] | Series: Stanford studies in Middle Eastern and Islamic societies and cultures | Includes bibliographical references and index.
Identifiers: LCCN 2025034917 (print) | LCCN 2025034918 (ebook) | ISBN 9781503636484 cloth | ISBN 9781503646063 paperback | ISBN 9781503646070 ebook
Subjects: LCSH: Iranians—Race identity | National characteristics, Iranian | Group identity—Iran | Black people—Iran | Iran—Race relations | Iran—Intellectual life
Classification: LCC DS268 .M68 2026 (print) | LCC DS268 (ebook)
LC record available at https://lccn.loc.gov/2025034917
LC ebook record available at https://lccn.loc.gov/2025034918

Cover design: Lee Friedman / LF Studio
Cover art: Sara Dolatabadi
Typeset by Newgen in 10.5/14.4 Brill

The authorized representative in the EU for product safety and compliance is: Mare Nostrum Group B.V. | Mauritskade 21D | 1091 GC Amsterdam | The Netherlands | Email address: gpsr@mare-nostrum.co.uk | KVK chamber of commerce number: 96249943

Contents

	Acknowledgments	vii
Introduction	To What Ends Do We Recover (or Discover) Blackness?	1
One	Iranian Aryanism and Racial Thinking	26
Two	Racial Realism	43
Three	The Longing for Black Radical Thought	69
Four	Performing Blackness on Stage and Screen	92
Five	Documenting Race and Iranian Identity	121
Six	Curating Blackness	148
Conclusion	To What Ends Do We Recover the Voices of the Enslaved?	174
	Notes	193
	Bibliography	231
	Index	251

Acknowledgments

I started to collect the material that gave rise to this project when I was a graduate student at Princeton University. A long time elapsed between that time and now. Given the length of that period (more than twenty years!), my thanks are due to many.

First, I need to thank Sherene Seikaly, who gave me the gift of her time, her incisive critical eye, and her enormous generosity in believing that we are forging a new field together. Thank you for the hope and the spirit of equanimity that you model every day.

I would also like to thank Ira Dworkin and Hanan Kholoussy, two colleagues who shared many of my years (2008–2017) at the American University in Cairo (AUC) and read early versions and variants of this work. My thanks both to Ira (in his capacity as associate director of the Center for American Studies and Research [CASAR] at AUC) and to Alex Lubin, then director of CASAR's sister entity at American University in Beirut (AUB), for including me in a series of exchanges between AUC and AUB faculty to discuss how to bring the fields of American Studies and Middle East Studies into more productive dialogue.

At UC Davis, thanks are owed to many. The Bita Daryabari Endowment in Persian Language and Literature at UC Davis brought me back to the US and into an environment where I came into daily contact with racial thinking in the Iranian diaspora. A Center for the Advancement of Multicultural

Perspectives in the Social Sciences and Humanities (CAMPSSAH) writing retreat gave me time and space to jumpstart the project, and also introduced me to the incomparable Elena Abbot, to whom I am so grateful. A UC Davis Faculty Development grant gave me a course release at a key moment. The Davis Humanities Institute at UC Davis provided another course release and the feedback of wonderful, incredibly smart colleagues (thank you, especially, to Lucy Corin, Erin Grey, and Ben Weber). A quarter of sabbatical leave and a Revitalization grant pushed me into the end zone. Among UC Davis colleagues, I have many to thank: Suad Joseph, for mentorship and support; Noah Guynn, for excellent advice at a key moment; Cheri Ross for her support and generosity; Jocelyn Sharlet for sympathy, support, and friendship. Thanks also to Talinn Grigor; to Bettina Ng'weno and the Mellon Indian Ocean Initiative at UC Davis; to Michael Subialka, for tea and sympathy; and to my COM and ME/SA colleagues all.

Thank you to Persis Karim and Nasrin Rahimieh for mentorship and the opportunity to share this work in its early stages. Thank you also to Ahmad Karimi-Hakkak, who generously told me at an early stage that this work was important to continue. Many thanks, as always, to Afsaneh Najmabadi, for the example of her brilliance and her refusal to accept the limits of the field as it is; and to Michael Beard, who is always willing to patiently answer questions and think with one about odd topics in Iranian Studies.

Friends inside and outside of academia (and some in between) have succored me during this writing process. Thank you to Kelli Moore for our long friendship and many conversations over the years, and to friends and neighbors in Davis for their encouragement: Sahar Pirmoradian, Mesi Parker, and Shelly Buchanan, and Barbara Zadra and Kent Bradford. My thanks also to KL Halls for accessing the Daneshvar-Stegner correspondence at Stanford when I was unable to do so.

I am deeply impressed by and grateful to a new generation of colleagues—among them, Beeta Baghoolizadeh, Parisa Vaziri, Neda Maghbouleh, Shadee Malaklou, Mira Schwerda, and Belle Cheves—who I've had the pleasure of meeting since I returned to the US in 2017, and whose work is redefining the field of Iranian Studies. Parisa's and Beeta's monographs were published when the first version of this book was already finished, and meant going back and thinking through it again. Their interventions have sharpened my own.

I am grateful to my undergraduate and graduate students in Comparative Literature and Middle East/South Asia Studies at UC Davis for conversations in classes and during office hours that shed light on intellectual problems I was working through in the book. In particular, I want to acknowledge conversations with Laura Catterson, Elina Sadeghian, and Henna Bayat for their insights into diasporic sensibilities around loss of culture.

My thanks as always to Kate Wahl, who read an early pitch of this book in 2017 and has waited patiently as it evolved in the intervening years.

Sincere thanks to Sara Dolatabadi, who generously allowed me to adapt one of her remarkable works of art for the cover of this book.

Although she probably does not remember me, I wish to acknowledge and thank Phyllis Jackson. I took her "Black Woman(ist) Feminisms" class at Pomona College in 1998 and could never look at the world the same way again.

My brother David has been thinking with me sympathetically and compassionately about many of the ideas that found expression in this book for years—our whole lives, really. Thanks, Dave.

I lost my first and most patient interlocutor on Iran during the writing of this book: my father, Hossein Motlagh. This book is dedicated to his memory, and to the memory of two other people who changed my life forever by taking me into theirs: Toni Clark and Larry Thornton.

To Mimi, Lennart, and Mom, who have been the patient, loving, and enduring foundation on which this project was built, my love and endless thanks.

COLORBLIND

Introduction
TO WHAT ENDS DO WE RECOVER (OR DISCOVER) BLACKNESS?

"In the beginning, there was the word...*Persian*."

—Porochista Khakpour

THE 1979 REVOLUTION IN IRAN SENT WAVES OF IRANIANS INTO voluntary or forced exile. They were not altogether cast upon unfamiliar shores, however: because of the educational diaspora that had been created by the Pahlavis' drive to create an educated, modern middle class through foreign education, almost 70,000 Iranians were studying at foreign universities (the vast majority—55,000—in the US) when the revolution broke out in 1978.[1] Iranians who left permanently after the revolution, therefore, often had either spent time abroad themselves or knew someone else who had. Following these established networks, many Iranian immigrants who left in the first wave of immigration during and after the revolution settled in the US, with smaller numbers settling in Europe, Canada, and the UK. In the US, they quickly set about becoming a model minority that was highly integrated into professional and educational realms.

Yet, in their host country, Iranian immigrants were forced to confront a widespread and angry perception that Iran was a country of violent religious fanatics. Bumper stickers with messages like "Kick the Shi'ite out of Khomeini," "Free the Hostages," and "Hey, Iran!" (with a cartoon Mickey Mouse giving the middle finger) proliferated in American suburbs. During the Iran Hostage Crisis (1979–1981), everyday Americans tied yellow ribbons around their trees in a "bring them home" gesture. Even after the crisis ended, they kept their ribbons up in remembrance of an event widely seen as a terrible breach of trust and what would today be understood as an act of terror sanctioned by the new Iranian government. It was considered by many to be a national trauma—a moment when the US could not protect its diplomatic staff and their families abroad—and is still widely regarded as a key component of Ronald Reagan's successful bid to unseat Jimmy Carter in 1980. The crisis was more broadly construed as a sign of American vulnerability in its sprawling empire of democracy.

In light of these circumstances, it was not an easy time to be an Iranian immigrant in the United States. Iranian parents encouraged their children to blend in, to cling fast to the ideas of whiteness and assimilation as the keys to success, and to call themselves "Persian" to dissociate themselves from "Iran," the much-maligned state that was constantly in the news. In *The Brown Album*, a collection of personal essays, Iranian-American novelist Porochista Khakpour evokes the almost sacred quality of this practice. "In the beginning," she writes, "there was the word...*Persian*."[2] Iranians carried this venerated word with them from home into exile and diaspora, much as the Shah of Iran packed a small box of Iranian soil that he put in his pocket before he boarded the plane that would take him into permanent exile in 1979. However theatrical or performative the Shah's gesture, it nonetheless resonated with many. Similarly, Iranian immigrants carried this small word, "Persian," from their imaginative national earth and packed it into their own pockets. It was one of the few things some of them could bring as they fled—a talisman they hoped might protect them and their children in a sometimes hostile new environment.

Why did the word *Persian* have such importance in the diaspora? The question is especially striking when we consider that many of the Iranians using this term were actually not, strictly speaking, members of the ethnic group known in Iran as "Fars" or "Pars" (Persian).[3] Beyond using this word to distance themselves from "Iran" during a time of tense international politics, Iranian-Americans used it to signal a range of socio-cultural investments in their new home. They believed it differentiated them from their Arab neighbors in the Middle East, for example, and associated them with more positive connotations. Unlike the word "Iranian," *Persian* tended to be correlated with luxury goods—carpets, cats, pistachios, rugs, and empire, both ancient and more recent.[4] Perhaps most importantly, they saw the assertion of *Persian* affiliation as a quiet reminder of their racial pedigree while exiled in a nation where understanding of Iran's social and cultural history had been flattened to encompass only the recent political turmoil.[5]

For Iranians in the modern era, "Persian-ness" reflects the purest form of Iranian heritage. It is connected to the national language but also, more importantly, to ancient Iran, which many see as the height of their civilization—a heritage lost to the Arab-Islamic conquest. Indeed, prior to the 1979 Revolution, Iranians had spent most of the previous hundred years distinguishing themselves from Arabs. In the pre-revolutionary Iranian context, the preoccupation with Persian-ness was connected to a process of Aryanist nationalism with roots in the nineteenth century. Drawing on the discoveries of European philologists, intellectuals in Iran during the reign of the Qajars began to imagine a lineage for Iran and Iranians that connected them ethnically, linguistically, and culturally to the ancients. These intellectuals found in the work of European scholars and writers the language to both describe and dissociate themselves from Arab-Islamic culture, which they rejected as backward and primitive. Instead, they embraced the idea of being connected to the Aryan language (and race), which they believed found its fullest expression in ancient, pre-Islamic Persian civilization.

While the practice of insisting on the cultural and racial significance of being "Persian" was clearly not new, the post-1979 diasporic audience for this specific narrative was certainly different and perhaps less receptive. As immigrants abroad, many Iranians insist that the distinction of being connected to the pre-Islamic Persian past is ethno-linguistic rather than racial (or racist). This claim, however, has proved tenuous in a diasporic context where Iranian-Americans are frequently seen by European Americans as non-white. In a diasporic milieu characterized by socio-political hostility and a new and multilayered history of racial discrimination, the narrative of

Persian-ness has taken on new resonance. Finding themselves in an uncomfortable position in an unfamiliar racial hierarchy, Iranian-Americans began to use *Persian* to assert a Middle Eastern form of whiteness.

If Iranians in the nineteenth and twentieth centuries believed themselves to be an ethnic elite (descendants "of the original Aryans")[6], an important nuance to this—and one that Iranian reformist intellectuals capitalized on as they sought to cast off the so-called "yoke of Islam" during this period—was that Aryans were not Arabs. Ipso facto, Islam, an Arab religion, was foreign and inauthentic in Iran. Positioning Iran as the cousin of Europeans rather than the sibling of Arabs thus "dislocate[ed]" Iran from the Middle East, as Reza Zia-Ebrahimi aptly puts it.[7] In this way, intellectuals sought to style Iran as the long-lost relative of Europe who could be welcomed back into the fold of Enlightenment civilization. And in this fashioning of self (to borrow Mohamad Targhi-Tavakoli's term), the racial element is and was a crucial aspect.[8]

Notably, it is only in the last twenty years or so that Iranians living outside of Iran have begun to recognize themselves as part of a "diaspora"—a globally dispersed collectivity displaced by national trauma. *Persian* evokes the same sense of ancient lineage in this contemporary diasporic context, but it is also connected to a performative and fitful form of diasporic nationalism that has changed with successive generations of immigrants and their children.[9] Iranian immigrants who came to the US in the first revolutionary reaction wave were confused at being (in their view) incorrectly racialized as non-white, Arab, and black.[10] They have used the word "Persian" as a stick with which to beat back such misrecognition. Then, in the early part of the new millennium, an additional, new, and different urgency arose in the wake of the 9/11 attacks on the World Trade Center. 9/11 gave new life to American prejudices toward Middle Easterners, Muslims, and anyone thought to resemble them (a Sikh American, for example, was killed in Arizona by someone who mistook his traditional turban for a Muslim marker). In the wake of such a monumental terrorist act, the United States created institutional forms of discrimination that were—at least initially—broadly embraced by a frightened American public that was horrified to be attacked on domestic soil for the first time in over a hundred years.

With the 9/11 aggressors identified as belonging to a group called al-Qaeda, invasions were launched into Afghanistan and, eventually, Iraq. The

Islamicate world and Central Asia, a region with its own distinctive history and culture connected to East and South Asia, were subsumed for rhetorical convenience into the "Middle East," and Iran—which was never out of the American news as a bad guy—found itself the neighbor of two countries invaded by the US. Even though Iran had played no role in the 9/11 attacks, it became part of the "axis of evil" identified by George W. Bush as the imminent target of American military power. More than ever, Iranian-Americans found themselves conflated with the home-country neighbors they had long tried to distinguish themselves from. They were targeted as part of an ever-enlarging group of Muslim/Middle Eastern/brown Americans who were being pulled aside at airports, glared at on airplanes, and told to "go home."

Iran, of course, had long been part of the geopolitical designation "Middle East"—in American estimations, at least. Yet to the extent that it was part of that category, Iran was the exceptional member of the group. It was blessed with natural resources such as oil as well as a varied topography that included ports and arable land. It had historical ties to East and West that distinguished it (according to Iranians) from its neighbors, and it felt itself positioned in the twentieth century to take its place among the leaders of the world. Its aspirations, however, did not come to pass. And Iranians who were forced to leave Iran with this consciousness of (and/or belief in) their special status as the elite of the Middle East found themselves in degraded positions once in exile.

For many, the exilic condition was either tacitly or explicitly thrust upon them by a threat of violence, incarceration, and/or loss because of their profession, religion, politics, or ethnicity; for others, it was a move to preserve wealth and status. (These motivations were not always mutually exclusive.) The first wave of exile and immigration from Iran was thus largely comprised of a particular type of elite. In subsequent years, the immigrants and causes of dislocation changed, and while the revolution can still be considered the "first cause" of immigration, in the sense that it gave rise to the later economic, educational, and social conditions that cause Iranians to continue to immigrate or seek dual citizenship, Iranian immigrants cite reasons related to educational and professional prospects, as well as social conditions for their children.[11] Indeed, diaspora itself is a term that is associated with a certain type of permanence that did not always fit the character of Iranian immigrant groups, many of whom still hoped to return to Iran in their lifetimes; it did not emerge as a term used by Iranian immigrants or their offspring until the late 1990s. Nonetheless, across generations and immigrant experiences, a sense of ethnic distinction has pervaded the ways that Iranian immigrants have sought to carve out space for themselves in their new homes.

In the US, where they have encountered confusion about their ethnic status and unexpected forms of racialization in diaspora, new alliances and identities among diasporic Iranians are constantly being formed. As sociologist Neda Maghbouleh describes in *The Limits of Whiteness*, Iranians have been racialized in North America in ways that they often reject, and they have adopted different strategies to reconcile the conflict between their self- and family/immigrant community perception of what it means to be Iranian with the perceptions of Iranians held and enforced by the host culture.[12] In this context, some have sought identification with black Americans, trying to highlight the ways that they, too, are oppressed by American society—particularly in the aftermath of 9/11.[13] It is notable, however, that in this effort to form identifications or solidarities with black Americans based on their status as a permanently oppressed, permanently oppositional group, diasporic Iranians are actually following the trend of an earlier, older, and more established diasporic group: Arab-Americans.

Pointing as it does to Iranian immigrants' shifting priorities in the increasingly racialized landscape of the twenty-first-century US—as well the shifting generational imperatives experienced among Iranian-American youth—this comparison is worth emphasizing. Unlike Iranian-Americans, Arab-Americans have historically tended to be highly politicized around the issue of Palestine in the US, and they have sought to explain the Palestinian struggle to the American public using the frameworks of black and Native American justice movements.[14] This point of view positions Palestinian displacement by the establishment of the state of Israel as an analogous story of "settler colonialism" through which a European colonial power displaces an indigenous population. By contrast, during the first decades following the Iranian Revolution and the exile, voluntary or forced, of many Iranians (primarily to the US), Iranian-Americans had not often voiced support for Palestine or made common cause with Arab-Americans.[15] They only began to seek out such solidarities and to be more vocal about Palestine after 9/11, perhaps seeing a way in which to make their own minority legible within US racial hierarchies.

Significantly, such expressions of alliance to pro-Palestinian and black freedom/rights movements tend to come from urban-based, highly educated, and/or younger Iranian-Americans who have spent their entire lives in the US and been educated in coastal state public school systems. Some, but not all, are children of Iranian leftists who had supported the 1979 Revolution but were forced to flee for their lives after the consolidation of power under Khomeini and the purging of political dissidents that continued through the 1980s.[16] Unlike their parents' generation, younger Iranian-Americans, oftentimes born and entirely educated in the US, realize that the nuances their parents and grandparents sought to put across in terms of their ethnic history would only be understood as hollow racist/racial gestures in the American context. Faced with entrenched racial politics that paint brown- and black-skinned bodies with a wide brush, they understand that the assertion of a "Persian" identity is neither enough to claim a seat at the table of whiteness nor an identity upon which to build racial solidarity in diaspora.

An amusing demonstration of this truth is reflected in an episode of comedian Pamela Adlon's FX show *Better Things*, "Father's Day." An illustration of the peculiar fruits born of earlier generations' efforts to teach Americans to call them Persian, "Father's Day" finds particular resonance due to its setting in Los Angeles—a diasporic site where there is a high concentration of Iranian-Americans. Featuring one of Adlon's daughters and her capriciously badly behaved but endearing grandmother, the episode dramatizes the two having lunch in a "Tehrangeles" restaurant on the eve of the granddaughter's "Batcañera" (a mashup of a bat mitzvah and a quincañera).[17] The overtly woke granddaughter's "Batcañera" is a compromise: she has agreed to honor her mother's Jewish heritage with a bat mitzvah, but only if she can simultaneously celebrate the Mexican-Angeleno heritage of their gardener, whose daughter will be celebrating her quincañera on the same occasion.

Part of the humor of the episode is that Adlon's daughter, a symbol/stereotype for her generation, wants to retain the financial and class privilege of her whiteness but also longs to possess the cultural authenticity she sees as belonging to "ethnic" Americans. This tension reverberates in her response to her grandmother's engagement with the Iranian-American restaurant waiter. After delivering a brief summary of Iran's modern history, the (white, gentile) grandmother proceeds to educate the waiter on why he should let go of the word "Persian" and just call himself Iranian. Adlon's daughter, who is anxious to distance herself from attitudes born of racial and ethnic hierarchies, is at first pleased by her grandmother's engagement with the waiter. However, once the grandmother has established her superior understanding of this arcane bit of Iranian pride and history, she abruptly proceeds to treat the waiter rudely and like a servant, embarrassing the granddaughter with an overt assertion of both class and racial privilege. This comedic collision of race, class, and generational perspective in a heavily Iranian neighborhood of Los Angeles offers an apt demonstration of what diasporic Iranians have so often found to be true: no matter how strongly they assert their Persian exceptionalism, and however much Americans appear to understand the distinction, Iranian-Americans will nonetheless be understood and treated as inferiors in the racial privilege schema of the US.

It is this awareness that has increasingly led a younger generation of diasporic Iranians to explore affiliation and alliance with historically marginalized groups and identities in "host" societies. Yet these efforts often collide with the legacy of a Persian exceptionalism that has rooted itself in particular modes of race and racialization, not just in distancing Iran from the Arab world but in the troubling ways Iranians and Iranian-Americans continue to disavow, downplay, or simply ignore Iran's own history of African slavery and the existence of black Iranians in the home country. While we might attribute the denial/downplaying of enslavement and the relevance of blackness in Iran to a regime of censorship, examining spaces of expression outside of Iran reveals the degree to which Iranians in the diaspora—particularly in places with continuing tension over the histories of slavery and racial justice—manifest a high degree of ambivalence about race even as they probe where they fit in and to what end.

This book aims to bridge the gap between understandings of race-making in Iran and in sites of the Iranian diaspora—particularly in North America—by examining explorations of race, racialization, and group identification that are legible in cultural criticism, ethnographic studies, historical scholarship, films, memoirs, and social media/websites produced by Iranians in the home country as well as by diasporic Iranians. This is a project that is bound up in the historical legacy of the Aryan disavowal of Arab affiliation, but, I argue, it receives particularly insidious expression in the complex ways that the history of African slavery in Iran is disavowed or exceptionalized both in Iran and by Iranians in diaspora. In attempting to forge solidarities with black justice movements, in particular, diasporic Iranians enact a form of historical amnesia (or, as Parisa Vaziri puts it, anamnesia) that either minimizes (or effaces entirely) the history of African slavery in Iran or produces it only to obscure it.[18] In both cases, they obfuscate the way that racial thinking continues to structure social hierarchies in Iran and among Iranians in diaspora, even as they try to make common cause with those who have experienced race-based injustice in the United States.

Reflecting and replicating the longstanding narratives about Iranian exceptionalism with regard to race and slavery that this book takes as its central concern, Iranians and Iranian-Americans have developed and continue to cultivate a distinct form of dissonance. We see a prime example of this in a story in Sayeh Dashti's *You Belong*, a self-published memoir by an Iranian woman who, like many affluent Iranians, has lived a life between Iran and various diasporic locations (including Los Angeles and Toronto) since the revolution.[19] Dashti demonstrates an awareness of rhetoric around race in the US and outside of Iran more generally, and her writing offers insight into her dissonant efforts to navigate differing generational perspectives on the matter. She begins her chapter entitled "Black Members of Our Family" with an odd anecdote about her mother (for whom she uses the affectionate term "Bibi"). Set in the diaspora, the story unfolds at the Bullock's department store in Los Angeles:

> Bibi embarrassed me every time we were in Bullock's Department Store in Los Angeles and she stopped an African American woman shopper telling her that she loved her. She insisted that I translate her message, "We love our blacks." She literally followed them around and continued to say:
>
> Tell her that we are mad at American for having had slavery. Shame on them! They can never clean this stain off their history. Our blacks are members of our families; never slaves, not in our family nor in the history of our country.[20]

Dashti continues:

> Obviously, I could not convey such an inherently prejudiced message. Instead, I would try to compliment the ladies, as they could not understand why my mother was holding on to their arms and smiling at them so compassionately. "She says you are so beautiful and she loves your elegant blouse," I would say. I could tell, however, that they knew there was much more to it than I was saying.[21]

This anecdote is clearly meant to signal the distance between Bibi's privileged and dated Iranian frame of reference and the perception that Dashti herself is aware will be assigned to it, but Dashti does some selective editing in translation that reveals as much about her own racial understanding in diaspora as it does her mother's. What she means by "inherently prejudiced" is never unpacked, but she uses it in reference to Bibi telling the story of "our blacks"—the enslaved (or formerly enslaved) persons in their household. Notably, Dashti echoes her mother's rhetoric when she describes such individuals as occupying a status characterized in familial terms rather than in terms of servitude or bondage; indeed, she calls them "the black members of our family."[22] On the strength of Dashti's own description, however, these people do in fact appear to have been enslaved. Moreover, they came into the family's life as children—Dashti describes them as part of one of her aunts' dowries, suggesting that the family understood them as property first and humans second.

In other words, Bibi is not alone in her obfuscation. In her memoir, Dashti herself is also at pains to emphasize that these children were "part of our family" and that they were *not* slaves, despite all indications from her own description confirming that they were. The chapter title, "Black Members of Our Family," attempts to further banish any possible misapprehension on the part of the reader that these people were enslaved. Yet what Dashti goes on to recount is clearly the story of a southern Iranian slaveholding family that, after abolition, discursively repositioned the account to elide the aspect of slavery from their collective memory even while preserving it in the documentary evidence of the family's marriage and death documents.

In a related mode of narrative, consider the story related to me by an Iranian-American writer. They heard about the project I was undertaking on racial thinking in Iran (this book) and proceeded to tell me about the "black sister" their family had "adopted" in the 1960s in a southern city in Iran. The writer's grandfather had allegedly found this child on the street, begging with her grandmother. The grandfather "offered to take her," and the child's grandmother apparently acquiesced. This child was then raised alongside the writer and their siblings, but she was not treated as a child of the household. Although she was brought into exile with the family when they left Iran, she was not offered the same educational opportunities as the blood children of the family. Instead of the university degree the writer acquired, the "black sister" was sent to hairdressing school. The author confided in me that they still "did a lot" for this sister, who had been married, had an unhappy divorce, and was now a single mom with children of her own and seemed in constant need of financial and emotional support. The intersection in this story of the common tropes of "good treatment" and benevolence toward enslaved Africans and their descendants in Iran—as well as the trope of the American "welfare queen" narrative in the US—is striking. More specifically, they demonstrate the way in which Iranian-Americans have (perhaps unconsciously) adopted stereotypes associated with blackness in the US to explain in a diasporic context the presence and problems that articulate relationships between (former) enslavers and the people they erstwhile enslaved.

As this book argues, the idea of Iranian exceptionalism expressed through the idea of being "Persian" has also manifested in relation to Iranian perceptions of its own history of and relationship to slavery and servitude. The very existence of enslavement in Iranian history continues to be a subject of debate. Indeed, despite clear evidence to the contrary, Iranians seem able to simultaneously believe that slavery never existed in Iran and insist on what Ehud Toledano mildly calls the "good treatment" thesis—that is, that insofar as slavery existed in Iran, it was benign compared to the Atlantic context and that slaves were treated like members of the family.[23] (Scholars of Iran often echo this note in the historiography of Indian Ocean slavery, suggesting that it was fundamentally different from and unconnected to the transatlantic slave trade and that the treatment and experience of enslavement in the one ought not to be conflated with the other. They also insist there are no living descendants of the enslaved to contradict such an assertion.) Stories such as those highlighted here thus illuminate how diasporic Iranians have been living at the intersection of a profound contradiction and double-consciousness around race and identity that has arisen in no small part from bringing longstanding national Iranian prejudices about race and class into a diaspora with its own complex history of racialized oppression.

It is common to see this phenomenon manifested in memoir. Clearly unbeknownst to both Dashti and the writer telling me about their own "black family," for example, their stories bear startling resonances with accounts like Miriam Behnam's, which was published in the 1990s as *Zelzelah: A Woman Before Her Time*. The text offers a familiar spin:

> Once when I was quite young, a little girl of about five was left on our doorstep with a note pinned to her bonnet: she was being given to us in exchange for a trade debt. In those days little or no account was generally taken of the feelings or emotions of the zar-kharids [a commonly used word for "slave," meaning "bought with gold"], or how cruel it was to separate small children from their parents. My family, however, did not like this sort of arrangement. Grandfather tried to find this poor child's parents, but learned that they had already sailed away with their master so, although he would gladly have foregone his claims, he couldn't do anything else but bring her into our house.
>
> The little girl's large, dark eyes clearly showed how terrified she felt. I remember my sisters and I, barely older than this little one, sympathizing with a child in such a situation. We named her Hasina, meaning "beauty", and despite her childhood trauma she responded to our love and affection, growing into a happy and charming person.[24]

Once again, we see the power of the "good treatment" narrative trope that surrounds master–servant relations in Iran articulated through the lens of "benevolent" families taking in needy black children. In Behnam's account, moreover, there is an implied assumption that such black children are not themselves Iranian and that they are ipso facto the descendants of enslaved persons (note here the contrast with the assertion that there are no descendants of enslaved people in Iran to attest to that history; this is an issue addressed by Beeta Baghoolizadeh in *The Color Black*).[25] These are pervasive presumptions about the contours and scope of enslaved labor that erase the very notion and historical reality of slavery in Iran, replacing it with depictions of quasi-familial ties that are at once more palatable to Iranians themselves and that seem, on the face of it, more acceptable in a diasporic context linked to the history of the transatlantic slave trade. The rhetorical gesture also suggests, importantly, that loyalty on the part of "servants" (not slaves) demonstrates the goodness of the masters, as does the happiness of "family members" consistently distinguished by their race and class distinctions.

The erasure and substitution at the core of such narratives only underscore the absence of critical engagement by Iranians at home and in the diaspora with global discourses on slavery and its aftermath—even as they seek to negotiate their own status within the racial hierarchies they encounter. In this space of ambivalent identification and suppressed histories, many diasporic Iranians simultaneously feel themselves to be marginalized and misunderstood by the host country and believe themselves to be from a racially superior culture. They decry the evils of "chattel slavery" and its ongoing connections to racial injustice in the US while telling stories about their own families' beloved black slaves/servants. They vociferously disavow any connection or comparison between the two, and this contradictory thinking has manifested in their varied efforts to claim their place in American society. For years, diasporic Iranians armored themselves with the connotations of the word "Persian" while eschewing political alliances with oppressed or "disadvantaged" groups in the US (e.g., Arabs, black Americans, Latinos) for fear of being conflated with them. Now, younger generations and activist groups like the Collective for Black Iranians strive to craft new affiliations and alliances to protest the racial conflations they have been unable to avoid. In both cases, the national and familial disavowal of African slavery in Iran itself has undergone noticeably little change.

Today, operating at the intersection of the longstanding circumstances, histories, and imperatives described here, we are currently witnessing something new: a self-interested process of self-fashioning and self-positioning by way of both scholarly and popular efforts to re(dis)cover Iran's history and legacy of enslavement. By closely examining these efforts, as well as the cultural and historical foundations they build upon, this book reveals how heretofore unacknowledged ideas about race and slavery in Iran have helped forge a specific conception of modern Iranian cultural identity at "home" and in the diaspora.

The history of racial thinking in Iran is connected to its long history of enslavement, but not in the ways one might think. Iranians engaged in a variety of enslaving practices but were likewise themselves enslaved. One of the most famous episodes in modern Iranian history, in fact, involves enslavement. The subject of a book by Afsaneh Najmabadi entitled *The Daughters of Quchan*,[26] it involves Iranian girls being kidnapped by Turkoman raiders operating at the northern border. The episode became the object of a parliamentary debate in which (Najmabadi persuasively argues) the girls' captivity and sale was equated with Iran's compromised sovereignty. Given how emotionally disturbing the idea of Iranian girls being enslaved and sold was to the Iranian public, it is notable that, at virtually the same moment, Iran was still itself dealing in the human trafficking of enslaved Africans.

Much of *Colorblind* addresses the legacy of the last years of slavery in Iran, and the legacy of those years in popular memory and culture. The long twilight of slavery in Iran began in the nineteenth century, when the practices of acquiring and keeping slaves changed substantially in the Iranian realm. Russian conquests of Qajar territories prompted a curtailing of the trade in enslaved ethnic minorities from the Caucasus (e.g., Circassians, Georgians, and Armenians) who had historically been trafficked in Iran. This put new pressures and demands on the trade in captives from Africa at the very moment that European powers were moving to abolish the slave trade in the Atlantic, as well as in the Indian Ocean and the Persian Gulf. Britain, in particular, was exercising its power in these regions through its outposts in the Gulf along the routes to South Asia, where British power was at its peak.

During this time, Iran came into contact with Britain's abolition campaign through British possessions/colonies in the Persian Gulf and India, and it was forced to accept terms that ostensibly outlawed slave trading in the Persian Gulf. However, slavery wasn't officially abolished in Iran until 1929, at which point it was abolished through a decree by Reza Pahlavi. Yet even after abolition, black Iranians who had been enslaved or were born of enslaved persons (and even those who weren't) were stigmatized as distinctive and different from other members of the population. Unable to assimilate racially and untrained for work other than that which they had performed in their status as enslaved persons, they were often forced to remain in quasi-enslaved positions long after slavery was formally abolished. Accounts like Miriam Behnam's, mentioned above, and those of Haleh Afshar and Sayeh Dashti, which are explored in chapter 5, as well as stories like Simin Daneshvar's (examined in chapter 3) all attest to this reality, as do myriad family photographs from the early post-abolition period visible in digital archives like Women's Worlds in Qajar Iran, which is housed at Harvard University. While this post-abolition circumstance was not specific to Iran, it is one that has seldom been acknowledged in the scholarship of that country despite being widely attested to in the cultural record.

Historians of slavery in Qajar Iran have leaned hard on the "good treatment" thesis, particularly emphasizing the idea that slaves were treated well in these contexts, especially when compared to the treatment of plantation slaves in the Americas. This is a move to mitigate or diminish the fundamental brutality and cruelty of this history and the inherent violence of enslavement itself. Slavery in Iran was undoubtedly distinct from slavery in the Americas, with many of its basic contours and practices different from the characteristics of slavery in the Atlantic context, but this does not detract from the underlying vulnerability inherent in this status. From the documentary evidence that exists, the Africans enslaved and traded or sold into Iran were largely acquired by elite households in urban environments.[27] Indeed, the primary documentary evidence we have about the lives of slaves during the Qajar period is from their appearance in legal contracts (e.g., for dowries) of elite families, on the one hand, and memoirs written by members of the royal household and court or from photographs from the royal household, on the other. Some of the latter were taken by Nasser al-Din Shah Qajar himself (I discuss these photos and their contemporary circulation in chapter 6).

There is a broad assumption, often reinforced by memoirs like those of Taj al-Saltaneh, one of Nasser al-Din Shah's daughters, that such "palace slaves" lived lives of relative contentment and power—aside, that is, from the fact of their enslavement.[28] Their enslavement is tacitly acknowledged, but the violence it almost certainly entailed is glossed over or ignored altogether. Diving deeper into Taj al-Saltaneh's account, we see her spending time detailing the extensiveness of her black staff—considered requisite for royal Qajar children and wives—and the importance of her enslaved nanny to her, particularly in the absence of a loving mother. However, she also spends substantial amounts of space detailing how much she hated her husband's black nanny, who seems to have had as much or more power over him. Both of these enslaved women appear to have had significant influence over their royal wards/charges, leading to the possibly false conclusion that they led lives of relative empowerment (Haleh Afshar's account of her nanny Sonbol in the post-abolition period, discussed in chapter 5, makes similar false connections/attributions). In fact, it is probably worth noting that most of those who read and interpret Taj al-Saltaneh's memoir (which was not actually published until 1969) tend to use Atlantic/New World slavery as their benchmark for "cruelty," which effectively lowers the bar for what could qualify in the Iranian context as "good treatment." Slavery in the Qajar realm was clearly different from that practiced in the Americas: in scale, scope, and the kind of labor demanded of enslaved people. Yet subsequent generations of Iranians and scholars of Iran have sought to make "different" mean "exceptional" or "better" or even "not really slavery."

Significantly, there are almost no written accounts by enslaved persons or their descendants in Iran. What can be gathered from the accounts that do exist (e.g., the memoirs of elites mentioned above) is that Iranians in the Qajar era not only enslaved conquered peoples but also imported slaves. The cruelty of these practices—typical in neighboring and coeval dynasties, as well—has not become the stuff of national anguish as has America's history of enslavement, yet there is enough material to demonstrate that the "good treatment" thesis rings hollow. Neither Islam nor any special quality of kindness substantially mitigated the essential cruelty of the practice of enslavement, no matter how hard historians gesture toward them in the Iranian context.[29]

In the century since the official abolition of slavery, Iran and Iranians have also invested significant cache in identifying themselves as "colorblind" or "race-blind" despite the existence of black Iranians and the long socio-economic shadow of African enslavement. More specifically, although Iranians and scholars of Iran may countenance the existence of people of different skin colors in Iran, they simultaneously disavow any racialization of such difference and insist that these differences have no importance politically or socially. These attitudes have been variably adopted in the diaspora. We see evidence in curator-scholars and curator-creators examined in chapter 6 continuing with the narrative of colorblindness, for example, while in other coeval sites, we see Iranian-American scholars and content-creators not only acknowledging that race exists, but racializing themselves strategically as "brown" or black. With competing narratives of Aryanism, colorblindness, and Persian exceptionalism, the content of dialogue within diasporic communities on race is, to say the least, overdetermined, and has tended to produce another iteration of the dissonance I highlight throughout this book. In this case, it is a dissonance that has profoundly shaped scholarship on the history of racialization and political engagement in the twentieth century.

Like many other third-world nations in the 1960s, Iran watched the development of black freedom movements with interest and, in some cases, as inspiration to revolutionary action. The rejection of American nationalism as racist seemed to offer a way to name and act against the influence that American imperialism had played in Iran. Part of the Islamic Republic's discourse of radical equality and resistance to (American) imperialism involves positioning itself as the antithesis of US racialization, racial practices, and racial thinking. Indeed, the Islamic Republic of Iran (IRI) developed a discourse on blackness that built upon pre-revolutionary intellectuals' deployment of blackness to put the lie to US promises of freedom and equality, and it continues to recruit and use black Americans to attest to and demonstrate the IRI's superior racial politics.[30]

Scholars often point to Franz Fanon, positioned in Algeria, as a conduit through which Iranians (especially the lay socialist Islamist 'Ali Shari'ati) absorbed this critique. But Iranian intellectuals of this period also spent time in the US and observed the Civil Rights movement firsthand, an example of which is discussed in chapter 3. Yet this engagement with blackness as a revolutionary force in the 1960s and 1970s never translated to an explicit engagement with the history or legacy of enslavement of Africans in Iran. Even in spaces where some of these concerns might be presumed to overlap—in spaces like Kharg, for example, where critic Jalal Al-e Ahmad observed the culture of descendants of Africans on the island—we can't find evidence of the connection being made.[31] Although intellectuals in Iran were reading black cosmopolitan intellectuals like Fanon, Malcolm X, and James Baldwin, they did not seem to connect the forms of political blackness/radical blackness embraced by these authors with the black Iranians they encountered in spaces like the port cities of the Persian Gulf or Kharg Island.[32] The lure of twentieth-century black cosmopolitanism still endures, however, and in the bodies of work and cultural output examined in this book, we can see that increased sensitivity to race in the diaspora has occasioned a fraught engagement with Iran's past.

The desire to demonstrate both that Iranians understand race but also that race is not meaningful to them has created significant problems for diasporic Iranians. Both at home and in the diaspora, Iranians continue to emphasize Iranian (Aryan) exceptionalism as a core part of their self-understanding. Drawing on exempla chosen from a variety of media throughout the nineteenth, twentieth, and twenty-first centuries, this book argues that a kind of "colorblind" modern Iranian cultural identity in fact emerged as a consequence of the simultaneous erasure of the history of slavery and of black personhood. To call it simply "racism" is too simple and easy to dismiss; instead, I use the term "colorblind" through this book in a tongue-in-cheek way to describe the *willingness* to not see the implications of race that manifest themselves in so many different cultural forms in Iran and the diaspora. Informed by methodologies from critical race scholarship, cultural studies, and comparative literature, the book examines a range of prominent Iranian authors, filmmakers, and cultural producers to explore the way in which the delineation of what is "modern" in Iran is connected to the suppression of black subjectivity and a strategic use of blackness. In addition, it explores the ways that ideas about slavery and blackness in Iran have been transmitted into the Iranian diaspora, where they have often been challenged in cultural spaces where diasporic Iranians themselves are viewed as racially liminal and non-white.

Iran's practices of racial thinking have either resonated with or been directly influenced by other histories of racialization and enslavement. There are resonances between the imagination of magical realism in the oil-rich South of Iran, for example, and the purported home of magical realism in South America. These resonances help us draw intriguing connections between the two histories of oil and enslavement. So, too, are there explicit moments of interaction and influence between and among Iranian authors and artists whose work was directly influenced by US culture during the era of the Civil Rights movement. Today, diasporic artists and scholars operating in the globalized space of the internet grapple with the nationalist narrative of slavery and abolition in modern Iran through visual narratives like documentary film and photographs, both archival and contemporary. To make these disparate examples, which include both "high" and "low" culture/cultural products as well as scholarly writing and production, comprehensible within a common framework, I draw on the robust scholarship that has developed in other contexts (and is beginning to develop in Iranian Studies, too) to read against the grain of Iranian nationalist narratives that reflect willful colorblindness in relation to Iranian culture and politics.

The speculative and imaginative strategies that characterize this method for recovering the histories of enslaved persons and their descendants has largely adhered to the context of the US. While it may draw raised eyebrows from some critics, the refusal to allow the understood limits of the archive to set the parameters for engagement with the subject is salutary and finds echoes in the work of historians of Iran like Afsaneh Najmabadi, whose refusal to allow the perception that there are limited sources on women's lives in Qajar Iran be the end to the debate over whether or not it was possible to write substantive histories of women in that society. Such methods are also required when tackling the topics of racial thinking and the legacy of slavery in Iran, as both have remained largely unseen and unspoken due to their limited archival presence.

At present, slavery's racialized legacies in Iran and the Iranian diaspora are unreckoned with. They are largely sites of silence and discomfort. The very nearness of slavery's long shadow in the lives of many elite Iranians and their descendants in the diaspora is a source of unease that permeates the scholarship on the topic in a field largely peopled with elites of Iranian descent. At the same time, it complicates the racial hierarchies Iranians grapple with in the diaspora as they intermarry and grow more distant from the home country. In these contexts, I suggest, the enslavement of Africans in Iran has become a site of fascination and wonder—both of which are reactions to its putative "discovery" after having been so strenuously disavowed in Iranian culture. We see this fascination and wonder in not only ephemeral sites like Instagram accounts but also earlier documents, including the personal, historical, and fictional accounts of figures as varied as amateur historian Massoumeh Price, distinguished anthropologist Haleh Afshar, elite former ambassador Miriam Behnam, author Simin Daneshvar, and diasporic memoirist Sayeh Dashti. We also see it in the family photographs collected by the Women's Worlds in Qajar Iran archive and by individual curators. This wonder and fascination arise, quite simply, from the exceptionalist dissonance that has simultaneously blinded itself to the history of slavery while drawing on its socio-political implications as a strategy of self-positioning in Iran and in diaspora.

The field of Iranian Studies, and Middle East Studies more broadly, has changed rapidly over the past twenty years to reflect contemporary preoccupations with race and questions about why racialization had not been recognized or scrutinized meaningfully in previous scholarship. Bernard Lewis's seminal 1990 *Race and Slavery in the Middle East* was a work that invited response not only in terms of its innovativeness at its historical moment but also and subsequently because of the terms with which Lewis engaged race.[33] The thinking about race and racial thinking—and its role in history and culture in the Middle East—has only deepened and become more complex in the years since. In Iran, race is typically only mentioned in relationship to the history of enslaving Africans or in discussions about the Aryanist nationalism popularized during the Pahlavi period. Many studies of Iranian history and literature focus on the importance of "authenticity" and the "Aryan turn" in Iranian conceptions of self, but in doing so, they tend to ignore the development of racial thinking in relation to blackness. This focus on the authentic Iranian-as-Aryan has been challenged by other ethnic minorities in Iran and critiqued for cutting off Iran from its historical cultural neighbors and influences. But these efforts, too, forget the *internal* "others" who have been suppressed and silenced, focusing instead on the nearby Turks, Arabs, and Indians.

Iran is a place of enormous ethnic and linguistic heterogeneity, but it has been successful in uniting most of its population under the aegis of a "Persian" identity and language. Notably, an 1867 census reported that almost 12 percent of the population in Tehran was comprised of African servants and slaves, yet no mention of these persons is made in almost any account of Iranian ethnicity or race in later studies. This 12 percent simply disappears. The presence of black Iranians thus presents itself as anomalous and, in existing studies, difficult to categorize. When it is acknowledged, scholars and critics typically position this presence as a relic of the past rather than a persistent reality in the present. Some scholars indeed suggest that "blackness," as such, does not exist in Iran because of the so-called Iranian colorblindness I have pointed to here. The concept of "race," they suggest, simply does not exist in Iran as it does in the US.

While such assertions may hold a grain of truth, they demonstrate the unease and difficulty of attempting to understand racial thinking in Iran. These ideas are maintained, for example, by Behnaz Mirzai in her 2017 monograph *A History of Slavery and Emancipation in Iran, 1800–1929*.[34] Offering the most substantive digest of the archival resources on slavery in Iran to date, she insists on Iran's exceptionality and the impossibility of making comparisons with other coeval legacies of enslavement. She refuses to acknowledge the violence of slavery in Iran or its connections to anti-blackness in Iran and the diaspora. That said, Mirzai's study demonstrates that there is a readership for works on this topic both inside and outside of the discipline of Iranian Studies. Thus, in conjunction with the myriad texts and cultural products explored in the coming chapters, it demands the kind of reply presented here: a critical reading of the cultural scaffolding that enabled the persistence of slavery in Iran, a denial of its inherent violence, and an ongoing refusal to acknowledge the ways that black Iranians—whether or not they are, in fact, descended from slaves—shoulder this history and legacy.

While this book's insights into Iranian racial thinking are made even more pressing in light of recent scholarly interest in the subject of Iranian slavery, they are also bolstered by efforts made to shed more critical light on what remains an underdeveloped topic of analysis. Anthony Lee's scholarship on enslaved Africans in Iran, for example, has helped complicate the optimistic picture of slavery and abolition that celebrates the nation-state as the freer of slaves. Revisiting the few documents that record the lives and roles of individual African and African-descent slaves in elite and royal households, Lee's work invites us to read between the lines of elite memoirs, bills of sale, and petitions for refuge and demonstrates how future historians might usefully re-engage such documents. Beeta Baghoolizadeh's recent monograph *The Color Black* (2024) takes up the arc of Lee's work but goes further and deeper, arguing that there has been a systematic "erasure" of the history of slavery and abolition in Iran, as well as a concomitant (and in her view, mistaken) conflation of "blackness" with "enslavement." A scholar as well as the "resident historian" for the Collective for Black Iranians, an activist group comprised of people of Iranian and African heritage, Baghoolizadeh attempts not only to make an intervention in the historiography on slavery but also to suggest new and more positive directions for representations of black Iranian heritage in the future. Inflected by comparative and diasporic sensibilities, Lee's and Baghoolizadeh's works constitute important interventions in the scholarship on race and legacies of enslavement in Iran, attempting to put these areas of scholarship into comparative perspective against discourses around race and enslavement in the Indian Ocean and Atlantic.

Other, earlier publications on enslavement and/or blackness in Iran include chapters in Joseph E. Harris's 1971 monograph *The African Presence in Asia* and Lewis's aforementioned *Race and Slavery in the Middle East*. Harris and Lewis were among the first to write comparatively about enslavement in Iran as part of the slave trade that persisted into the twentieth century in several Islamicate societies but were seldom openly discussed and had heretofore not been the subject of scholarly attention. Historian Thomas Ricks made an important contribution by publishing some of the earliest archival work on slavery in Iran, but his efforts are primarily documentary and do not propose substantive frameworks for understanding the very useful data he presents.[35] More recently, historian Jerzy Zdanowski used archival material from the British archives to document the lives of slaves who sought refuge at British consular offices in the Gulf (including in Bushehr), but, as he acknowledges, the special arrangements between the British and the Iranian government effectively meant that Iranian slaves were largely returned to their owners and their testimonies not recorded.[36] While in no way comprehensive individually or together, these texts have offered important insights and directions for future scholars to build on.

Recent work oriented to a different set of regional and theoretical questions bears mention. Stephanie Cronin's article "Islam, slave agency and abolitionism in Iran, the Middle East and North Africa," which became a chapter in her monograph *Social Histories of Iran: Modernism and Marginality in the Middle East* (2021), rightly situates enslavement in Iran as part of a history of marginalized actors and communities that has largely been excluded from the historiography on Iran.[37] Cronin thoughtfully suggests that the transatlantic slave trade may be used comparatively to help shed light on the history of slavery in Iran and in Islamicate societies of this period more broadly. *Colorblind* takes up her proposal and broadens it, arguing that drawing on the scholarship developed around racialization (and not exclusively the history of slavery) in the US and other cultures can help scholars of other societies better understand Iran's history of racial thinking. On this front, Neda Maghbouleh's aforementioned *The Limits of Whiteness* was a significant watershed in the scholarship on Iranian diasporic conceptions of race, in that it acknowledged and documented the racial dilemma of Iranian immigrants in the US, who are often "misrecognized" as black. As Maghbouleh demonstrates, Iranian-Americans have alternately eschewed and embraced the consequences of this misrecognition. However, the roots of these practices in the immigrants' home country were beyond the scope and disciplinary area of Maghbouleh's study. Also, as a primarily ethnographic study of Iranian-Americans, *The Limits of Whiteness* grounds itself in contemporary diasporic experiences of racialization and does not address the textual cultural production of blackness in Iran or the diaspora. Deepening and broadening this shared project in the chapters to come, I identify the roots of these ideologies in twentieth-century Iranian intellectuals' ostensibly nationalist writings and filmmaking and build a bridge between practices and ideas in the home and host contexts of Iran *and* the diaspora.

Parisa Vaziri's *Racial Blackness and Indian Ocean Slavery: Iran's Cinematic Archive* marks an important departure from earlier approaches to the topic of racial blackness in Iran by putting her theoretically rich consideration of Iran's visual legacies of enslavement in film into the context of Indian Ocean slavery—a broader and more extensively theorized area of study.[38] Immersed in the black radical tradition, Vaziri draws on Afropessimism and other insights of critical race theory in the US to argue that much of the way in which blackness has been engaged so far in Iranian cultural production is simultaneously invested in erasure and the production of an alternate and digestible form of this history. Her superb monograph argues that this limited and problematic engagement must be challenged, and she models a compelling way to do so. More than any other work yet published, hers points a way forward in the field by demonstrating how studies of blackness in Iran can and should be informed by the body of black radical and feminist thought developed globally.

In scholarship on race more broadly in the Middle East, several other key texts stand out. Eve Troutt Powell's *A Different Shade of Colonialism* remains an important turning point in the study of colonialism and blackness in the Middle East, outlining the way in which Egypt based its own anti-colonial claims on its right to be a colonizer itself.[39] Powell examines the way in which Egypt's relationship to Sudan was instrumental in helping Egyptians develop an idea of themselves as having the right not only to be free but also to colonize others. In other words, Egypt overthrew a colonizer by becoming one. With regard to histories of enslavement in the Ottoman domains, Ehud Toledano's *Slavery and Abolition in the Ottoman Middle East* and later *As If Silent and Absent*,[40] as well as Madeline Zilfi's *Women and Slavery in the Late Ottoman Empire*,[41] are significant works that gave language to ideas like the "good treatment" thesis. Scholarship on Morocco has also offered important insights into how to write histories of race and enslavement, with Mohammad Ennaji's *Serving the Master*[42] and Chouki El Hamel's *Black Morocco: A History of Slavery, Race, and Islam*[43] offering useful comparative histories on the phenomenon of the active denial of the history of enslavement in the Maghreb. Also focused on the Maghreb, M'hamed Oualdi's *A Slave Between Empires: A Transnational History*[44] documents the exceptional life of one enslaved individual, a Circassian man known as General Husayn, who was sold into slavery in Istanbul but went on to lead a "transimperial" life in his journeys from slave to dignitary among several empires.[45] The case of Circassian slaves, while seemingly unique, offers important counter examples of the way in which some slaves circulating in Islamicate societies were able to racially assimilate and "disappear," in contrast to descendants of enslaved Africans, who—however culturally Iranian their habitus—remain visually distinctive and thus potentially vulnerable.

Building on these earlier studies, *Colorblind* traces through folklore, ethnography, literature, letters, and films the specific ways in which racial thinking—particularly surrounding blackness and its connection to the history of slavery in Iran—was and is memorialized and deployed in the cultural work of Iranian and diasporic Iranian intellectuals. It takes up some of the same issues addressed in the literatures highlighted above but positions them differently by identifying in the post-1979 Iranian diaspora and its historical circumstances a key to understanding racial thinking in Iran as well as among people of Iranian heritage living outside of Iran. *Colorblind* brings to the fore practices of forgetting and identity construction that have concealed a troubling but important aspect of Iran's modern history. However, while acknowledging that the suppressed history of slavery and its related cultural practices is essential to understanding Iran's literary and cultural history, this book is not intended to present a "new" history of enslavement in Iran. Rather, it offers an intervention in the ongoing dialogues on racial thinking that are taking place globally. It performs the important work of addressing ideologies and practices related to race in Iran that are connected with practices and thinking in the diaspora, which no existing study has yet fully attempted to do.

If the Iranian Revolution of 1979 was the beginning of a long exodus during which Iranians would be dispersed across the globe—primarily to sites like the US and Europe—it was also a moment in which their idealistic national colorblindness was brought into contact with notions of race in highly racialized societies. The idea of being "Persian" that they brought with them carried with it an unacknowledged racial dimension that has prevented a full accounting of race and its connection to slavery in Iran. Moreover, it has prevented Iranians in the diaspora from fully interrogating their own racial thinking. By critically examining how these phenomena have manifested in and continue to shape cultural identity in Iran and the diaspora, *Colorblind* offers the beginnings of a racial reckoning by critically examining how these phenomena have manifested in and continue to shape the modern Iranian cultural identity.

One
IRANIAN ARYANISM AND RACIAL THINKING

IN 1971, THE SECOND (AND LAST) PAHLAVI KING, MOHAMMAD REZA Shah, staged a celebration titled "2,500 Years of Iranian Monarchy." The event has become the stuff of legend, and indeed it is impossible to view or read recordings of the event without some sense that the question of its excess was answered with the 1979 Revolution. Though frequently criticized for their displays of excess, the Shah and his court outdid themselves on this occasion, and the spectacle is often characterized as the tipping point that inspired his political opponents to start mobilizing in earnest for his overthrow. It remains a favorite anecdote to demonstrate the corruption and senseless profligacy of the doomed Pahlavis, such that we might liken its repeated telling to the horrified glee with which historians of Rome relate the stories of Caligula or Elagabalus.

Unlike stories of Roman excess, however, we needn't just imagine it. There is extensive footage that was recorded at the Shah's behest in order to make a propaganda film about the momentous occasion. The film itself was narrated by Orson Welles—again, no expense spared. As a result, we can actually watch as the event unfolds. We can see the costly French-made tents go up to house the guest list of hundreds of royals and other state dignitaries from around the world, the sumptuous meals prepared by Maxim's of Paris, and the extravagantly costumed participants as they filed into the receiving line to shake hands with the Shah and his wife. The Shah's wife herself wore a crown adorned with so many diamonds that her neck seemed unable to support its weight.[1]

With his extravagant hospitality and expensive props, Mohammad Reza Pahlavi sought to achieve his dream of having contemporary Iran recognized internationally as not only an important player on the world stage but also the world's oldest monarchy. At his coronation four years earlier (1967), he had proclaimed himself the heir of the millennia-old mantle of Iranian kingship, although he was only the second Pahlavi king upon the throne. In fact, his father (who reigned from 1926 to 1941) had chosen "Pahlavi" as the name of his dynasty specifically to signal their lineage as Persians and connections to pre-Islamic Iran. Known to linguists as "Middle Persian," Pahlavi was the language of the Sassanian dynasty ruling Iran at the time of the Arab-Islamic invasions and conquest in the seventh century. Like modern or "new" Persian, the Pahlavi language was connected to an "Indo-Aryan" mother language from which all versions of Persian derived. This linguistic lineage reinforced a strain of thinking that styled Iranian people as being of "Aryan" descent, and the strategic decision to choose the name "Pahlavi" thus connected Reza Shah's new dynasty to the idea of a glorious pre-Islamic, Indo-Aryan past.

Mohammad Reza Pahlavi, however, took things further. From the moment of his coronation, he began to style himself as the "Shahanshah" (king of kings) and the "Aryamehr" (light of the Aryans)—titles that no modern Iranian king had ever claimed.[2] And now, on the occasion of celebrating the Iranian monarchy's purported 2,500 years of continuous existence, he ended his public remarks by stage-whispering to the tomb of Cyrus the Great: "Sleep, Korosh [Cyrus], we are awake [watching over (Iran) for you]."[3] In using these titles and performatively calling upon the father of the Persian Empire, the Shah was not only continuing his father's work of distinguishing Iran as a nation defined more by its Indo-Aryan pre-Islamic past than by its Islamic present, he was also connecting himself and his reign to a number of potent racial histories and symbols. In calling himself the "Shahanshah," Mohammad Reza Pahlavi evoked the grandeur of the Achaemenid and Sassanian pasts and a kind of grandiose religious connotation: the "king of kings" in Judeo-Christian parlance refers to the promised messiah, while

"Aryamehr" summons the grandiosity and racial pedigree of an ancient empire.[4]

It was in suggesting that he had a direct connection to Cyrus, however, that Mohammad Reza Pahlavi made his boldest claim. By doing so, he grafted his very young monarchy (scarcely fifty years old at the time) to that of the Achaemenid kings who had arguably ruled the known world. For many Iranians, both at the time of the Shah and today, Cyrus (Korosh) the Great, the founder of the Achaemenid dynasty (559–330 BC), is not only the greatest symbol of Iran's ancient splendor and the epitome of what the putative ancestors of Iran had achieved in antiquity (and lost as a consequence of the Arab-Islamic invasions), he is also the symbol of their cultural superiority to their neighbors and the source of their supposed racial purity. Cyrus's ethnicity is disputed (though he was certainly from a Persian nomadic tribe), but his heir, Darius the Great, the third king of the Achaemenid dynasty, made things clear for posterity: he identified himself on his tomb at Behistun in Iran as "an Achaemenian, a Persian, son of a Persian, an Aryan Iranian, having Aryan lineage."[5] It was this lineage and identity that Mohammed Reza Shah thus assumed as he ascended the throne and sought to establish a form of secular state nationalism that would confirm Iran's place in the modern world order and support a project of reinforcing Iranian geographic integrity under Pahlavi rule.

For the Iranians who embraced the Pahlavis' vision, the "Aryanness" propounded by Darius the Great would have had specifically racial valences that resonated in their own moment: it signaled a rejection of cultural ties to Arabs and Islamic culture, both of which they viewed as backward and anti-modern. Notably, contemporary Iranians who subscribe to this idea are at pains to distinguish "their" Aryanism and belief in their racial superiority from that of the Nazi vision for Aryan dominance, which advanced an even more stringent idea of racial purity and insisted on the destruction of non-Aryans in German society. However, the distinctions between these ideologies have not always been clear. As journalist Edward Polsue points out, the German soccer team's visit to Iran in 2004 raised the obvious specter of Nazism when some fans of Team Melli (Iran's national soccer team) sang the Deutschlandlied (the national anthem of the Third Reich) and offered the Nazi salute.[6] Through their actions, these Iranian fans did not seem to identify themselves with the "nice" version of Aryanism (which Iranians base on ethno-linguistic premises), but rather with the highly racialized version that was promulgated by the Third Reich. Such "slippages" between the ostensibly anodyne, academic ethno-linguistic Aryanism of Iran and the violent racialist thinking of Nazi Aryanism showcase how easily Iran's claim to a unique status of racial and ethnic purity dovetails with exclusionary racial thinking.

While the distinction of racial purity offered by Aryanism was certainly a big part of the Achaemenids' appeal to Mohammed Reza Shah, it wasn't all of it. Iran's inheritance of ancient glory, the new Shah believed, demanded Iran's international recognition and a place in the global community. In a post-WWII world in which the idea of "universal human rights" had become increasingly important and a potent virtue for modern nations to signal, Mohammad Reza Shah was keen to establish Iran's historical role in developing the idea. To do this, he pointed to the so-called Cyrus Cylinder, a sixth-century BC Achaemenid clay cylinder with a royal inscription announcing Cyrus the Great as the descendant of many kings and declaring that he would allow his subjects to live in peace. There is a great deal of dispute over the meaning of these words, and scholars have noted that it is in keeping with other royal declarations of the same period. Yet Mohammad Reza Shah made it a major cornerstone of his post-coup reign. He insisted that Iranians weren't just human rights adherents, they had *invented* human rights.

At home, Mohammad Reza Shah named Cyrus and Darius as the inspirations and models for his White Revolution reforms (ca. 1963), a vast campaign of economic, land, social, and political reforms that sought to redistribute land, nationalize forests, improve literacy and health, and enfranchise women, among other aspirational changes meant to signal Iran's consonance with the values of the Western nations it sought to style as its peers. He tried to sell these reforms to his people by claiming they were modeled on the just rule of the kings of old (i.e., Cyrus and Darius) and at least partly motivated by his and their human rights considerations. Of course, it was an idea that many found ironic in the light of proliferating evidence of the torture techniques regularly used by the Shah's secret police against political dissidents. Meanwhile, his twin sister, Ashraf Pahlavi, who was often deputized for the Shah abroad, presented the UN secretary with a copy of the Cyrus Cylinder.

At a UN conference on human rights in Tehran in 1968, the Shah called the cylinder the first evidence of codified human rights in the world—another feather in the cap of the ancient Aryan nation reclaiming its international place under the leadership of the Pahlavi dynasty.

While it is easy to decry the excesses of the Pahlavis and to reject their over-the-top evocations of Aryanist symbols and ceremony, the underpinnings of that ideology have endured beyond the end of their dynasty, even in the unlikeliest of places. At first, the early post-revolutionary IRI rejected Iranian Aryanism as part of the racist Pahlavi propaganda that excluded from its nationalist framework the huge swath of Iran's population that did not identify as ethnically "Persian" and in many cases lived in communities where Persian was only a state-imposed language. Yet the Islamic Republic had already begun to backtrack by the 1990s. Initially, the regime attempted to supplant the idea of a Persian-unified Iran with the idea of an Iranian *ummah*, the community of Muslim believers that transcends ethno-linguistic divisions. Disenchanted with the revolution, however, contemporary Iranians have not shown much enthusiasm for the idea of the *ummah*, often rejecting calls for solidarity with countries in the region based on any kind of pan-Islamic kinship. The regime thus found that it needed recourse to a more potent and enduring evocation of national community, and Iran as a nation of pre-Islamic ancient splendor (still on display at sites such as Persepolis) still has great cachet.

A labile and adaptable concept, Iranian Aryanism had so usefully served the project of Iranian nationalism under the Pahlavis that even the Islamic Republic could embrace it to suit their agenda. Turning a blind eye to the anti-Arab racial underpinnings the government had originally denounced, the IRI has used the idea of Iranian Aryanism as a platform for ensuring Iranian geographical integrity and projecting a neo-imperial Iranian influence in the region. Moreover, the Islamic Republic has come to strategically leverage the version of the ethno-linguistic Aryanist theory of Persian racial purity—as well as its glorification of an ancient world ruled by Iran—that has contributed to a contemporary sense of national loss and nostalgia as well as a collective desire for restitution.[7]

Meanwhile, trying to understand the roots of the Iranian Revolution while confronting a different scholarly milieu and zeitgeist in the post-revolutionary period, scholars of Iran in the diaspora have been more attentive to Iranian Aryanism as an important type of chauvinism or bigotry to be addressed, particularly in relation to its role in the Pahlavis' nation-building project. Yet even within their efforts to untangle the ideological investments and political uses of Iranian Aryanism, diasporic Iranian scholars frequently stumble into a reification of the very category they intend to critically examine. Professing Iranian Aryanism to be something that is apocryphal, their public comments and social media presence sometimes contradict their scholarly averments that they reject Aryanist thinking. In other words, while they decry Aryanism in their scholarship, they might re-post or like a post from Facebook groups such as "IRAN HOME OF THE ORIGINAL ARYANS," which aggregates a dizzying assortment of cultural goods and ideas under this characterization.

Tangled up in the ethnic, religious, nationalistic, and/or economic aspirations of many different groups, Aryanism has thus proved an enduring preoccupation in Iran. Animating a supra-nationalism as well as a nascent irredentism, Aryanism is so fully absorbed and so useful in an Iranian national context that one can understand why it is so difficult to critically engage, even where we see concerted efforts to identify it as a problematic ideology. We might discern in this dynamic the long shadow of colonialism/imperialism in the region: although the desire is expressed in different ways than in the nineteenth or twentieth centuries, Iranians today still want to be seen as the equals of Europeans and other Western imperial forces, and they believe that their racial credentials are part of what entitles them to that equality. Aryanism, therefore, remains a central concern in the Iranian cultural sphere, as both a lineage to be celebrated and a problem to be explored.

What has been missed within this preoccupation with Aryanism is the fact that the ideology has been deployed and engaged in such a way that scholars and critics have been unable to identify and name other forms of racial thinking in Iran. Remaining at the center of all debates about race and ethnicity in Iran and the diaspora, the focus on Aryanism as a true-but-not-true site of Iranian cultural identity has come at the expense of seeing the broader picture of how troubling attitudes toward minorities persist in contemporary scholarly and popular discourse in Iran and the diaspora. It has prevented any meaningful scrutiny into discriminatory and/or hostile attitudes toward minorities who defy or cannot be successfully absorbed into the Aryanist version of a "Persian" Iran, including, but not exclusive to, black Iranians. This failure to fully countenance the long-term implications of Aryanist thinking in Iran and the diaspora also contributes to and reflects a broader tendency to look away from racial and ethnic complexity or uncertainty, which in turn perpetuates the cultural ethos of Iran being "race-blind."

To begin a process of illuminating and examining the history and contemporary/enduring implications of Iranian Aryanism, the remainder of this chapter focuses on the figure often identified as its founding father: Mirza Fath'ali Akhundzadeh (1812–1878). Akhundzadeh was an *adib* and critic who personally embodied both a complex and possibly very different racial past and a modernizing force who perhaps ushered in a new era of racial thinking alongside the modern literary forms he experimented with. Highlighting unfamiliar facets of this well-known cultural figure helps us understand the way in which willful ignorance of racial thinking prevents us from seeing how it has articulated the development of modern literature and culture in Iran.

AFRICAN—BUT NOT BLACK

It was not Akhundzadeh himself but one of his admirers who most fully brought the idea of Aryanism—and its concomitant racism—into Iranian discourse. But Mirza Abdol Hossein Agha Khan Kermani, as generations of historians (and indeed Kermani himself) have acknowledged, came into contact with the ideas that he distilled into Aryanism through the figure of Akhundzadeh. Although Akhundzadeh did not use the term "Aryan" or "Aryanist" (or their Azeri or Persian translations) in his writing, there is little question that his "cultural revivalism," as Talinn Grigor terms it, was instrumental in ushering in the golden era of Iranian Aryanism.[8] He was an advocate for cultural reforms of many kinds, from the reform of the Persian alphabet (he recommended replacing the Perso-Arabic characters with the Latin alphabet) to the introduction of modern, European-style drama. But his most lasting contribution is undoubtedly the rejection of Islam and the Arab-Semitic culture he saw as accompanying it. As Akhundzadeh outlined in a fictionalized correspondence between two Iranian and Indian princes (known as the *Letters of Kamal al-dowleh to Prince Jamal al-dowleh*), Iran's best days had all come before the dawn of Islam.⁹ What remained in the nineteenth-century present was the sad ruin of that civilization. It had been tainted, he believed, by contact with Arab-Islamic culture, and only through a rejection of Islam and Arab culture—accompanied by the rediscovery of Iran's glorious pre-Islamic past—could Iran move forward into the future as a peer of modern European civilizations.¹⁰

Clearly aware of European racial thinking connected to the linguistic research on Indo-European languages and their connection to an Aryan master race, Akhundzadeh opened the door through which Kermani ran. Although both men were, in their own ways, marginal figures—literally living large portions of their lives on the margins of the Iranian cultural sphere, in Tiflis/Tblisi, on the one hand, and Istanbul, on the other—they nonetheless effected a massive change in the way that Iranians would come to view themselves. It was Kermani's advancement of Aryanism that was fully taken up and developed in the state ideology of nationalism propounded by the Pahlavis, but it was Akhundzadeh who lay the groundwork.

Significantly, studies of Akhundzadeh staged within an Iranian Studies context demonstrate the difficulties of categorizing him according to contemporary ideas of nationality and ethnicity. They also reflect the desire of Iranian diasporic scholars to demonstrate their own enlightened rejection of Aryanism while implicitly maintaining the apocryphal reinforcement of Aryanism as a meaningful category. Akhundzadeh's life and biography are substantially more complex and riddled with contradictions than is typically acknowledged. Though considered a founder of Iran's modern (Persian) literary traditions (including drama, criticism, and satire), Akhundzadeh was not himself ethnically "Persian." He was from an Azeri Turkish family and born in a region that, during his childhood, changed from Iranian to Russian territory. It is now part of Azerbaijan. Furthermore, while he is regarded as a founder of Iran's modern literary traditions, he wrote primarily in Azeri Turkish rather than in Persian. To add another dimension of complexity, Akhundzadeh was a Russophile, an admirer of Russian culture and literature. In Tblisi, he worked as a translator for the Russian viceroy, an obvious enemy of Iranians in the aftermath of the Perso-Russian wars of the eighteenth and nineteenth centuries. Finally—and perhaps most notably for our purposes here—his mother, according to at least one authoritative account, was reputedly the descendant of an African man enslaved in the court of Nader Shah (August 1688–19 June 1747). Either Akhundzadeh is a testament to Iranians' putative "color blindness" or to the ways that our own racial myopia prevents us from seeing how racial and ethnic complexities have been homogenized into Iranian nationalist historiography in spite of the seeming contradictions they pose.

The complexities of Akhundzadeh's identity are nowhere more fascinatingly revealed than in his admiration for the Russian poet Alexander Pushkin. In his *Encyclopædia Iranica* entry on Akhundzadeh, historian Hamid Algar notes that Akhundzadeh's first published work was an elegiac poem in Persian written on the occasion of Pushkin's death: "Poema-ye sharq dar vafat-e Pushkin" ("Eastern poem on the death of Pushkin," more commonly referred to as "Oriental Poem" or "Eastern Poem").[11] It was one of a minority of his works that he wrote in Persian rather than Azeri Turkish. Making special note of the poem, Algar implies that Akhundzadeh identified with Pushkin on the basis of their common African heritage: "Ākūndzāda's mother was descended from an African who had been in the *service* of Nāder Shah, and consciousness of this African element in his ancestry served to give Ākūndzāda a feeling of affinity with his great Russian contemporary, Pushkin."[12] Because Algar does not cite a source for this notion—and there is nothing in the poem to indicate it—Algar's reader is left to infer that Akhundzadeh's admiration for Pushkin is racial, rather than one of common literary or aesthetic sensibility.

If taken as true—or partly true, or just plausible—that Akhundzadeh's common tie to Pushkin was racial rather than aesthetic, the similarities (or dissimilarities) to Pushkin's own treatment in literary historiography invite examination. Pushkin, like Akhundzadeh, is a highly canonical figure. Yet part of his fame or celebrity derived from the fact that he was the grandson of Abram Petrovich Gannibal, a person of African origin who was enslaved and gifted to the Ottoman sultan Ahmet III and later purchased and gifted again to the czar Peter the Great.[13] A substantial body of scholarship has emerged in Russian and other European languages that engages Pushkin's blackness thematically. A 2006 book called *Under the*

Sky of My Africa is a collection of essays devoted to Pushkin's blackness;[14] a French-published work called *Pouchkine et le Monde Noir* (*Pushkin and the Black World*) draws together essays that approach Pushkin's racialization through different lenses.[15] A 1999 dissertation written at Ohio State University by Raquelle Greene entitled "The African-Aristocrat: Alexander S. Pushkin's Dual Poetic Persona" proposes that "Pushkin produced many works which, upon close examination, reveal an ambiguous, but ultimately positive attitude toward both sides of his lineage."[16]

These works take a variety of approaches. They look, for example, at Pushkin's own work that explicitly engaged blackness (such as his unfinished novel *The Blackamoor of Peter the Great*), letters both to and from Pushkin, and discussion of his race in the contemporary press, among other sources.[17] Russian authors like Marina Tsvetaeva (1892–1941) devoted a good deal of thinking and writing to the subject. For Tsvetaeva, what she describes as Pushkin's "blackness"—which she construes as a kind of meaningful alterity—was what was important to her about his work. Writing in the early twentieth century, Tsvetaeva identified it as a positive form of otherness set against the racism of normative whiteness in Russia. Even a scholar as far from Russia as W. E. B. Du Bois (who was an approximate contemporary of Tsvetaeva) included Pushkin in his *Encyclopedia Africana*. In a postscript to his entry on Pushkin, published in *Phylon*, Du Bois notes, "A pertinent question arises in this case as to whether an Encyclopaedia of the Negro should include a person like Pushkin. In the narrow sense of the word and according to continental usage, Pushkin was in no sense a Negro; and the mere fact that he was an octoroon had little to do with his cultural development. On the other hand, according to usage in America and according to the biological school of racial theory, the fact that great literary figure was the result of miscegenation is of vital interest."[18]

Today, Pushkin continues to be engaged as a sporadic flashpoint for scholars and writers in Russia, Europe, and the US who wish to reflect on the relationship of Russia and the Soviet Union to racism and blackness. In 2013, for example, a group of scholars convened at the Jordan Center for Russian Studies at New York University to discuss "connections of various forms between Russian and Africa."[19] There, historian Peter Gatrell observed that looking at Pushkin and the way in which he is understood by many Russians as being "African, and Russian—but not black" is demonstrative of broader thinking about race in the USSR and Russia. His African ancestor is acknowledged, but the connection to global conceptions of blackness, particularly American ones, are refused.

This idea—"African. . .but not black"—resonates with thinking about Akhundzadeh's putative ancestry as well. Algar could bring himself as far as recognizing an African ancestor, but not far enough to engage any discussion of race in Iran, or why this might have complicated Akhundzadeh's understanding of European racial theories of the nineteenth century. The difference between the engagement of race by and about the two authors, both of whom had an African great-grandfather enslaved at a royal court (possibly through similar processes), is notable: proliferation in the case of Pushkin; silence in the case of Akhundzadeh.[20] Unlike Pushkin, however, Akhundzadeh never wrote about his own African heritage. His writings that do engage the presence of Africans largely do so in the form of including black eunuchs in Persianate courts in his plays. His writings show sympathy for this character type but betray no clear sense of personal identification.[21]

A few scholars have noted this apparent sympathy for the "African" in his work. Historian Janet Afary observes, for example, that "Akhundzadeh was an outspoken critic of the African slave trade in the Middle East who penned a searing critique of castration of slave boys in Mecca, one of the first such criticisms by a prominent Muslim intellectual."[22] She goes on to quote Akhundzadeh at length:

> There are many humans in Africa who capture young boys, castrate them with great cruelty, then sell them like animals in Muslim lands. . . . In a village near Mecca, slaveowners have a hospital for such innocent children, complete with surgeons and barbers. First the barber cuts off one hundred percent of the boy's organ, then the surgeon struggles to save the boy. A third of the boys do not survive. The rest are sold at three to four times the price to make up for the loss. Who is the cause of such misery of the boys? Muslim pilgrims who purchase them during Hajj and other events.[23]

Here, of course, Akhundzadeh works his criticism of enslavement into a larger criticism of Muslim pilgrims, who continued to buy enslaved persons and bring them back to Iran even after measures were taken by the Qajar king to curtail the traffic in slaves via the Persian Gulf.[24]

In her dissertation *Seeing Race*—an important work in its own right—Beeta Baghoolizadeh devotes a substantial portion of a chapter to Akhundzadeh's sympathetic treatment of African eunuchs in some of his principal literary works:

> Akhundzadeh set his plays and short story in Persianate courts, using eunuchs to critique the politics of Iran's governing elites. Contrary to base forms of entertainment that rested on the eunuch's physique and impotence, *Akhundzadeh did not mock the bodies of the eunuchs*. Avoiding caricatures of eunuchs, he critiqued society at large. His critique included a realistic portrayal of the enslavement of eunuchs. Akhundzadeh's pieces portray Iranian society as abnormal and backwards with black individuals as some of the only redeeming characters.[25]

Both Baghoolizadeh and Afary see Akhundzadeh's engagement with African eunuchs as sympathetic. In their view, he expresses what seem like nascent abolitionist sentiments, which they view as laudable in a reformist Iranian male intellectual. Noticeably, however, neither mentions Akhundzadeh's own possible African heritage nor his own possible connection to the legacy of slavery.[26] Rather, Afary calls him an "Azeri linguist and playwright"[27] and Baghoolizadeh terms Akhundzadeh "[a]n outsider—an Azeri intellectual who worked as a translator of the Russian bureaucracy."[28] Positioning Akhundzadeh as an "outsider" to the cultural order that connived with the treatment of African slaves, Baghoolizadeh finds in him a proto-abolitionist critic of practices surrounding the enslavement of Africans.

Baghoolizadeh's original reading of Akhundzadeh is a wistful one, searching for an historical figure who could call out the racism that Baghoolizadeh herself sees in the Qajar period and connects to the present. But to read either of the plays that Baghoolizadeh cites in support of her argument is to find shifting sands. Baghoolizadeh suggests that Akhundzadeh's representation of eunuchs avoids "mocking." This is significant in her reading because it suggests he avoids a core convention of *siah bazi*, the clownish satirical performances in which the *siah* (literally, "black") character (typically, though not always, a eunuch) is the butt of the joke. She points out that during his lifetime, Akhundzadeh's plays were never performed on stage in Iran, as a culture of theater performance and theater-going had not yet developed there. This reading upholds the fiction that Akhundzadeh's dramatic works were truly "new" and "imported," rather than any kind of adaptation or assimilation of existing forms like *siah bazi*. It would go against the grain of nationalist/conventional thought to see Akhundzadeh as someone who was synthesizing existing and problematic forms like *siah bazi* with reforming European ones.

Some of Akhundzadeh's plays were, however, performed in Tiflis (Tblisi) during his lifetime, and he received word of their performance in other sites. They continue to be performed in present-day Azerbaijan, as well, where Akhundzadeh is considered a national icon best known as the father of the Azerbaijani national theater. Of particular note is the fact that in a recent (2014) performance of *The Vizier of Lankaran* in Baku,[29] the figure of the eunuch, Mobarak, was played by a woman who—though she did not don blackface makeup for the performance—certainly played it in a farcical and mocking way. Indeed, there are no stage directions, no notes that suggest the eunuch *should* be played "sympathetically." Clearly the role is now played for comedy, even if the blackface that historically accompanied it has been erased. An equally likely reading of the work, then, could be that Akhundzadeh deployed the figure of the black eunuch as it had traditionally been played, synthesizing an indigenous or existing practice with a new one. The *siah* in *howzeh takhti* is a comical figure and, absent explicit stage direction, would likely have been played as such even in Akhundzadeh's "European" style plays.

Understood variously by scholars as a proto-Aryanist, a nascent abolitionist, the father of modern Azerbaijani and Iranian theater, a native informant to the Russian empire, and a cosmopolitan intellectual—but never a black one—Akhundzadeh has become the ultimate ethno-racial cipher. The refusal to countenance the additional valence of Akhundzadeh's purported racial complexity is thus reflective of the ways in which anxieties about race related to the legacies of enslavement in Iran have been conveniently displaced onto the more comfortably identified (and rejected) problems of anti-Arab, pro-Aryan discourses. Indeed, the general tendency among contemporary scholars to reject the premise of Aryanism in order to demonstrate their own cultural enlightenment is haunted by the myopia about Akhundzadeh that accompanies it. And, notably, the same unwillingness to engage with the full complexity of the man himself has contributed to a troubling lack of acknowledgment for the ways that other (albeit related) forms of racial thinking have informed the intellectual traditions his writing gave rise to.

REFORM, REALISM, AND THE UNSPOKEN CULTURAL LEGACY OF ARYANISM

Partly owing to the judgment of figures like Akhundzadeh, who saw the Qajar period—particularly the Nasseri period (1848–1896)—as characterized by backwardness and decay, historians of Iran for many years viewed the Qajar era as a time characterized by humiliating military defeats and increasingly self-indulgent monarchs. More recently, historians have revised this general conception. Now, they concede that while Iran's military defeats in the Russo-Persian Wars of the early nineteenth century (1804–1813 and 1826–1828) meant a massive loss of territory, including Georgia, Armenia, and northern Azerbaijan, these defeats also led to the reform of the military and the development of a new educational system (albeit one intended to improve the acumen of the officers leading that military). While Nasser al-Din Shah certainly was self-indulgent, scholars now also give him more credit for ushering in important cultural reforms, among them an interest in translation, photography, European literature, and art more broadly. Far from leading simply to slavish imitation, the contact with European art forms also led to the development of indigenous practices that were both innovative and exciting.

Akhundzadeh was part of the resulting efflorescence of translation, new writing practices and genres, artistic forms, and ways of thinking that arose among Iranian intellectuals in the nineteenth and early twentieth centuries. His writings demonstrate the way in which the political, historical, linguistic, and literary were profoundly intertwined. Moreover, they reflect the fact that literary writing was not just a vehicle for many of the new political and philosophical ideas circulating in Iran during this period. Rather, literary writing of the era also uniquely encapsulated the spirit of cultural reformation in which experimentation was the rule, rather than the exception. Up to this point, Persian literature was defined and distinguished largely by its centuries-old poetic traditions. Now, new literary forms began to circulate. Anxious to try out and introduce new artistic and cultural forms and not be bound by static ideas about genre, authors like Akhundzadeh felt free to write across genres, including what we now conceive of as academic disciplines, deploying characteristics and practices of one genre in another.

Akhundzadeh, of course, was famous for his utilization of the European dramatic form to represent the situation of the Iranian court and other Persianate courts. Like Akhundzadeh, other Persophone or Iran-identified authors began to critique the social and political order. They looked to their neighbors, real and imagined, for alternative models of governance and expression, calling for reform of the government and of society. In doing so, they began to take note of the social conditions of the lower classes—the putative "people"—and found them to be characterized by poverty and what these intellectuals saw as an unhealthy attachment to religion and superstition. Consequently, they began to write and call for political and social reform that would replace the prevailing idea of the monarch as "God's shadow on Earth" with one of a ruler constrained by the will of his people. Concomitantly, they sought to identify Islam and its Arab taint as the source of Iran's fall from its past glory and the cause of the decay, backwardness, and corruption of the present. The way forward to a future that could redeem the pre-Islamic past would, in their view, be charted through secularism (or at least a reformed religion), reform of language and literature, and a monarch constrained by a constitution.

In order for audiences to understand clearly their view of conditions in Iran, these reformist intellectuals did not want the ornate metaphors, forms, and styles of poetry. Instead, prose, and a particular mode of prose, was necessary: realism. As in other national contexts, realism developed with a focus and interest in the "people." Choosing a Persian word, *mardom*, to replace the existing words, which were of Arabic origin, writers began to "document" vernacular speech and to record folklore, recognizing in these forms vessels that had preserved pieces of an indigenous Iranian culture that could be distinguished from Arab influences and would also distinguish it from Iran's other cultural siblings in the Persianate world. Akhundzadeh is seen by historians as the prime mover in many of these developments, though many of his reforms did not come fully to fruition until after the Constitutional Revolution (1911–1915).

During this later period, there was also an increasingly marked interest and investment among writers and scholars in examining folklore practices and vernacular speech patterns. This trend is perhaps best encapsulated in Mohammad Ali Jamalzadeh's *Farsi shekar ast (Persian Is Sweet)*, a collection of stories written in a realistic style that has been celebrated almost universally for the past one hundred years for its clever use of the colloquial and vernacular to mark out differences of class, piety, and ethnicity. Although their racial thinking is almost never remarked upon, Jamalzadeh's stories reinforce common mainstream Iranian prejudices, elevating them to the level of truth through their representation in a highly "realistic" form of fiction. His representation of the different "types" of Iranian—the foppish Europeanized *fokoli*, the Arabized *mullah*, and the good-but-simple "common man" Ramezan (who is the "true" Iranian)—have become so naturalized that no one asks if they had a basis in truth. Similarly, the original rhyme from which the story and volume's title took their names is almost forgotten to contemporary readers: "Arabic is a language, Turkish is an art, and Persian is sugar; the other languages are for donkeys."

Within the genre of Iranian realism, Jamalzadeh helped give form to the Aryanist thinking Akhundzadeh opened the door to. Theirs was a cultural endeavor laden with problematic assumptions about race and purity in Iran that have yet to be fully interrogated by scholars in Iran or the diaspora. Indeed, while there is broad acknowledgment that the nineteenth century planted the seeds of the racial thinking that flowered in the twentieth century (through interest in cultural "refashioning," as Tavakoli-Targhi puts it[30]), little has been said of the problematic forms of representation that grew out of this kind of racial thinking in Iran or of the *scholarship* on this phenomenon.

Just as the complexities around Akhundzadeh's racial thinking has either been ignored or addressed in ways that ultimately reify Aryanism as a legitimate facet of Iranian identity, popular and scholarly engagements with Iranian realism have failed to address how racial thinking that both informed and stemmed from Iranian Aryanism shaped a literary genre considered foundational to Iran's modern cultural identity. While the overtly racial underpinnings of the Aryanism embraced by the Pahlavis have increasingly been identified as problematic by a new generation of scholars and critics, there is clearly significant work to be done to untangle the overlapping investments scholars in Iran and the diaspora retain in relationship to nationalism, national history, and cultural identity. By focusing on the figure often identified as Iranian Aryanism's founding father, Mirza Fath'ali Akhundzadeh, this chapter has offered a suggestive exploration of the multifaceted ways in which willful ignorance of race and racial thinking in Iran has prevented us from seeing its influence on modern Iranian cultural identity—a central contention of this book. Building on this initial introduction and assessment, the next chapter turns to the ways Iranian racial thinking was articulated in different forms of study, preservation, and literary endeavor that sought to capture the "essence" of the Iranian "people"—and how critics and scholars have struggled to fully grapple with the more troubling texts by esteemed literary figures.

Two
RACIAL REALISM

AUTHOR SADEQ HEDAYAT (1903–1951) IS WIDELY EXTOLLED IN criticism as the cultural figure most foundational to the development of the forms of realism that characterized twentieth-century literature in Iran. Recognized during his lifetime as the foremost modernist writer of Iran and a proponent of folkloric study and preservation, Hedayat was keenly interested in documenting Iranian folklore. However, his interest was riven with contradictions and underwritten with a belief in the Aryanist idea that Iranians were in fact a superior race that had been tainted by contact with Arabo-Islamic civilizations. Although Hedayat's writings were largely focused on urban milieus, his successors transplanted his methods onto a variety of rural and littoral contexts. They were particularly interested in the Iranian South as a fertile site for anthropological writing of various kinds. These Iranian author-creators and their contemporaries were deeply engaged in folklore and ethnography, both of which have historically been mobilized in the promotion of nationalist racial thinking in many contexts. The folklorist impulse persisted well into the twentieth century, inspiring subsequent generations to "discover" and "preserve" (or "salvage") indigenous Iranian cultures.

This chapter examines how a modern national Iranian identity and literature was forged through the movement to "preserve culture" (i.e., to collect folklore and other ethnographic miscellany). This movement became the foundation of modern Persian fiction, but especially of the so-called Southern School that sought to document life in the southern provinces of Iran, a region where slavery survived longest and left its most enduring mark. The authors I examine in this chapter worked among different genres to experiment with how to portray a coherent Iranian identity. They used ethnographic and folkloric practices to "document" the language of the "common people," in fact creating an idea of the common people and common language that was fabricated, using race and blackness as a kind of a foil to a normatively non-black, Persian-oriented national identity.

Hedayat himself led an idiosyncratic life that has come to symbolize Iranian modernity: born to a family of learned Qajar courtiers at the end of that dynasty's era, he is often called a "child of the Constitutional Revolution" (1905–1911). He was among the first generation of Iranians to be educated abroad, spending time at universities in France and Belgium, where it was intended that he should study engineering. Instead, he became an admirer (as well as, later, a translator and imitator) of Edgar Allen Poe (through Baudelaire's translations), Franz Kafka, and Rainer Marie Rilke. His most famous work, *The Blind Owl*, is heavily inflected by these authors; in some cases, it even samples from their writings, as Michael Beard and Manoutchehr Mohandessi have documented.[1] His commentary on the classical poet Omar Khayyam was seen to reclaim Khayyam from Orientalist translation and appropriation. In addition to being an experimenter who tried on the genres of Gothic, satirical, and naturalistic fiction, Hedayat is characterized by some as a founder of anthropology in Iran because of his folkloric interests and efforts. While it is difficult to know just which lens to view Hedayat through, he is commonly recognized as Iran's first modernist writer of prose, which has led to him being used retroactively (and in the aftermath of the Iranian Revolution) as one of several mascots for Iran's failed project of secular modernity. Unfortunately, he was dead by his own hand at age 48.

In *The History of Literary Criticism in Iran*, literary historian Iraj Parsinejad places Hedayat among the stars of the Iranian/Persianate intellectual constellation, considering him the heir to the intellectual legacies of Akhundzadeh, as well as of Kermani, Malkom, Talebof, Maraghe'i, and Kasravi—all pillars of a modern Iranian cultural sphere and authors of Iranian Aryanism.[2] While Parsinejad focuses on the development of the practice of literary criticism as a positive phenomenon, we should not ignore the way that criticism in Iran (as elsewhere) can be a vehicle for racial thinking. Hedayat's work has been amply considered in comparison to earlier Iranian thinkers like Akhundzadeh, and it has also been studied for its connections to the American and European authors who inspired him (like Poe, Rilke and Kafka). Notably, however, and in contrast to these American and European literary figures, Hedayat's work has never been fully scrutinized in terms of the racial and ethno-linguistic politics of his moment beyond his pro-Aryan sentiments—and this only in passing. Indeed, as with Akhundzadeh and his contemporaries and heirs, Hedayat's Aryanism/anti-Arab sentiments have simply been identified, if not fully examined, and his other forms of racial thinking have gone unremarked altogether.

Much of the criticism and historiography on Hedayat, which locates him as a blighted sun in the solar system of modernist writers, focuses primarily on what is perceived as his magnum opus: the cryptic novel *The Blind Owl*.[3] This strange book, part pastiche and part legend/myth/fable, surrealist and violent, has puzzled and fascinated critics for decades and is one of very few Iranian novels to be recognized as a work of "world literature." Critics are less interested in his other writings, which document a range of characters, periods, and types and range in emphasis from the fervently nationalist to the uncomfortably classist (although critics have understood the latter as a way of realistically representing the lower classes). But it is in his broader oeuvre that we see the full expression of a racial ideology prevalent (if typically unremarked) in his work and among his contemporaries.

While Hedayat was indeed influenced by, and built upon, the ideas about the role of cultural criticism (*qeritika*) cultivated by the cluster of writers identified by Parsinejad, his most significant (and overlooked) development of their ideas was to deploy the racialization they fomented in works of creative writing and to locate it "naturally" in proto-ethnographic work that "recovered" the purity of the Iranian past against the soiled/disheveled/tainted racial present. One of the earliest expressions of this interest was Hedayat's collection and publication of folklore. In fact, his oeuvre of folkloric writing is perhaps the most neglected area of his writing, remaining for most critics an aberration in the scope of his authorial corpus. When attention *is* paid to Hedayat's folkloric efforts, these works are often chalked up as an aspect of his (over)zealous Aryanist nationalism, which critics believe was part of a youthful immaturity. Yet the folkloric writings are a rich and strange vein of Hedayat's broader oeuvre and foreshadow the ethnographic turn that so many Iranian writers would take in the twentieth century. This turn produced both amateur ethnographies, like those penned by Al-e Ahmad and Saʻedi in the 1960s and 1970s, but also other catalogs of folklore, expressions, and idiomatic speech, like those undertaken by Jamalzadeh, Dehkhoda, and later, Ahmad Shamlu.

These works, understood in aggregate, reveal a desire to record and preserve the "real" Iran: that of the *mardom* (a concept closely tied to the German notion of *Volk* expounded by Nazi ideology, as discussed in chapter 1). At times, moreover, their efforts overlapped with and/or were motivated by nationalist sentiments. Exploring Hedayat's folkloric work and the ways it influenced subsequent generations of ethnographic and literary writing foreshadows the way that race, and blackness in particular, has emerged as an unacknowledged foil for a Persian-oriented national identity premised on the cultural and racial purity of Aryan heritage.

REPRESENTING THE "COMMON PEOPLE"

One of the most striking contradictions in Hedayat's enduring interest in preserving and documenting Iranian folklore is that while representing himself as a documenter of the speech of the "common man," he was himself from an aristocratic family closely allied with the Qajar court.[4] Another striking contradiction is that although the tenor of Hedayat's folkloric writings was essentially nativist and Aryanist, he disclosed to confidantes that an black servant (*kaniz*) was a major source of his material—possibly for all of his folkloric writing, but certainly for much of *Neyrangestan*, his catalogue of rituals and proverbs.[5] In *Zaban va farhang-e mardom* (*The Language and Culture of the People*), critic Mahmud Katira'i writes:

> he [Hedayat] told me himself that the Hedayat family had a *khanehzad* [born in the household; used to refer to children born of enslaved people who remained in one household or family][6] servant (*kaniz*) who was half black by the name of "Omm Layla;" her father was white (*sefid pust*), her mother black (*siah*). A portion of the material that he published in *Neyrangestan* was from the sayings of that servant and some from other hangers-on of the Hedayat family. Another portion was from Sadeq Hedayat's mother, who was a superstitious woman.[7]

Like the Grimms' Huguenot-descended informant Dorothea Viehmann (born Katharina Dorothea Pierson), whose "German" folklore the Grimms recorded as representing the stories of the German *Volk*, "Omm-e Layla" was thus the source for what generations of Iranians took to be quintessentially Iranian folk traditions (albeit Arab-inflected, since Hedayat was writing them down in order to refute them as examples of a tainted culture).

Indeed, Hedayat's *Neyrangestan* was part of a larger cultural movement to distance Iran from its historical connections to the Arab, Turkish, and South Asian worlds. However, while Dorothea Viehmann's French influence on the Grimms' German folktales has now become the stuff of scholarly legend, and a lesson in the folly of efforts to demonstrate cultural purity, Hedayat's *khanehzad* servant informant has been erased from the story of what most critics will acknowledge were racially motivated efforts to record a national Iranian folklore. Moreover, the racism these critics detect is only directed, in their estimation, at Arabs. Yet, the presence of Omm-e Layla as an influence or source demands a reconsideration of Hedayat's racially encoded writings, not only his folkloric writing but also his fictional writing of the same period. Her participation, and indeed her complex existence as a person produced through a practice of enslavement and sexual coercion in aristocratic and affluent households, has been entirely effaced from the history of Hedayat's "achievement" as a folklorist, and the irony/denial of such a person playing a generative role in his success as a folklorist has been studiously ignored.

Lauded as the "first serious book in Persian on Iranian folklore. . .published in 1933 at a time when most Iranian intellectuals looked down on popular literature,"[8] but also dismissed by cultural critic and Hedayat biographer Homa Katouzian as "short on rigor,"[9] Hedayat's *Neyrangestan* is a strange text. Nematollah Fazeli, meanwhile, suggests that its preface offers "one of the best representations of Iranian nationalist Aryanism."[10] Since it was only recently translated into English for the first time in 2023 (almost 100 years after its publication), it is worthwhile to spend some time elaborating its contents. An introduction by Hedayat explains that if the superstitions and beliefs it recorded were left documented, "others," "outsiders," and "foreigners" coming to Iran might ascribe them to Iranians rather than properly understanding them as the influence of the foreign invaders (i.e., Arabs and Mongols) who destroyed Iran's indigenous (Aryan) culture. Individual chapters of inconsistent lengths are often broken up into smaller subsections. The first chapter examines the "Customs and Ceremonies of Women," which are broken down into "Wedding Customs," "The Pregnant Woman," and "The Child." The next chapter is called "Various Beliefs and Ceremonies" and is divided into subsections like "Travel," "Honorary Sisterhood," "Sacrifice," "Snake Stone," "How to Find a Thief," and "Throwing Goat's Feet." The next chapter is "Unpleasant Manners [or Customs]," which includes "Hunger Disease." The next chapter, titled "To Meet One's Needs," consists of subsections like "To Smell Good" and "Nuts that Cure Problems," as well as several surrounding Shi'i-derived rituals. The chapter "Sleep" is followed by "Death," "Results Inferred/Derived from Parts of the Body," and "Fortune-Telling, Souls, Good Omens, Bad Omens." From there, Hedayat moves to "Hours, Time, Days," "General Rules," "Scientific Orders and Rules," and "A Few Expressions and Sayings/Idioms." "Things and Their Characteristics" is followed by "Vegetables and Seeds," "Reptiles and Rodents," "Birds and Fowls," and "Traps and Predators/Beasts." There are also chapters for "Some Ancient Celebrations," "Famous Places and Things," "Common Legends," and "Miscellany."[11] As these fascinatingly wide-ranging titles and subsections suggest, it is an eclectic book in the extreme, and it is difficult to discern much organization.

Hedayat presented *Neyrangestan* as the second part of a series of writings on folklore in Iran. The first was *Owsaneh* (Legend, 1932), a collection of what heretofore had been oral folk songs. He promised further writing in the same vein, as well as an index for *Neyrangestan* that would help readers navigate what he acknowledged was a somewhat disorganized text. Ultimately, he followed up these "folkloric" writings with "Persian Expressions" (1939), "Folk Songs" (1939), and "Folklore or the Culture of Masses" (1944–1945).

We can see *Neyrangestan* in some ways as a struggle to find the right form for collecting and conveying the wide-ranging material within. In fact, Hedayat tried out other forms for disseminating information about Iran's pre-Islamic/Arab past: in the same year that *Neyrangestan* appeared (1933), Hedayat also published both *Maziyar*, a pro-Iranian/anti-Arab historical drama about an allegedly Zoroastrian uprising against the Abbasid caliphate, and *'Alaviyeh Khanom*, arguably a work that most clearly conveys both his fascination with and contempt for the (Arabized) lower classes.[12] The latter story is full of the most viscerally repulsive descriptions of the lower classes, their hygiene, and lax morals. It includes as a character an black former slave, a woman named Fezzeh Baji (Sister Silver—precious metals or gems often being used to name enslaved persons, presumably because of their value or cost[13]), who is described in unflattering terms and accused by another character of being a procurer. The intersection of race and class in Hedayat's stereotyped and often grotesque descriptions of the masses is, in fact, quite hard to miss.

Critics have a hard time dealing with this part of Hedayat's oeuvre and, in particular, figuring out how to reconcile it with his reputation as a cosmopolitan modernist. What little critical engagement there is with *'Alaviyeh Khanom* is conditioned by the idea that Hedayat was somehow doing a service to Iran and its lower classes by "recording" or representing their speech. Most recently, this interpretation of Hedayat's work was repeated by literary scholar Omid Azadibougar in *Sadeq Hedayat and World Literature* (2020), where he characterizes *'Alaviyeh Khanom* as "a linguistically rich work and proof of his unrivaled mastery over ordinary Persian language: common expressions, idioms, and slangs are used in the narrative, pushing the boundaries of literary language and dramatizing lower-class characters."[14] Azadibougar goes on to suggest that *'Alaviyeh Khanom*'s "primary merit *is not narrative but linguistic* because it registers a language that is unprecedented in Persian literary history. Besides using coarse expressions, there are many nuances, such as slangs [sic], colloquial expressions, and idioms that contribute to characterization and *make understanding the story for a reader unfamiliar with common, lower class, language quite difficult, regardless of how well they know standard Persian.*"[15]

In contrast, historian Mohamad Tavakoli-Targhi's assessment recognizes the racism inherent in this story: "Hidayat scapegoated the Arabs as the destroyers of Iran's ancient grandeur. He called them the corrupters of pure Iranian blood, who, through miscegenation, left behind 'filthy Semites' (*kesafat-ha-ye sami*) who were held responsible for the dissemination of "cheating, treason, thievery and bribery'."[16] However, Tavakoli-Targhi's critical stance on Hedayat's obvious racism toward Arabs (and Muslims, who he sees as accepting or adopting Arab culture) is the clear exception; generations of critics uncritically (and even gratefully, as in the case of Azadibougar) accepted the idea that Hedayat's "representation of the speech of common people" truly corresponded to the *actual* speech of the so-called common people. Moreover, they have long accepted Hedayat's overarching portrayal of the people whose speech he recorded at face value. In 1949, for example, Henry D.G. Law averred that "it is useless to look for the 'happy ending' in Hedayat, for the lot of the common people in Persian about whom he chiefly writes is not usually happy."[17] This perspective was confirmed by Homa Katouzian in various forms, including in 2006, when he suggested that the pilgrims in Alavoyeh [sic] Khanom are "simple folk [. . .] so largely devoid of hidden psychological constraints that they normally speak and behave with the utmost openness."[18] Here, as elsewhere, the literature and the criticism are conditioned by a practice of denying the existence of racial thinking— with no attention whatsoever to thinking about blackness.

Subsequent generations of Iranian writers, critics, and folklorists were drawn from a somewhat more socioeconomically diverse group, but Hedayat was indisputably from an aristocratic, highly literate family of courtiers who lived among and married into the extended Qajar family.[19] Notably, the question of how he would have had access to the speech of the "common people" in order to represent it and them is never seriously considered by critics. Azadibougar characterizes the Iranian literati as titillated and impressed by Hedayat's show of vernacular speech and vulgarity, but he does not wonder whether it was truly reflective of the speech and behaviors of the lower classes depicted. Rather, he only wonders at how Hedayat got it past the censor.[20] This scholarly refusal to look more closely at where this purported speech came from and how and why it became part of Hedayat's realism is particularly noticeable in light of Hedayat's significance to modern Persian literature and the extensive criticism on his work. In celebrating his transgressive representation of "the people's" speech, we seem to have missed a step in understanding who the people were and how they were conveying their speech to Hedayat—as well as how and why realism depended on it.

Meanwhile, anthropologist Nematollah Fazeli believes that Hedayat's legacy and impact are a significant aspect of the history of anthropology in Iran, although he does not seriously consider Hedayat's literary works as truly anthropological writing. Fazeli goes so far as to suggest that Hedayat facilitated the development of secular studies of folklore in Iran with *Owsaneh*,

Neyrangestan, and a series of essays published in *Majaleh-ye Musiqi* (*Journal of Music*) in the 1930s. He summarizes Hedayat's estimation of Iranian culture as being "comprised [of] two distinctive elements: non-Iranian and Iranian. Islamic cultural elements were treated as 'alien', irrational and anti-modern, whereas the cultural elements remaining from the pre-Islamic period were taken as 'genuine culture', suited to a modern society based on European civilization."[21] No less than his influence on realism, Hedayat's contributions to a developing secular study of anthropology enabled his perspective to long outlast him. Indeed, his would become the enduring point of view in the twentieth century, and Fazeli documents how his approach was easily assimilated into the statist nationalism of the Pahlavis.

While Hedayat and the Pahlavis agreed on Aryanism as something that should be a core component of a national Iranian identity, however, Hedayat deplored the clumsy and superficial attempts by the government to institutionalize its ideas. Moreover, he saw Reza Shah as a dictator, punching down reforms rather than teasing them out organically. Yet, in Fazeli's view, writers like Hedayat, however much they may have opposed Reza Pahlavi politically, nonetheless provided the ideology that the state would appropriate and foster as its own. For his part, Hedayat viewed institutions intended to reform Iran's Persian linguistic heritage along the lines of statist nationalism to be ill-conceived and worse-executed. Among these institutions was the Farhangestan-e Zaban-e Iran (the Culture Institute for the Iranian Language), a body charged with the replacement of Arabic words with Persian words. Hedayat viewed such efforts with skepticism at best and contempt at worst.[22] Similarly, Hedayat viewed the Pahlavi regime's halfhearted effort to systematically gather folk narratives from provincial children to be a misguided and empty gesture with no "scientific value."[23] Like other efforts of the Pahlavi period, this was, in Hedayat's view, a "loathsome caricature" of proper folkloric research.[24] Hedayat viewed his own work as distinct from these clownish forays into folklore collection.

Regardless of Hedayat's contempt for their efforts, the Pahlavi state continued to co-opt authors and intellectuals into their project of statist nationalism, offering various forms of emoluments to secure their work. Although Hedayat died by suicide on April 9, 1951, his peers and successors did not abandon his folkloric impulse, even if they often proved more susceptible to the emoluments offered by the state. They pursued Hedayat's interest in folklore in other genres, utilizing new forms of media (film, audio/radio) as well as older forms (travelogues-cum-ethnographic-essays and translations) to continue the work of documenting so-called indigenous Iranian culture.[25] The turbulence of this period in Iran's history, which included two world wars, the 1953 coup, the so-called White Revolution, the development of anti-Shah/revolutionary feeling (if not a coherent movement), and ultimately, a revolution that ended monarchical rule in Iran and replaced it with an Islamic Republic, meant that the work was produced fitfully and ambivalently. It often feels incomplete, confusing, or unfamiliar if one is looking for conventional anthropological or cultural preservation work. Nonetheless, it represents a legacy of racial thinking and discursive—if unremarked—engagement with blackness that has proved remarkably enduring even in a time of dynamic social and political change.

"A WIND FROM AFRICA": RACE AND THE SOUTHERN SCHOOL/STYLE

As Iranian intellectuals turned their attention away from urban areas and toward sites more distant from the national center of Tehran, their abiding interest in documenting "the common people" intersected with a different form of racial thinking around the presence of "otherness." The growing attention focused on the Iranian South, which developed concomitantly with the region's developing oil industry, showed tendencies toward representation that were both intimately connected to and slightly distinct from the Aryanist emphasis on an anti-Arab/anti-Islam Persian past. In the south of Iran, the social and racial legacy of slavery remained evident in the black communities and individuals whose rituals and dialects proved fascinating to amateur ethnographers from other parts of Iran where slavery had faded away into the distant past.

In Iran, the "South" encompasses Khuzestan, Bushehr, Hormozgan, and Sistan-Baluchistan, and to some extent Fars and Kerman insomuch as these cities were part of the region's cultural and political economies. These provinces have a history that differs substantially from other parts/provinces of Iran by virtue of overlapping historical realities: the proximity to the Persian Gulf and their status as border provinces.[26] Now the site of a burgeoning oil industry and thus a place where foreigners are more common than anywhere else outside Tehran, the deep regional history of the South nonetheless persisted alongside the new oil cosmopolitanism. The region's significance to Iran largely lay in its maritime trade and its commodities. Significantly, this included its trade in enslaved Africans—although this particular history is often denied or obscured. These ports were the gateway for the trafficking of captive East Africans, who were moved from Iran's southern ports northward toward other slave entrepots in the hinterland, such as Shiraz. The legacy of that trade was and is still visible here, with populations of Iranians who acknowledge African heritage and connection to this past. In demographic characterizations of this region, however, the term "Arab" is often used to subsume this population, thus (wittingly or unwittingly) perpetuating the obfuscation of this heritage.

Writer and intellectual Jalal Al-e Ahmad, who was one of the most famous writers of the pre-revolutionary period and in whose emphasis on the vernacular we can see Hedayat's ethnographic influence, wrote about the Iranian South in his book *Jazireh-ye Kharg: Dorr-e yatim-e khalij-e fars* (*The Island of Kharg: The Orphan Pearl of the Persian Gulf*). Specifically, he wrote about the island of Kharg and its Afro-Iranian inhabitants in the Persian Gulf. Although from a dramatically different background from Hedayat's—Al-e Ahmad was from a clerical family and grew up working in the bazaar while sneaking off to take classes at the new Dar al-Fonun—he was nonetheless invested in many of the same concerns, particularly in the early stage of his career. Although stylistically very different from Hedayat, Al-e Ahmad is similarly famous for the use of colloquial speech in his writings. In one noteworthy departure from Hedayat's influence, though, he doesn't seem as determined to convey the "vulgarity" of the masses; only, perhaps, their abjection. In addition to the use of the vernacular, Al-e Ahmad, too, endorsed realism in literature, and, like Hedayat, believed that intellectuals were called to preserve the indigenous culture of Iran, which needed to be documented before it disappeared in the eclipse of the modernity being imposed on Iran by the Pahlavis.

In 1954, for reasons both cultural and pecuniary, Al-e Ahmad took up the state's call to preserve culture and began to publish ethnographic writings. His writing was initially commissioned by a state organ, the Mo'assaseh-ye motale'at ya tahqiqat-e ejtemai (Institute of Social Studies), although Al-e Ahmad became disenchanted with this association and ultimately abandoned it. The first piece to appear through the Institute of

Social Studies, *Owrazan*, focused on the village that Al-e Ahmad's paternal family came from. He then went on to write *Tatneshin-e Boluk-e Zahra (The Tatis of Boluk-e Zahra)*, followed by *The Orphan Pearl*. The latter was a study of Kharq (Kharg), a Persian Gulf island that was historically a site of slave-trading but at the time of Al-e Ahmad's visit had become important for the oil trade. Little-studied (and entirely excluded from the *Encyclopædia Iranica* entry on Kharg), Al-e Ahmad's booklet on the gulf island included chapters on its history from antiquity up to the near-present. He offered descriptions of the island dwellers, their homes, their means of living, their way of life, their rituals and religion; stories; songs; and an index of words used by the islanders in their speech, which he described as similar to the dialect of the city of Tangestan, in the mainland province of Bushehr. The words are given in Persian script, with the Persian equivalent as well as a pronunciation guide in Latin characters—suggesting an audience that, if not European, was educated sufficiently in European languages to make such a pronunciation guide useful.

Al-e Ahmad's descriptions of the dress and physiognomy of the Khargis are, in accordance with the style he had already begun to establish, typically blunt. He thus notes that several of the inhabitants are "completely black." He describes the conservatism of dress, observing that (in contrast to the urban centers of the mainland) the women were heavily veiled in long cotton gowns, black chadors, and a face covering they call a "burqeh." He goes on to say that it is difficult to tell "whether the women are pretty or ugly" because of these coverings. Although he did recognize that the presence of Africans and/or those of African descent represented the legacy of Persian Gulf slave routes, he does not comment on it substantively:

> I saw eight to ten or so [*hasht dah tayi*] who were completely black. Children and adults. And there were more of another kind of face that didn't seem black but had black lips and noses. Probably these are the remnants [*baqaya*] of the Zanzibarians who had comings and goings in the Gulf. Especially if we bear in mind that the Persian Gulf was one of the major centers for slavery (*bardeh forushi*). And it's interesting that Hartzfield observed that the majority of the inhabitants of the island were black at the beginning of the century (Gregorian calendar).[27]

The ethnographic urge to document and the belief in the possibility of neutrality are clear in these descriptions. Al-e Ahmad continues by observing that the island's inhabitants use the water pipe heavily and do not drink coffee, only tea. He describes some common illnesses on the island (boils; eye diseases such as conjunctivitis and trachoma; shortness of breath; leg pain that he calls a "type of rheumatism") and speculates that some of these are the legacy of pearl diving, which was the livelihood for the Khargis for many years—until, he notes "approximately 1932."[28]

Al-e Ahmad's understanding of (or desire to describe) the way that slavery has shaped the island is ambivalent. He either does not seem to realize or does not particularly credit the fact that the decline in pearl-diving coincided with the abolition of slavery in Iran (1929), which likely meant that fewer slaves could be imported to dive. Instead, he prefers to attribute the decline to a rise of cultivated pearls and the incursions of the oil industry (both also true). He is clear, however, in noting the presence of black people, whom he calls "sīāh" or "Zanzibarians," and recognizes that they are connected to Africa. He notes, for example, that "they have a special dance called the 'Shaykh Faraj' dance that is special to blacks and is a memento of Africa; everyone participates in this who can."[29]

Dorr-e yatim is an odd document—like much of Al-e Ahmad's work, it seems to be several things at once: ethnography, fiction, personal essay. Iranian-American cultural critic Hamid Dabashi observed the following of this work: "as always with Al-e Ahmad (*The Orphan Pearl*) reads like a compendium of researched and observed material awaiting a final draft. Through his experimentations he arrives at a particular prose that resembles ethnography."[30] Dabashi does not spend much time on Al-e Ahmad's ethnographic writing, moving quickly to situate this writing as mercenary work he did only out of financial desperation (to paint his house and buy a heater), and about which he felt uncomfortable given that the pay came from the Iranian Oil Consortium. Dabashi's analysis culminates in a sweeping indictment of the discipline of anthropology, in fact, with an invocation of Edward Said's comments on the discipline. Yet oddly, here as elsewhere, Dabashi is complicit (despite a substantial show of his virtue credentials as a dissident) in refusing to acknowledge what even Al-e Ahmad himself noted: the island's history as a slave entrepot and the legacy that Al-e Ahmad observed in the faces of its inhabitants.[31]

Gholam-Hossein Sa'edi, sometimes described as Al-e Ahmad's protégé, also explored the legacy of blackness in the Iranian South, where evidence of its slave history lingered long after the trade in slaves was outlawed. The presence and practices of black Iranians appear in both his ethnographic work, *zar, Ahl-e hava (People of the Wind*, 1966),[32] and in his collection of stories titled *Tars va larz (Fear and Trembling*, 1968).[33] Sa'edi's work, like that of Al-e Ahmad, foregrounded colloquial and regional speech, and *Fear and Trembling* clearly drew from the ethnographic research of *People in the Wind*, particularly in its attention to the presence of black Iranians in the south. *Fear and Trembling*'s stories reflect black Iranians' marginal status as well as the villagers' dependence on the rituals they control that can protect the village from the forces of the wind and sea.

Neither of these works by Sa'edi has been seriously engaged by critics, and the element of blackness in them is almost never addressed.[34] Yet the opening story of *Fear and Trembling* features a black man (possibly a ghost or spirit) who is taken to be a malevolent spirit by the villagers in whose midst he suddenly appears. Although all he asks for is food, drink, and company, they treat him as a haunting to be expelled. When that effort does not work, they stone him to death. It is hard to miss the racial messaging of this story, yet, this racially charged conflict framing the book of stories is rarely engaged. Indeed, the little scholarship that exists in Persian and English seems to almost self-consciously turn away from such engagement.

Significantly, Sa'edi's *Fear and Trembling* is arguably the first literary collection to evince characteristics of an Iranian "magical realism," which had echoes in the phenomenon that developed in Latin America. In her magnum opus *Decline and Fall of the Lettered City*, literary scholar Jean Franco contends that the development of magical realism in Latin America was an effort on the part of *criollo* (European-descent, Hispanic) intellectuals to develop an indigenous national narrative style that they could control and was distinct from the European modernisms that they both aspired to and felt excluded from. "The lure of 'magical realism,'" asserts Franco, "was that it reenchanted the world by drawing into literature popular beliefs and practices as a form of dissent from post-Enlightenment rationalism."[35] She goes on to acknowledge that she was (at the time of *Decline and Fall*'s publication) alone in "thinking of 'magical realism' as an appropriation of racial difference," but avers that "it is a reasonable assumption given the fact that race has been and continues to be one of the most persistent blind spots of Latin American politics and culture."[36]

While the histories of Iran and Latin America are obviously different in many ways, there are some notable affinities—among them, histories of enslavement of Africans that are generally suppressed or papered over, and the discovery and development of oil that created economic inequalities that tended to be racialized in ways that extended the legacy of colonialism and/or gave new life to Western imperialism in those countries. It is also worth noting that although works by authors like Sa'edi would not be termed "magical realism" until much later, *Fear and Trembling*, his most "magically realistic" work, was published in the same year as Gabriel Garcia Marquez's *One Hundred Years of Solitude*—1968.

At the moment of *Decline and Fall*'s publication more than twenty years ago, Franco acknowledged that her views on the role of race in magical realism's development represented a "departure" from the accepted opinions of others looking at magical realism as a style, form, or school. She persuasively argues, however, that it was this very suppression of race in the culture that produced both the writers and the critics that facilitated race's determinative role in the literature of this phenomenon. Similarly, while I acknowledge the general silence on race in the context of Iranian letters, I argue that race clearly plays a suppressed role in a number of now-canonical works that are considered part of the "Southern School" (*maktab-e jonubi*) in Iran. In what follows, I consider the ways in which the Southern School was a development of the social realist style that Hedayat played a key role in pioneering and which so clearly reflects pervasive tropes of racial thinking in Iran that are connected to ideas about "folklore" and ethnography.

Al-e Ahmad himself, though never considered part of the Southern School, meets the criterion for having written about it. (As I discuss later in the chapter, Hassan Mir-Abedini proposes that authors who are from the South or write about the South can both be considered part of this "school.") Yet the style emerged more fully when authors like Sa'edi took up the call to record evidence of Iran's various cultures, which were disappearing in the drive towards modernization and standardization of "Persian" culture and language that accompanied it. Critic Fatemah Shams offers the following definition:

The School of the South was a literary trend that gave rise to a distinctive style of writing from the 1960s onwards, featuring the myths, rituals, dialects and customs of the south with a constant emphasis on the impacts of modernization and industrialization on the southern lifestyle. The discovery of oil and the British presence in the southern provinces have been touched upon in some of the works that belong to this trend.[37]

Sa'edi himself is best known for the stories that became the film *Gav* (*The Cow*, 1969), the film that became iconic as an early product of the so-called Iranian New Wave (and later, ironically, became the prototype for post-revolutionary films produced under the aegis of the Islamic Republic's efforts to create an "Islamic cinema"). But he also produced the first ethnographic work in Persian on the practice of *zar*, one of the rituals that has consistently drawn the eye of amateur ethnographers in Iran. Sa'edi called this particular type of wind "the most dangerous and common of the winds [...] most of which come from the east coast of Africa"[38]—disowning it as an Iranian ritual/tradition at the same time that he participated in the ethnographic pattern of appropriating it to distill and signify blackness in Iran. The work in question, *People of the Wind* (*Ahl-e hava*), is an informal study of *zar* practices he called in the work's subtitle "assorted notes on the coastal dwellers of the south."[39] The *zar* ritual, which both Al-e Ahmad and Sa'edi document their knowledge of and interest in through their writings, is one major manifestation of the magic living as part and parcel of the landscape in the Iranian South.[40]

It is because of the settings of his works that Sa'edi's writings on the South have been subsumed into the category of the Southern School. Also sometimes known as "Southern Style" (*sabk-e jonubi*), the genre is in fact a nebulous notion that recalls the category of "southern literature" and even "southern Gothic" in the US.[41] Within the US context, however, problems with using "southern" as a meaningful category of analysis have been confronted within discussions around literary regionalisms as well as in the context of racial thinking. In Iran and the diaspora, by contrast, this category has received little scrutiny or interrogation. One critic, Hassan Mirabedini, proposes that the *sabk-e jonubi* includes both writers who originated from the provinces of Fars, Bushehr, and Khuzestan *and* authors who write about those regions. He goes on to describe the Southern Style as influenced by American writers such as Erskine Caldwell and William Faulkner, as well as Ernest Hemingway, but neither he nor any other Iranian critic has acknowledged or delved into the obvious similarities between ideations of the *sabk-e jonubi* and concepts like Southern Gothic or other types of style attributed to the American South.[42]

The similarities between these regional literatures are not only derived from common environmental factors like extremes of heat and storms; they are visible in the way that the legacy of enslavement, represented through blackness, haunts the regions and the literatures. It is perhaps no surprise that Iranian authors would find in writers of the American South some affinity, as their letters and translations clearly indicate they do, yet their influence has been overlooked or ignored. This has partly been because of a stalwart rejection of the idea of American influence and a privileging of nativist readings that insist on the originality of Iranian literary production.[43] Where critics do agree is that a characteristic of at least one important strain of "Southern Style" is the presence of magic or the fantastic (though typically not the marvelous) that is part and parcel of the world in which the characters live.

In *Fear and Trembling*, this element of the fantastic is also the element that most reflects the region's history of slavery and its distinctive demographic makeup: the sudden appearance of a "siah" man (in the original, literally, "a black") in the home of a community member. As discussed above, he is immediately understood by the village as a visitation by an evil or rapacious spirit.[44] However, this character is not the only person of African descent featured in Sa'edi's opening story. The villagers call upon another black man in the community, Zahed, to expel the spirit by beating drums. When this doesn't work, they kill the man who is ostensibly the spirit and bury him under a pile of rocks—a murder spearheaded by a seemingly important, if marginal, member of the community: Ibrahim, who is also termed a *siah*.[45]

Here and elsewhere in the Southern School, magical realism is often deployed around issues of race or racial difference. Yet the obvious presence of black and/or Arab Iranians seems to be an elusive subtext in critical writings on "Southern Style." Black and Arab Iranians are clearly represented as such in the stories as characters but are never identified as such in the criticism. Mirabedini, in examining this collection of stories by Sa'edi, discusses the presence of a "stranger" (what in American academic parlance might be termed an "other") as the catalyst that motivates and animates these stories. Yet at no time does he mention the clearly marked racial difference of the "strangers."[46] The obvious and clear racialization of some characters is passed over silently in other critics' writing as well. This noteworthy and consistent omission superficially confirms the notion that Iranians are "race blind" or "colorblind"—but in effect, rather, it only confirms their *insistence* on being blind to the racial thinking so clearly visible in their own canonical literature.

The Iranian South thus serves as a "site of national fantasy" or, as Jennifer Greeson describes the American South, "an idyllic habitat with mythical overtones."[47] Here, as in magically realistic sites of the Yoknapatawpha County in the US South or Macondo in Latin America, the haunting legacy of slavery and racial difference serves as foil for expressing the magical or supernatural. Yet scholars of Latin American and American South literature have been able to more thoroughly engage the complexities of these legacies by acknowledging the profound role that racialized enslavement—however historically denied at any given political moment—played in shaping the history of these regions and their literatures. Although scholars' attention to the particularities of the landscape in the Iranian South is often acute—as it is one of the distinguishing marks of this literature—they either refuse to see the *racial* landscape or engage it only fitfully and obscurely. To date, scholars who attempt to place the literature of the Iranian South in the broader scope of twentieth-century fiction's development in Iran miss the intersection of ethnographic and realistic fiction in the deployment of racial tropes, as well as the clear implications of this intersection on Iranian racial thinking.

The Blackness of Oil

Oil, of course, brought the wealth that enabled a "modern" Iran at the very same time that it prevented other forms of development and permanently stunted the possibilities for particular communities in the South. It is also the case that oil became Iran's principal asset and the basis of its modern economy at virtually the same moment that slavery was abolished in Iran.

Alongside the history of slavery and its unacknowledged legacy in Iran's cultural identity, oil is an animating force in the modern life of the Middle East that has been dramatized in Southern School literature in ways that have not yet been fully engaged by scholars.[48] Focusing too much on style and its connection to the cosmopolitan, critics who turn their attention to this literature have missed the opportunity to address the entanglements and resonances of oil and enslavement. Both are extractive and exploitative industries with a particular historical connection in the Iranian South.

Recently, in a review essay on M.R. Ghanoonparvar's translation of Moniro Ravanipur's novel *Ahl-e gharq* (*The Drowned*),[49] Fatemeh Shams took issue with the use of comparison between South American and Iranian "alternative realisms," which she sees as a belittling critical impulse intended to diminish the originality and creativity of Iranian authors.[50] *The Drowned* is the story of a coastal fishing village, Jofreh, in the South, where the inhabitants live in isolation from the rest of Iran and the surrounding region. They rely upon the sea for their livelihoods and are also enmeshed in the sea's complex magical politics. In particular, they fear the wrath of Bu Salma (a spirit also documented in Sa'edi's *Ahl-e Hava*), who tempts human fishermen into drowning by setting them the impossible task of recovering a rare pearl. The inhabitants of Jofreh also have traffic with the mermaids who are Bu Salma's paramours and sometimes tempt young men into undersea liaisons from which they never return. The profound dependency of the villagers and the sea people can only be mediated by a kind of messianic figure, Mah Jamal, who is the child of a fisherman and a mermaid. The timeframe of the book plays a significant role in these dynamics. Over the time period of the book, the inhabitants of the village are brought into greater contact with the world outside of the village, owing to the incursion of the oil industry and the revolution of 1979.

In her review essay, Shams attempts to refute critics of *The Drowned* who saw it as a derivative implementation of magical realism. Houra Yavari, for example, calls Ravanipur an author "distinguished by focusing on local scenes, customs, and folklore" who writes "in a language strongly colored by her local dialect and influenced by magical realism."[51] Shams proposes in her review essay, however, that "[f]ar from being a diluted version of a western literary trend, *The Drowned* is a work deeply rooted in ancient and modern forms of Persian storytelling."[52] A recent doctoral dissertation by Shervin Emami takes a similarly nativist stance, attempting to demonstrate that Iranian magical realism is actually a direct descendant of earlier forms of narrative and not derived from or influenced by the magical realism of Latin America.[53] Yet Shams's interpretation is particularly noteworthy in the way it oddly poses work from elsewhere in the global South (Colombia) as "Western" but moves "to ground the book in its place of origin" (Iran).[54]

In her analysis of *The Drowned*, Shams draws heavily on an earlier critical essay by Nasrin Rahimieh, which sought to explicate why one might use magical realism both to describe the narrative mode in *The Drowned* and to disrupt the assertion that Gabriel Garcia Marquez was the only South American practitioner (or inventor) of magical realism.[55] Yet even as she makes this critical intervention, Rahimieh acknowledges that Marquez was clearly an influence for Ravanipur, if not the only model for her work. Rahimieh carefully steers clear of the reductive nativist impulse embraced by Shams, wherein magical realism can only be seen as "good" or appropriate in the Iranian context if it is understood as indigenous to Iran. Indeed, Rahimieh points out that at the time her article was published, a number of postcolonial critics (e.g., Spivak, Said, Bal) had all cautioned against the type of nativist responses that tended to follow anti-colonial movements. They could perhaps not have foreseen how enduring such responses would be.

The critical engagement of *The Drowned* tends—like much of the criticism on the Southern Style—to be focused on modernization and the crisis of oil discovery and extraction that plays out in the novel. It also tends to straightforwardly engage issues of magical inter-species coupling and births, missing completely the idea of miscegenation that is obviously present in such representations.[56] As in *Fear and Trembling*, the sea in *The Drowned* is both friend and foe: the enslavement (and drowning) of human fishermen by the underwater spirit is a major theme in the novel, and the mixed race child of a fisherman and a sea sprite is the only human who can mediate the conflict between the realms of earth and sea. And yet no critic has tied these plot elements to the history of enslavement, whose legacy is still seen in much of the Gulf coast and littoral.[57]

The preferred critical reading of *The Drowned*, as with *Fear and Trembling*, is an anti-colonial/anti-imperialist one in which the villains are the foreign oil companies and the Iranian government that collaborates with them to exploit the South. Even a recent article (2017) by Monir Gholamzadeh Bazarbash and Alireza Akbari, which presciently attempts to elucidate the importance of oil in *The Drowned*, does not correlate the enslavement that is a core element of the novel with the practices of slavery that were a principal trade of the area before the advent of oil. Rather, their discussion prefers to situate oil within the more acceptable contemporary critical parlance of "trauma" and the "Anthropocene."[58] It is a glaring omission. The legacy of historical enslavement in the novel is visible not only in the economic traffic between humans and non-humans, which we see in relation to the merpeople and other characters in the story, but also possibly in personal names like Zayyer Gholam (slave), which may indicate the legacy of enslavement in the village. In other words, even if no character is identified as "black" in *The Drowned*, the location in which the novel is set—the geographical spaces of Jofreh and Bushehr—are historical sites for trafficking captive Africans. The themes introduced warrant exploration in light of this connection.[59]

Perhaps unsurprisingly given the visible influence of Hedayat on Ravanipur's other work, Ravanipur herself reflects the enduring power of Hedayat's preoccupation with the preservation of folklore and its relationship to narrative in Iran. And, like Hedayat, she reflected the urge to efface or downplay the legacy of enslavement in documenting while still utilizing folkloric material in fictional writing. In the introduction to *Afsaneh'ha va bavarha-ye jonub* (*Legends and Beliefs of the South*), a collection published in 1989, she states that after the publication of *The Drowned*, she received letters from readers asking if the myths and beliefs expressed by characters in the novel were "true" or the product of the author's imagination. "I wasn't able to give an accurate reply," she writes, "so I decided to publish some of the stories [I had collected in my research] so that when the second edition of *The Drowned* came out, the reader could easily judge for himself."[60] The idea that recording the myths and folktales of a region gives unmediated access to the inhabitants' beliefs is clearly an enduring one in Persian letters.

Nonetheless, the legacy of slavery is made clear in *Folktales of the South* in a way that it is not in her novels. If critics overlook the possible allegories of slavery and its legacy in the South when reading *The Drowned*, the folktales that Ravanipur claims animated that novel make the connection clear. In the collection's first chapter, "Gofteguyi kutah ba..." ("A brief conversation with..."), Ravanipur's local informant relates a story attributed to 'Amu 'Abbas of a night he woke from sleep to the rattle (*jelang jelang*) of chains. When he got up, he found a "tall black (*sia* [sic])...it was human but crawling on all fours and two of its legs were in chains...." This chained black man delivers a message commanding 'Amu 'Abbas to go to the sea "*ta maro did*" (until you see us; or, now that you've seen us). The man then returns to the sea himself.[61] Like Sa'edi's "siah" in *Fear and Trembling*, the story hinges on a quotidian but ghostly black figure connected to the sea—a spirit who haunts the fishermen that dwell in villages by the shore. While these oral narratives don't have a narrative arc or clarity in meaning or intention, it captures the effort of the author to record and reflect the speech and stories she is collecting.

In the Iranian Southern School, the memory of enslaved Africans has been hidden in plain sight. Cultural critics and popular audiences alike refuse to engage with the blackness embedded in now canonical works of this literary tradition, opting instead to read them through the lens of oil's socially and environmentally deleterious effects. But if we follow Jean Franco and explore the idea that, in Iran as in Latin America, "magical realism" constitutes an appropriation of racial difference in a cultural and literary landscape, we can see that here, too, "race has been and continues to be one of the most persistent blind spots."[62] This disavowal, which I have provocatively called "color blindness," enables the suppression of meaningful engagement with blackness as a constitutive aspect of Iranian cultural identity and encourages the uncritical continuation of nativist and nationalist ethnographic practices and identity articulation. This modern Iranian cultural identity echoes the concerns and investments of Aryanism up through the present day as a troubling phenomenon that permeates cultural production in all forms.

THE LIVING AND THE DEAD IN IRANIAN LITERARY CULTURE: KAKA ROSTAM'S STUTTER

The folkloric nimbus surrounding Hedayat's 1933 story *Dash Akol* is perhaps the most startling example of a haunting in plain sight. One of the stories in the collection *Seh qatreh khun* (*Three Drops of Blood*),[63] which took its name from a folkloric fragment in *Neyrangestan*, *Dash Akol* is now a canonical tale that has enjoyed enduring appeal for readers and critics. Often read as an exemplar of an historico-mythical time that has passed, it tells a "luti" story: a story of a local tough/Robin Hood type (*luti*), the protagonist Dash Akol, whose good-doing ultimately can't save him from his nemesis Kaka Rostam, a tough characterized by his coarseness and, importantly, by a stutter. His inability to be taken seriously is, we are meant to understand in the story, part of what triggers his aggression; as readers, we are invited by Hedayat both to disregard the stutter ("Everyone knew that Kaka Rostam stuttered; that wasn't why they laughed at him") and to attend to it, because Hedayat insists on representing it orthographically and repeatedly in dialogue.[64] Generally interpreted as the story of "good" and "bad" historical masculinity, *Dash Akol* has been translated into English more than once and made into a film twice: first as a *jaheli* ("tough guy") film by Masoud Kimiai in 1971 and again as a period drama in 2018 by Mohammad Arab.

In his 1985 article on *Dash Akol*, which was refined into his broader study *A Social History of Iranian Cinema*, sociologist and film polymath Naficy offers a fascinating commentary of the making of the 1971 film.[65] Naficy provides insight into not only the film itself but also the oral legend or folklore that Hedayat allegedly drew on to write his story, documenting the excess, the folkloric detritus, that Hedayat may have excised from the myth to create his realistic short story.[66] For Naficy (at least in his first draft of this essay, which was published in the journal *Iranian Studies* in 1985), the most important elision was the homoeroticism that Naficy knew was associated with *lutigari*.[67] This association was endorsed by the oral testimony of Bahman Mofid, the actor who played Kaka Rostam in blackface in the 1971 film, and who Naficy interviewed years later about the making of the film. Through talking to "elders of Shiraz," Mofid discovered that homoeroticism was, indeed, a part of the "real" Dash Akol's story. According to Mofid, the historical Dash Akol was a *"bachehbaz,"* or pederast, whose "boy lover" impregnated the daughter of a Shirazi landowner. The *luti* in Persian literature and Iranian history is an ambiguous figure associated with both homosocial and homosexual practices and places (e.g., the *zurkhaneh*, a fraternal space of ritual exercise and "ancient" masculine culture), as well as with folk heroism. Yet in Hedayat's version, Dash Akol is a tragic heterosexual: he longs for Marjan, the girl whose upbringing is entrusted to him when her father dies, but who is out of reach to him (in the logic of the story) because of their differences in age, class, and beauty.[68]

Naficy later revised his essay for inclusion in his monumental *Social History of Iranian Cinema*, where he elaborates further on the folkloric background of Dash Akol's nemesis, Kaka Rostam.[69] In the earlier version, Naficy recounts Mofid's story by calling Kaka Rostam the child of "servants of a wealthy Shirazi landowner," who had been killed through exposure to cold when Rostam's father would not allow the landowner sexual access to Rostam's mother.[70] In *Social History*, however, he acknowledges that Mofid believed that Kaka Rostam was not merely the child of "servants" but of "black slaves" in the Qavam household, and therefore (Naficy implies) decided to play the character in blackface.[71] (The Qavams, who had helped bring the Qajars to power, were reputed to originally have been Jewish, making them "*jadid al-Islam*," or "newly converted to Islam"—a smear on an ostensibly Muslim family trotted out to impugn the family as needed—a fact that was used against them when convenient, but that aspect is left out of any version of the story I have discovered.) In Naficy's reading, the film's director Kimiai and Mofid himself undertook what they believed to be a restorative history, and the fact that Mofid played Kaka Rostam in the 1971 film in blackface has been overlooked by virtually every engagement of the film except to be noted in passing in Naficy's revised version.[72]

A new film version of the story was made in Iran by director Mohammad Arab in 2018, which was followed by a stage interpretation of the story developed by Iranian dramaturge and director in exile Bahram Beyzai. Both attest to Dash Akol's enduring fascination, at home and in the diaspora. Both Arab's and Beyzai's interpretations have superficially dispensed with the blackface element of the story, preferring instead to return to a fuller heterosexual/heteronormative reorientation of the story of *lut* vs. *lat*. The homoerotic traces that Hedayat cut from the version that Naficy believed was the "true" story are not picked up at all in these versions, with Beyzai focusing on a possible love interest between Dash Akol and Marjan's mother, and Arab's film also opting for the heterosexual emphasis by foregrounding the unrequited and tragic heterosexual romance with Marjan at the heart of Hedayat's story. And yet, and yet: Beyzai, perhaps in a nod or wink to the history of the Kaka Rostam character, casts an actor who is clearly not black, but sports curly hair that comes fairly close to being an Afro; in the meantime, Arab's film presents both characters (Dash Akol and Kaka Rostam) with attributes that could be read as visual cues to read African descent: the men wear wigs that conceal their own hair and instead present to the viewer frizzy, kinky hair stereotypically associated with blackness.[73] Once again, we see the unspoken just beneath the surface. The ambivalence reflected in dramatic renditions of the characters' racial heritage is yet another example of how Iranian cultural producers consistently avoid substantive engagement with Iran's slave past while simultaneously winking at it in passing. They remain willfully and troublingly "colorblind."

As this chapter demonstrates, Hedayat, the canonical figure who engendered the kind of ethnographic writing and fictionalized material examined here, not only knew of the history of enslavement in Iran but it was also part of his family's domestic history. He leaves traces of it—consciously or unconsciously—in the social world of the *mardom* he represents in *'Alaviyeh Khanom*,[74] and also in *Neyrangestan*, which he acknowledged existed because of the folkloric knowledge of the *khanehzad* woman in his family's household, Omm-e Layla. Omm-e Layla and Hedayat would have been born before abolition, in Tehran, in the household of a family that was part of the larger realm of the Qajar court where so much photographic evidence of enslavement was recorded by the Qajar shahs and their photographers.

We do not know what became of Omm-e Layla; we do not even know her real name, only that she was at some point a mother: "Omm-e Layla" literally means "Layla's mother." Who was Layla? Was she, too, a *khanehzad* child? Could she have been, as many *khanehzad* children were, not just servants, but blood relatives—born of an enslaved woman and a male member of the enslaving family? Did she live beyond abolition, and if so, where? We do not know. But Omm-e Layla haunts *Neyrangestan* like the ghost that menaces villagers in Ravanipur's ethnographic documentation of the South, reminding those who would canonize Hedayat-the-Aryanist of the ghost of the intimate forms of enslavement perpetrated by elite families of the Qajar period. While forever afterwards forcibly forgotten, she nonetheless persists in the repository of Iranian folkloric memory Hedayat produced. An obviously liminal figure in the Hedayat household remembered by a son of that household in the post-abolition period, her presence in *Neyrangestan*, like the ambiguous figure of the *siah* that persists in modern literature (and the cinema it influenced), haunts not only Persian literature but also the criticism that responds to it.

As this chapter demonstrates, folkloric memory is a form of racialized memory that has, through the ethnographic and literary work of Hedayat, Al-e Ahmad, Sa'edi, and their contemporaries, been central to the formation of Iranian national memory, ensuring a persistent refusal of meaningful engagement with race in not only Iran but also the myriad sites of Iranian diaspora. The insistence on Iranian originality and authenticity that always emerges in relation to Iran's modern history prevents us from perceiving the racial dimensions of ethnographic and literary writing in the twentieth century, as well as the historical legacies and mechanisms that connected them to Aryanist racial thinking. As a result, we have racially informed and inflected texts that are revered and yet critically disavowed in terms of their racial dimensions, and the ways that cultural criticism has remained "race blind" have prevented an effective reckoning with Iran's slave past even in Iranian literature based in the very region where slave trading proliferated.

Three
THE LONGING FOR BLACK RADICAL THOUGHT

IN THE 1950S, THE ELECTION OF POPULIST PRIME MINISTER MOHAMMAD Mossadeq was a significant event in Iranian political life and consciousness. His goal of reclaiming Iran's major source of wealth—oil—as a national asset (rather than a semi-colonial artifice) seemed to signal a new era for Iran. In 1951, Mossadeq joined the ranks of other third-world leaders in deciding to decolonize Iran at once, rather than later. In response, British and US forces swiftly intervened by orchestrating a coup in 1953 to remove him from his post and to restore Mohammad Reza Shah to power (he had fled the country in fear of his life during the tumult). It was a moment of intense hope and utter disillusionment for many Iranians, and one that would leave an indelible mark on their political consciousness.

One underappreciated outcome of this moment is the way that it forever reoriented Iranians' impressions of the US as a champion of freedom, as well as their understanding of how they themselves were seen by western colonizing powers. Whereas the US had, heretofore, been mostly seen as an advocate of freedom by Iranians (a notion idealistically embodied by the voluntary participation of American Howard Baskerville in the Iranian Constitutional Revolution of 1905–1911, and later somewhat eroded by the role of the US in the occupation of Iran during World War II), its starring role in a coup that wrested power from a popular prime minister put an end to any idealism Iranians cherished about this new world power. Moreover, while Iran in the nineteenth and early twentieth centuries had sought to align itself with Europe through the narrative of ethno-linguistic Aryanism, Iranian intellectuals from at least the Mossadeq period onward began to see that they were just another site of imperialist play and, furthermore, were racialized in the world in a way that foreclosed racial solidarity with Europe and North America. Indeed, the series of events punctuated by the 1953 coup marked an acceleration in intellectuals' interest in political blackness and a shift in the way that Iranians understood themselves and the world racially. Yet even while reading and writing with the ideas of various anti-colonial movements, including the Third Worldist movement, the consciousness of their own racialization was accompanied by a willful ignorance, misunderstanding, and mis-engagement with articulations of political blackness more generally. As a result, their work reflects a complex relationship to blackness that permeates Iranian cultural identity in the home country and in diaspora: cognizant of their own racialization in diaspora, Iranian intellectuals drew from traditions of black radical thought to understand their positionality in diaspora while refusing to turn the lens back to examine the ways that racial thinking manifests in Iran. Without an accounting for this sort of diasporic double-consciousness among Iranian intellectuals, the significant role that blackness has played in the intellectual tradition of Iranian nationalism, anti-colonialism, and resistance to imperialism has been almost entirely overlooked.

This chapter examines how tangible and documented contact with American ideas about race in the context of the Civil Rights movement transformed the thinking of a major Iranian ideologue: Jalal Al-e Ahmad. This contact—mediated through his wife, the writer Simin Daneshvar—has been left unnoticed and disregarded in the existing scholarship on Al-e Ahmad. While Al-e Ahmad's visit to Harvard and his efforts to establish connections with black radical thought (oftentimes through the Third Worldist movement) have received scholarly engagement, this work not only misses the point of actual connection but also fails to address the notable ways that figures like Al-e Ahmad demonstrated their attention to blackness in the American context and how this thinking shaped their writings in the Iranian cultural milieu.[1] While Al-e Ahmad is often cited as an anti-colonial, anti-imperialist intellectual whose wildly diverse body of work reflected the intellectual ferment and experimentation of the moment, his work also evinced a shallow engagement with political ideology—a characteristic of his work we can easily see in relation to his contact with and investment in racial thinking. By recognizing points of direct contact and influence, we can not only better understand the subtle ways that racial thinking in diaspora inflected Iranian scholars' insistence on maintaining their "colorblindness" but also, significantly, better appreciate Daneshvar's importance as a twentieth-century intellectual in her own right and the influential role her experiences and writing played in the political thinking that is generally just ascribed to Al-e Ahmad.

IRANIAN INTELLECTUALS AND THE SEARCH FOR BLACK RADICALISM

Jalal Al-e Ahmad has long been considered a leftist-intellectual-cum-accidental-nativist by historians of the Iranian Revolution. Brought up in a Shi'ite clerical family in Tehran, Al-e Ahmad secretly enrolled himself in the state's prestigious Dar al-Fonun school while he continued to fulfill his father's wish for him to pursue a more traditional career in the bazaar (to which his family, like many clerical families, had longstanding ties). His eclectic education led him to be involved with intellectuals, writers, and reformists, but his familial connection to the clergy and the bazaar gave him a breadth of knowledge of those spheres that few secular intellectuals possessed. As a consequence of this wide exposure, he had observations to offer on almost every aspect of Iranian society.

Al-e Ahmad wrote copiously and widely, not feeling bound to produce work in any one genre. He offered his views on whatever took his fancy, from the poetics of Nima Yushij, Nowruz (New Year's) traditions, and the status of women in Iranian society to his *hajj* experience in Mecca. His writings, if not always internally coherent, were nonetheless provocative, and they inspired many Iranians of his era and after to view him as an individual who would always speak truth to power.[2] He also, as noted in the previous chapter, was among a group of writers engaged in observing and recording their views on indigenous cultures in villages situated in different parts of Iran. That said, it was his most generically amorphous work that captured the imagination of would-be revolutionaries in the 1960s and 1970s: *Gharbzadegi* (*Westoxication*, originally circulated around 1962).³ Enormously influential, it would later be called the "playbook" for the Iranian Revolution.

On the strength of not only *Gharbzadegi* but also his other writings, Al-e Ahmad has typically been viewed by history as a nativist—one of the intellectuals who was willing to make a Faustian bargain with organized religion in Iran in order to achieve a revolution. The nativism, in this framing, is seen as an unfortunate outcome of his historical situation: when all other spaces of political reform had been colonized by the Pahlavis, the only space left was nativism. At this historical moment, nativism expressed itself as a kind of Islamism, since the nativism of Aryanism had also been colonized by the Pahlavis. Although Al-e Ahmad did not live to see the revolution, he would nonetheless come to symbolize the ambivalent and problematic role that intellectuals played in facilitating it, as well as their regret at how it turned out. Notably, despite being a nativist who is upheld as an ideologue and hero of the revolution (albeit posthumously), Al-e Ahmad was in touch with a broad swath of society and international movements during his lifetime—facets of his life that have enabled recent moves to recast him as a more complex figure.

As the fate of the revolution began to bend toward the authoritarian and the idealist project of the Islamic Republic looked less and less like a utopia, scholars who had initially supported the revolution were driven out of Iran (an exile that included their children). In this context, scholars began to reconsider Al-e Ahmad in order to make sense of how a leftist revolution had become an Islamist one. For scholars based in the race-sensitive context of the US, where engagement of race—and particularly blackness—tends to be valorized and is considered not only a legitimate but also a desirable subject of knowledge production, a natural place to look was at the wider global milieu of protest in the 1960s. During this time, anti- and de-colonial movements, protests against foreign wars, the Non-Aligned Movement, and Third Worldism were important forces in the world. Black liberation movements in various contexts, including the US, demonstrated the legibility and potential of political organizing around racial injustice. In light of these global dynamics, scholars outside of Iran have attempted to rehabilitate Al-e Ahmad as not only a more suitably cosmopolitan figure but also specifically one who was conscious of critiques of racialization, racial thinking, and their connection to colonialism in Europe and the Americas.

Diasporic Iranian scholars, in particular, have recently begun to try to place Al-e Ahmad within the global radicalism of the 1960s and within the tradition of black radical thought. Historian Golnar Nikpour, for example, staged a reading of Al-e Ahmad's *hajj* narrative *Khasi dar miqat* (translated into English as *Alone in the Crowd*) in relation to Malcom X's *hajj* narrative in *The Autobiography of Malcom X* through the lens of "affinities" between the two authors and the dates of their *hajj* trips.[4] However, Nikpour proposes only a convergence of ideas rather than identifying points of actual influence. In a more recent and abstruse reading, historian Eskandar Sadeghi-Boroujerdi attempted to revise the "parochialism" and "nativism" with which he suggests Al-e Ahmad has been stamped by suggesting that Al-e Ahmad somehow intuited the argument made by W. E. B. Du Bois in *The Souls of Black Folk* (1903) regarding the "color line." In this article, Sadeghi-Boroujerdi reads Al-e Ahmad within the "series of common preoccupations [that he shares] with more familiar anti-colonial thinkers who have since emerged as both the beneficiaries and victims of 'canonisation'."[5] Here, too, the effort seems to be on identifying convergence and putting Al-e Ahmad in a framework that will be more comprehensible to contemporary academics in the West. Sadeghi-Boroujerdi specifically contends that Al-e Ahmad "can be read profitably through the critical approach to race and the manifold logics of racialization."[6] While the critical move to read Al-e Ahmad within these traditions is laudatory, the framing of "affinities" or "convergence" does not live up to the projects' potential because they fall short of identifying—and thus exploring—the fact that Al-e Ahmad had a *direct* point of influence with regard to the black radical politics circulating at the time.

Sociologist and general culture critic Hamid Dabashi's approach in his biography of Al-e Ahmad, *The Last Muslim Intellectual*, is the most sweeping as well as the most mysterious, suggesting that it was both Western myopia and Iranian (diasporic) naïveté that prevented critics from understanding Al-e Ahmad properly as an heir to black radical consciousness:

> The phenomenon Al-e Ahmad had diagnosed and briefly articulated was integral to all these arguments long before and long after the publication of his *Gharbzadegi*. But the pathologically Eurocentric obsession of his [Iranian] contemporaries could not see any of these links. [. . .] In

mapping this globality we must keep in mind how as early as Richard Wright's *Native Son* (1939), and certainly by the time James Baldwin had published his *Notes of a Native Son* (1955) or when Ralph Ellison published his *Invisible Man* (1952), the issue of conflicted and traumatised soul of the colonised, enslaved, abused and brutalised people was widely on the literary and critical map of racist white supremacy at the heart of European colonialism. The whole phenomenon of the *Négritude Movement* had decidedly scaled the globality of this condition of revolt against the colonial theft of character and culture. [...] These movements revolutionised colonised nations' awareness and pride in who and what they were, and in the process, they crafted an entire alternative universe of being, of existence, of rebellious consciousness, of will to resist power, and certainty not opting for what the Iranian critics of Al-e Ahmad still call "nativism."[7]

The arguments of these critics, while provocative, substitute *similarity* for *contact*, and Dabashi in particular argues tautologically that Al-e Ahmad must have been aware of these thinkers because he must have been aware of these thinkers. And by focusing so narrowly on Al-e Ahmad as the intellectual giant, they miss the most likely conduit through which these ideas actually reached Al-e Ahmad: his wife. Dabashi, for example, does not even countenance the idea that his awareness of them might have come through Daneshvar, herself a renowned and cosmopolitan intellectual and author. Instead, these critics endeavor to find readings of Al-e Ahmad's thinking that converge with black thought regarding anti-colonialism and anti-imperialism at different periods: during the Civil Rights era (Nikpour); in Reconstruction, with Al-e Ahmad thinking like W. E. B. Du Bois in *The Souls of Black Folk* (Sadeghi-Boroujerdi); and in Dabashi's case, the entirety of the twentieth century, as though Al-e Ahmad were omnisciently and intangibly aware of the whole of black radical thought (without ever showing *how* Al-e Ahmad would have achieved such a feat).[8]

It is this last issue—the *how* of such knowledge acquisition—that stymies the success and impact of these efforts. Left as such, these scholars can construct only partial and suggestive readings and cannot successfully disrupt the dominant understanding of Al-e Ahmad as a suggestible and, finally, incoherent thinker.[9] Indeed, they seem intent on finding in Al-e Ahmad a mirror of their own radical predilections, desiring to locate in the Iranian past an intellectual who, like themselves, perceived the radical possibility of forging alliances with black resistance politics as early as the 1960s. This kind of presentism confirms Al-e Ahmad as a "Third-Worldist," Bandung-inflected intellectual who was (like they are themselves) enraptured by the cosmopolitan notion of a global anti-colonial struggle and concomitant solidarity. Yet were critics to overcome the widespread belief that Daneshvar was merely his helpmeet rather than a major shaper of his ideas, they would find the link between Al-e Ahmad and black radical thought that they have been searching for.

While attending the University of Tehran, Al-e Ahmad famously met and married a woman from a completely different background to his own clerical family's. This woman, Simin Daneshvar, would go on to complete a doctorate and become a scholar, writer, and translator, as well as Al-e Ahmad's wife and lifelong companion. If we appropriately credit Daneshvar with the significant influence she had on Al-e Ahmad's thinking, which is demonstrated not only through Daneshvar's published writings but also in the letters that the couple exchanged, we can see the complex and compelling ways she mediated Al-e Ahmad's understanding of the Civil Rights movement in the US and its connection to global anti-colonial black radicalism.

Yet there is another facet of this connection that is noteworthy in its own right: the often-overlooked context of Daneshvar's own racial liminality and frequent public discussions of her color, which she and others described as "dark," "dusky," etc. Within the scholarship on Al-e Ahmand and Daneshvar herself, these markers of racial liminality and the social context in which they were made to matter are frequently disavowed or denied. Here, I read Daneshvar's own and others' attention to her skin as reflective of broader anxieties about race and racialization in the context of modernization and national consolidation, particularly in the context of Daneshvar's native Shiraz, an erstwhile "clearing center" for the slave trade.[10] Equally, Daneshvar's fellowship periods in the US and her own introduction to American racial thinking, typically relegated to footnotes in Daneshvar scholarship, clearly had a profound impact on her own writing and on Al-e Ahmad's.

The post-WWII period in Iran saw intense effort on the part of the US to control Iran's "modernization" and to steer it toward affiliation with the West. International programs sponsored by the US, including the Fulbright program, the Franklin Books Project, the Harvard International Fellows program, and others had a profound effect on the work of Iranian intellectuals. Daneshvar's career, in particular, demonstrates the direct influence that cultural exchange between the US and Iran during the Cold War period had on Iranian writers and intellectuals. Indeed, far from there being no demonstrable connection between Iranian and American racial thinking, influential Iranian intellectuals and writers knew about the history of Atlantic slavery and the Civil Rights movement, interacted with black American intellectuals, and wrote about it directly in their letters and indirectly in their writings for Iranians and about Iran. They observed the Civil Rights movement, in particular, in surprising ways: Daneshvar, for example, witnessed and wrote in letters to Al-e Ahmad about black protests at local eateries in Palo Alto and San Francisco, remarked on working conditions for black laborers and social conditions for black students at Stanford, and was moved to participate in the March on Washington on her second visit to the US. First Daneshvar, and then Al-e Ahmad, read and met with noted black intellectuals in the US, leading them to engage racial liberalism in different ways.

I argue that the Fulbright year Daneshvar spent at Stanford, as well as the later periods both Daneshvar and Al-e Ahmad spent at Harvard, had a lasting effect on both authors. In combination with the pernicious presence of American culture in Iran in the post-WWII period, these experiences and connections led them not only to identify with the black American struggle for equal rights in the US in the 1960s but also to deploy blackness as a metaphor in their work in ways that would continue to trouble Iranian racial thinking well beyond the 1979 Revolution. For both authors, blackness in the US came to be useful as a metaphor for the victimization of suppressed classes, including the suppression of Iranian intellectuals at the hands of the Pahlavi state. Although they never drew explicit connections between Iranian legacies of enslavement—with which both Daneshvar and Al-e Ahmad had personal contact—and the American history of enslavement that produced the Civil Rights movement, Daneshvar and Al-e Ahmad both identified with the position of subjection and exclusion expressed by black

Americans including Martin Luther King Jr., Malcolm X, Ralph Ellison, and James Baldwin. Reflecting the limits of this affiliation, however, they simultaneously expressed ambivalent feelings about being seen as black in the US and about individual black Americans.

DANESHVAR ON THE STEGNERIAN FRONTIER

Born in 1921 in Shiraz, eight years before the formal abolition of slavery by Reza Shah in 1929, Daneshvar later acknowledged that many of her stories came out of her childhood.[11] Daneshvar attended a British missionary school in Shiraz that enabled her to learn English at a very high level of competency at a time when it was not common even for affluent Iranians to do so. She published her first collection of short stories, *Atash-e khamush* (*Extinguished Fire*), in 1948, but later insisted that it not be reissued; she was embarrassed by this early effort. She started work as a translator and writer of occasional pieces for newspapers and radio to earn money while she was a university student, and she would continue to be a prolific translator for the duration of her life. Her translations include not only literary works such as *The Scarlet Letter*; *Cry, the Beloved Country*; and *The Human Comedy*, but also bestselling self-help works like *Men Are From Mars, Women Are From Venus*. While she remained interested in the implications of translation as a profession and a practice in Iran throughout her life, perhaps her most complicated negotiation with translation was her engagement with ideas of race between an American context and an Iranian one.

At the very beginning of her literary career, Daneshvar spent a formative Fulbright year at Stanford University in 1952–3. Daneshvar always acknowledged the important impact the Fulbright year had on her writing, and she credited one of her teachers at Stanford, Wallace Stegner (1909–1993), with changing the way she wrote entirely.[12] Stegner was an important architect of the development of a masculine mythology of the New West, and Stegner's work has been both celebrated and critiqued for its depiction of the American West and of white masculinity.[13] Stegner's most famous novel of the American West, *Angle of Repose* (1971), was yet to come when Daneshvar met him, but he was already acknowledged by that time for a multitude of writings on the West, including *Big Rock Candy Mountain* (1943). Notably, he had recently finished a book of essays commissioned by LOOK! Magazine entitled *One Nation* (1948), which examined racial, ethnic, and religious prejudice in the US. In *One Nation*, there is a section entitled "NEGROES" (in all caps) that contains the chapters "Faces of Jim Crow," "Black Wave," and "The Trapdoor in the Ceiling," which generated an associated film entitled "American Negro."[14]

Contact with Stegner clearly coincided with her introduction to American literature's partiality for the "power of blackness," a phenomenon that Toni Morrison critiques in *Playing in the Dark*.[15] Although she did not translate any of Stegner's work, Daneshvar was clearly influenced by his worldview and style, and she continued to seek his patronage long after her Fulbright year ended.[16] Beyond her stalwart adoption of the by-now hackneyed phrase "show, don't tell," which she associated with her American "program year," Daneshvar continued to correspond with Stegner for many years and clearly regarded him as an important mentor.[17]

The legacy of this fellowship period and Stegner's influence in her fiction is particularly legible in her deployment of racial difference in the first story collection she published after her Fulbright: *Shahri chawn behesht* (*A City Like Paradise*).[18] Unlike her previous collection of short stories, *A City Like Paradise* expands the scope of its characters. Three stories in the collection prominently foreground themes of blackness: the eponymous "A City Like Paradise ("Shahri chawn behest"), "The Iranians' New Year" ("'Ayd-e iraniha"), and "The Playhouse" ("Suratkhaneh"). In the first, Daneshvar related the story of an enslaved Afro-Iranian woman who has fallen on hard times in ways that narratively resonate with "true" accounts of such persons (e.g., Haleh Afshar's and Mariam Behnam's accounts of enslaved persons in their households). In "The Iranians' New Year," two American expatriate children are fascinated by a young man in their neighborhood whose job is to play the blackface Hajji Firuz character associated with the Nowruz, or New Year, in Iran. The volume's final story, "The Playhouse," revolves around an actor playing the *siah* blackface character in a traditional Iranian theater.

Taken together, these stories reflect a significant change in Daneshvar's sensibilities regarding race and racialization. As Daneshvar tried to translate concepts from the US to Iran and vice-versa (a process evident in her letters to Al-e Ahmad), one of those concepts was racialization.[19] She could not understand what determined why she was or was not seen as black by Americans.[20] Daneshvar was one of the first, if not the only, Iranian to record experiences of racial encounters during the height of the Civil Rights movement, and the language she uses is tentative and does not conform to any preconceived or prescribed vocabulary for discussing race.[21] Her letters suggest her fascination with race as an operative concept in the United States structuring relations between black and white Americans. She struggles to see how she herself is understood within this paradigm, referring to herself as "just a shade" lighter than the black Americans she meets.[22] Against this uncertainty about where she falls in the American color continuum, we must also acknowledge the fact that Daneshvar and Al-e Ahmad, whose family was from northern Iran, clearly had a running private joke regarding her color. He sometimes refers to her in their letters as his "black girl from Shiraz" (*dokhtar-e siah-e Shiraz*) or "my black one" (*siah sukhteh-ye man*), and she frequently signs herself in the same way, or as "your black Simin" (*Simin-e siah-e to*).[23]

Yet Daneshvar is at times patronizing toward the black Americans she meets: she seems confused and, at times, horrified or bemused at some of the situations racism in the United States engenders. Returning to Daneshvar's own racial liminality and the affect it prompted her to adopt in her first trip to the US, we can see in her early letters to Al-e Ahmad that she is moved to identify with the black Americans she sees protesting their treatment by white business owners but simultaneously sees herself as distinct from them. This dynamic is unmissable, for example, in a letter wherein she recounts a memorable experience at a Palo Alto diner:

> My dear Jalal, now I am sitting here and a black [man; *yek siah*] is protesting and I see him. This black man who is just about my own color, meaning maybe just a shade darker, wants an apology from the diner and he has hung something around his neck upon which is written "Don't go to this diner, they were cruel to me." I went to him and asked what happened. I said, Can I help you? He said, Just the fact that you have asked is the best thing you could do for me. I said, Has anyone else looked at your sign? He said that those who are themselves without money and alone pay attention but the women in furs and the men in pressed suits never look at him.[24]

In this anecdote, Daneshvar figures as the ideal and surprising receiver of the black protester's message. Rather than ignoring him, like the white American patrons of the diner, she engages him and asks what she can do to "help"—a question that can be read through the lens of the "white savior" mentality as much as it can be read as sympathy.

She also recounts for Al-e Ahmad in a later letter the story of Dorothy, a young black woman who lived in Daneshvar's dormitory at Stanford and figured in the letters as someone who was remarkable for her beauty.[25] In this particular story, Dorothy answers a phone call intended for another girl in the dorm, and when that girl is not available, the caller asks if he can take Dorothy out for a date. She accepts and waits for the caller in the dormitory's lobby. When he arrives and discovers that she is black, however, he berates her and refuses to take her out. At that point, Daneshvar relates, a black female custodian for the dormitory, who is unnamed but frequently referred to in Daneshvar's letters, yells at the man and threatens him. Daneshvar ends the story by relating how she and another (white) friend intervene by coming home from the cinema and telling the custodian to stop or she might be fired. In her relation of the events, Daneshvar clearly sees herself as having helpfully intervened.[26] But how to parse the difference here between identification and disidentification? It is clear that to Daneshvar, the behavior of all of these people is foreign, and that she once again sees herself as a white savior of sorts, intervening sympathetically and helpfully to prevent greater harm being done to the black persons whose stories these actually are. In the re-telling, notably, they become Daneshvar's stories, and she plays a quotidian heroic role, mediating racial conflict for the benighted Americans.

Daneshvar's difficulty placing herself on the color spectrum in the US, as well as her ambivalent (dis)identification with black Americans, is clearly not singular. Writing about the post-1979 Iranian diasporic population in the US, Neda Maghbouleh observes that "[t]he specter of Iran was a racial hinge between white Europe and non-white Asia"—in other words, Iranians could be construed as and could self-present as white when needed.[27] And indeed, Daneshvar's descriptions of her interactions with Americans, as in the account above, show that her "blackness" is something she elects to participate in but can step back from when she wants to in order to take the position of white ally. Most importantly, she seems to have been more interested in the history and social implications of slavery in the US as a way to explore her own civilizational progressiveness while in the US than to illuminate and examine the complexities of history and racism in Iran.

In a comparable history, Egyptian intellectuals of the same period selectively courted and rejected both the idea of Egypt as an "African" (for which we can read "black") nation and the implications of black radical activism and thought in the US. In her article "A Complicated Embrace," Ebony Coletu examines the reception and translation of Alex Haley's novel *Roots* (1976) in the Arab world in the 1970s and 1980s, where it was enormously popular.[28] The plight of protagonist Kunta Kinte became a metaphor for the condition of Egyptians, especially Egyptians working in the Gulf, at the same time that Egypt was practicing racist policies directed at Sudanese refugees and Nubian Egyptians.[29] Coletu compares this use of *Roots* to Eve Troutt Powell's powerful investigation, in *A Different Shade of Colonialism*, of racial politics in Egypt during the period of the Anglo-Egyptian condominium (1899–1956). Coletu comments that while the use of blackface in Egypt at the time Powell investigates was a way to "visualize stubborn resistance to the 'civilizing mission' of the British colonial project while reifying support for Egyptian cultural transformation under European influence [...] [t]he rhetorical plasticity of Kunta Kinte as a resistant figure and a slave marked by blackness resonates with this local history even as it conveys a distinct story about Atlantic slavery and diasporic survival in the United States."[30] Coletu goes on to explain that the use of *Roots* by Egyptian intellectuals such as Sonallah Ibrahim tended to exploit the metaphor of slavery outside of Egypt (e.g., in the US) to dramatize the plight of intellectuals such as himself, rather than to shed light on contemporary practices of racism. She also points out that "legacies of slavery are also reworked over time and in Egypt, reference to slavery as debasement has been visually coded to blackness in the last century."[31] This last point is echoed in Beeta Baghoolizadeh's examination of racial artifacts and discourse in Iran in the nineteenth and early twentieth centuries.[32]

The personal history and writings of Radwa Ashour (1946–2014) tell a similar story.[33] Ashour, an Egyptian intellectual and writer married to prominent Palestinian poet, writer, and activist Mourid Barghouti, had long been interested in black political movements before she began work on a doctoral degree in 1973 at the University of Massachusetts, Amherst. Ira Dworkin argues that it was her long association with W. E. B. Du Bois's widow, Shirley Graham Du Bois (who lived in Cairo for many years) that led her to choose UM Amherst's Department of English. Once there, she specialized in African American literature and was closely associated with the Department of Afro-American Studies. Ashour's dissertation discussed in depth the First International Congress of Negro Writers and Artists in September 1956 and, specifically, the "applicability" of the "colonial thesis"—as put forward by writers like Aimé Césaire—to the situation in the United States.[34] Dworkin uses Ashour's 1983 autobiography and the later quasi-historical novel *Siraaj: An Arab Tale* (1992), which relates the tale of a slave rebellion on a fictional east African island, to argue that Ashour's engagement of black American cultural politics influenced her fictional and autobiographical writing in Arabic in ways that had broader (but largely unexamined) consequences for the modern Arabic novel. Her profound interest in African American politics notwithstanding, Dworkin notes that Ashour was unable to endorse the critique made by her mentor and friend Shirley Du Bois of racism in contemporary Egypt. Along similar lines to those suggested by Coletu, Dworkin argues that "the particular appeal of black American culture [for Ashour] lies more in its broad-based engagement with colonial histories of oppression than with the particular contours of racism within the modern state."[35]

Like her Egyptian contemporaries, Daneshvar was inspired by the metaphor of enslavement and the metaphorical possibilities of blackness, but she was unwilling (or unable) to connect it meaningfully to any Iranian history of enslavement. Daneshvar was not interested in looking closely at how Iranians racialized black Iranians or other minorities. However, she did see the condition of black intellectuals in the United States as having some parallel to the situation of dissident intellectuals and artists in Pahlavi Iran, where any critique of the shah was censored and the author blacklisted or flagged for surveillance. Insofar as Daneshvar did see the condition of black Americans as a metaphor for some Iranian experiences, however, she clearly conflated blackness with degradation or abjection. And while her writerly sympathies remained with the politically downtrodden, they did not always embrace those who were suppressed in relation to class or race. Her representations of non-Persians (and specifically Indians and Azeri Turks) in *Savushun* can be charitably described as "Othering," and her treatment of lower-class women, especially, was often contemptuous and deployed for satire.

The dissonance in Daneshvar's perception of race relations in the US and her perspective on race and slavery in Iran was particularly evident once her fictional work began to incorporate themes of blackness in the period after her Fulbright year. When Daneshvar published *A City Like Paradise* in 1961, the eponymous story of the collection thematized the status of an enslaved black woman in the household of an elite family in the early post-abolition era. It follows the tragic life and finally the death of Mehrangiz, a slave-cum-servant who is now serving as a nanny, maid-of-all-work, and de facto concubine in the middle-class home of her former master's daughter, to whom she was given as a wedding gift.[36] With the onset of modernity and Reza Shah's reforms, which included land reforms and the Manumission Law of 1929, elite slaveholders saw a rearrangement of their fortunes. Here, we see this dramatized in the case of this married daughter, who cannot afford another person in her household. She resents Mehrangiz's sanctioned intimacy with her children (and unsanctioned intimacy with her husband), treating Mehrangiz as subhuman and with immense cruelty. Although the story clearly evinces sympathy for Mehrangiz, the character portrayed as the true victim is Ali, the son of Mehrangiz's mistress, who loves Mehrangiz more than he does his mother. In the end, Ali's inability to achieve the signposts of manhood (e.g., profitable employment, marriage) is obviously signaled as the true tragedy of the story, even though the story itself concludes with Mehrangiz's abject death.

In "The Iranians' New Year," another story in *A City Like Paradise*, the focalizing sensibility is that of two American expatriate children in Iran in the 1950s, when Americans were beginning to be present in Iran in larger numbers. But the site of sympathy in the narrative is the Iranian young man they patronize. The two children, Ted and John Michaelson, are fascinated by the blackface Hajji Firuz character, which is an important ritual aspect of the Nowruz holiday. They become, by extension, fascinated with the young man living on the margins of their neighborhood who plays this character professionally. The boys adopt a charitable attitude toward the young man and his father, who is a shoeshine, and build—unbidden—a kiosk shack for the men. They decorate it with American symbols such as the American flag and Mickey Mouse.

One day, the boys find the shack abandoned and open to the rain and wind, which has destroyed their decorations. The younger boy first imagines that "red Indians" have attacked the place; then, when his brother pooh-poohs this idea, insists that it must have been "black men with masks" and that they must be "lynched."[37] The story is very obviously a critique of American influence and expatriates in Iran in the 1950s, at a point when they had begun to look like representatives of a colonial presence—especially after the 1953 coup engineered by the CIA and MI6 to oust Mossadegh. The evocation of blackness here comes in the form of the Hajji Firuz character, as well as in the comments made by the two boys in their mistaken understanding of what has happened in the kiosk. The young man's father has died, and the boys do not understand the reasons for the poverty in which the young man and his father lived. They also do not understand that their "help" does not, in fact, save a man who has spent his life shining shoes by the side of the road.

As in "A City Like Paradise," it is not the plight of any black *person* that is dramatized (or a critique of the strangeness of the Hajji Firuz blackface tradition); rather, it is the abased condition of non-black male Iranians. The boys are foolish (if naïve) white Americans, but in the story, they take on sinister qualities nonetheless: their innocence, which is protected by their whiteness and their privilege as Americans, enables them to feel self-satisfied at the pathetic help they offer impoverished members of a society whose language they don't speak and whose customs they don't understand. With the readers's sympathy firmly directed toward in the characters of the non-black Iranian father and son, Daneshvar does not at all attempt to unpack the Hajji Firuz tradition or the two white boys' dog whistle to the threat of masked black men and the idea of applying American racial "lynch law" to solve the problem. In other words, she deploys blackface to tell us something about non-black Iranians, but she does not interrogate blackface as a problematic or dehumanizing practice in Iranian culture.[38]

Her approach is similar in the final story, "Suratkhaneh" ("The Playhouse"), which takes as its focus players in the "low" theatrical tradition of *siah bazi*. The story narrates several days in the life of a blackface performer, Mehdi Siah (which literally means "Mehdi the black"), in the dramatic tradition that was still popular at the time of the story's creation. In this tradition, as the story relates, the *siah* is the mediating, jester-like character with whom audiences are invited to identify.[39] Widely admired for his skill in this role, the actor Mehdi Siah is mentoring a young man from an upper-class background who has gotten the idea that he wants to be an actor. Mehdi becomes caught up in trying to teach this young man the importance of the *siah* figure in the tradition, while at the same time trying to help one of the regular players, a young woman who has become pregnant out of wedlock. Mehdi is ultimately coopted into the woman's scheme to try to seduce Mehdi's mentee, the amateur who has recently joined the troop. Although Mehdi forms a relationship with the young man, he ultimately chooses class solidarity by allowing the subterfuge. Here, as in "A City Like Paradise" and "The Iranians' New Year," the reader's sympathy is elicited by black or "blackened" figures, but it is ultimately directed toward a disenfranchised non-black Iranian male.

In Daneshvar's literary representation and deployment of blackness, there is a trace of her racial thinking that she may not have intended or been able to see herself. Indeed, in her letters and other self-conscious revelations of self, she does not appear able to critique the racialist thinking she absorbs through contact with Americans who saw her as neither white nor black. It is impossible to overlook the fact that in her letters and her fiction, black Iranians and black Americans remain Others who cannot be fully humanized through narration; yet we can surmise that, for Daneshvar, the liminal space in society that she observed many black Americans occupying resonated with her own experiences in Iran. We can see her, especially during her first trip to the US, trying to feel a way toward identification with black Americans. Her own literary deployment of blackness must have seemed to her both apt and timely—a move that dramatized and put into proper perspective the degradation of Iranians under the repressive and pro-American policies of the Pahlavi regime. That she later foreclosed effective identification with black Americans by growing fully into the affect of an elite Iranian intellectual (with all of the attendant persecution and poverty that entailed) does not change the fact that in that earlier moment, the liminality she occupied was a place of rich literary possibilities, if also of ethical and moral contradictions.

PLAYING IN THE DARK

In the summer of 1963, Daneshvar returned to the United States for a second extended stay, where she participated in the Harvard International Seminar and again recorded her impressions in letters to Al-e Ahmad. (While on her trip, she writes irritably to Al-e Ahmad of an unfavorable review, written and published two years earlier, of *A City Like Paradise* by a young man she didn't know.⁴⁰) During this visit to the US, she writes on several occasions, and at length, about the Civil Rights movement in the United States, which was foregrounded in the seminar. The filmmaker Richard Leacock, for example, screened and discussed his documentary *The Chair* (1962), which follows the attempt to commute the death sentence for Paul Crump, a black man convicted for his participation in the killing of a security guard during an armed robbery in Chicago. The seminar participants were taken to a Boston "slum" (Daneshvar's word) to see conditions of life there, and they were offered social experiences in self-consciously integrated settings.⁴¹

Daneshvar also wrote about Ralph Ellison's visit and presentation to the seminar, which was clearly an important part of her experience that summer. Ellison, author of *Invisible Man*, made a profound impression on Daneshvar, and she spoke of his work with great respect and interest, recording quotations from his speech to the seminar. She observed that he was someone who had used literature to overcome the enormous obstacle of race, which "might otherwise have defined him."⁴² She described to Al-e Ahmad how she had begun reading Ellison's novel and was so impressed by it that she ordered it for Al-e Ahmad in French (he could not read fluently in English).⁴³ She also discussed how Ellison, in spite of being made financially comfortable by the success of *Invisible Man*, continued to teach. She clearly saw him as a kind of comrade—a model for herself and for Al-e Ahmad. Later in the letters, having finished *Invisible Man* in its entirety, she indeed compares Ellison's style to Al-e Ahmad's.⁴⁴

In Ellison, the avowed engagé writer, Daneshvar recognizes a commonality.⁴⁵ Yet in trying to find parallels between the struggle to end racism and confront the legacies of slavery in the US with the contemporary situation in Iran, Daneshvar falters. She describes Ellison to Al-e Ahmad as a "serious" writer and goes on to characterize *Invisible Man* as a work that is focused on the hopelessness and exhaustion of (American) intellectuals who are worn down by the petty battles of right and left politics. While *Invisible Man* may tangentially be about intellectuals, Daneshvar fails to describe it in its most glaring and obvious terms: a book about the non-humanity, the "invisibility," of a black man living in the US during that period. In trying to find common ground with Ellison, Daneshvar elides the critique of racial thinking that is central to the novel, revising its meaning in her letters to Al-e Ahmad to reflect their own political predicament.⁴⁶ In this mischaracterization, can we find the link to Al-e Ahmad's own ostensible deployment of "black radical thought"? Meanwhile, how might we read, in context, the fact that Daneshvar and Al-e Ahmad refer to Ellison—whom they otherwise seem to admire— as *mardak* (meaning "little man," a derogatory term in Persian)? While this can simply be a highly colloquial expression, it feels unusual and jarring in Daneshvar's writing (if not in Al-e Ahmad's).⁴⁷ In a context inherently mediated by US racial politics—and in a discussion fundamentally about Iranian intellectuals' latent racial thinking—it is worth exploring the dimensions of colloquial usage even if no malice was intended or can be ascribed.

Daneshvar also comments on James Baldwin, whose work she had already come into contact with during her Fulbright year. During this later visit, however, she met a story of his that caught her eye. When the writer and academic Jack Ludwig (the humanities group chairman who Daneshvar called "our professor") gave her a copy of the *Atlantic* in which his own work appears, Daneshvar didn't really care for it. But she admired a story by Baldwin in the same issue (she doesn't name it, but from her description and the date, it must be "This Morning, This Evening, So Soon," 1960). She declared the story a "masterpiece" (*shahkar*).⁴⁸ Nonetheless, she later compared him unfavorably to Ellison.⁴⁹ Both Daneshvar and Al-e Ahmad are snide and condescending about Baldwin's open homosexuality; meanwhile, they seem to admire what they see as Ellison's desire to transcend race. Al-e Ahmad comments, for example, that while Ellison will always be black, he doesn't have to always be a "black writer" like Baldwin; he can just be a writer.⁵⁰

Read together, Daneshvar's comments suggest a sense of being above, and separate from, what she saw as an American problem. She was clearly attracted to the powerful social and political criticisms, as well as the elegance of style, present in Ellison's and Baldwin's work. She was also exposed to issues of racism in the Harvard Seminar, where a large part of the program focused on racial conflict in the United States. Yet she summarizes the situation for Al-e Ahmad flippantly as follows: "In summary, right now the most difficult political issue in America is the solution of the case between whites and blacks, and the Don Juans of the [American] universities and colleges are thick-necked blacks, and the white and blonde girls who don't have a black friend have lost their chance. But my dear, I'm sure you're weary of hearing my explanations."[51] The casual racism with which she reflects a stereotype about black sexuality and the fraught issue of interracial relationships in this era is profoundly disturbing and hard to reconcile with the image scholars have tried to make of Al-e Ahmad and Daneshvar as cosmopolitan radicals.

Still, Daneshvar was clearly drawn to aspects of this struggle, and indeed traveled from Boston to DC to attend the March on Washington. As she records it in the letters, she wanted to "be part of history, be a witness to history."[52] She goes on to say that it had a profound effect on her: the march was organized and peaceful, and the police, both black and white, were helpful. She observes that "the black race is truly a beautiful one," and that the black and white people participating in the march, to her surprise, "were kissing each other."[53] For Daneshvar, the march and the Civil Rights movement that it was part of are a fascinating spectacle: something to be deployed, but not something to truly be part of.

Al-e Ahmad's personal understanding of race, and his apprehension, if any, of his wife's racialization, is less clear. His access to American ideologies of race was more mediated, less direct. He had not himself visited the US before he published *Gharbzadegi*, but he was clearly influenced by American ideas, as the epigraph to the treatise as well as numerous references to black Americans within the book show. (On a more banal level, he and Daneshvar exchange letters about using American architecture as a model for the home they planned to build in the northern part of Tehran, Tajrish.) His later story, "The American Husband," shows further evidence of his interpretation of the status of black Americans as a kind of caste issue, representing them as deployed to do jobs that white Americans would not touch, such as grave digging. The titular "American husband" of the story is depicted as benignly evil, not only because he clearly worked for military intelligence in Iran but because, once home in the US, he secretly works as a gravedigger—a tainted class of work only black men will undertake. Al-e Ahmad's troubling representations of American social life and organization are both strangely detailed and trenchant, as well as reflective of the racial logics this chapter traces.

While scholars of Daneshvar have largely overlooked her time in the US and its influence on her writing and thinking, it is even more notable that the efforts by diasporic Iranians to connect Al-e Ahmad—and themselves—to the black radical tradition in the US seem to miss these important nodes of connection. In this context, they seem to be assigning Al-e Ahmad a racial consciousness that he did not, in fact, possess on his own. Rather, Al-e Ahmad expressed a consciousness of race and racial inequality that were demonstrably mediated by Daneshvar's time in the US and articulated through their letters to one another. Al-e Ahmad's reflections on American racism in his own writing do not suggest a nuanced engagement or a willingness to explore or unpack Iranian racism in a meaningful way.

Why have Daneshvar's letters, which have been clearly recognized in recent accounts like Dabashi's *The Last Muslim Intellectual*, been overlooked in the understanding of both Al-e Ahmad's and Daneshvar's racial thinking and political writing? Surprisingly, given her historical marginality and exclusion from most accounts of the ideologies of the revolutionary period, Daneshvar's perspective on race would in fact become a dominant one in Iran. Following her lead, writers like Al-e Ahmad used race as a metaphor for abjection and marginalization in the global scheme of colonialism/imperialism. Her role in developing such a point of view has been overlooked because critics like Nikpour, Sadeghi-Eskandari, and Dabashi, even when they are ostensibly looking at literary documents like the *hajj* memoirs, cannot see the literary as a valid source for understanding historical development. They fail to see the important role that Daneshvar played in shaping Al-e Ahmad's racial thinking. This pattern is one that recurs in scholarship on Iran: when scholars turn their attention to race, readings attentive to gender or sexuality tend to fall by the wayside, and vice-versa. While the call to intersectionality has in some ways become a hollow or empty gesture, here we see a compelling reason to demand it: if we use an intersectional strategy, we can perceive in Daneshvar and Al-e Ahmad's relationship not only the complicated and uneven "companionate" marriage it has often been celebrated for being, but also the racial logic within a marriage where she was styled "your black Simin." It is through their letters to one another in conjunction with their published writings that we see them navigate their ambivalent relationship to blackness and their uneven and often self-serving identification with black radical politics. In short, it is only through his intimate correspondence and connection with Daneshvar that Al-e Ahmad's (limited) racial consciousness becomes legible.

A COMPLEX HERITAGE

The desire on the part of Iranians for filiation with the black intellectual tradition ambivalently demonstrated by Daneshvar and Al-e Ahmad did not end with the Iranian Revolution. It reappears in the scholarship I mentioned at the beginning of the chapter but also in the 2019 video proceeds of the conference "Forty Years After" (i.e., after the Iranian Revolution) held at the Center for Iranian Diaspora Studies at San Francisco State University.[54] Some of the conference attendees were invited to narrate their experiences on camera; these recordings were then disseminated online via YouTube. In her recorded interview, Ida Yalzadeh, a second-generation Iranian-American reflects:

> I was born in Torrance, California; both of my parents were born in Iran...I remember when I was younger, and we were learning about the Civil Rights Movement, for example, I would see pictures of...the sit-ins at the diners... [...] and thinking *where would I have been...were there any people like me in this moment at time in the United States*? [...] Were there any Iranians back then? That was when I was probably in elementary school and these questions were in the back of my mind....[...] And then I remember when I was applying to colleges, I checked "other" [for race] and then my mom [...] was like, why did you check "other"? We're white! And I am like, No, we're not! What's happening?[55]

This Iranian-American woman narrates a generational divide between first- and second-generation Iranian immigrants who see themselves translated into US racial schemes quite differently. As sociologist Neda Maghbouleh suggests in *The Limits of Whiteness*, such signaling of racial filiation is an important but often overlooked aspect of Iranian immigrants' negotiation of assimilation in their host countries. Whereas the diasporic Iranian's mother, a first-generation immigrant, is at pains to establish Iranians as white, the second-generation child of that immigrant demonstrates a desire to affiliate her ethnic difference with blackness. Although her expression of this feeling is presented by the speaker as novel, when viewed in the longer scope of Iranian contact and identification with black radicalism, it becomes a fascinating echo of the observations made by Daneshvar, who was, in fact, a witness to the Civil Rights movement in the US in the 1950s and 1960s.

Daneshvar's attraction to discourses around Civil Rights made for a heady combination in conjunction with her ambivalence about black people. She lauded individual black American authors, yet disparaged their emphasis on *being* black; she wrote about blackness and black people in her short stories, but only as a foil for eliciting sympathy for non-black Iranians; and she wrote in glaring stereotypes about race relations in US higher education while evincing an inability to fully scrutinize her own racialization in Iran. At one point, she also wrote into her fiction her memories of a black nanny who had likely (given Daneshvar's birth before abolition) been enslaved, signaling a different but equally suggestive personal connection to the practices of enslavement. Collectively, these seeming contradictions show us the complexity of the cognitive dissonance that could be employed by Iranians enmeshed in the legacy of enslavement when they confronted the parameters of American discourse around slavery, emancipation, and rights. Daneshvar could or would not connect the struggle of the black man wearing the sandwich board of protest in front of a Palo Alto diner to the woman who gave her the character Mehrangiz, and she found it strategic to deploy blackness as a trope in her work without ever scrutinizing it as a meaningful category of analysis in Iran. For her, black people—even the nanny who lived in her home—were always foreign and always a symbol of something else.

In the Pahlavi era, young Iranians were disseminated into the world through their modernizing campaign, charged with going abroad to be educated and returning home to renew and develop their country. Daneshvar was both part of that project and also interpellated in the American Cold War project of educational propaganda through her Fulbright fellowship. However, while she did bring her experience of American racial politics back to Iran both in the form of her own writing and in the ways her experiences informed the thinking of her husband, she brought back a self-serving version of political affiliation between Iranian and black intellectuals rather than a more robust engagement with race as a useful category of socio-cultural analysis in Iran. We continue to see this dynamic today—replicated and iterated across a range of cultural forms that manage to leverage the potential of black radical politics in diaspora while remaining willfully blind to its application in Iran.

Four
PERFORMING BLACKNESS ON STAGE AND SCREEN

IN APRIL 2013, THE NOTED IRANIAN ACTOR SA'DI AFSHAR DIED. Eulogized in Iran and in diasporic sites around the world, obituaries recounted how Afshar had won fame in theaters playing the *siah*, the black slave character (sometimes a eunuch) that gave the name to the Iranian dramatic tradition called *siah bazi*—a farcical historical comedy notable for its eponymous blackface performance. Notably, Afshar was not himself a black person; rather, like all actors who appeared in this role, he was a practitioner of a blackface tradition that had flourished in Iran for untold years. While obituaries acknowledged Afshar's repute as a *siah* performer, they did not attempt to describe what this character was or how it fit into the dramatic tradition of *siah bazi*. Rather, the obituaries invariably assumed that anyone reading the article in Persian would already know what a *siah* character was. Afshar's career had faded as live audiences dwindled in the era of the Islamic Republic of Iran—he was, in fact, one of the last Iranian actors to make his reputation playing the *siah*—but the tradition has remained a familiar part of the Iranian cultural landscape.

The dating of its origins is uncertain, but *siah bazi* has lived on in national memory up through the present.[1] Indeed, *siah bazi* is a theatrical tradition that Iranians at home and in the diaspora continue to nostalgize and value. A "low" or popular form of theater, it can also be classified as *takht hawzi* or *ru hawzi* (both names deriving from the site of the performances) or as *mazhakeh*, meaning comical. The premise of this type of performance is the interaction of the *siah*, or blackface character, with members of a pre-modern royal court. Through humor, the male *siah* character—typically a slave (*gholam*) or eunuch slave (*khvajeh*)—challenges the authority of those in power. The audience is invited to identify with the *siah* as a jester character who frequently speaks directly to the audience, inviting their alignment with his perspective.

Siah bazi's ongoing relevance in the contemporary Iranian imaginary was confirmed by dramaturge Nasser Rahmaninejad in 2014 at a lecture and cultural event entitled "In Search of Laleh-Zar" at Stanford University. In the presentation, he spoke sadly about the life and death of the theater district in Lalehzar, a street in Tehran full of famous cafes, theaters, and shops. It is renowned for its modernist, European, and cosmopolitan glamour, and it has been memorialized in many Iranians' recollections of the world before the revolution.[2] Rahmaninejad, now in exile in the US, recalled Lalehzar's glory to his audience. In the course of his remarks, he included *siah bazi* only in passing, but the theatrical tradition that had been a major facet of Lalehzar's cultural life took on a more prominent role following his lecture. The evening included a screening of Paris-based filmmaker Maryam Khakipour's *Siah Bazi: The Joymakers*, a 2010 documentary film that is a nostalgic paean to Afshar, his troupe, and the Theater Nasr, which was perhaps the last site in Iran of *siah bazi* performances. If the connection between the nostalgia for Lalehzar and *siah bazi* were not already clear to those attending the talk, the website describing and advertising the event, which now offers a link to the lecture recording,[3] is accompanied by a thumbnail of a *siah* actor costumed and in full blackface. The actor's gaze is just slightly away from the camera, and his head rests at a quizzical angle, suggesting an ironic pose. The requisite jar of blackening paste sits in front of him on the dressing table.

In his 2020 memoir, *A Man of the Theater*, Rahmaninejad spends much more time reminiscing about *siah bazi*. He recounts both the tradition itself and its centrality in Iranian social life, disclosing that his own first experience of theater was playing the *siah* character in the amateur productions he and his siblings would stage with other children in their southern Tehran neighborhood. He describes the *siah*'s history and theatrical role as follows:

> I do not think anyone knows the exact origins of the Siah-bazi, but its roots are obviously in slavery, *although the character is not a slave*. He is a servant who lives in the master's house. He's funny, he has an accent, and under the guise of not understanding certain words he turns them cleverly against the master. The audience understands that he is clever, that he is purposely mistaking the meaning of the words in order to use them as weapons.
>
> This character has different names—Almas (diamond), Mobarak, or Firouz—and during the show he slyly says or does wrong things in order to aggravate his master so as to get laughs from the audience. When the master calls him—"Fi-i-i-rouz!"—the audience laughs, because they know something funny will likely happen soon. *This black character serves as a metaphor for the Iranian masses.* The audience always sympathizes with him; he is their hero, always outwitting the master. Also, he acts as a confidante to whoever is relatively powerless or oppressed in the play. If the master's son has difficulties—loves a girl whose father won't let her out of the house, for example—Firouz will act as a go-between. The son and the daughter always trust him. When my brother formed the theater group with the neighborhood kids, I was always the one who played this black hero. *Siah-bazi was the style of theater we knew best. All kids would see it at wedding ceremonies and knew the stories and characters, especially the black character and his master, Haji.*⁴

Although *siah bazi*, like other popular dramatic traditions in Iran, no longer occupies the central place it once did among Iranian social/public entertainments, it has not disappeared because of any anti-racist sentiment or movement. Indeed, as Rahmaninejad's words suggest, many Iranians disavow any actual connection of this tradition to slavery and don't find significance in its racial underpinnings. Rather, its decline owes more to repressive conditions for artists and restrictions on performance under the Islamic Republic. And regardless of its performative death, it lives on in the collective imagination and memory of Iranians at home and in the diaspora. Indeed, its reverberation in collective memory reflects and refracts the deep cultural tension over Iran's long legacy of slavery and its contemporary efforts to define and refine its national identity.

As with Rahmaninejad's reminiscences, Khakipour's *Siah Bazi: The Joymakers* memorializes the passing of this dramatic tradition. Along with the film's sequel, *Shadi*, in which the troupe travels by invitation to France to stage a performance with avant-garde director Ariane Mnouchkin, it also mourns the decay of the theater tradition symbolized by Lalehzar. Khakipour's films do not attempt to historicize this tradition in any way or to tie the dramatic practice to practices of enslavement. Nor do her films compare *siah bazi* to American or other traditions of blackface or minstrelsy (or even to other Iranian dramatic traditions, high or low). Instead, Khakipour takes the tradition of *siah bazi* to be both chthonic and *sui generis*. She views it through the nostalgic lens of a cultural dramatic tradition being lost in the contemporary post-revolutionary world of the Islamic Republic, where public performances—dramatic, musical, etc.—are censored, policed, and/or prohibited.[5]

In the first of the films, the approximately 45-minute documentary *Siah Bazi*, Khakipour intersperses on-stage and behind-the-scenes shots of performers at the Nasr Theater, one of the last troupes to perform *siah bazi* live in Iran, with scenes of former *siah* actors gathering to talk about what happened to the practice. The presence of Sa'di Afshar is notable among them. Through Khakipour's lens, we see the poverty and degradation into which many of these actors have fallen since the revolution. Interestingly, in scenes shot outside of the theater and in poorer neighborhoods of Tehran, there is some intimation that many of the *siah* actors were in fact Iranian Jews. While this potentially fascinating history of Iranian Jews' involvement in the facilitation of this tradition is touched upon in passing, however, it is ultimately lost in the narrative sweep. Overall, the film evinces nostalgia for an era not of *convivencia* but rather Persian cultural dominance. Many other important and interesting aspects of this tradition's story are similarly obscured or ignored. Most strikingly, the fate of the enslaved Africans who gave the tradition its "hero"—its "voice of the people"—is entirely excluded from this sentimental commemoration of an all-but-dead dramatic tradition. Instead, the film ends with a focus on the plight of a young woman, a member of the troupe, who had once hoped to make her life in the world of this "low" theater tradition. She feels like this possibility has been foreclosed, and it is her agony, her sadness, that gives the film its sounding note.[6]

Perhaps unsurprisingly, the sentimental post-revolutionary lens used by both Rahmaninejad and Khakipour offers a distorted and limited view of this dramatic tradition. Seen through their eyes, the end of *siah bazi* is representative of the loss of Lalehzar and of Iran's glamorous modernity—one of many other cultural losses caused by the revolution and the purge, which are to be mourned. Such positioning effaces the need for critique, making the narrative about *siah bazi* an elegy, not an investigation nor even a history. Seeing the demise of *siah bazi* as a consequence of the IRI's policies and practices around the arts not only prevents us from seeing its fundamental racism, it also obscures other relevant aspects of why or when the tradition came about, how it persisted, and other reasons that may have contributed to its cessation.

Indeed, to search for information about Lalehzar is to open the door to a profound nostalgia for the pre-revolutionary past. Often characterized as Tehran's "Champs Élysées," Lalehzar symbolizes the hopes of a lost modernity. Lalehzar: the "tulip garden" —a name redolent of the Qajar past. One popular story often repeated is that Lalehzar was established when Nasser al-Din Shah Qajar (with whom so many stories about lost modernities begin) traveled abroad and became enamored of European-style walkways/streets and theaters, and wanted to establish such a district in Iran. In reality, the development of this district, which had, prior to the mid-nineteenth century, been a private royal pleasure garden, had to do with the economic corners Nasser al-Din Shah backed himself into. When he had to revoke an unpopular concession he had granted to a European for tobacco, he had to make good on the funds and did so by selling off the land in and around Lalehzar.[7] Almost from its beginning, Lalehzar was thus associated with wealth, cosmopolitanism, and foreign goods and people.

Yet, by the first decade of the new millennium, the street had been declared culturally "dead" because of the many closures and general decline of the street. Scholar Jane Lewisohn examines the "downfall" of Lalehzar from its pre-revolutionary grandeur and cosmopolitan beginnings to its later status as "working men's district" and finally a district dominated by wholesale electrical goods.[8] Nevertheless, as Iranians at home and abroad witnessed the closure of the last two theaters on the street, Pars (in 2005) and Nasr (2011), it catalyzed a sense of high nostalgia for Lalehzar.[9] A site of several live drama theaters, it had also become known as "cinema street," boasting no fewer than eight cinemas—a literal manifestation of the proximity between popular dramatic and cinematic traditions in Iran. Cinema clearly grew out of Iran's dramatic traditions, and also grew into them—a truth demonstrated by the texts examined in this chapter.

It is this Lalehzar, the Lalehzar that was once the center of Iranian theater and film, that Iranians remember fondly. In fact, a stage set of Lalehzar now resides in a studio city on the outskirts of Tehran. Created by filmmaker Ali Hatami and used in many historical films and TV shows (including, most recently, *Shahrzad*, which was wildly popular in Iran and the diaspora), the set elicits deep nostalgia and is a national treasure of sorts. And recently, an architectural group established a kind of pop-up museum in Nasr Theater, offering patrons "old school tickets" and a "symbolic tea token" to help them remember (or in most cases, imagine) what it was like to attend a show there. The internet, meanwhile, is full of Lalehzar tributes from the first two decades of the twenty-first century, some of them professionally produced, others more amateurish; some narrated, some not. Those that are unnarrated simply show footage taken by a person carrying a handheld phone camera and walking through the street, the lack of vocalized impressions suggesting that there is no need to narrate—any Iranian will understand the tragedy of Lalehzar's decline.

Lalehzar's fall from beauty is a narrative arc that mirrors the nostalgia, sadness, and loss that many diasporic Iranians feel for the world before the revolution. And if Lalehzar is representative for many Iranians (especially diasporic Iranians) of the lost modernity of the pre-revolutionary period, it only takes a short step to understand how references to the past glory of *siah bazi* and its blackface "voice of the people" operate metonymically to convey that nostalgia and sense of loss.[10] Taking the proximity of cinema and theater represented by Lalehzar as a kind of map for the close relationship between drama and cinema in Iran, this chapter takes that short step to examine how *siah bazi*—and the specter of blackness more generally—continue to inflect artistic explorations of Iranian modernity and identity. Focusing on the utilization and critical engagement of performative blackness in key works from director/dramatist Bahram Beyzai and filmmakers Mohsen Makhmalbaf and Marzieh Meshkini, I suggest that their work demonstrates how culture makers in Iran and the Iranian diaspora romanticize and nostalgize blackness through *siah bazi*-inspired comedic performances and through the use of black actors, operating from a space of exceptionalist nostalgia that seemingly precludes any critical reevaluation of how these traditions have emerged and take meaning from Iran's legacy of slavery. By exploring these makers' artistic productions and critical reception, we can see how blackness is deployed to help cue and recreate lost cultural concepts and landscapes and to explore the limits of revolutionary ideology without ever engaging the historical contours or contemporary experiences of race and racialization as a constitutive facet of cultural identity in Iran.

THE BLACK THAT "WON'T SCRUB OFF"

Dramatist and cinematographer Bahram Beyzai has been involved both with the theatrical tradition of *siah bazi* and its afterlives in cinema.[11] The child of a renowned poet, Beyzai regards himself, and is widely regarded by critics, as one of the most important Iranian filmmakers and culture producers of the twentieth century. Beyzai's writing on the history of *siah bazi* in his monograph on the history of drama in Iran, *Namayesh dar Iran* (*Drama in Iran*), comprises one of the earliest scholarly monographs on the subject.[12] It is still considered an authoritative text today. Beyzai is also a human bridge between the older traditions of drama and the newer artistic tradition of cinema. Now residing permanently in the US, he is regarded and extolled as a national treasure in exile, guarded and maintained in an honorary professorship at Stanford University by Abbas Milani, who has himself played a complex role in the political and cultural wars over the meaning of Iran in the twentieth and twenty-first centuries.[13] Even Milani's ideological enemy Hamid Dabashi avers, in his typically *entre-nous* style, "I have always thought of Beizai as the most 'Iranian' filmmaker, for something about him is almost archaic or archetypal in his iconic representation of Iranian culture. When he makes a film, it is as if Hafez or Ferdowsi had come back to life, had learned the techniques, and were now making a film. I think you get the picture."[14] Beyzai also demonstrates how porous the distinction is between "Iran" and "diaspora" in an era in which so many Iranian nationals and their children possess two passports, allowing them to move back and forth between Iran and a second nation, often the US or Canada.

Beyzai's film *Bashu: The Little Stranger* (1988) is famous for its deployment of racial misapprehension in Iran to stage a conflict-and-resolution story about the unity of Iranians around the Persian language. It chronicles the development of a quasi-familial relationship between an orphaned black Arabophone Iranian boy from southern Iran and the white Gilaki Iranian woman in the Caspian region who adopts him. Throughout the film, the eponymous character, Bashu, is racialized through the identification of his "blackness," which is understood by the inhabitants (including, initially, the protagonist Naii) of the Mazandaran village where Bashu arrives as something that makes him inhuman. Naii asks "What are you?" and tries to forcibly scrub off Bashu's blackness in a pond. When she can't remove his skin color, she cries out, "It doesn't wash off!" and "You are as black as coal!"

Naii herself is an extremely fair-skinned northerner from the Mazandaran region near the Caspian Sea. As literature scholar Nasrin Rahimieh proposes, Naii, as a Gilaki speaker, exists outside of the dominant, normative realm of Persian language.[15] Moreover, the story is staged in a location that is literally marginal, being located at the northern edge of Iran. Bashu, who speaks an Arabic dialect common to southern Iran and the Gulf, is likewise from a geographically decentered location. They are therefore both marked as "others" in Iranian society, but in different ways: Naii linguistically, Bashu by his "blackness." In focusing on language, Rahimieh is able to sidestep the obvious ethnic/racial implications that exist and does not need to examine the fact that Naii is not only a Gilaki speaker but is obviously *ethnically* Gilaki—belonging to the group of Caucasian people settled near the Caspian Sea. As we are shown through footage at the beginning of the film and in flashbacks, Bashu, in contrast, is not just a speaker of an Arabic dialect but also is a member of a population of black Arabophone Iranians who live in the South of Iran.

By setting this story outside of the altered cityscapes of 1980s Iran, the film recreates a pre-urban, pastoral, "lost" cultural landscape where the idea of a reclaimed supra-Iranian identity can be demonstrated and acted out. *Bashu* evokes nostalgia for a moment when Iranians could imagine themselves united around something other than the revolution, other than the war, other than religion. Diasporic critics, perhaps even more than critics based in Iran, took the bait. For example, while astute in many ways, Rahimieh's focus on the way the film stages various forms of reconciliation through language effaces the profoundly disturbing ways in which the allegorical assimilation of Bashu (and black Iranians) into the "family of Iran" can only be achieved through the death of his natal family and his assimilation into a white Iranian family. The focus on language also seems to follow a general nationalist tendency to believe that language can overcome ethnic or racial conflict. Reading with Beyzai's intentions, then, Rahimieh agrees with his narrative directive to see blackness only as a prop or a red herring—a useful tool to tell a story about a supra-Iranian identity that can be supported through a common use of the Persian language and the feeling of fellowship it foments. She thus reinforces the avoidance of seeing race as a noteworthy facet of Iranian cultural negotiation, and she does not confront the racial thinking in the film. Like the film itself, this critical evaluation ultimately facilitates the fantasy of a "race-free" or "colorblind" Iran, a place where everyone can live together in Persian.

Rahimieh is not alone in this reading. Notably, *Bashu*'s reception in Iran is difficult to accurately assess since it was suppressed domestically and banned for four years because of its anti-war content. It received only one censored screening in Iran.[16] But its reception in the Iranian diaspora has been enduringly enthusiastic. Indeed, the existing scholarship on *Bashu* is written almost exclusively by diasporic Iranians and tends, as in the case of Rahimieh, to reinforce optimistic perceptions of Iran as a race-blind culture and to ignore the problems that arise from the film's staging. In "Treacherous Memory: *Bashu the Little Stranger* and the Sacred Defense," scholar Kamran Rastegar overlooks available racial readings entirely.[17] Rastegar interprets *Bashu* in the context of the Sacred Defense, the Islamic Republic's "trauma production" of the war, and reads it primarily as a "product of the memory practices around the Iran-Iraq War."[18] While otherwise an attentive and astute reading, Rastegar characterizes Bashu only as "Arab," eliding reference to the scenes in which racialized blackness is significant. Such a positioning seems, once again, to demonstrate race-blindness on the part of both the film and the critic as a particular kind of virtue. Similarly, in the same edited volume, *Moments of Silence: Authenticity in the Cultural Expressions* of the Iran–Iraq War, 1980–1988, co-editor Shouleh Vatanabadi comments on the way in which *Bashu* "exposes the interconnections of race, gender, and cultural divides," but declines to explain what constitutes these divides to begin with or why they persist.[19]

Film scholar Negar Mottahedeh's reading is ostensibly more oriented to the question of race.[20] She names the legacy of slavery and its presence in *Bashu*, but her reading eventually sidesteps any practical engagement with or critique of Beyzai's representations of race and allusions to enslavement, which include his deployment of the motif of the wind through *zar*, the Afro-Iranian ritual practiced in southern Iran. Mottahedeh is right both to identify the winds in Beyzai's films as betraying a consciousness of the legacy of enslavement and in suggesting (albeit uncritically) that Beyzai, to the extent he is aware of it, sees enslavement and racism as metaphors for the condition of white Iranians rather than real historical conditions to be addressed. Yet Mottahedeh seems to congratulate Beyzai for appropriating and deploying the *zar* ritual in *Bashu*, choosing not to see it as an exploitative use of blackness in a film that ultimately does not critique racial thinking in Iran. Instead, her reading moves transcendentally, positioning Beyzai's films (even the pre-revolutionary ones) as a vindication of her general thesis about Iranian cinema: that its ironic surprise is that it is "unconstrained by the voyeuristic look and the spatio-temporal coordinates that prescribe its realism."[21]

While viewers in Iran likely identify with Naii, diasporic Iranians express sympathy for Bashu.[22] We might speculate that that this is so because of the racial misapprehension he experiences. Like many diasporic Iranians, the child Bashu is not accurately understood racially in his own national context. As Neda Maghbouleh demonstrates, Iranian immigrants and their children in the US have been understood as black, Latino, and other racial/ethnic categories, which not only offends many Iranians' sense of their own racial superiority as putative Aryans but has also in fact reawakened the discourse of nationalist linguistic unity in sites of high diasporic aggregation, like California, where the population of Iranians is estimated to be over 200,000 (the highest population in the US).[23] Hamid Naficy observes, "In the film's screenings abroad, this scene [in which Bashu reads in Persian from a textbook and Naii's village understands for the first time that he is indeed Iranian] proved to be highly cathartic for Iranian exiles, who tearfully identified with both

Bashu and Nai as exilic characters. The film offers to both diegetic characters and exilic spectators the healing and unifying power of a national language as an antidote to difference and displacement."²⁴

Beyzai's treatment (or non-treatment) of race in *Bashu* is lauded by diasporic audiences and critics like Mottahedeh and Rahimieh for suggesting that the commonalities that unite Iranians across their racial and ethno-linguistic differences far surpass their differences, but the film remains curiously deaf to the issue of race it raises. Although racial difference is, arguably, the very problem the film sets its characters to overcome, a deeply nuanced fact is that both the filmmaker himself and the critics agree to pass silently over its significance, opting to see the film's solution to the problem as a solution to any racial difference or conflict in Iran. When Naii's husband returns from the war disfigured by the loss of a hand (a fatal problem for a farmer), Bashu essentially offers to become that hand—not so much to become a son (Naii and her husband already have one), but rather a useful tool. It is thus perhaps unsurprising that critics invested in the myth of racial blindness accept the offered sop of national-unity-through-language and step away from meaningful engagement with the presence of blackness. They choose instead to note it and leave it to the reader's interpretation.

"AN ANCIENT COMIC GENRE"

Almost twenty years after *Bashu*'s release, Beyzai brought to the stage a play that both makes clear the problems with racial thinking in Iranian and Iranian diasporic communities and casts a shadow on the racial terms enacted in *Bashu*. *Tarabnameh: A Modern Interpretation of a Traditional Play* was staged in two parts at De Anza College in March and October 2016 with support from the Iranian Studies Program at Stanford. According to Beyzai, this play was written much earlier, in 1994, but he could not find a venue or audience for it until 2016 when Abbas Milani championed it and arranged for its production and performance.²⁵ Stanford University's Iranian Studies program website offers the following laudatory description of the production:

> Bahram Beyzaie's new play *Tarabnameh* was performed in two parts to nearly sold-out audiences. A cast of 37 actors, more than a year of rehearsals, and hundreds of hand-made costumes!

Tarabnameh has its genealogy in the tradition of Takhte-Hozi plays—a tradition of popular plays, combinining [sic] comedy and music, dance and poetry. Centuries of despotism have rendered this form bereft of content. In Tarabnameh, a play with a cast of thirty-seven actors, this ancient comic genre keeps its joyous ambiance but takes on new form and meaning, underscoring the possibilities of once forgotten traditions becoming rich, robust, and lively modern forms of theater.[26]

Tarabnameh seems to pull in every character trope of pre-modern narrative in Persianate society, reflecting that, at its core, it is a story structured by the logic of slavery. The principal tale around which the play's other stories unfold is the journey of an old man, a *haji* (a title given to those who have made the pilgrimage to Mecca, typically denoting, therefore, someone wealthy enough to do so). He is traveling to market to sell his black male slave Mobarak (presumably, by the appearance of this character, a eunuch) and to replace him with an attractive white slave girl, Nobar, who will become his concubine. The haji's wife—herself a trope of the toothsome middle-aged wife about to be supplanted by a younger woman—tries to interfere, and the whole group becomes enmeshed with local politics, an execution, and more in a setting that is clearly from "before" modernity. In its comic nature and deployment of a clownish enslaved black character, it also fits the loose requirements for *siah bazi*.

For the average viewer, the play is hard to watch—not least because of its length: it is a ten-hour production, staged in two five-hour performances. Although there is plenty of easily comprehended physical humor, the play traffics in tropes that are likely unfamiliar to many younger viewers and completely unfamiliar to the non-Iranian viewer. Perhaps anticipating such misapprehension, the production was heavily scaffolded in informational presentations and websites like the one cited above. In a presentation in Persian at Stanford several weeks before the play's performance, Beyzai's champion, 'Abbas Milani, introduced a lecture by Beyzai proposing that Beyzai was saving a vital aspect of Iranian culture from loss through his writing and production of *Tarabnameh*, as well as through his larger artistic oeuvre. Indeed, Beyzai's works encompasses more than fifty plays, twelve films, and several monographs. Beyzai himself then went on to speak at length (for over an hour) about his efforts to recreate the *ru hawzi* and *mazhakeh* (humorous, comedic, popular) genre of performance outside of Iran and outside its temporal origins. He also discussed his work on drama more broadly. In his remarks, he framed diaspora and exile in the US as a necessary evil, a place where the new Iranian regime cannot suppress his art and where there is an outlet for a form of cultural nostalgia that hearkened back to pre-revolutionary Iran.

Notably, Beyzai spent significant time refuting any connection between racism and the *siah* performance, suggesting that attempts to draw such connections are "simple-minded."[27] Rather, he insists, the *siah* has been a presence in Iranian performative traditions since time immemorial and is derived from a color symbolism figured in the *Shahnameh* (Book of Kings), a medieval epic poem with ancient roots that relates the story of Persian civilization and kinghood since the beginning of time (literally). According to Beyzai, in the *Shahnameh*, blackness is associated with the hero-king Fereydun, while whiteness is a characteristic of the villainous usurper king Zahhak. (Beyzai has a great deal of interest in this story, which I return to below.) The dancing and "joy-making" (*shad avari*) associated with blackness is about the triumph of Fereydun over Zahhak, as is (according to Beyzai) attested by as lofty a source as Abu Reyhan Biruni, the tenth–eleventh-century CE polymath.[28]

Having refuted any racial inflections, Beyzai did not, of course, acknowledge or address similarities of the *siah bazi* in *Tarabnameh* to blackface traditions in the US, or the potential conflicts or concerns that might arise from staging a production with blackface characters in twenty-first century America. But he had good reason to believe that his staging would not land uncomfortably with his core audience. Iranians in the diaspora have largely refused such comparisons as well, asserting, as Beyzai did, that *siah bazi* has nothing to do with black people themselves or even with slaves—despite the fact that these assertions are manifestly untrue.[29] Still, whatever its origins, it is clear from the costuming, speech, and gestures of the *siah* in such performances that at some point in its performative history, the practice took on an unambiguous connection to slavery and, specifically, African enslavement in Iran.[30]

Following the lead of Beyzai and Milani, who both clearly hoped to avoid any genuine confrontation around this core aspect of *Tarabnameh*'s production, not a single one of the thirty photo stills on Stanford University's Iranian Studies program website shows the blackface performers who were integral to the play. But the fact remains: two characters, Mobarak and Golzar, were played by actors who used artificial means to blacken their faces and revealed skin. In *Tarabnameh*, these characters are humorous foils to the principal characters' love story, and clips of the performance available online reinforce the sense that the blackface minstrelsy of the US has either clearly influenced this production or that there is convergence between the two traditions. This is especially apparent in the degree to which exaggerated sexualized behaviors are part of the role of the blackface character(s). And, in fact, we can see from Khakipour's *Siah Bazi: The Joymakers* documentary that the performance of blackface in *Tarabnameh* clearly differs from the performance of the *siah* role in Iran's Nasr Theater, at least up through the early 2000s. In Beyzai's *Tarabnameh* production, the male *siah*, Mobarak, is almost certainly played by a woman, and uses exaggerated physical gestures that mark him out from the other actors: the character simpers, dances, bends forward while speaking to stick out his bottom. By contrast, in a production captured by Khakipour in her documentary, the actions of the *siah* are more subdued. While this may be attributable to restrictions on reference to or suggestion of any kind of sexuality in the Islamic Republic, it is equally possible that an actor playing a blackface character in the US would have access to—indeed could likely not avoid—exposure to historical or contemporary American performances of blackface.

Indeed, despite Beyzai's presumptions of his audience's understanding and approbation of the tradition—as well as his efforts to stave off criticism—his production struck a nerve. In an online review of *Tarabnameh* hosted on the Ajam Media Collective's website (ajam.com), an Iranian-American community member attending the production wondered, "Why are Iranian-Americans still laughing at blackface in 2016?" The author, Maziar Shirazi, a physician based in the Bay Area, expressed shock at the director's complete denial of racist elements within this form of representation. Shirazi notes:

> After the play, exhausted and hungry, we drove home from San Jose, a car-full of Iranian people who collectively have been racialized and discriminated against in multiple countries and contexts over the course of our lives. We discussed *Tarabnameh* and its vivid racist imagery, which had left the most durable impression of the whole production.[31]

Interestingly, what seemed to compound Shirazi's dismay at *Tarabnameh*'s racial representations was his knowledge of Beyzai's reputation as a filmmaker. He points out:

> It was no less disconcerting to see this work coming from an artist acknowledged in the Iranian community for his race-consciousness. Director Beyzaie is an acclaimed filmmaker and playwright who won recognition for his treatment of complex social and cultural issues through his work, including race. His 1989 film "Bashu", was lauded for its portrayal of Afro-Iranian identity and racism present within Iran during the Iran-Iraq War (1980–1989), and is considered by some to be one of the best Iranian films of all time.[32]

Only in the aftermath of the play's production (and perhaps after Beyzai was called out in the op-ed piece for the tone-deafness of the blackface performances) was a thirteen-minute short documentary released to respond to the issue. Made available on tamasha.com, a Persian-language video site similar to YouTube, it features Beyzai directly addressing the question of the *siah* and racism, if only briefly (less than a minute):

> The black [character] has a name of [i.e. indicating] prestige, such as Mobarak (Blessed), or Almas (Diamond), or some other jewel. . .it's always a name that expresses their role as makers of joy. It is a blessed, joy-making character. The color of his face has no connection to racism, or race, or that kind of thing. He's the hero of the story. . .it doesn't have anything to do with race. . .he's a good hero of the story.[33]

Beyzai goes on to describe the function of the *siah* in this kind of drama but refuses to acknowledge in any way the problems that might arise in producing a blackface play in California in 2016—or how this connects to Iran's own troubling legacies of slavery and racial thinking.

In *Tarabnameh*, as with *Bashu*, the "tearful identification" with "exilic characters" by diasporic Iranians proves to be at the core of how Beyzai's art is understood and extolled within the Iranian diasporic community. In this sense, then, Shirazi's critical review reads as a sort of outlier to the main thrust of how Beyzai's work has been reviewed and received. Shirazi asks, "In a time when institutionalized racism and police brutality against black

Americans are a matter of widespread national protest and debate, what does it mean that Iranian-American audiences are laughing at a blackface performance put on by a supposedly race-conscious director?"[34] But the question was never answered. Beyzai was not "canceled" because of *Tarabnameh*; far from it. Rather, Beyzai continues to enjoy— in both Iran and perhaps even more the diaspora—the kind of respect and reverence known to few academics or artists in today's world. 'Abbas Milani himself avers that Beyzai is a singular individual who has "lived a life devoted to the dignity of the artist and the scholar."[35]

Indeed, it is because Beyzai is such a major figure in twentieth-century Iranian drama, cinema, and the arts that we must recognize the ways in which he encompasses and is in fact representative of the way Iranians at "home" and in the diaspora see race and how they interpret it through the lens of a distinct cultural identity. In his defense of blackness in *Tarabnameh* and more broadly in the *mazhakeh* tradition, Beyzai brought in a lineage of blackness from the Persian epic, the *Shahnameh*, which is widely regarded as an authoritative text on "pure" Persian culture. His engagement with the *Shahnameh* runs deep, as he has engaged in a sustained effort to prove that the *1,001 Nights*, a text whose development and circulation has been credited to Arabophone societies, was in fact a corruption of the *Shahnameh*—an argument primarily invested in establishing a Persian provenance and highlighting the text as yet another iteration of Arab cooptation and corruption of a pure Iranian culture. Where the *Shahnameh* is undisputed as a text of Persian provenance, the *1,001 Nights* is a contested text: Iranians insist (and most scholars acknowledge) that the text is connected to, and likely came from, Iran, given that the names of the frame story's characters (Shahrzad, Dinarzad, Shahzaman, Shah) are Persian. But many scholars give credit for its development and circulation to Arabophone societies. Iranians chafe at this, seeing it as yet another theft of Iranian cultural patrimony by "the Arabs." Beyzai himself has spent considerable time in recent years trying to establish Iran's cultural claim to this tradition, writing two monographs on the topic that apparently derive from his dramaturgy (he also wrote and staged two plays based on the *Nights*). Moreover, Beyzai's interpretation of the *Shahnameh* not only reflects the nationalistic terms with which it was commonly read in the nineteenth and (especially) twentieth centuries in

Iran—as a parable of the Arab conquest and the ultimate victory of Iranian culture over Arabo-Islamic cultural incursion—but also positions it to possess a more sweeping authority: by suggesting that the story is pre-Arab and Indo-Aryan (and, importantly, pre-*Nights*), he tries to wrest back the cultural authority/capital (however dubious) that European translation has given the *Nights* and to claim it for Iran instead.

Significantly, Beyzai's efforts to reclaim the *Nights* as "Persian" deracinate the story, which is focused on themes of adultery, slavery, blackness, and tyranny. In Beyzai's interpretation, the frame tale of the *Nights* is a corruption of the story of Zahhak and Fereydoun from the *Shahnameh*, a story that does not include any reference to slavery or race (or, for that matter, adultery). In his view, the Arabs have not only stolen this story, they have corrupted it. In a kind of perverse interpretation of the contemporary call to "decolonize" academia, Beyzai stretches into the medieval world in which a pure Persian culture was colonized by Arabs and Islam. In so doing, he reinserts the Aryan myth/Aryanism back into contemporary Iranian discourse on culture and race while managing to remove the specter of race altogether. In fact, despite Beyzai's silence on race and insistence on its inapplicability to the *Shahnameh*, the *Shahnameh* has plenty of color symbolism and hierarchy, albeit with disputed meanings. Critics suggest, for example, that the presence of blackness is not always negative or clearly tied to race, though it has undoubtedly become tied to race in the modern imagination and interpretation of these stories. So it stands out that in his commentary on *siah bazi* and his various remarks on *Tarabnameh* that Beyzai denies the racial hierarchies embedded in these traditions. Eschewing and in some cases blatantly rejecting engagement with race, Beyzai refuses to see a way that he might usefully engage, critique, or even acknowledge it as meaningful.

Seen in the light of Beyzai's passionate engagement with the *Shahnameh* and his efforts to reclaim the *Nights* as originally of Persian provenance, his oeuvre signals among Iranian intellectuals a broader sense of cultural loss caused (or accelerated) by the revolution, as well as the desire to reclaim what is rightfully Iran's heritage and due. Reaffirming Iranians' place in a racial hierarchy (or outside the US racial hierarchy) is significant in this regard. In *Bashu*, the Persian language can unify Iranians and efface the significance of any racial differences; in *Tarabnameh*, the logic of the play leads to happy endings and a place where the *siah* character is "beloved," "the hero," and "has nothing to do with racism." His work recreates, fleetingly, the cultural spaces perceived as lost to the revolution and to time, offering on screen, on page, and in the diaspora the opportunity to forget the past decades and feel connected to a past untainted by the revolution and racially conflicted sites of exile.

THE TRUTH ABOUT HASSAN

Bashu and Beyzai's work on drama may represent the most longstanding interest in the tradition of *siah bazi* by a modern "high art" director, but other films produced by contemporary Iranian directors also exhibit a strange consciousness of Iran's history of *siah bazi* and deploy it to curious ends. Director Mohsen Makhmalbaf began his cinematic career as a staunch (even rabid) supporter of the revolution and its cultural reforms, as well as a vociferous opponent of directors like Beyzai, who he termed "idolatrous" (*taquti*).[36] As time went on, however, Makhmalbaf would eventually repent of his support for the Islamic Republic. He broke with the regime publicly in 1989 with the film *Marriage of the Blessed* (*'Arusi-ye khuban*), which follows the plight of a veteran of the Iran–Iraq War in an effort to expose the hypocrisy of the regime's treatment of "martyrs," the name given to those injured or killed in the conflict.

Like Al-e Ahmad in the pre-revolutionary period, Makhmalbaf's engagements of blackness superficially appear peripheral to his projects, yet his commitment to oppositional positions and his interest in forms of alterity are legendary: several of the films he made in the 1990s exposed enormous gaps between the rhetoric of the revolutionary government and its actions. In spite of his break with the Islamic Republic, however, he remains devoted to many of the ideals that animated the 1979 revolution, including a rejection of US imperialism in its many forms. In an interview in Nader Homayoun's documentary film *Iran: A Cinematographic Revolution*, Makhmalbaf applauds the expulsion of Hollywood films from Iran after the revolution and asks, "Why should we let someone else dream our dreams for us?"[37]

In spaces like Homayoun's documentary and beyond, Makhmalbaf demonstrates that he is aware of the frustrations in black Americans' struggle for equality and justice, but he does not connect this to his gestural use of blackface and enslavement in his films. For example, he introduces blackface and enslavement repeatedly in films like the satirical (and nostalgic) *Once Upon a Time, Cinema*, which Hamid Dabashi has called Makhmalbaf's "love letter to Iranian cinema."[38] Here, as in traditional and cinematic *siah bazi* performances, blackness is deployed largely for critical comedic effect, such as when, at one point in the film, a black child is handed to Nasser al-Din Shah in the harem to create the occasion for the punchline, "Is this child mine, too?" The child is used to stage a joke about the Shah's profligacy—the joke being that his harem was so large and varied that he could not possibly have kept track of how many or who his wives were, or how many or what race of children he had.

Indeed, while Makhmalbaf has never staged a performance of *siah bazi*, its style inflects his cinematic productions. When Makhmalbaf uses blackness in his films, it is typically deployed humorously and for comedic effect while offering subtle social critique. At the same time, the recurrence of blackness in *Once Upon a Time, Cinema* is a reminder of aspects of Iranian history that have been swept under the rug. In an interaction with Anis al-Dawleh, one of Nasser al-Din Shah's most (in)famous wives, the Cinematographer (the main character in the film) is brought blindfolded into the harem and offered a black slave girl for his use if he will cooperate to help Anis al-Dowleh regain the shah's favor. That Anis al-Dowleh, a consort recognized through marriage, could offer to the court photographer a black slave girl as a gift suggests the way in which Iranian viewers would have understood that black slaves were considered chattel. The film also includes a montage tribute to classical Iranian cinema in which several highlighted films (including *The Black Slave and the Hunchback*) are blackface comedies. Taken in aggregate, the instances of blackness in *Once Upon a Time, Cinema* comprise a wink and nod to a history of enslavement and minstrelsy that post-emancipation generations of Iranians have been complicit in forgetting.

As his growing separation from the regime continued, and his celebration at international film festivals meant that he was marginalized in Iran and would eventually go into permanent exile, Makhmalbaf increasingly made films set in other locations. He continued, however, to make films that were critical of the regime. His 2001 *Safar-e Qandahar (Kandahar)* is ostensibly set in Afghanistan, but was in fact filmed in a border territory between Iran and Afghanistan.[39] Made *before* but released *after* the 2001

American-led invasion of Afghanistan that followed the 9/11 attacks on the World Trade Center, the timing of *Kandahar*'s production and release have proved confusing and feel prophetic. Although the film could not have addressed an invasion that had not yet happened, the film has the quality of a space already besieged and dangerous, heightening the qualities of irony and prescience that are this cryptic film's hallmarks. The aspect of this cryptic quality that enters into a discussion of blackness is Makhmalbaf's casting of Teddy Belfield/Dawud Salahuddin in the role of Tabib Shahid (credited as "Hassan Tantai"). The character played by Salahuddin is a black American disguised as a Muslim doctor who is practicing medicine in a village in Afghanistan. Here, Makhmalbaf offers up a character who, like black performers in *Once Upon a Time, Cinema*, is in some ways peripheral to the plot yet feels essential to the film's oblique (and unexpectedly anticipatory) critique of the US and its predatory (and future) involvement in Afghanistan.

Dawud Salahuddin's personal biography warrants brief consideration. A black American born in 1950 as David Theodore Belfield, he moved to the Washington, DC, area to attend Howard College. Soon thereafter, he became involved with various Islamic movements, including the Nation of Islam (which he says he eventually rejected because of its corruption—he likens it to the Mafia). According to his own account in Jacques Lafond's film *The Trouble with Hassan*, he became a Muslim because he saw it as a "color-blind" religion. Through association with Iranian supporters of the revolutionary regime in the DC area, who he met at a local mosque, he eventually agreed to assassinate a Pahlavi-era Iranian diplomat on behalf of the revolutionary government of Iran. (Again by his own account, his preference would have been to assassinate a high-profile American who had been involved with interference in Iranian politics, such as Kermit Roosevelt.)

The diplomat selected for assassination, Ali Akbar Tabataba'i, was believed to be organizing a counter-revolution with the support of the US government. Belfield/Salahuddin, dressed as a postman, rang the doorbell of Tabataba'i's home in Bethesda, Maryland, and when Tabataba'i was summoned, shot him point blank and fled. He drove into Canada and flew to Switzerland, where he was aided in flying on to Iran. Since his escape, he has been resident (possibly in a form of captivity) in Iran, although he has spent periods of time in other places, such as Afghanistan. To this day, the

IRI uses him propagandistically as a symbol of their rejection of US racism and the systematic degradation of black people in the US. In reality, however, Belfield/Salahuddin has led a complicated life in Iran, and in Lafond's documentary, appears as a quasi-prisoner of the IRI.[40]

In *Kandahar*, blackness is, as in Makhmalbaf's earlier films, deployed comically, to reveal absurdities in both the situation of the film and Iranian contemporary history. Belfield/Salahuddin appears in the film in the guise of an Afghan physician living under the Taliban. We first see him addressing a little girl who is relaying her ill mother's symptoms to the doctor; the mother herself is off camera. Eventually the mother comes into the makeshift office to sit behind a curtain with a hole in it; when prompted via the child intermediary, the mother puts her mouth, then her eye, to the hole so the doctor can examine her. The scene is played for absurdity: the mother can obviously hear what the doctor is saying and the doctor can obviously hear what the mother is saying, but they must use the pretense that the child—not yet sexually mature as a woman, and therefore permitted to speak to this male stranger—is the mediator between them. The next patient is Nafas (the film's protagonist), with Khak, her child guide (though not her own child), relaying her symptoms to the doctor. Throughout, Belfield/Salahuddin speaks to himself and the viewing audience in English, commenting that these people aren't sick; they're hungry. Overhearing his asides to himself, Nafas eventually asks him in English who he is.

Salahuddin/Belfield/Hassan's presence in the film bisects it, both temporally, coming at the almost exact halfway point in the film, and also in terms of its plot, since his character, Hassan, offers to take Nafas to her destination of Kandahar by cart and urges her to dismiss her child guide. Hassan warns her that people in Afghanistan are so hungry and impoverished that she should not trust anyone and urges her to pay the child off and send him home. All the while, he keeps up the pretense of giving directions to Khak in Persian while speaking quietly to Nafas in English. This character becomes a major one in the second half of the film, offering a strange counterpart/contrast to Nafas. Like her, Hassan has come to Afghanistan from North America in search of meaning, but whereas she comes to effect a rescue and prevent the suicide of her sister, he has come in search of God and to fight on the side of God with the mujahedin against the Soviets. Like her, he is horrified by the poverty and desperation he sees.

Then, at 1:10:39, Hassan abruptly exits as an onscreen character, offering nothing more than the cheerful American exhortation of "Take care!" What could be more banal? Yet his voice returns minutes later (1:12:50) as Nafas turns on the tape recorder she has carried with her throughout the film, and in which she confides to her sister the elements of her journey. Hassan had borrowed it from her and she plays it back to listen to what he has recorded: "This is the voice of a man who has been searching for eternal love all his life, but has always fallen in love with another human being. This is the voice of a man. . ." This evocation of love is then abruptly cut off, and Nafas begins to speak over Hassan's voice. Their meeting and brief union evince the hallmarks of an odd "meet-cute," but the film moves quickly to curtail what otherwise seems like an obvious romantic possibility and instead returns Nafas to her mission to locate and rescue her sister.

Oddly comedic in a film that is overtly not a comedy, the use of Belfield/Salahuddin as the character of Hassan appears both unnecessary and significant. Hamid Naficy observes that this casting was "controversial."[41] Makhmalbaf maintained that he knew Belfield/Salahuddin had killed someone, but claimed ignorance of his exact crimes until after the film's production. After the film was released, notices of his appearance peppered various American periodicals. When questioned about whether he knew of Belfield/Salahuddin's past, Makhmalbaf demurred: "I have always chosen my actors from crowded streets and barren deserts."[42] However, after being pressed further, Makhmalbaf revealed a complicated genealogy of justification for his decision, arguing that he (Makhmalbaf) had been tortured by SAVAK, of which the person assassinated by Salahuddin was a member; Makhmalbaf, therefore, owed Tabatabai no loyalty.[43]

Several other articles on the film in the mainstream American press focused on this strange appearance, wondering why Makhmalbaf would cast such a person and why Salahuddin/Belfield would choose to reappear publicly in this way after living for so long in exile to escape prosecution in the US. It was, indeed, a noteworthy casting choice. *Kandahar* was never screened publicly in Iran or in Afghanistan. It was manifestly a film made for foreign, rather than Iranian, audiences. Yet it would be a mistake to assume that it wasn't a Parthian shot at the regime as much as it was a critique of American and Soviet imperialisms and their legacies in Afghanistan. Belfield/Saluhuddin has lived in Iran for more than forty years, and older Iranians at least are aware of his existence as a kind of footnote to the revolution and the ongoing conflict with the US that was at its height in the early 1980s. Used by Iranian authorities as a symbol of the regime's rejection of American political and racial hypocrisy and an example of the revolutionary promise of Islam (as well as the use of strategic violence to enable systemic change), Belfield/Salahuddin is an apt symbol of Iranians' blindness to their own racial thinking about black Iranians. Celebrated and sheltered by an Iranian government that denies any history of enslavement of Africans in Iran, he is celebrated by the IRI as someone who puts the lie to both American boasts of "liberty for all" and the promises of American foreign policy, which uses notions of "human rights" to advance geopolitical exploitation.

Makhmalbaf's casting of Salahuddin in *Kandahar*—however subconsciously—thus calls out both the Iranian government's hypocrisy and the society's hypocrisy more generally. Belfield/Salahuddin's presence in the film, set against his presence in post-revolutionary Iranian society and culture, offers a way of understanding Iranian attitudes toward race, which seem split into two: attitudes towards what Iranians consider "our own Africans"[44] vs. attitudes toward black Americans. The latter are seen (at least publicly) as heroic, oppressed, and as symbols of America's failure as a democratic society. Yet at the same time this deployment adds—through the overt use of a black person to give the film its moment of comedy—the touch of *siah bazi* that makes the viewer squirm.

Unlike Beyzai, Makhmalbaf is not a dramaturge and he does not use blackface in his representations of blackness; his deployment of blackness involves black actors. However, his comedic moves are clearly inflected by the practices of *siah bazi*, wherein blackness is deployed satirically. They are derived from the same genre, married here to Makhmalbaf's political sensibility. The results are strange, and the viewer is left with an uncertainty about whether Makhmalbaf truly empathizes with black people or if he is merely using them—as did generations of authors and dramatists that preceded him—metaphorically, to reveal truths about non-black Iranians.

THE DAY I BECAME A (WHITE) WOMAN

Whatever their other ideological differences, Makhmalbaf and Beyzai appear to have reached the common conclusion that blackness can be usefully deployed to develop the central subjectivity of a non-black character. Makhmalbaf's wife and collaborator Marzieh Meshkini, who is part of his family production house, picks up this strategy and develops it further, if obliquely, in her directorial debut *Ruzi keh zan shodam* (*The Day I Became a Woman*; henceforth referred to as *TDBW*).[45] Here, the deployment of blackness reads as a move to develop the subjectivity of the central, non-black woman character, who is seen at three stages of life: childhood (but on the cusp of "womanhood" at age nine); maturity; and old age.

Meshkini's film—overtly billed as a "feminist" film—uses blackness as a metaphor or foil to represent the plight of Iranian women in the Islamic Republic. Released a year before *Kandahar*, Meshkini's *TDBW* was also produced by Makhmalbaf Film House and was banned upon release in Iran.[46] A non-linear narrative offered in a style that critics have called "fable-like," "allegorical," and "consisting of parables," the film shows the stories of three female characters (Hava, Ahu, and Hura) who represent the different stages of the life and engendering of an Iranian woman. Set on the island of Kish, an Iranian possession in the Persian Gulf that is a "free-trade" zone and former slave entrepot, the film exhibits and uses blackness without comment or explanation, relying on viewers to draw their own conclusions about its strangeness and meaning. Sited in this marginal, liminal national space, the film also negotiates the liminality and uncertainty related to the film's creation.

In spite of these elements, which mark it out as exceptional within an Iranian context, the presence of black people in the film seems to elicit indifference (or at best a general shrug) from both Iranian and foreign critics, who are not interested in getting into the weeds of racial politics in Iran when they know so little about them to begin with. The rare exception is Jonathan Rosenbaum, who observes:

> I've been told that Iranians can be just as color conscious as Americans, so there's some reason to observe that most of the boys in this movie are black and that Havva herself is fairly dark skinned—hints that there's an underclass in Iran and *maybe that being black and being female are two versions of the same thing.*[47]

Rosenbaum's comments illustrate at least an awareness that there *are* racial subcurrents in the film that he does not understand. To be fair, not all of the racialized language makes it into the subtitles, which overall tend to sanitize the content of characters' speech where any mention of race is concerned. Critics instead tend to focus on the manifest intent of the film: its critique of women's rights in Iran, which is where Rosenbaum's analysis takes him in the end, too. This is a point we will return to below.

The first engagement of what the film clearly sees as an oppressive device is in the opening story of Hava, who is arguing with her mother and grandmother about the necessity of wearing a veil and new restrictions on her movements on the occasion of her ninth birthday. (In strict interpretations of Islamic law, nine is the age at which a girl becomes a woman and, consequently, the age at which she must begin to wear a veil.) At the beginning of the film, Hava is trying to prevail with her plan to go out for ice cream with her best friend, a boy named Hassan. As the story begins, Hassan is lingering at the threshold of Hava's house, urging her to come with him, and her mother and grandmother try to convince her that she is a woman today and must accept the new rules that apply: she can't play with boys, and she must wear a veil. Hava eventually negotiates a compromise and can go out, as long as she wears her new veil and returns home by a particular time. By now, however, it turns out that Hassan must stay home because he has homework to do. The actor playing Hassan is a black child, while the one playing Hava is perhaps not. The actor playing her mother, however, is black, suggesting a complex racial scheme that is further elaborated in the next vignette, which seems at first to have nothing to do with Hava's story.

But here again, the casting draws our attention to racial elements. The second story features Ahu, who is competing in a women's bicycle race on the island. She is pursued on horseback, first by her husband, who is black, and then by other male members of the community as well—first a mullah, then the male members of Ahu's family. They are trying to convince her to give up the race. Her husband threatens her with divorce, but Ahu refuses to give in. Finally, in a sinister and overly determined confrontation between "modernity" (woman on bicycle) and "tradition" (men on horseback), she is surrounded by the horses at the end of the film segment. In contrast to the family in Hava's vignette, Ahu and her family appear, phenotypically and dialectically, to be Afghan rather than Iranian. (Kish was and is a site of asylum for Afghan refugees.) Yet here and throughout, the music that accompanies the film is clearly marked out as "African." A keening song introduces and concludes Hava's story and is reprised at the conclusion of the film; a didgeridoo accompanies Ahu as she cycles through her story, except at the very end when she is forced off her bicycle by the men of her family.

Finally, the last story features Hura, who disembarks from an airplane and proceeds to do what mainlander Iranians come to Kish—a designated "free trade zone"—to do: shop. She has ribbons tied around her fingers to remind her of what to buy, and she proceeds by wheelchair to spend literally fistfuls of cash on home furnishings and appliances, which she asks the cadre of black boys who have been assisting her with her purchases to set up in a makeshift home on the beach. Dissatisfied with the "naked" glass tea pot the boy has helped her purchase, Hura insists he wheel her back to the store to return it. The shopkeeper refuses, and she pulls her old tea pot out of her purse and says it is full of memories of "that black man." She then tells the young black boy who is pushing her wheelchair that if "that awful woman" hadn't gotten in the way, she would have a "black son like you." She then asks if he will be her son, which he politely declines, pointing out that he has his own mother.[48]

The racial dimensions of this story continue to unfold on the beach as Hura tries to return her tea pot. Left unsupervised, the children who had assisted her with setting up her beach household have seen her absence as an opportunity to use all of the goods in a party-like atmosphere, eating everything in the refrigerator, turning on the washing machine, and dressing up in her clothes. One black child looks at himself in the mirror as he thickly applies pink lipstick to his own face, then applies "whiteface," putting on her foundation. Another black child puts on a wedding dress and veil, and is tackled into bed by yet another child, who cries out, "Bilal has become a bride!" (Bilal is the name of the black companion of the Prophet Mohammad, and is often upheld by black Muslims as a model and ideal.) Here we have the specter of both suppressed racialization and suppressed homoeroticism reappearing at once.

In another spotlight on the racial dimensions of this tableau, Hura asks the child who is, in her words, "the white one with Afghan clothes," to make her tea—rejecting the offers of the black children. As the "white" child makes her tea, Hura says, "I wanted a son like you, white. Do you want to be my son?" He shrugs. She asks repeatedly, and he says, "Take one of these black boys." She responds, "But I like you, you're handsome, you're white." Importantly, the subtitles do not cover this exchange—and when they do, none of the racial language is translated. In Hura's confused evocations of the black man she wanted as a husband, and in her prevarication about whether she wants a black son or a white son, we see a dimension of racial thinking that is entirely ignored in all of the film's criticism.[49]

Even critics who have access to the Persian largely ignore the racial content. In his sweeping and grandiose assessment of Meshkini's film in *Masters and Masterpieces of Iranian Cinema*, Hamid Dabashi ignores the racial content completely. He suggests that Meshkini's film is exemplary of what he calls "parabolic realism," which he believes is the third stage (following the "actual realism" of Kiarostami and the "virtual realism" of Makhmalbaf) of Iranian cinema. In his view, it is the "culmination of women's contributions to cinema."[50] Dabashi sees Meshkini as the heir of a lineage of "female filmmakers" beginning with Forugh Farrokhzad and her documentary *The House Is Black*. However, far from demonstrating a "parabolic realism" that is transcendent and connected to generations of Iranian women (itself a profoundly sexist assertion that suggests women filmmakers can only inherit their art from other women), Meshkini's film seems rather to affirm a bevy of tropes of Western liberal feminist thinking about the Middle East, tropes that scholar Nima Naghibi calls out in *Rethinking Global Sisterhood* (2007).

Naghibi's monograph explores the ways in which Western feminist discourse has historically exploited, and continues to exploit, the abjection of a monolithic Muslim woman to its own ends—namely the consolidation of a white feminist subjectivity. Echoing Gayatri Spivak and Leila Abu-Lughod's observations about US interventions in the Middle East ("white men saving brown women from brown men"),[51] Naghibi's book attends to some of the lacunae in this history. Since Iran often falls between the cracks in studies of women's history in the Middle East, where the focus tends to be on the Arab world, it offers a welcome consideration of the ways in which Iranian women have been useful to Western feminism's projects without themselves benefiting from such exposure or use.

Rethinking Global Sisterhood was published at a moment of outrage in the academy over the invasion of Afghanistan and Iraq and the way it had been accomplished with the help of figures within academe who provided gender-inflected ideological scaffolding and justification for these wars. In this context, it documented how the imagination of the subjugated Muslim woman served an instrumental purpose for the Western/American feminist, and the ways in which these feminists became complicit in the post-9/11 wars of the George W. Bush administration. In the rhetoric of the Bush administration, Muslim women and girls figured as "the abject"—objects in need of rescue, both ideological and literal.

Women's abjection has received substantial attention in discourse on Iran, but little attention has been paid to sites of black abjection. Even in monographs like Naghibi's, the goal of which is ostensibly to "decolonize" scholarship on Iranian feminism(s), the discourse on the (veiled) Muslim woman and her abjection remains profoundly enmeshed in discourses of colonialism and imperialism, wherein the "Iranian" is viewed as the racialized and blackened subject vis-à-vis Euro-American feminisms. Meshkini's *The Day I Became a Woman* is an apt echo and demonstration of this framing in its manipulation of foreign audiences' anticipated reactions to veiling and the actual characterization and action in the film to exploit stereotypes surrounding the veiling of women. Like Naghibi, the film does not remark on the ways in which feminism—Euro-American and Iranian—has remained profoundly non-intersectional, refusing to countenance the ways in which abjection reaches across gender and into poverty and race. Nonetheless, it does leave in its cataloguing of women's abjection a racial trace.

Iranian laws pertaining to women's public modesty are part of the film's raison d'être, but it uses blackness as a foil for this consideration in a way that is almost completely unremarked upon. By focusing on the veiling of women, Meshkini forecloses any dialogue surrounding race, even though she foregrounds it by setting the film on the island of Kish. Moreover, while several stylistic aspects of the film mark it out as made for a foreign rather than domestic Iranian audience (including the veil being repeatedly deployed as an oppressive garment), the near invisibility of its racial dynamics to foreigners and the silence on it by Iranians mark it out as something that is made in Iran, by Iranians. By both foregrounding racial elements in the persons of

Afghan and black Iranian actors and including racialized language, the film invites scrutiny of race even as it forecloses the possibility. Mediating the space between Iranian and non-Iranian understandings of race and racialization, the film suggests that racial identity is not intersectional, but parallel to gender.

If the success of Western feminism depended, as Naghibi argues, on the continued abjection of Iranian and other women in the third world, we can see in this film how the success of Iranian feminism relies equally on black abjection. An Afghan woman can be subsumed in the feminism offered in the film, but the blackness of Hava's mother and the boys she plays with will remain unquestioned, unpoliticized, and unrelated to their poverty. It simply is. Thus, women's rights in *The Day I Became a Woman* are staged at the expense of seeing the color-based racism that surrounds the debate in the film. It's a seeming failure of the intersectional thinking that ostensibly underpins the project of transnational feminism. Thus, like the works of Beyzai and Makhmalbaf, it showcases yet another dimension of how Iranian cultural identity is predicated on a sense of Persian exceptionalism that precludes close scrutiny of how blackness and race operate in Iranian society.

Five
DOCUMENTING RACE AND IRANIAN IDENTITY

NASSER TAQVAI'S DOCUMENTARY FILM *BAD-E JIN* (*SPIRIT WIND*) opens with scenes of a tumultuous sea and ruined architectural sites.¹ It is narrated by the somber voice of poet Ahmad Shamlu (1925–2000), whose widely circulated vocal recordings of his own work and that of many other poets have made him one of the most recognizable voices of the Iranian twentieth century.² In *Spirit Wind*, however, Shamlu is not reciting poems; he is narrating the action of an ethnographic film. At twenty-two minutes long, the film is very short. It opens with the sound and sight of waves beating the coastal shore of a southern Iranian city. Shamlu's voice intones, "Man can endure much...but when the pain is too great to bear, the blacks of the South turn to their *zar*..." (0–00:00:19).

No humans appear for the first several minutes of the film, but the waves and Shamlu are replaced by footage of a ruined city and the otherworldly sound of two women vocalists singing softly. As the fourth minute begins, the haunting female voices stop and a *dohol* drum begins to sound, as if to usher in the entry of a black woman wearing a veil and face mask characteristic of the South. The woman walks purposefully through the ruins, stopping here and there. She eventually enters a dwelling. Within, a ritual is underway. A group of black men and women of different ages sit around the perimeter of the small room, chanting and moving. The ritual is unnarrated until the twelfth minute of the film, when Shamlu's voice returns to inform us that the ritual is *zar*—translated as "bad winds," which he explains were brought long ago with the "black Africans" who came to the southern Iranian coast. The wind is a destructive one, we are told, and the viewer seems meant to infer that it is responsible for the urban wreckage shown in the film.

The *zar* ritual has become a continuing preoccupation in educational films and writings on the Iranian South and African diaspora communities in the Middle East.³ *Zar* has become a black mirror into which Iranian ethnographers gaze.⁴ It is the most "other," the most "un-Iranian" of rituals. It is characterized as African, uncivilized, and pre-culture/pre-civilization. It fascinates and horrifies. The soundscape of *zar*—an insistent drumming—is one that haunts the Iranian imagination of the past and of the South. Broadly considered a healing ritual of "African" origin, *zar* is not so much practiced as believed in and/or observed in various sites of Iran and West Asia where enslavement took place. The *Encyclopædia Iranica* entry on "ZĀR" by Maria Sabaye Moghaddam focuses on Qeshm Island in the Persian Gulf, but the practice is demonstrably more widespread.⁵ Although the sickness caused by the bad winds can take weeks to treat, it is the final stage of the treatment, the ritual of exorcism, that draws the attention of documentarian ethnographers. This last stage is characterized by a communal ceremony presided over by a "mama zar" or "baba zar" and can take several days, with drumming and singing comprising important parts of the ritual. Often, the documentaries that have sought to capture this phenomenon have compared it to voodoo.

In the austere cinematography, with the imprint of Shamlu's resonant, poetic narration and the music of the drums, we see the influence of poet Forugh Farrokhzad's earlier film *The House Is Black*, which introduced many of these motifs to the genre of Iranian ethnographic documentary.⁶ This film, Farrokhzad's only solo directorial credit, is not focused on *zar* but on another marginal community: a leper colony. Now a touchstone in Iranian documentary film history, *The House Is Black* in many ways set the style and tone for depicting marginalized communities in Iran on film. This is not only due to Farrokhzad's innovative techniques in filming, narration, and editing, but also because of her enduring popularity in the Iranian diaspora as a symbol of a secular, feminist modernity that is one of the cultural losses effected by the Iranian Revolution.⁷

Although she never appears onscreen in the film, Farrokhzad herself recites her poetry as a sonic backdrop to many scenes, just as Shamlu's voice overlays *Spirit Wind*. Prayer-like, her voice offers "a mixture of her own verses and translated passages from the Bible and Qur'an" that together invoke and narrate a listening God who is merciful and a creator of beauty as well as despair and illness.[8] Visually, Farrokhzad uses strategies like repetition and close-ups to make real, singular, and meaningful to the viewer the lives of the isolated members of the leper community. The film is not unlike an imagist poem, using distinctive and isolated images of individuals and objects as metaphors for the condition of the colony's inhabitants. The other narrator of the film, Ibrahim Golestan, repeatedly notes that "leprosy is not an incurable disease." The fact that the film documents people suffering from such severe affliction from it thus suggests that their abjection is man-made and can be man-cured. Farrokhzad's and Golestan's voices form the harmonious, contrapuntal voices of beauty and reason, respectively, and the sounds of the colony and its inhabitants are the discordant noises that emphasize the narrators' humanity.[9]

Like the other ethnographic films and texts considered in this chapter, *The House Is Black* was ostensibly intended to humanize a dehumanized and misunderstood marginal community in Iran (i.e., people afflicted by leprosy), but it nonetheless does at times feel voyeuristic and exploitative of its subjects, lingering uncomfortably on their bodies and deformities. They are not allowed to speak in the film except when cued, and then only in short excerpts that are staged to assume a meaning for the audience that they almost certainly didn't have for those documented. Instead of the subjects' voices, we hear the voices of Farrokhzad and Golestan. Further, there is a quality of the personal that troubles this film, such as the use of Farrokhzad's voice and poetry and the fact that it includes the voice of her lover Golestan. As Naficy observes, *The House Is Black* "leaves an impression of Farrokhzad's extreme sympathy," but it also reflects "an almost total identification with the lepers."[10] And while their images never appear in the films, their voices—particularly Farrokhzad's, both literally and figuratively—shape the narrative and insist on a particular interpretation of the film's subjects.

Such elements have come to characterize the Iranian "new wave," which would become an exilic/diasporic style in artistic and academic representations of Iran as well. Although Farrokhzad, Golestan, Taqvai, and Shamlu were not themselves in exile from Iran, these films nonetheless coined key conventions that we see in Iranian exiles' representations of Iran from sites of cultural production abroad. For example, diasporic film and cultural production also tend to be fundamentally solipsistic in ways that undermine the representation of the ostensible subject. Taken together and considered with the later ethnographic films and texts examined in this chapter, the iconic films of *Spirit Wind* and *The House Is Black* suggest a practice of self-centering in documentary filmmaking that could be understood positively as "reflexivity," a catchphrase of the late twentieth century in ethnographic endeavors. Less charitably, this practice can be seen as a habit or practice of documenting marginalized communities in Iran that unselfconsciously foregrounds the filmmaker and tends to re-assert the very class, ethno-national, and racial hierarchies that the films seemingly want to overcome by offering up the abject of Iranian society for sympathetic consumption.[11] Viewed either way, these films and the complicated and imperially/colonially inflected qualities of documentary filmmaking in Iran reveal a tension in artistic production and scholarly reflection that has continued to trouble documentary works across film and text in diaspora.[12]

Understanding, recognizing, and contextualizing this tension in documentary filmmaking and texts helps us see the ways in which the representation of racial others in Iran has developed onscreen and off, and helps us understand how representing slavery, in particular, has played a key role in nationalist and diasporic racial thinking. By figuring the subjects as abject and voiceless, the documentarians examined here use *zar* and blackness in their films to convey non-black Iranians' own sense of global/international liminality and otherness. Meanwhile, the scholars and authors who share the stories of their "own" enslaved persons do so to suggest the moral superiority of Iranian slavery while also establishing themselves as non-black in a diasporic context. Although these films and texts ostensibly foreground the plight of marginalized others, they nonetheless erase the viewer's ability to truly *see* the subjects, instead always returning through the use of personal voice to the subjectivity of the filmmaker/author themself, who is invariably an ethnic majority Iranian.

AFRO-IRANIAN LIVES

The Iranian Revolution of 1979 created a population of Iranians living in the in-between zone of dual citizenship and residency, and the difficulties of conducting research in post-revolutionary Iran—particularly ethnographic research—virtually purged non-Iranian scholars from the field of Iranian Studies. Only scholars who are Iranian or dual citizens are in a position to do extended research, which is often conducted surreptitiously to avoid persecution by the state. These circumstances have created a strange scholarly situation in which ethnographic material about Iran is partial and often grows out of other kinds of research and social activity.[13] The ethnographic research that does emerge is oftentimes highly personal.

When it comes to the issue of black Iranians and the enslavement of those presumed to be their ancestors, the stakes are even higher and more fraught. As we saw in the case of Al-e Ahmad and Daneshvar (see chapter 3), accounts of black Iranians and interest in Iran's history of enslavement are invested in diasporic Iranian scholars' concerns about their own racialization in their host countries as much or more than they are in representing the facts on the ground. Such accounts by diasporic scholars decry the evils of slavery while at the same time making a distinction between "elite" or "limited" or "benign" slavery (which they present as the norm in Iran) and "plantation" or "chattel" slavery, which they assign to the US and the transatlantic slave trade propagated (and ultimately dismantled) by Britain. In performing the demands of this distinction, they position themselves as enlightened arbiters of the past as well as saviors of the black Iranians whose lives they purport to represent.

Historian Behnaz Mirzai's educational productions about the population she describes as "descendants of African slaves" seem to embody all of these characteristics. Her two short films, *Afro-Iranian Lives* (2007)[14] and *The African-Baluchi Trance Dance* (2012),[15] are visual supplements to the extensive archival work undertaken by Mirzai for her dissertation (and monograph) on the history of slavery in Iran.[16] In terms of method and material, the ethnographic documentary *Afro-Iranian Lives* moves between footage of Mirzai on site in southern Iran, footage of contemporary Iranians whom she racializes as "black," maps, and archival photographs of enslaved persons, primarily from the Qajar period. She also includes footage of slave memorials; however, these are not located in Iran and she does not disclose their locations. (The footage is, in fact, from Stone Town, Zanzibar.[17]) The filming of contemporary Afro-Iranians is primarily in color, though at some moments (as she transitions from discussion of the Qajar period to the present), the footage is de-colorized to black and white. On the film website, Mirzai describes the film's goals as follows:

> *Afro-Iranian Lives* is a documentary produced and directed by Dr. Behnaz Mirzai. Born and raised in Iran, Mirzai moved to Canada in 1997, where she studied slavery and the African Diaspora in Iran. Since then, she has conducted extensive research in European and Iranian archives, fieldwork and interviews in Iran, and published numerous academic articles resulting in this documentary. The movie explores the history of the African slave trade as well as African cultural tradition in Iran, and pays particular attention to socio-economic activities, performances and rituals of the descendants of African slaves in rural and urban communities in the provinces of Sistan va Baluchistan, Hurmuzgan, and Khuzestan. Mirzai's aim was *to visualize the lives of Afro-Iranians*, who were widely scattered throughout southern regions along the Persian Gulf, and at the same time could *preserve and blend African cultural heritage* with local religious and traditional elements. By producing this documentary, she intended *to demonstrate both the diversity of Iranian society as well as the reconstruction of a new identity of African communities in Iran.*[18]

The scope of her second film, *African-Baluchi Trance Dance*, is smaller, with Mirzai primarily filming the exorcism rituals, including a *zar*, that she characterizes in the film as "African" and "animist." For *The African-Baluchi Trance Dance*, she offers these explanatory comments:

> The spirit possession cults are a blend of local Iranian culture, shamanistic cults, Sufism and traditional African rituals, and have a few elements in common: the belief in living spirits, the importance of the leader, and the use of music and dance to enter an ecstatic state. The similarity of many of these rituals with those of African origin is due to the influx of peoples to Iran through the slave trade that began in the late eighteenth century. Likewise, their Central Asian Sufi and Shamanistic roots are the result of historical migration within closer geographical areas.

Written and produced by Dr. Behnaz Mirzai, this documentary film is about the belief in supernatural forces that can cause illnesses and the healing rituals held to cure the afflicted person. The practice of the rituals remains widespread in remote areas of Baluchistan, especially among poor and illiterate communities where modern medicine is not easily available or has been proven ineffective.[19]

In both the films and the accompanying commentary, Mirzai is foregrounded as an authority, by virtue of being "born in Iran" as well as because of her "extensive research in European and Iranian archives."[20] It is also worth noting that although none of her films' subjects ever mention the word "slave" or "slavery" (or any of the related variants) in their brief self-accounts (many in fact rejecting Mirzai's verbal nudges toward relating such a history), the characterization of black persons in Iran is always necessarily described in her productions as deriving from slavery; no possibility of indigeneity is posited, and no other form of migratory entrance to Iran is entertained. While Mirzai seems intent on "recovering" this history, it is intriguing that the people to whom it supposedly belongs would prefer not to discuss it.

Drawing attention to the centering of self in Mirzai's films, anthropologist Pedram Khosronejad notes in a review that her films are based on minimal contact with the subjects: both of Mirzai's films were the product of a single trip that Mirzai took to the region.[21] Comparing them to other ethnographic films about the Gulf cultures of Iran, Khosronejad points out that the "films are heavily based on voice-over narration and interviews" and use "her [Mirzai's] voice in the nostalgic manner of 'returning home from afar'."[22] He goes on to say that "her techniques of participation observation and questioning clearly demonstrate that she is unfamiliar with the basic elements of field ethnography, and therefore has placed her protagonists in a difficult position." He suggests that "the use of slow-motion technique in both films during the healing ceremonies and rituals undermines the importance and value of these socio-religious gatherings."[23]

We can indeed see verification of Khosronejad's allegations visually in the fear that shows in the faces of many of Mirzai's subjects in the films, as well as in the absence of any kind of discussion or disclosure or consent that she has achieved in interacting with these subjects. In *The African-Baluchi*

Trance Dance (a strange title for what appears to be a complex set of ritual practices that may not best be lumped together as "trance dance"), Mirzai indeed insists that they reveal their confessional affiliations (they are Sunnis, not Shi'ites, a status that could bring them and their clearly unorthodox rituals to the attention of the watchful Iranian state). She also tries to get them to confess to gendered practices (i.e., female leadership, an admission that could also bring them to the attention of the Iranian authorities, who oppose female leadership in religious ceremonies).[24] Such insistence suggests that there is a particular narrative about the lives of black Iranians that Mirzai wants to elicit: she wants to suggest that these people live outside of culture, outside of Iranian modernity, and are aberrant in their practice of this strange ritual (the "trance dance"—a sing-songy characterization that does not seem to take the practice seriously) and in their other practices as well. This position compromises her ability to be objective (or even curious) with regard to these subjects.

There are other investments to be discerned as well. For Mirzai, the abolition of slavery by Reza Shah Pahlavi in 1929 is a story of the triumph of the modernizing and secularizing Pahlavi state—a story that echoes the feelings of many Iranians living in the diaspora, who prefer the modernizing despotism of the Pahlavis to the anti-modern despotism of the Islamic Republic. In Mirzai's work, the people she depicts were "saved" by the modern nation-state that refused to permit the backward and outdated practice of slavery. That we are witnessing the long afterlife of slavery and abolition in the poverty and abjection of her subjects—no provision was made for the education or employment of slaves after they were "freed"—appears to be beyond the scope of her analysis, here or in her monograph.

Indeed, her goal in these films does not seem to be cooperative documentation of the lives of these communities. Nor does it seem to be an attempt to use her work to materially assist them (many of these communities are characterized by poverty). Rather, Mirzai's work demonstrates the way in which she uses the history of enslaved Africans in Iran to construct a racial identity and position of professional authority for herself in the diaspora.[25] Her effort to render the history of slavery in Iran a "fascinating," benign, and triumphant story of nationalism's success results in two dissonant and uncomfortable films that reveal more about her construction of her own positionality than they do about the persons or communities whose lives she purports to represent pedagogically.

Afro-Iranian Lives, significantly, begins with an invitation to understand Mirzai as the film's focus. To cheerful flute music, the title screen appears: a black background with "Behnaz Mirzai presents" in large white lettering. Mirzai, as narrator, is immediately centralized: at 00:00:48 Mirzai's voice is heard and her image introduced. She quickly becomes the film's subject: even when she is not onscreen, her breathy narration insists on her centrality. By way of opening comments, she centers herself: "It was not until 1997 when I left my country Iran for Canada that I first became conscious of the terms "whites" and "blacks" in terms of ethnicity and race. As a teacher and writer about the African diaspora, I have returned to Iran to conduct more research about this little known topic. The shores of the Persian Gulf have witnessed the forced and voluntary immigration of Africans for many centuries."[26] A shot of Mirzai in the foreground and one of her "Afro-Iranian" subjects operating and steering the boat in a servile position behind her accompanies this narration.

The film cuts from this dramatic autobiographical narration (00:01:24) to cheerful flute music once again. This is followed by a discussion of "Iranian society," which she suggests is "characterized by great ethnic diversity and heterogeneity." "Ethnic diversity" is a point Mirzai also emphasizes in *The African-Baluchi Trance Dance*. And at least one American reviewer of Mirzai's films responds positively to this cue: "The films thus not only emphasize cultural and ethnic diversity in Iran, but even cultural variations among people whom one might think of as a uniform group—the Afro-Iranians, depending on where and among whom they live and their socio-economic existence and organization."[27] Neither Mirzai nor the reviewer mention that while "diversity" is a notion with a particular kind of cultural cachet in the US, it does not have the same meaning in Persian discourse; one would indeed be hard put to find its usage equivalent in Persian. For the communities that she documents, there is no intrinsic value in contributing to "diversity"; rather, it is Mirzai herself who extracts this value as a diasporic Iranian representing this population for foreign audiences in countries where "diversity" is part of the lingua franca of virtue.[28]

The impulse toward memoir/autobiography has profoundly shaped Iranian cultural and scholarly production in the diaspora, subjecting would-be narrators of Iranian history, anthropology, film, and other disciplines to the insistence of a relentless "I."[29] Many of these efforts are in fact moves toward assimilation and a way to secure a place for themselves in the host country, a strategy in keeping with (and in some cases imitating) the work of earlier immigrant communities in the US.[30] Mirzai's films clearly fit within this pattern, yet they take on a more sinister quality in that the populations she visually documents still live in Iran and are still subject to interpellation and retribution by the Iranian state. By contrast, Mirzai has escaped any consequences of her representations through her immigration to North America.

Mirzai's autobiographical impulse also interferes with a clear accounting for the violence to which these communities were (and may still be) subjected, as well as the historical circumstances of their presence in Iran. By privileging her memory and subjectivity as narrator, Mirzai's representations jeopardize her ability to represent these communities accurately or to appropriately allow them to self-represent in these venues. This is doubly problematic in the case of representing black Iranians, since there are no substantive written testimonies from either enslaved African persons or their descendants in Iran (beyond those recorded by the British consul in the Gulf, which were orally recounted) that might challenge,[31] make more complex, or offer more nuance to the narratives offered by enslavers or by contemporary historians. (As *Colorblind* went to press, Mirzai published her translation of what she terms "the only known account by a former African slave in Iran:" i.e., The *Autobiography of Mahboob Qirvanian*. While there was not time to integrate an analysis of this new work into Colorblind, a quick review indicates that the analysis offered alongside the translation accords with Mirzai's critical positions in her earlier work, and she lists herself as co-author rather than following the more accepted practice for translations—even annotated ones—of listing the author of the work first and translator second.) Instead, the dominant voice (and narrative) in these films is that of figures like Mirzai, who clearly sees herself as a savior and/or self-appointed spokesperson for a "forgotten" people.[32] Her effort to listen to the voices of the black Iranians whose lives she documents is partial and filtered through the notion of her own centrality to this narrative.

DISAVOWING SLAVERY'S VIOLENCE

Mirzai is not alone in the way that she engages the history and legacy of enslavement in Iran. Though frequently overlooked, there is documentary evidence of enslavement in odd genres—academic articles, memoirs, fiction, and interviews—and contextualizing ethnographic films like Mirzai's in light of other (textual) forms of documentary production helps illuminate the ways that racial thinking and the representation of slavery in Iran has developed and manifested. Haleh Afshar's 2000 article "Age, Gender and Slavery In and Out of the Persian Harem: A Different Story" is one such narrative.[33] Published in a scholarly journal (clearly on the basis of Afshar's by-then established academic reputation), the piece offers a peculiar autobiographical reflection on Afshar's nanny's life story. Afshar claims she is motivated in this representation by a desire to demonstrate the agency of women in the "harem" and to document alternative histories of this realm. Thus Afshar, an Iranian-British sociologist and peeress, offers an account of a woman known to her (and us) only as "Sonbol Baji" (sonbol means "hyacinth" and "baji" is a familiar title akin to "sister"). Sonbol Baji was a black woman enslaved and sold to a Qajar family. She grew up in the *andaruni* of that family, but, with the declining fortunes of the Qajars, the family could no longer keep its slaves. Afshar's family "generously" took her in.

The bare outlines above may already make obvious some of the problems with this narrative. However, Afshar goes on to insist on the way in which her "nanny's" story is special and distinct from the lives of enslaved Africans elsewhere. Indeed, Afshar suggests that Sonbol's story is a metaphor for the larger problem facing scholarship that attempts to portray female slaves and members of harems alike as "victims." She notes:

> In writing this story I feel hampered by the terminology as well as by the narratives. In English language sociological discourse slavery, when not focused on the fabricated sexuality of "black" women (Stott 1992), has been largely defined in terms of the harrowing lives of "black" American slave women and their subjugation (Stetson 1982).[34]

Afshar asserts that far from being a "victim," Sonbol Baji's experience offers a supplementary and excluded history of the harem that demonstrates a form of subjectivity that even feminist accounts have failed to acknowledge.

Notably, Afshar seems to be only peripherally aware that she is using a person who had come into the royal harem through enslavement, not through marriage, and that however brutal or patriarchal arranged marriages or the lives of royal wives may have seemed, that violence pales in comparison to the processes that would have brought a child like Sonbol Baji into such a household. Afshar deploys scare quotes to mark off words she deems objectionable in this context—for instance, "black," "slave," and even "job." Thus anchored in her project, Afshar goes on to "translate" Sonbol's memories (as shared with Afshar at some time in the past) into a version of her life. The story goes on to aggrandize the role of Afshar's family in housing her (there is no mention of payment) and giving her post-emancipation life meaning. She even manages to suggest that Sonbol Baji is, indirectly, a feminist nationalist, insofar as she made it possible for Afshar's own mother to forego the responsibilities of mothering. Instead, Afshar's mother participated in the feminist salons and activism available to elite women at that time.[35]

Although she superficially emphasizes her inability to be "an impartial observer," Afshar insists that her version of Sonbol's history is true and real—an antidote to one-sided understandings of enslaved and racialized feminine subjectivity. In fact, if we read between the lines of Afshar's self-congratulatory narrative, we learn that Sonbol remained illiterate even after her assimilation into the Afshar household. She was able to leave no oral or written record of her own story. Without recognizing the profoundly disturbing ventriloquism that she is performing for Sonbol, Afshar dismisses the possibility that Sonbol could or would want to create such a document. Afshar characterizes Sonbol as a "woman who experienced the impact of the harem 'education'. [. . .and] talked about it long afterwards *without offering any analysis and with no intention of producing a 'history'.*"[36] Did Sonbol have children or other relatives who might wish to tell this story themselves, or wish for it not to be known? Afshar does not say. The stories that matter are Afshar's own, her family's, and the nation's. In her view, they were Sonbol's protectors, enabling her to participate in women's emancipation in Iran (though, sadly, not her own).

Afshar cannot confront the violence of the processes that brought Sonbol Baji into her household, and she cannot stop using this woman even years beyond her death to celebrate her own elite family's alleged role in modernization and its concomitant gifts to Iran. Among these, of course, were emancipation and feminism.[37] This odd and profoundly jarring appropriation and mischaracterization of this enslaved woman's story, as well as the dismissal of any intention Sonbol may have had in framing or owning her own story, seems to create no dissonance for Afshar.

Noticeably, in both Afshar's and Mirzai's accounts, there is an effort to separate the "Atlantic slave trade," which they associate with violence and horror, from what they see as the more benign practices of enslavement in Iran. In both cases, it leads to limitations in their critical perspective. Mirzai, for example, writing more than twenty years after Afshar, writes in the introduction to *A History of Slavery and Emancipation in Iran, 1800–1929*:

> It is important to realize therefore that the exigencies characterizing the slave trade in the Atlantic were *quite different* than those in Iran: indeed, where the divide between slave holder and enslaved for the former *was always racial*, for the latter *it was tended to be more subtle and to rely on a range of cultural, social, and geographical considerations*. As such, it is important not to overemphasize the fact that enslaved people from certain racial backgrounds tended to be found in certain positions. Instead, one must look at the socioeconomic factors that found them in these roles. For instance, it was common for African eunuchs, who were highly prized because of their functions, to be chosen for the harems.[38]

Up to this point in her introductory chapter, Mirzai had seemed conscious of some of the problems with characterizing the enslavement of Africans as benign. Indeed, in the excerpt above, she asserts the importance of being attentive to "socioeconomic factors" that would lead people of particular ethnic or racial backgrounds to be enslaved for particular roles. However, she declines to scrutinize (or even to explain) the circumstances that created one of the most horrific conditions of enslavement in Iran: "African eunuchs" (who she implies are an actual *type* of human, rather than a *condition* imposed through physical violence and mutilation). One might speculate that because of their racial and/or geographic origins, enslaved African boys were more vulnerable to such forms of violence, and the fact that they were "prized" in this role only serves to once again efface the violence of the circumstances that created and perpetuated such value. Yet, in spite of suggesting the need for socio-economic analysis, Mirzai herself declines to undertake it.

In Afshar's case, this emphasis is worked out through her representation of the formerly enslaved person's "celebration" of her "education" in the harem and her fond memories of that time, as well as Afshar's own valuing of this woman for her role in Afshar's life. (In spite of Afshar's assertions that Sonbol led a comfortable life with the Afshar household, we might speculate on how degraded the conditions of her employment in that household must have been if she looked back longingly to a time of overt enslavement.) Part of what is so disturbing about Afshar's method in relating this story, however, is her odd use of existing scholarship and theories. Afshar moves rhetorically, using Islamic feminist sociologist Fatemeh Mernissi's comments about the enslaved status of several caliphs' mothers to conflate enslavement of black Africans in Iran in the nineteenth and twentieth centuries with concubinage among West Asian and African women in the distant past.[39] Such a move is an attempt to efface the specificity, historicity, and violence of Sonbol's enslavement—which manifestly continued beyond abolition. Mernissi's work, while considered groundbreaking in its moment, has since been criticized for being sweepingly over-general and apologist in nature. Here, we can see how it facilitates a facile conflation of the distantly located "mothers of caliphs" with a woman like Sonbol Baji in the early twentieth century without attending to massive historical differences of condition. Afshar's conflation of such experiences seems willfully naïve at best, and disingenuous at worst.

In a more blatant example of this narrative impulse toward rags-to-riches, slave-to-princess (or "mother-of-caliph") framings, memoirist Mariam Behnam recounts the story of one of her family's slaves in *Zelzelah: A Woman Before Her Time*. She recounts, "Another story about our slaves has the enchantment of a fairy tale."[40] This story centers around an enslaved woman in Behnam's family's household named Saleha and her infant daughter, Zuleika. They were "given" to Behnam's great uncle and "passed. . .on to his father-in-law, Mohammad Mohamood in Dubai."[41] (The geographical scope of this context is not unusual. Many southern Iranian families had homes and family connections elsewhere in the Gulf and along the trade route. Behnam's family, for example, had connections in India/Pakistan. In the Emirates, these families are known as "Khaliji.") Behnam continues, "They were treated well in this household. . .the baby [Zuleika] was even suckled by the mistress who had a baby of her own."[42] However, this "idyllic" enslavement soon came to an end: "As she blossomed into maturity, however, Mohammad Mahmood [her owner] was concerned that, with a house full of gholooms [sic;

this is the colloquial form of "gholam," or "slave"], life would be difficult for her. With great sadness he took her and her mother to a slave dealer, who supplied rich and noble families in Saudi Arabia. After being raped or near-raped, the mother and daughter are eventually sold into the royal Saudi court."[43] Lest we forget that Behnam oddly sees this story of an enslaved woman as a "fairy tale," this was not the end: "Zuleika, always the image of modesty, was pouring water for Malik Saud [future king of Saudi Arabia] to wash his hands after a meal, he saw for himself how beautiful she was. She soon became his favorite; later he married her and she was renamed Maleka Turkiya."[44]

Throughout her account of the family's slaves, Behnam's narrative emphasizes how "well treated" the slaves in her household were; how she even "envied" them their lighter-weight clothing. This attitude, like Afshar's—which adopts the position that enslaved girls were "luckier" or "freer" than the daughters of the household—is a bizarre one, but one can see how it is extracted from the logic of apologist Islamic feminism like Mernissi's. Mernissi, herself from an elite Moroccan family, tended to see the problem in her own and other Islamicate societies as being one of patriarchy, and her concerns for liberation were largely for elite women, not for the servants and slaves that served them. But the women like Sonbol and Zuleika (later known to her as "Maleka Turkiya"—the race-obscuring name she was given by her Saudi prince husband, which means "Turkish queen") who are recounted fondly and nostalgically in these stories of diasporic Iranians were, like other East Africans, enslaved for specific purposes in Iran. Their stories—even Zuleika's—are hardly "fairy stories." They do not, as a rule, go on to become "mothers of kings." Moreover, if black Iranian children were born of sexual contact between royal persons and enslaved persons, they would not become royalty; rather, as recounted in the story of Chaman Andam (discussed below), the children born of such contact were often treated as cruelly and callously as the enslaved persons themselves.

Ignoring the evidence, Mirzai optimistically suggests in *Afro-Iranian Lives*, "In the cities, African slaves were mainly employed in the harems of shahs and princes. . . .female slaves served the wives. . . .a female slave who looked after children was called a *dadeh* or *dayeh*. . . .they were considered second mothers. . . . The children of slaves born into the household were termed *khanehzad* and became members of the master's family."[45] This narration is offered as the camera cuts from a map of the Persian Gulf and Iran to archival footage of Qajar families and their slaves, shown as an extradiegetic soundtrack of "Oriental" music begins. The language chosen by Mirzai for her ethnographic documentary is significant and resonates with both her own historiographical scholarship and with Afshar's and Behnam's autobiographical accounts. All three center the Iranian diasporic subject and emphasize that "domestic" slaves (who are contrasted to "plantation" slaves—a kind of shorthand for the type of enslavement practiced in the US and against which these writers position Iranian slavery as benign) led peaceful lives as quasi-members of the master's family. Mirzai proposes that slavery was simply part of the "commercial and geographic exchanges" in the Gulf and emphasizes it as a form of trade akin to that of the other goods like spices and building materials that circulated through the region. She refers to slaves as being "transferred" or "distributed," thus effacing the violence of such movements. Mirzai does not in any way examine or acknowledge the documented violence or bodily harm that accompanies, for example, wet nursing or the birth of children to enslaved persons.

Notably, not all stories of Iranian slavery turn away from the violence. Consider the story of Chaman Andam, recorded by amateur historian and diasporic Iranian Massoumeh Price and subsequently recounted by historians Janet Afary and Staci Gem Scheiwiller in their monographs:

> Chaman Andam was born in Africa; she did not know where or when. All she remembered was the day when armed men attacked their village, killed many adults and took the young and the children. The haunting memoirs of the assault were the only memories left of all she was before that gory day. With her siblings she was taken to Mecca, the most flourishing slave market at the time, where they were sold separately. An Iranian merchant while on pilgrimage bought her; he was to be known as Hajji. She was so young that she lost her language and most memories of her past. The Hajji gave her a new name, Chaman Andam. Once in Tehran, she lived with the other servants in squalid quarters outside the main house. When she was 10 or 12, she did not know the exact age; one day she was given the task of taking Hajji's bath accessories to the private bathhouse somewhere near the outer walls of the expansive garden. She was terrified, this had never happened before; furthermore, Hajji was

going to the bathhouse alone without her [sic] sons or other male servants. She walked behind the seemingly huge man while carrying the accessories in her little hands. The normally short distance seemed miles away and with every step her heart was pounding louder and louder. When at the bathhouse, she was ordered to bath and wash the old man, in tears and shunned she did as she was told and resisted little when she was raped by the Hajji. The memory of the incident was as horrific as that bloody day in Africa and wounded her little soul even more.

Hajji's sexual adventures with the little slave girl created resentment in the family and turned Hajji's wife and their children against her with increased humiliation and abuse. Hajji continued his sexual abuses but never treated her like a lover or a favorite concubine or even a person. She got pregnant and gave birth, the newborn girl never received any attention, kindness or money from Hajji. Chaman Andam called her little daughter Jahan and as soon as she turned 9, Jahan was married off to a construction worker who would not want to have anything to do with a black African slave as his mother-in-law. Chaman Andam never saw her daughter again.

Soon after her daughter's wedding, just before No Ruz, Hajji died from a heart attack. Right after his death, she was kicked out of the house without a penny or any compensation. Desperate with nowhere to go she knocked on neighbors' doors and asked for help. No one wanted to have a young slave girl in the household and she was refused till she got to Monir joon's house. Her father, a patriotic diplomat and an advocate of modern political systems, was furious with the situation, he took Chaman Andam in and threatened to sue Hajji's family for practicing slavery that was against the new constitution of 1907. Chaman Andam joined the household and no one noticed that she always stayed in the kitchen and never came into the house. Just before No Ruz, as was the custom, Khanum Jaan the matriarch of the household went shopping and bought new clothes, shoes and treats for everyone. Again no one noted when Chaman Andam did not join the other servants and stayed away. Once every one had received their presents, Khanum Jaan realized that Chaman Andam was absent. She sent for her, she came frightened and shaken, they asked what was wrong and told her they wanted to give her the new cloths [sic]. She exploded and burst into tears and told them that in Hajji's house they only called her in when they wanted to punish her or humiliate her. She held the new fabric to her face and chocked [sic] with tears and emotion and told them "no one had ever bought me anything new".

They calmed her down and gave her tea and sweets; she became a permanent member of the household and was called Hajji Khanum as a sign of respect. She was asked a few times if she wanted to marry and each time she had said "it is all trouble, Khanum Jaan," and refused any suggestions of the kind. She died peacefully in her middle age and was remembered by the children of the family as the kind but sad black servant from Africa.[46]

Although not unproblematic (dying "peacefully in middle age" glosses over the reality of shortened lives for persons subjected to this kind of violence), Price's recording of this story generally does not shy away from the violence of enslavement and concubinage (indeed, in some cases it tends toward the sensational). Afary's re-telling acknowledges these factors as well, although her chapter (and monograph) does not focus on slavery but rather examines slave concubinage as a pre-modern form of sexual practice that persisted into the twentieth century.[47] Scheiwiller's version, too, acknowledges the violence, but summarizes the ending by saying that the enslaved woman was "rescued by a constitutionalist patriot."[48] Each version of Chaman Andam's story, in re-telling, seems to unwittingly confirm the chain of pro-state/nationalist historiography posited by Afshar in her story of Sonbol Baji, in which the modern state (and its acolytes in modernizing families) is the savior of the enslaved person, especially the enslaved woman/concubine, whose sexual violation neatly fits into other contemporaneous nationalistic narratives about the state's duty to protect the virtue and chastity of girls/women.[49]

For Mirzai, whose research became a monograph covering a 100-year period ending with the abolition of slavery in Iran, the stakes are similar: Iran must be dissociated from the violence of the "Atlantic slave trade," and the Iranian nation must be posited as the freer of slaves. For both sets of scholars, the point is to refute any similarity between Iranian histories of enslavement and the history of the British-American enslavement of Africans and persons of African descent in the Americas. Consistently, they deny any connection to American practices of enslavement—though Mirzai oddly suggests that the Africans enslaved in the Americas were the "kinsmen" of those enslaved in Iran.[50]

All of these non-filmic "documentary" accounts (Mirzai, Afshar, Massoumeh Price, etc.) are also at pains to separate these histories from the present, and to distinguish between their respective motivations in the distant past—that is, to establish that the impetus for American slavery was plantation economics whereas the impetus for the Iranian enslavement of Africans was to signal royal refinement and affluence. Moreover, all of these scholars' accounts converge in that they are, at their core, about the present racialization of diasporic Iranians in their adopted countries. For these scholars, whose work helps form the ideological foundation of "good treatment" so readily visible in Mirzai's *Afro-Iranian Lives*, denying any connection to enslavement is an important way of establishing the superiority of their home country against prevalent understandings of race and blackness in their host countries. It is also how they signal that diasporic Iranians are not themselves black.

DINGOMARO: IRAN'S BLACK SOUTH

Kamran Heidari's documentary film *Dingomaro* (subtitled "Iran's Black South") offers a very different perspective on blackness and legacies of enslavement in Iran that is well worth exploring in its own right.[51] Taking as his subject black musician Hamid Sa'id, Heidari, a professional documentarian, attempts to let the subject tell his own story.[52] Whereas Mirzai's films centralize her as narrator and arbiter, Heidari is conspicuously absent from *Dingomaro*. Instead, the protagonist (henceforth referred to as "Hamid" in keeping with the use of first names used by the filmmaker for the other individuals in the film) is foregrounded, and his sensibility is offered as the mediating consciousness in the film. That said, several different versions of the film—dubbed, undubbed; subtitled in English; subtitled in German—offer notably different framing of the film's content. In attempting to make this story legible to these different linguistic audiences, the filmmaker alters the story to suit each diasporic context's racial thinking.

Heidari follows Hamid as he travels around the southern province of Hormozgan on his motorcycle to organize a concert featuring black (or, in Hamid's characterization, "Afriqayi," African) musicians.[53] Principal among the individuals he meets are Hossein, a ten-year-old with nascent musical talent who Hamid wants to mentor; Gholam ("Gholam Siah" in this context—a name that literally means "black [male] slave"), a performer who sings, dances, and leads chants from the stands for the Hormozgan soccer team to stir up spirit at the matches; Carlos, a retired Afro-diaspora musician; and Carlos's son Omid, an aspiring rap artist. Gholam's mother, Mama Safi (a *zar* priestess, or mama zar), also plays an important role. The audience is introduced in passing to several other members of the black community that Hamid wants to recruit, but Hossein, Gholam, Carlos, and their families, together with Hamid, are the principal characters developed in the film.

The premise the film pursues broadly is that Hamid feels that "Afriqayi" music is not understood or fully appreciated by mainstream Iranian culture in spite of the popularity of *bandari* music in Iran. He worries that it is in danger of dying out altogether. Unlike Mirzai's films, *Dingomaro* introduces a group of people that the film spends time establishing as not simply "Afro-Iranians" but also a community in which the subjects are sons, fathers, and husbands. Hossein's family wants to protect him from what they see as unwanted attention from Hamid, which will distract Hossein from his schoolwork and from learning to be a fisherman; Gholam is Hossein's uncle and Mama Safi's son; Carlos (whose given name is revealed to be Hossein) was forced into retirement after the 1979 Revolution, when his music was judged too "Western." His son Omid, though clearly not as talented as Carlos, wants to be a rapper and seeks his father's approval, which is not readily forthcoming. The "plot" staged by Heidari to frame the film (Hamid traveling to organize a concert involving these men) sometimes feels imposed on the film and a bit stiffly acted out by the principals, but it nonetheless attempts to show these individuals as persons with complex lives and relationships. They are not on film exclusively in terms of a filmmaker's perception of them as marginal, Other, or in need of representation.

Like Mirzai, Heidari also chooses to feature *zar* as a prominent aspect of the story of the black community, finding it a seemingly compulsory aspect of documenting the lives of black Iranians. Yet whereas *zar* in Mirzai's films is a deterministic and "foreign" animistic ritual, here it is an important aspect of the subjects' socio-religious life in ways that are comprehensible to the audience. It is possible to see *zar* here as a form of self-representation and expression. This becomes particularly clear when we compare the treatment of two persons who appear both in Mirzai's films and in *Dingomaro*: Mama Safi, the *zar* priestess, and her son Gholam. In Mirzai's films, these characters appear namelessly, or only partially named, whereas they appear in *Dingomaro* as people with lives, families, and professions. Heidari highlights the importance of *zar* by using the name of one spirit associated with it—Dingomaro—for the film, but he attempts to contextualize this focus on *zar* in a way that Mirzai rejects.

Still, even though Heidari is more conscious of the problems inherent in representing *zar*, the film cannot entirely forego the opportunity to exploit the allure of this "exotic" ritual. Indeed, in an interview, Heidari discloses that this allure has led him to his next film project, which focuses more closely on Gholam Zarei and the exoticism of *zar* that he captured in *Dingomaro*:

> I am filming one of the characters in Dingomaro, Gholam Zarei who dances in the stadium and Zar ceremonies. He is so called "Ahle Hava" (Air People) and have [sic] been captured by magical and mysterious wind Zar. They think there is air in their bodies, so they perform a ceremony to control the air in their bodies[...] *It's a very exotic film because it's about the Africans in the South who came to Iran 800 years ago from Zanzibar***.[54]

In a trenchant analysis of Iranian ethnographic films' obsession with *zar*, Parisa Vaziri proposes that *zar* provides a useful metaphor for an essential problem of modernity—namely, that it "visually indexes the perennial modern philosophical problem of the meaning of interiority and exteriority."[55] She goes on to propose that in Iranian ethnographic films of the pre-revolutionary period, "the thematic of slavery [is used] to elaborate modern concerns about human alienation in an increasingly industrialized and nascently modernizing Iran."[56] The consequence of this usage, in her view, is the erasure of the history of slavery; it remains as a trace that becomes "a problem for or of Iranian modernity."[57] In other words, Vaziri proposes that *zar* becomes a central preoccupation of Iranian modernity because it enables simultaneous attention to and forgetting of enslavement in Southwest Asia (including Iran).

Vaziri reads this preoccupation through ethnographic filmmaking of the 1960s and 1970s in Iran. But in the contemporary diasporic landscape for Iranian documentary filmmaking, we see this "anthropological fascination" with zar continuing. It enables not only what Vaziri identifies *but also* permits blackness in Iran to become a subject that erases both the historical present and the historical past. Diasporic Iranians have carried into their sites of dispersal the preoccupation with blackness that Vaziri believes derives from a problem with Iranian engagements with modernity in the twentieth century. In the diaspora, however, the focus on race in ethnographic film has taken on the additional burden of clarifying diasporic Iranians' own possible racialization as non-white Others.

Zar, in its representation in Mirzai's films and in *Dingomaro*, also indexes the differences the filmmakers want to establish between transatlantic slavery and Indian Ocean slavery. As we have seen, establishing and maintaining the distinction between these two historical phenomena is key to Mirzai, who wants Iranian slavery to be understood as benign and resolved into cultural "diversity" by the intervention of the modern nation-state. Heidari, on the other hand, wants to do the opposite: to establish similarities between American legacies of enslavement and those of Iran/the Gulf that will make the story of black communities legible to foreign—and especially American—audiences. Even so, Heidari looks away from the violence of enslavement, emphasizing music and cultural similarities between black populations in Iran and the US rather than the histories of violence that enslavement entails.

Heidari's intent to find comparisons between these histories of enslavement is evident from the first moments of the dubbed version of *Dingomaro*. Indeed, the film's subtitle is "Iran's Black South"—a comparison to the American South that the filmmaker continues to develop. Within moments of the film's beginning, we are shown footage of men participating in Moharram rituals, and the narrator comments that "a Shi'ite mourning ceremony resembles a procession in New Orleans."[58] When we are introduced to the woman who becomes central to the story *Dingomaro* tells, the narrator explains that "Mama Zafi (sic) is the spirit healer of Bandar Abbas. . . .a kind of high Voodoo priestess."⁵⁹ The narrator continuously cues viewers to understand that what they are seeing is part of a larger story of African diaspora, in which New Orleans and Bandar Abbas are just two sites. Importantly, New Orleans, an internationally recognized site for culture tourism and of positive associations with Afro-Caribbean/American culture, is selected for comparison, rather than, say, Charleston or Atlanta—places where the violence of enslavement has not produced the cultural efflorescence of Mardi Gras Indians or second line parades.

Another aspect of the film that seems intended to connect it specifically to African diaspora in US culture is the casting of voice actors who either have or are putting on American regional accents. The voices and choice of words used for dubbing suggest that the filmmaker and his team may have been intending to cast voices suggestive of black American dialects. (Oddly, however, the woman playing the child Hossein's mother sounds like she has a New Jersey accent.) Another odd dissonance comes when Hamid is talking to Carlos, who tries to dissuade him from staging the concert. First, Carlos remonstrates with Hamid about black Iranians' denial of their heritage, which makes it unlikely that they would want to attend a concert focused on that heritage. He then suggests that Hamid is trying to exploit his "race" to stage the concert. The voice actor for Carlos concludes that the concert will be a "flop," and finishes with a flourish: "Man, your bubble's gonna burst."⁶⁰

This clumsy effort to create a phrase that *sounds* like black American slang serves to draw attention to the way the dubbed film insists on "black" identities for these individuals. In the Anglophone version, Carlos's real name, Hossein, is never used, and the audience cannot hear his actual voice; instead, the dubbed version attempts to give him the stereotypical speech and voice of what the filmmaker believes a black American who came of age in the 1970s would have sounded like. When we are able to literally hear Carlos/Hossein's own voice in the Persian version, we hear the voice of a cranky older Iranian man, complaining about "youth today." The "jive" quality that the English dubbed voice accords him is gone, and it is hard to reconcile his actual voice with the stereotype the Anglophone version seeks to present.

What makes the dubbed Anglophone version's odd choices even more conspicuous is the fact that other versions of *Dingomaro* were produced and distributed. If we look at the Persian-language version that is undubbed but has English subtitles, the intent of the dubbed version becomes very clear: to make the Anglophone version a film to educate foreign audiences about slavery in Iran and to draw parallels to the American legacy of slavery. Heidari includes segments in the Anglophone version (excluded from the undubbed version) that self-consciously connect the present to the history of slavery. Important among them are segments that I would term *pseudo-historical* footage—that is, contemporary footage that has been treated with an "age" filter to give the impression that it is historical/archival. There are also segments that show Hamid reflecting specifically on slavery and his own ancestors' enslavement. The first such sequence occurs early in the film,[61] where men on a fishing boat are depicted wearing *galabiyya*-style attire associated with the Gulf and head wrappings to protect them from the sun.[62] The narrator intones, "In the 17th century, Portuguese and later, mostly Arab, sailors, brought slaves from East Africa to the Persian Gulf. Having survived the ordeal, the Africans were sold at the slave markets in southern Iran.... They had nothing left but their songs. This was the only way they could express themselves." Another episode of "historical" footage comes at 26:30–27:00, with the narrator explaining: "The women of Minab have collected water in them [the *jaghleh*, water jugs used as drums] since time immemorial...one day someone had the idea of drumming on them to accompany singing...this is how the jug came to be used as an instrument. This tradition can also be found in parts of Africa. Tribespeople from Nigeria, for example, thought they could hear the voices of their ancestors in the sound of the *wuduh* [the ritual washing, presumably in this case using the water jugs referenced, before prescribed prayers in Islam]." Through these techniques—voiceover, subtitling, pseudo-historical footage, citation of actual historical photographs—Heidari practices a kind of *hypomnesis* (technical inscription of memory; the opposite of "anamnesis") to describe and/or create a superficially historicized "Africanness" that is tied to enslavement in the Iranian South.

Hearkening back to Mirzai's use of archival Qajar-era photographs in *Afro-Iranian Lives*, we can see that while Mirzai is at pains to understand slavery as something that occurred in the past, Heidari insists on the overlay of slavery upon the present in the Anglophone version. Indeed, one of the first lines spoken by the narrator is, "The African influence is hardly recognized, and yet it can be found everywhere you look, not just in the faces of its inhabitants."[63] Moreover, Heidari's filming of possible histories for black Iranians (rather than using archival photographs of domestic slaves used by Mirzai's films) and including dialogue among his subjects allow for the ambivalence that black Iranians might feel about their heritage being seen and heard. By contrast, notwithstanding Mirzai's insistence on the *pastness* of slavery, her film reflects her insistence that the people she meets are/must be the descendants of enslaved persons.

In Hamid's fascination with Gholam's performative talents as well as Carlos and Hamid's argument over whether or not the people of Hormozgan genuinely regard themselves as African descendants and would want to participate in or attend a concert focused on "African" music, we can see that the subjects themselves disagree to some extent on what blackness means to them and what it signifies more generally. Does it tie them to Africa? Does it make them different from other Iranians? Whereas Mirzai might unequivocally say yes, *Dingomaro* suggests that among different persons identifying with or being identified as having African heritage, there is a rejection of monolithic blackness. This ambivalence should give pause to those documenting the contemporary experiences of black Iranians and also to those engaged in the present with curating representations of those experiences.

AN ENDURING IMPRINT

The very first ethnographic film produced about Iran was *Grass: A Nation's Battle for Life* (1925), which followed the journeys of the Bakhtiari tribes on their annual migration.[64] This film, created by three Americans (Merian C. Cooper, Ernest B. Schoedsack, and Marguerite E. Harrison—Cooper and Harrison would go on to make "King Kong"), was grand in scope and featured no dialogue, only the sound of dramatic and sweeping music.[65] Nonetheless, it uses a contrived "plot" to tell the story of the tribes, representing them as historical artifacts trapped in the past rather than a living, changing group of people.[66] Although created by foreigners, *Grass* left an enduring imprint on ethnographic filmmaking internationally, including in Iran. *Grass* offered a kind of grand (ahistorical) narrative about the Bakhtiaris that romanticized the tribe and suggested that pre-modern Iranian civilizations were more civilized than the modern one(s).

In the 1970s, a new set of foreign filmmakers returned to the Bakhtiari to make a film entitled *People of the Wind* (1976).[67] It is hard not to hear in this title the name Gholam-Hossein Sa'edi gave to his ethnographic study of *zar* in southern Iran—*Ahl-e havā*—but the filmmakers do not acknowledge the influence, suggesting instead that it is the punishing winds of the migratory route that give the film its title.[68] Yet the Bakhtiaris, a group of nomadic tribes whose range extended from the southwestern region of Iran near the border with Iraq northeast through the Zagros Mountains, exist at the center of the history of the oil industry and the creation of the Anglo-Iranian Oil Company in the early twentieth century, a history that is shadowed by the specter of slavery even though that shadow is rarely acknowledged even in postcolonial histories of the oil industry.[69]

Unlike *Grass*, *People of the Wind* did not enjoy enduring praise and repute, and it is rarely called "majestic" or "sweeping." In fact, it is perhaps best known for its foibles and awkwardness: a "folk disco" soundtrack and the production and editing disputes that beset the film.[70] Iranian singer-songwriter Shusha Guppy, who had served as a consultant on the film and originally narrated and scored the film, objected to the decision to dub the main Bakhtiari figure's narration with the voice of James Mason, the well-known British actor. Set in relation to the oddly dubbed versions of *Dingomaro* and the insistent voiceovers in Mirzai's films, we can once again hear the echo of the "colonial modernity" that haunted Iran not only throughout the twentieth century but long after it was ostensibly freed from imperialism by the 1979 Revolution.[71] Indeed, the imperialism of *Grass* has been extensively critiqued by Iranian diasporic scholars, but it is perhaps nowhere better revealed than in light of this "remake." *Grass* simultaneously exoticizes and domesticates the Bakhtiari, but *People of the Wind* reveals the way in which the personal voice (literal or figurative) of the filmmaker can profoundly distort the subject.

Released fifty years after *Grass*, *People of the Wind* reinforced the practice of ethnographic filmmaking about Iran that centered the subjectivity of the director/observer in relation to the marginalized Other they purported to represent. We see the long arm of these practices and perspectives iterated in the diasporic films and texts considered in this chapter, where they attest to the longevity of the legacy of "colonial modernity" and its aftermath, particularly in diasporic politics of self-representation. In addition to using the grandiloquent style of *Grass*, documentaries like those produced by Mirzai adopt and enlarge the solipsism of films like *Spirit Wind* and *The House Is Black*, layering in the intense self-focus that also characterizes much diasporic writing. Even in a film like *Dingomaro*, in which the black ethnographic subject is ostensibly speaking for himself, the voice and hand of the filmmaker/author leave a huge imprint on the film.

The complex cultural investments of filmmakers, scholars, and critics considered in this chapter reveal the tensions and dissonances that emerge when diasporic (and typically ethnic majority) Iranians have sought to engage the legacy of slavery and the contemporary lives of black Iranians in documentary and ethnographic work. Contending with the inheritance of Persian exceptionalism in spaces inflected with their own contentious histories of enslavement and racialization, these cultural producers have often sought to explore the phenomenon of blackness in Iran as the product of a more benign (and thus morally superior) form of slavery while self-consciously positioning themselves in relation to it. For Heidari, this meant positioning himself in a global cultural milieu of blackness; for most, however, including Mirzai and Afshar, they have done so by positioning themselves as unambiguously "not black." Through their various representations of racial others in Iran, these cultural producers showcase how various and complex forms of racial thinking have contributed to the construction of a nationalist and diasporic cultural identity premised on fashioning Iranians as somehow apart from and immune to the historical and contemporary legacies of African enslavement.

Six
CURATING BLACKNESS

IN 2021, A US FEDERAL COURT RULED AGAINST TAMARA LANIER IN her bid to have Harvard University release to her daguerreotypes of enslaved persons that had been commissioned by Harvard professor Louis Agassiz in 1850. The individuals captured by the daguerreotypes, she claimed, were her ancestors. Lanier sought not only to take possession of the daguerreotypes, but also to prevent Harvard from using or benefiting from these images in the future.[1]

Although adjudicated in favor of Harvard's right to own and use the images, Lanier's suit was widely sympathized with in the American press and on the internet.[2] At a moment of general unease about race in the US occasioned by police violence and its backlash in 2020, it also reopened difficult questions about the long and unfinished legacy of enslavement in the US. It raised questions about the ownership of coercively acquired images; about the degradation of enslaved people by scholars; about the deployment of such images in the contemporary world; and about the meaning of photographs that were commissioned in an environment that viewed such practices as appropriate and in the service of science. As many scholars of photography in the postbellum American South have asserted, photography is a site of power relations, and it "proved a powerful tool for slaveholders... [who] cast their regime as a benevolent world of interracial intimacy and harmony, run by paternalist masters who treated their slaves as people, not property."³

Arguments evinced about photographs of the enslaved in Iran during the Qajar period use a very similar narrative of benevolence when slavery is acknowledged at all (rather than being disguised with terms like "service" or "servant"). Unlike scholars of slavery in the Americas, scholars of the Qajar period in Iran have for the most part resisted thinking critically about the depiction of Africans in photographs. Some attention to photography during the Qajar period has developed in the last twenty years, but the scholarship has largely revolved around biographical attention to the Shah and his realm, and to a lesser extent on gender. Despite the visibility of enslaved black persons in the photographic archive, issues of enslavement have been almost entirely ignored until very recently. To the layperson, the photos that stand out most significantly are those of non-white subjects, although many of the archives also include photographs of enslaved white persons who "disappear" from interpretation because they are phenotypically more similar to the enslaver.⁴ While a recent spate of scholarly and non-scholarly efforts has sought to bring more attention to these photographs, they have not been accompanied by the kind of sustained engagement and scrutiny that might yield critical insight into the role of slavery and race at the heart of the royal palace at a time of modernizing nationalism in Iranian history. Instead, they offer a narrative that simultaneously presents the public with the fact of Iranian slavery while excusing it with platitudes about its benign nature.

This chapter considers archival photographic displays purporting to show black people—typically termed "Africans" by the curators—from the Nasseri period through the beginning of the early Pahlavi era. It places them alongside contemporary efforts to document the existence of black Iranians in the south of Iran, which began to appear in 2014 as assemblages of photos. These kinds of collections were presented in a variety of media forms and continue to circulate on the internet today. The primary curator-creators addressed in this chapter are anthropologist Pedram Khosronejad and photographer Mahdi Ehsaie. Both operating in the diaspora, Khosronejad's and Ehsaie's archival and curatorial practices often blur the lines between the category of creation and curation. Photographs of the enslaved and photographs of people racialized in other contexts have been heavily scrutinized and criticized within frameworks of ownership and the coercive circumstances for acquiring and preserving them. This has culminated in cases such as Harvard University vs. Lanier with litigation. Yet the curators of these Iranian photo archives/assemblages offer no such acknowledgment or scrutiny. Rather, they insist on their own surprise at "discovering" the existence of slavery in Iran, and subsequently, at the benevolence of that slavery. They seem to believe, significantly, that their discovery gives them ownership, or at least primary rights, to the documents and photographs.

This chapter suggests that we reconsider these photos, assemblages, and creator-archivist-curators with the recognition that photography is not only an *honorific* and *coercive* technology, as Alan Sekula asserts, but also an *affective* tool.[5] It elicits emotion for both participants in the process, and audiences, whether contemporary or successive. In the case of Iranian audiences, including the diasporic curators bringing them together for international audiences, the emotions elicited are tied to a sense of the world lost to the 1979 Revolution. The stories these photographs seem to tell is about that lost and mourned world and about the racialization of Iranians in the diaspora. For Iranians confronting (or in some cases inviting) challenges to their whiteness, the existence of a past they can "discover" in order to reject is another opportunity to establish their racial pedigree.

Twentieth- and twenty-first century Iran has experienced significant iterations of historical trauma. To wit, the multiple regime changes (from the Qajar monarchy to the Pahlavi monarchy, and from the Pahlavi monarchy to the Islamic Republic) as well as the revolutionary purges of the 1980s. These circumstances have led to continuous mass immigration from Iran and the creation of a diasporic population connected by trauma. The culture of diaspora that developed in the US and Europe following the Iranian Revolution of 1979 included those who had been imprisoned, dispossessed, and exiled. Yet they have been vilified and/or misunderstood as immigrants in the US and Europe, and they have found themselves at the center of various regimes of discrimination: color/race discrimination, Islamophobia, general xenophobia. Consequently, diasporic cultural rituals and displays by Iranians are often accompanied by nostalgia and melancholy. In the face of widespread stereotypes about Iranians as terrorists or rabid Islamists, Iranians in the diaspora are often at pains to demonstrate the superiority and antiquity of their culture.

Unfortunately, as this book has suggested, this effort often leads to a valorization of all aspects of Iranian culture, even those that would benefit from critical scrutiny. This comes to the fore nowhere more clearly than in the case of the assemblages of photographs of enslaved persons and their putative offspring in Iran. In examining the reception of such displays through comments and other written responses, one can gauge the degree to which diasporic Iranians are at pains to suppress the history of enslavement of Africans because they are fearful of being conflated with white supremacy—a worldview they nonetheless court in other contexts. Diasporic Iranians are, ironically, aided in the process of suppressing/denying the legacy of slavery by the Islamic Republic of Iran itself, which also denies any history of African enslavement in Iran. Thus, the regime and its opponents can agree on at least one thing: the black people who appear in photographs held in state and private archives from the Qajar period are not slaves, but valued servants.

Because of these circumstances of mutual agreement to suppress or ignore the actual histories of enslavement in Iran, access to archival materials related to such histories are often constrained or precluded, leading to a perception of an absent, inaccessible, or nonexistent archive. It is already difficult to conduct research in Iran of any kind, given the political circumstances and restrictions on gathering data or using libraries and archives. There is also the general surveillance that follows scholars, particularly diasporic Iranians (dual citizens) and foreign (primarily European) scholars. When scholars do achieve access to an archive, they often fetishize their access and invite audiences to view them as heroic for overcoming unusual obstacles to get there (the scholar, in other words, extols their skill and prowess in negotiating the system to subvert it). In turn, what they find is often heralded as a "discovery." (Of course, the flipside of this dynamic holds true as well: the difficulty of accessing archival material is often used as an excuse for ignorance or non-treatment of a subject when access is precluded.)

Critical examination of the assemblages of photographs that purport to show enslaved Africans during the Qajar period and their putative descendants in contemporary Iran shows that these contemporary assemblages are shaped by existing patterns of historiography and collective memory work (by which I mean cultural production related to history and memory) surrounding enslavement in Iran and West Asia more broadly. In particular, they reflect a troubling and entrenched perception of the figure of the African eunuch, who is a recurrent figure in such displays. The figure of the eunuch in these photographic displays, I argue, prompts in viewers an affect of *wonder* or *surprise* alongside horror and rejection. I propose that the treatment of the figure of the eunuch, which is often read in historiography of the Islamicate world as a metaphor for magical liminality, is in fact symbolic of the problems surrounding the representation of enslaved people in the historiography of Iran. Here, I connect this affect to an established literary convention: the medieval literary topos of *'ajab/'ajaib* literature, or "literature of wonder" and catalogs of wondrous things. I propose that it is activated in photographic assemblages in a way that reflects and replicates longstanding cultural efforts to neutralize and/or dismiss the history of enslavement in Iran. Seeing how curator/creators of these assemblages both mourn the general ignorance of Iran's history of enslavement while simultaneously refusing to engage with it critically helps us appreciate the complex ways that Iranian racial thinking around race and slavery contributes to diasporic expressions of Iranian cultural identity.

IN THE ABSENCE OF AN ARCHIVE

The problem of the archive is one that troubles several fields of humanistic inquiry, but perhaps no area more than that concerned with enslavement. Two of the most influential strands of debate have been delineated by French postmodernism and poststructuralism in the works of Jacques Derrida, who coined the term "archive fever" (*mal d'archive*) to explore a set of issues surrounding space, power, and memory, and in the writings of Michel Foucault, who examined the archive as an imaginative space of discursive power. For both of these thinkers, the problem of the archive was part of a larger consideration of power: who constructs the archive, who controls it, who has access to it, and what does it mean?

The problems presented to scholars by archives (or their absence) on the history of slavery have been engaged along parallel but different lines within the fields of African diaspora scholarship. In particular, the school of thinking associated with Afropessimism has made it a special field of inquiry and imagination.[6] In this perspective, the archive is straightforwardly an archive of oppression and enslavement, and the task of historians and scholars has been to grapple with the potential (or impossibility) of recovering black lives from such archives. The question of constructing knowledge and histories about the Middle East has been particularly vexed, as Edward Said articulated in *Orientalism*—and then perhaps more articulately in *Culture and Imperialism*. For scholars of Iran, the question of the archive is also fraught.

For the purposes of this chapter, I wish to draw attention to two important ways in which questions related to the archive haunt the Iranian case. First, there is general denial that enslavement existed in Iran; thus, it has no history and therefore no archive—at least no discrete one. There is not a collection entitled "Documents related to the history of slavery in Iran in the Qajar period." Concomitantly, the 1979 Revolution in Iran occasioned the massive destruction, loss, seizure, and subsequent reorganization and ideological reclassification of historical material, as well as the creation of new archives. Access to these archives, whether maintained by the state or privately, is variable and can be difficult to obtain.

Projects like historian Afsaneh Najmabadi's Women's Worlds in Qajar Iran digital archive encompass efforts on the part of diasporic scholars of Iran to enable broader access to family and state archives for purposes of scholarship. Najmabadi's efforts are a powerful counter to assertions of the "absence" of sources related to women's lives during the Qajar period. When faced with historians of the Qajar period proclaiming that "there are no sources" to help narrate or recreate the lives of women of this period, Najmabadi forcefully replied that the very silences around this topic were informative and a basis for historiography. Moreover, she pointed out, sources that are ostensibly "about men" could just as readily be used in service of scholarship to reveal aspects of women's lives.[7] In no small part as a result of her efforts, the subfield of gender studies in Iranian Studies has flourished. Her engagement with the archive is suggestive where enslavement is concerned, as well.

Efforts to create an archive of photography related to the enslavement of Africans in Iran have posed a complex problem, not least because of the denial that surrounds this history in many areas of study. Pedram

Khosronejad has repeatedly asserted that his efforts to draw documents (primarily photographs) out of existing state, university, and family archives to create an archive of African enslavement are an important and singular effort. He positions his creation of this archive as a service to the field. Yet, while acknowledging that this is partly true, his work sets out a series of questions that remain largely unanswered and methodological problems that remain uninterrogated. Underpinning his efforts—and indeed all of the current attention to race that is mediated through the lens of enslavement and blackness in Iran—is the question of recovery. The editors of a 2015 issue of *Social Text* entitled *The Question of Recovery: Slavery, Freedom, and the Archive*? address just this question in their introduction, suggesting that an exploration of the "the generative tension between *recovery* as an imperative that is fundamental to historical writing and research—an imperative infused with political urgency by generations of scholar-activists—and the *impossibility of recovery* when engaged with archives whose very assembly and organization occlude certain historical subjects."[8]

Yet while Khosronejad seems at least partially aware of some of the work done in the study of enslavement as it relates to archives and photographic evidence in other contexts, he seems unable to bring this research to bear on his own work except to pose questions that remain unaddressed. The question therefore remains: to what ends do we attempt to "recover" an archive of enslavement in Qajar Iran? Khosronejad suggests that examining such photographs is necessary because we must:

> listen for and [...] report the voices of African slaves; I believe that it is necessary to allow the subaltern actors in history to speak for themselves, if we are to respect their humanity. Until we recover the voices of enslaved Africans, they remain merely objects of our historical inquiry... It is only when they are allowed to speak that they become fully human. Even when their voice cannot be recovered, it must be listened for, taken seriously, and respected.[9]

Notably, how we might "listen" or "report" or "recover" and, finally, how to enable them to "become fully human," remains opaque in his efforts.

Possibly because of its proximity to both the pre-modern and modernizing periods in Iran, the period of the Qajars' reign occupies both a richly sourced and studied area of historiography as well as an undertheorized space in Iran scholarship. This may partly be because many of the contemporary scholars who have worked on the period are themselves Qajar descendants (e.g., Layla Diba, Nahid Mozaffari, Manoutcher Eskandari-Qajar, etc.), and are in familial possession of some key sources for scholarship on this period. The Qajars are regarded in the scholarship simultaneously and contradictorily as backward; innovative; anti-modern; modernizing. They are both reviled and nostalgized as the Oriental despots par excellence. Sentimentally resurrected in the diaspora through music, photography, cinema, and consumer goods, they are also important in Iran itself, where the likeness of Nasser al-Din Shah is still the predominant image on practical consumer objects such as *qaliyan* (Iranian water pipes for smoking) and tea pots.[10] In short, the Qajars comprise a complicated symbolic network to which many different meanings are ascribed.

The Qajars' slaveholding practices and their relationship to photography comprise the historical background for this chapter's investigation of contemporary practices of ownership, display, and interpretation related to archival images of enslavement in Iran. Indeed, the photograph is an especially important site for understanding the Qajar period, not only because the longest-ruling Qajar king, Nasser al-Din Shah, was an early and enthusiastic adopter of the technology but also because of the scholarly understanding this type of evidence can yield. Nasser al-Din Shah was himself a photographer and also enjoyed being photographed. He participated in staging himself, his court, and his family in photographs. Consequently, there is a large body of photographs of surprising subjects from his court and the *andaruni*/harem. There are also contemporaneous photographs taken by his children and his court photographers, and occasionally by a particular court photographer who became one of the most famous documenters of the era, Antoin Sevruguin.

Sevruguin's work, recovered (or re-engaged) by scholars of Iranian Studies beginning in the 1990s, is a major touchpoint for diasporic Iranians. As an historical figure, Sevruguin appeals to diasporic writers interested in investing their own identities with the reified Bhabhaian concept of "hybridity," a kind of positive outcome of colonialism, whereby new transcultural forms are created in spite and because of the violence of colonialism. It is a concept they identify in Sevruguin himself. As an Armenian Christian, Russophone, and Iranian-born person, Sevruguin can—like Mirza Fath'ali Akhundzadeh, who we met in chapter 1—claim or have ascribed to him myriad identities that seem contradictory in the contemporary world. Many diasporic writers see in him a mirror of their own experience. Consider Ali Behdad's comments on first seeing Sevruguin's photographs at the Sackler Gallery in Washington, DC:

> Without the usual background provided by a review of the scholarly literature, I initially approached Sevruguin's work in a personal and highly subjective manner, viewing the photographs not merely as a source of information, artistic expression, or historical evidence, but rather as a kind of tableau vivant that allowed the projection of my own identity and history as an Iranian into them. As an Iranian viewer, I could not help but read the photographs as representing a period and place similar to the setting of my own youth in a provincial town, inhabited by figures so seemingly similar to the people I was seeing in Sevruguin's images. [...] Viewing Sevruguin's photographs *gave me in a sense the experience of direct, visual contact with my own past*, a projection that transformed the viewing of a public image into an intensely personal experience.[11]

Behdad is perhaps one of the most sophisticated interpreters of Sevruguin, coming as he does from a scholarly background in the study of Orientalist writings about the Middle East. Even so, his account of this encounter with Sevruguin suggests the wonder or amazement with which Iranian diasporic viewers confront images of the Qajar past, as well as their desire to read their experiences of their own Iranian past into it.

Sevruguin's photographs are part of a sizable body of photography that straddles the royal court and the world beyond. His photographs depicted wide-ranging subjects, including photos of prostitutes, dervishes, criminals, and an otherwise broad cross-section of Iranian society. Among the most notable of these images are the staged photographs of criminals such as Reza Kermani, the assassin of Nasser al-Din Shah, who Sevruguin committed to film before and after his execution. Through the Orientalist photographs taken by Antoin Sevruguin and his imitators, as well as through the copious photographs taken by and of the Qajar family and household, we can see and more broadly conceptualize the composition of a "shadow archive" as conceived by Alan Sekula:[12] it not only reflects the whole spectrum of social positions in Qajar society but also reveals the hierarchy and relative power accorded by these positions.[13]

Yet the absence of mechanisms or methodologies for understanding Iranian racial thinking and the photography of enslaved persons together—especially in light of a rich body of such mechanisms and methodologies developed in other contexts—presents necessary questions. With such photographs available to us, what are we prepared to understand better or differently about the intersection of Iranian ideas regarding race and slavery, the actual history of race and slavery, and Iranians' ideas about national identity? Only by seriously addressing this tangle of investments—national and diasporic, historical and present—can we hope to forge a more constructive path through existing records and shadow archives.

THE QAJAR EUNUCH AS A SITE OF WONDER

Notably, in all of the discussion of photography during the reigns of Nasser al-Din Shah and his son Muzaffar al-Din Shah, little to no attention has been paid to the recurring figure of the enslaved person known as *agha* or *khvajeh*: the eunuch. Both readily apparent in the photographic archive and almost wholly absent from any description and discussion, the eunuch's critical role in the royal household has much to tell us both about the contours of enslavement and the collective commitment to eliding the history and legacy of slavery. Indeed, more than any other figure of the Qajar period, the African eunuch in particular is a site of silence and, when he elicits historical attention, *wonder*. In what follows, I examine the ways in which the curated representations of the eunuch in contemporary scholarship are meant to evoke feelings of both wonder and surprise before being rhetorically suppressed in historical narratives.

Diasporic Iranians are prompted to experience surprise when they encounter evidence of the enslavement of Africans by Iranians, a surprise that is conditioned by their knowledge of American histories of enslavement. This positioning allows Iranians to both successfully establish their whiteness vis-à-vis enslaved black people and to perform their shock and rejection of enslavement. The eunuch is an especially complex figure in this process because scholarship has enabled the complete ignorance of the facilitating violence that created his status as a specific kind of enslaved person. Simultaneously, it has set him up as a figure of beauty and wonder, and a site for nostalgia and melancholy.

In the world of classical Islam, the notion of *'ajab* (wonder) developed primarily within the realm of treatises on the natural world and cosmography. Perhaps the most famous treatise is al-Qazvini's fourteenth-century compendium *Aja'ib al-Makhlukat* (*Marvels of Creation*), but C. E. Dubler observes in his *Encyclopedia of Islam* entry on *aja'ib* that this genre (if it can be called such) or mode of writing became involved with other narrative styles/types in the centuries that followed.[14] By the time it resurfaced in the Qajar period, it was a genre of writing used in travelogues, a case eloquently discussed by Naghmeh Sohrabi in *Taken for Wonder* (2012), wherein she examines the travelogues of Iranians in Europe in the eighteenth and nineteenth centuries in an effort to disrupt the scholarly focus on Orientalist travelogues of European travelers in Iran and the Middle East.[15]

In her monograph *A History of Slavery and Emancipation in Iran*, Behnaz Mirzai reflects how common this attitude of wonder toward the existence of eunuchs is among diasporic Iranians. She asserts, "eunuchs guarded the honor and prestige of the royal family. Omniscient, they existed outside of time and space and often assumed almost mythic qualities."[16] In this characterization, she echoes earlier historiographical writing on eunuchs in Islamicate courts, such as Shaun Marmon's famous study, *Eunuchs and Sacred Boundaries in Islamic Society*, in which the eunuch is exceptionalized and imbued with a sense of household significance and prestige while being removed from the temporal plane that gives his role such meaning. Marmon goes even further into this mystifying impulse:

> Like the magical "drei Knaben" of Mozart's Magic Flute, who act as neutral messengers between the dangerous and disorderly female world of the Queen of the Night and the sunlit, rational male world of Sarastro, the eunuch/child is an intermediate being, safe in both worlds and belonging to neither.[17]

The eunuch is thus characterized as belonging to this world and yet not of it.

In the historiography of the Islamic world, such studies of the eunuch tend to emphasize the "strangeness" and "in-between-ness" of the category, and to exclude the sociohistorical. (David Ayalon's *Eunuchs, Caliphs and Sultans*[18] and Jane Hathaway's more recent *The Chief Eunuch of the Ottoman Harem: From African Slave to Power Broker*[19] are the exceptions that prove the rule). Partly owing to the lack of other studies on the topic, Shaun Marmon's study has become an authoritative work. It is, in many ways, a *sui generis* piece of scholarship on a particular group of eunuchs in medieval Islamic (specifically, Mamluk) society, and it combines a variety of odd methodologies. The result is a work that deprives the reader of any actual historical knowledge of the persons who became eunuchs and instead tends to see the eunuch as a kind of magical category, as her comparison to the figures in the *Magic Flute* suggests. The eunuchs in Marmon's (hi)story therefore seem to be rendered sacred and/or magical by virtue of their participation in the ritual practices that they were created to sustain.[20]

Fewer scholars still have looked closely and critically at the role of the eunuch in Qajar Iran, where they occupied an exceptional social space. Their position in this society was connected to historical royal practices in pre-Islamic Persian empires and to those of other antecedent and contemporaneous Islamicate societies with which Iran had cultural exchange, such as the Ottoman Empire. Eunuchs served in a variety of roles, including as guardians of boys affiliated with the court or military; tutors; guardians of the harem and enforcers of the *quruq*; and guardians of sacred spaces such as the tomb of the Prophet and its precincts in Medina.[21] They could even be regents, or advisors to regents.[22]

The historiography on the eunuch himself and on the practices related to the acquisition and use of eunuchs in the Qajar period tend to ignore this category of person unless it is impossible not to do so. Most troublingly, they seem to almost entirely efface or overlook the mutilation that marked the eunuch. This pattern is particularly notable in reference to the African eunuch, as these individuals experienced multiple registers of violence to be rendered into this status (I am not adding the word "enslaved" because the condition of being a eunuch was to be enslaved). Eunuchs made from boys purchased in Africa were routinely subjected to total castration—that is, removal of testicles and penis. The violence of this procedure killed a high number of the boys subjected to it. The ones who lived had to urinate with the aid of an instrument that would open their urethra.[23] This obviously painful aspect of the life of a eunuch has no place in the romanticized version of their lives that appears either in Islamic historiography generally or Qajar historiography specifically. Both are traditions that tend to view eunuchs as favored or "fortunate" slaves, a depiction that often focuses on the fact that they were able to acquire wealth and status.[24] But this rank/privilege was permanently conditioned by their status as eunuchs and the natal alienation that accompanied this status. They could not pass wealth to descendants or family because they were incapable of producing the former and had frequently been separated at the time of enslavement from the latter.[25]

In the absence of meaningful historical writing about such persons, photographs of eunuchs are thus frequently misread or mined for information that accords with the viewer's feelings and preferences about enslavement and the period more generally. They are at times viewed as signs of Qajar corruption and despotism, as an excess of humanity, or, teleologically, as harbingers of the coming loss of power for the Qajars. In these tellings, the eunuch has become a metaphor for enslavement in Qajar Iran even as their enslaved status has been downplayed in the literature—something glossed over in passing and strangely romanticized. They are made the aberrant symbol of a sterile and dead past. Other times, however, they go completely unremarked in photographic assemblages. This was the case, for example, in Bahman Jalali's collection of Qajar-era photographs published as *Ganj-e payda* (*Visible Treasure*), in which Mozaffar al-Din Shah's eunuch dwarf Khvajeh Mohammad (known as Faqir al-Ghameh, which literally means "impoverished in height") appears disporting himself in clown-like roles, lying on the ground in front of a royal hunting group, embracing a leopard that has been killed presumably by the king.[26] The creator of the volume makes no comment about either the content of these photos or Khvajeh Mohamad's status as a eunuch—his prominence in these photos dismissed into mere existence. Those who know what "khvajeh" (a common term in Persian for "eunuch") means will know; it is not translated.

In her impressive doctoral dissertation *Seeing Race* and her monograph *The Color Black*, Beeta Baghoolizadeh argues that Nasser al-Din Shah's photography and preservation of photographs of the African eunuchs in his court constitute an intentional project of "memorialization" of the lives of these men. She proposes that the shah "understood the fragility of the slave trade and its impact on the castration of eunuchs, and he used photography as the prime medium to preserve images of his slaves."[27] Baghoolizadeh suggests that "[a] few of these eunuchs appear particularly frail, approaching an age where their deaths were eminent [sic]. Their fragile status, paired with announcements of their death [consisting of the addition to the captioned names the word *marhum*, or "blessed"—which Baghoolizadeh glosses as "departed"], seem to overwhelm this series, which were likely taken to commemorate their manumission and their service."[28] Evocative as this depiction is, it seems to attribute to the shah too much foresight as well as a reflectiveness that is not apparent in the documentation of other aspects of his life and court. It also insists on a reading of these men as "fragile"—a subjective reading that, while sympathetic, does not seem justified by the evidence. The king documented and archived the photographs of his subjects and possessions, including his slaves. The addition of the word *marhum* to the captions does not necessarily mean that they were being "memorialized" at the time that the photographs were taken; rather, it could suggest that, as with other photographs, the Shah sought to preserve a record of his possessions as an aspect of his royal person. Understood in the broader context of Nasser al-Din Shah's album-keeping practices, this is perhaps more noteworthy for the consistency with which he recorded property in things and persons than it is indicative of particular acknowledgment.

However, although I may disagree with some of her conclusions, Baghoolizadeh rightly identifies the importance of the eunuchs in the court of Nasser al-Din Shah and his heirs. Most other historians of the period mention them only in passing or, like Mirzai, treat them as non-human non-slaves or magical creatures. Indeed, Mirzai's treatment of eunuchs embodies the most glaring evidence of willful misunderstanding among Iranian and diasporic scholars, who either ignore or misread the presence of eunuchs in nineteenth-century and twentieth-century Iranian life or insist that Iranian practices of enslavement did not involve or sanction violence. These stances consciously or unconsciously reinstate the "good treatment" thesis that scholars of contemporaneous contexts like the Ottoman Empire have rejected: i.e., that in the Islamic world, slaves were "part of the family" (see chapter 4). As an anchor for this troubling perspective, Mirzai intimates that slavery had virtually disappeared by the time of 1929 abolition decree and that there was no violence or cruelty involved in the slave trade.[29] All else aside, this position requires an active disregard for the presence of eunuchs in elite households and the violence through which that status adhered to them.

Notably, African eunuchs do occupy a central role in the collections of photographs published by Pedram Khosronejad, though he does not address the complexity of their position. Khosronejad, a visual anthropologist, acquired photographs of enslaved Africans from the Golestan Palace collection and from several private collections of Qajar families. He subsequently curated and presented this assemblage in a variety of media: in a special issue of the journal *Visual Anthropology of the Middle East*, which he edits; in the newspaper the *Guardian*; in a traveling photographic exhibition; and in an exhibition book entitled *Qajar African Nannies*. Over time, Khosronejad has styled himself as a creator and curator of an archive of photos of the enslaved as well as the person who has reawakened historical memory of African enslavement in Iran. Notably, he also jealously guards his rights to these photographs, and even engaged in a public dispute with journalist Mazyar Bahari regarding the latter's rights to use the images.

In 2016, Khosronejad cooperated with Denise Hassanzadeh Ajiri, a writer for the online PBS-affiliated *Tehran Bureau*, to publish an article in collaboration with the *Guardian* called "The Face of African Slavery in Iran—In Pictures."[30] Featuring sixteen photographs culled by Khosronejad from several private and state collections, the article opens as follows: "Despite its ancient roots, the topic of African slavery is rarely discussed or even acknowledged in Iran. This is partly because there has not been comprehensive research on either African slavery or the subsequent use of African domestic servants."[31] From this fuzzy quasi-historical summary, the article goes on to present the photographs as "sensitive," and suggests that Khosronejad is a pioneer for developing a "first-of-its-kind visual analysis book on African domestic servants in Iran" and "preparing several related exhibitions around the world."[32]

This "first-of-its-kind visual analysis" resulted in Khosronejad's book, *Qajar African Nannies* (2017), which features thirty-seven plates that include people he characterizes as African or Afro-Iranian persons.[33] Rather than showing the work of his "team" at Oklahoma State University, where they were "developing techniques for studying these strange photos," Khosronejad's "Notes for Readers" seems notably devoid of method and eschews historicization. Designed to visually mimic the Qajar family albums in which many of the photographs were originally situated, the volume seems to offer an oddly nostalgic assessment of the enslaved persons presented, characterizing them as "Qajar African nannies"—an odd move, not least because the men pictured are certainly not "nannies" in the English sense of the word. Indeed, the very premise of the feminizing title "Qajar African Nannies" seems to depend on the status of the eunuch as an emasculated man, yet Khosronejad only briefly touches on the idea of the eunuch and does not go on to explain any aspect of the circumstances that would have brought them into Qajar households. Skirting the issue of their castration almost completely, Khosronejad nevertheless seems to acknowledge some problems with their gender. He thus proposes that the men pictured in these photographs holding or standing with royal and affluent children were "nannies," although he also acknowledges that the conventional terms for nannies (*naneh, dadeh*) are not applied to them in the documents he has encountered.

Indeed, Khosronejad does not discuss or acknowledge the more obvious term that connects eunuchs to the practices of bringing up and tutoring male children in the Qajar court—*laleh*. This term and its deployment in the Qajar period present some issues, however, for not only Khosronejad but also other scholars as well. In an otherwise trenchant critique of the existing scholarship on eunuchs and concubinage in the Qajar period, for example, historian Wendy DeSouza suggests that a photograph held in an archive at the British Library shows a young boy with his "nanny," whereas the photo only identifies the person as his "*laleh*."[34] *Laleh* or *lalehsara* is another term for "eunuch" in Persian, but David Ayalon gives examples of this term (which he transliterates as *lālā*) being used in other Islamicate historical contexts to describe a eunuch who is a "guardian," "educator," or even the odd "upbringer."[35] Kathryn Babayan also attests to the role of the *lala* in the Safavid period as an educator-guardian of young boys in the service of the shah.[36] Therefore, we can see the slippage through which a term for a role that a eunuch *could* occupy became a synonym in modern Persian that was exclusively applied *to* eunuchs. (The confusion is compounded by the fact that *laleh* also means tulip in Persian, and African slaves were often given names of jewels or flowers.)

Eliding this complexity and opting instead for the misapplied and problematic term "nanny," Khosronejad also ignores a major facet of the eunuch's condition: as a castrated slave, he is doubly cut off from familial ties. In the "Notes for Readers" that introduce the photographs, Khosronejad focuses on just one form of familial connection lost to eunuch's, opining,

> The faces of all the Africans in the photographs of this collection confirm their deep sadness and the horror that encapsulated their entire lives. Holding those babies in their arms with those expressions perhaps reminded them of their own lost childhoods. We can look at these photographs at length while asking ourselves about the situation of their lives.[37]

He does not identify the other major sadness that might be induced in a eunuch holding his enslaver's children—that is, that he is the "absolute slave," severed from kin and the possibility of creating kin. In other words, his ability to procreate and have his own children has been violently removed; he has not only "lost his mother," he has been prevented from ever becoming a father.

Beyond the obfuscating use of terminology and the oversimplified assessment of violent familial disconnection, there is also an odd contradiction to the assertion of both "nanny" status *and* eunuch status as framing devices for these photographs, as seen illustratively in one of the most emphasized photos in the assemblage: Photo #29, which Khosronejad used as the exhibition poster image for his traveling exhibition. Unlike the other photos in Khosronejad's exhibition and book, which feature enslaved black men and women attired in the garb of aristocratic household servants, this plate shows a black man naked to the waist with a garment draped as a long skirt. He is holding a naked black child. The caption offered in English in the appendix by Khosronejad is "Haji Yagut Khan Sarhang (Zell-e Sultan's housekeeper,

Qomeshlou) with his son Iqbal." The credit is to the "Farhad and Firouzeh Diba Collection of Qajar Photographs," manifestly a private collection held by descendants of Zell-e Sultan.[38] But, even if enslaved, one cannot be the "nanny" of one's son, and if one has a biological son, one cannot be a eunuch. Why, then, use this photo as the cover for the book and for marketing an exhibition about eunuch "nannies?" Perhaps subconsciously, Khosronejad has made a choice that draws on and exploits tropes of nudity in the photography of enslaved Africans and people of African descent in the US—the very history of exploitative documentation and display memorialized in the daguerreotypes held by Harvard University and contested by Lanier.

When we contrast this book framing to the same photo's presentation in the *Guardian*, we notice some odd differences, especially in the comparison with the Persian caption:

> In this staged photo taken by Zell-e Soltan at his summer hunting palace near Isfahan, one of his African slaves holds his son. According to the caption, the infant (Iqbal) is the real son of the adult African slave, Haji Yaqut Khan, suggesting he wasn't a eunuch and could father his own children. The caption says that Yaqut Khan is in his ethnic clothes (*languteh*), which was mainly worn by Africans outside of Iran, 1904. Photograph: Zell-e-Soltan/Kimia Foundation.[39]

Here, we see acknowledgment of the fact that this enslaved man was not, in fact, a eunuch. We also see more attention paid the garment he is wearing, which is identified as African in origin. (*Languteh*, drawn from the Persian caption, is glossed in the *Guardian* caption as "ethnic clothes," whereas it simply means "loin cloth" in Persian.) Notably, a male slave working in the household of a Qajar prince would not typically be dressed in this manner. The photo, then, is manifestly staged, showing a background with what looks like studio draping, and the subjects are posed in front of a painted column and part of a building with an elaborate painted façade. The *Guardian* article acknowledges that the photo is "staged," but *Qajar African Nannies* does not. The photo is also differently attributed (to the Zell-e Soltan/Kimia Foundation rather than to the Diba Family) and offers a quite different descriptive caption. Individually and collectively, these disparities elicit additional questions about possession in relation to these photographs, methodology in relation to the collection, and the problems inherent in taking interpretive liberties in the photos' descriptions.

Because Khosronejad chose this photo as the poster image for his traveling exhibition, the interpretive choices he makes in describing the photo bear careful scrutiny. Khosronejad is strangely silent on the meaning of the nudity in this photograph, which stands in stark contrast to the other photos in the exhibition. This is particularly noticeable since, elsewhere, he waxes lyrical about how "well-dressed" the photographed African slaves are. How do we interpret this silence? Moreover, when the visual emphasis on (unspoken) nudity is deployed in the context of an exhibition traveling in the US, how can we ignore the way in which it evokes tropes of violence and savagery commonly associated with slavery in the New World? Since Khosronejad and other scholars of Iran are at pains to separate the Iranian history of enslavement from that of the transatlantic slave trade, it bears emphasis that Khosronejad nonetheless evokes these tropes to elicit interest from international audiences. Unfortunately, he refuses to explain the photo's meaning or his choice to deploy it as emblematic.

While Khosronejad has done a service in making these photographs available, the assertion of his rights to these photographs, his self-valorization of his role in "discovering" them, and their under-analysis have so far precluded Khosronejad or others from a more holistic analysis of what these photos might tell us about slavery in Iran and its legacy in the present. Further, in framing the eunuchs through the lens of wonder and attempting to relegate them to the doubly feminized role of "nanny," Khosronejad rhetorically suppresses closer analysis. As a result, what we *can* see is not Iranian slavery itself. It is how these photos can be leveraged as part of a diasporic identity effort to claim the mantle of "discovering" Iranian slavery (now a contested topic with the US academy) while simultaneously neutralizing the impact by framing it as a more benign institution not requiring the same level of close analytical contextualization. In this context, the eunuch is a repository of two conflicting realities: extreme violence and extreme privilege—only the very wealthiest families in Qajar Iran, or the royal family and its retainers, could afford to buy and keep for their households children who had been made into eunuchs. Both realities are effaced or lost in the superficial provision of detail offered in Khosronejad's presentations.

The eunuch has no descendants to claim these photographs; no descendants who can assert rights to control how, or when, or even *if* these photographs should be shown. As such, and through Khosronejad's use of these photographs, we can see Orlando Patterson's characterization of the eunuch as "ultimate slave" given new configuration, wherein the eunuch continues to labor posthumously as a site of wonder that unlocks (and then closes) the door to a part of Iranian history.[40] Even when brought to light through efforts like these, what lies behind the door is shown only partially. The handsome and beautifully attired royal eunuch of Qajar photographs become the distorted mirror in which diasporic Iranians see themselves not as possible descendants of enslavers (or of the enslaved) but of benevolent "employers."

AFRO-IRAN AND THE HYPHENATED IDENTITY

While scholar-curator Khosronejad's efforts to create a "digital archive" of photographs of enslaved Africans in the Qajar period demonstrate the desire to relegate slavery to the past in order to "discover" it archivally, Mahdi Ehsaie's work as a content-creator and photographer demonstrates an anthropological urge to rediscover slavery in the present through the documentation of communities of African descent in southern Iran. Ehsaie, like Khosronejad, uses the affect of "wonder" to draw attention to his photographic project, "Afro-Iran," which was staged across a variety of media: physical installations/exhibitions, Instagram curations, an exhibition book, and several websites.[41] He explains that his photographs, which are constituted and comprised of black Iranians posed in "real" situations—working, swimming, shopping—were inspired by Sevruguin's, who he (mis)understands in a highly presentist way as someone who "visually documented the diverse population of Iran for the first time."[42]

Much as literary critic Ali Behdad confesses to doing in *Camera Orientalis* (but without the later self-correction), Ehsaie uses Sevruguin "as a kind of tableau vivant that allow[s] the projection of [his] own identity and history as an Iranian into them."[43] This projection enables Ehsaie to see, as a self-identified "Iranian-German," the evidence of an endorsement of diversity in Sevruguin's photographs. Ehsaie further connects his own work to this lofty precedent, explaining that his interest in documenting "diversity" in Iran began on a family trip to Iran, where he saw "for the first time" a "black Iranian man" (whom readers will recognize as Gholam from the film *Dingomaro* discussed in chapter 5):

> Some years ago when we were on summer vacation in Iran with my family [. . .] I saw an Afro-Iranian man for the first time. We went to watch a football match in the Shiraz, where my father is from. [. . .] For the first time ever I saw a black Iranian man. He also happened to be the fan leader of the opposite Team from Hormozgan. I was quickly appealed [sic] by the way the opposite fans joyfully and rhythmically chanted for their team. Being someone who likes to record things, I decided to capture that moment on video.[44]

Expressing (and repeating) what was for him the strangeness and novelty of encountering a "black Iranian" for the first time—and connecting it to his own identity as a "hyphenated" diasporic Iranian—Ehsaie builds (and invites his viewer to share) his sense of wonder regarding this person (whom he never names) and the community and history he symbolizes.[45] This would be peculiar under any circumstances, but here it assumes additional oddness in that Gholam is manifestly a public figure—someone who is a kind of celebrity in Iran among soccer fans and who also appears in a significant role in the film *Dingomaro* (which was dubbed in German and released in Germany). Ehsaie grossly simplifies what we know from *Dingomaro* to be Gholam's complex life story, which is involved with music, performance, poverty, racial marginalization, and his family's leadership of the ritual practice of *zar* in their community. He offers only that "Afro-Iranians" are the descendants of Africans who were "employed" in Iran by "slave traders" until their "emancipation in 1928" (the decree is from 1929).[46] While it does superficially and awkwardly acknowledge the existence of slavery, albeit in a way that denies its actual nature through the use of words like "employment" (which suggests consensual, remunerated work), this vast oversimplification in characterizing the lives of his subjects typifies Ehsaie's strange engagement with this population.

Building on this gestural, euphemistic, and autobiographical foundation, Ehsaie's "Afro-Iran" project in its many media installation incarnations aptly demonstrates art cognoscenti Reese Greenberg, Bruce Ferguson, and Sandy Nairne's assertion that art exhibitions have "a tendency to be self-referential and didactic and. . .relatively unselfconscious and uncritical."[47] In each curation offered by Ehsaie—Instagram feed, physical installations, the exhibition book *Afro-Iran*, other online arrangements of the material, and his framing of it on various websites—Ehsaie offers only the most superficial information about the subjects of his photographs, choosing instead to make the actual subject his own diasporic self, conflating his status as an "Iranian-German" with that of people he identifies as "Afro-Iranian." In essence, he proposes that their "hyphenated identit[ies]" have the same meaning.

But these problems go largely unremarked by critics. Introductory comments to the *Afro-Iran* exhibition book by Joobin Bekhrad also emphasize the diasporic subject's wonder at encountering these photographs of black people and reinforces the superficial connection to Sevruguin. He suggests that for the majority of Iranians, Sevruguin's photograph showing a prostitute being served a water pipe (hookah) by a black man (presumably a eunuch) is the only—and sensational—evidence they have of black people existing in Iran. Though obviously intended to provide a requisite "context" for Ehsaie's photographs, Bekhrad's clumsy comments feel peculiarly wrong-footed. He first rehearses a series of stereotypes in a fashion that is obviously intended to be tongue-in-cheek but fails to overcome the actual surprise and wonder that Bekhrad himself (like Ehsaie) felt at seeing black Iranians. Foregrounding that sensation, he anticipates what other diasporic Iranians will also feel:

> Imagine my amazement, then, when I learned that no, not all Iranians are Persian, and that some aren't even—may I bite my tongue—Aryan, and even those we called "Turks" I believed to be of Persian lineage; they only happened to speak with a funny accent, and enjoy the status of the butt of all Iranian jokes. We sported fair to "olive" complexions, an abundance of dark hair (in all possible places), eye-brows joined in hirsute bliss, and of course—painfully large noses. Any other features and characteristics I deemed aberrations, deviations from the "norm." Slanted eyes? How quaint. Dark skin? *Far out*.[48]

Bekhrad goes on to praise Ehsaie's work by proposing that "In *Afro-Iran*, Mahdi Ehsaie lifts the aforesaid shroud of mystery that has for so long surrounded Afro-Iranians. Rather than presenting them as oddities or bizarre specimens to arouse non-Iranians and Iranians alike, he does the opposite, portraying them as, quite simply, Iranians. [. . .] Some even have blue eyes and blond hair, as well as Indo-Iranian features. . ."[49] In the qualifier *even have*, there is a wealth of information about Bekhrad's own perspective about the racial norm for Iranians.

Independent scholar (and Qajar descendant) Nahid Mozaffari's introductory comments to the volume, which follow Bekhrad's, are more sober and tactful but not much more illuminating. Rehearsing the now well-known tropes of the official history of enslavement in Iran, Mozaffari suggests that in the Middle East, both before and after the "advent of Islam" (which she also calls the "Arab invasions"), "slaves were considered to be human beings with rights that included adequate nourishment and clothing, training and education for the tasks they were expected to perform, and the right to inheritance."[50] She also steers her comments through the familiar contrast between benevolent Iranian slavery and "Atlantic slavery, where slaves were considered to be chattel—an article of personal property with no rights."[51] Mozaffari's comments seem intended to reassure the reader who is shocked to learn of slavery in Iran that *if* Africans were enslaved during the Qajar period, they were treated benevolently and have now been so successfully assimilated into contemporary Iranian culture that everyone has forgotten the whole matter.

This last point—a forgetting of the past that enables integration in the present—seems particularly important to Ehsaie, who insists in several of his online appearances that this "ethnic" minority is assimilated and accepted. For all of the emphasis on the hyphenated identity "Afro-Iranian," Ehsaie never offers on any platform a definition of what the term "Afro-Iran" means. Is it a place? A state of mind? Moreover, what it means to be an Afro-Iranian is unclear, aside from being of "ethnographic interest" to diasporic Iranians looking for the meaning of their own privileged hyphenated identities. There is no sense of what their "ethnic" identity or racialization in Iran means for them, or what significance, if any, they might attribute to this hyphenated identity. Ehsaie's refusal to countenance the word "race" or "racial," and his insistence on the status of his subjects as simply comprising just another form of "ethnicity" in Iran, is of a piece with the denial of racial thinking around blackness and the legacy of slavery in Iran documented throughout this book.

Like Khosronejad, Ehsaie chose a portrait of a naked black child as the signature image for his project. Through its use of the tropes of nudity and blackness, this photograph of a nearly naked child connects us to a long (but here unremarked) history of the use of black bodies to signal particular positions and attitudes. In the photographs and online installations that comprise the "Afro-Iran" collection, Ehsaie's work comes across as strangely naïve in its engagement with the subjects of his photography, as well as with the broader tradition of Orientalist and anthropological photography.

Although all of the images in the *Afro-Iran* project are clearly staged, suggesting that Ehsaie has obtained a kind of consent for the photographs to be taken, photographs like this one promote uneasiness in the viewer. This child is obviously posing for the camera, but is not of an age to give consent. He is wearing only a kind of cloth (possibly meant to evoke the "languteh" of the earlier Qajar-era photograph used by Khosronejad) and is otherwise naked. Despite this staging, the emphasis of the setting (a shoreline with horizon but no identifying markers) is on the "naturalness" of the subject, who is photographed in a nameless, un-geographic space that evokes the body of water through which enslaved Africans were trafficked. The affect of surprise works in two ways here: confronting images of Iranians who by virtue of their blackness are meant to appear strange, posed in Iranian environments that literally startle the viewer, who anticipates that Iranians will be non-black and live in urban or rural environments; at the same time, the subjects convey surprise at being caught in the midst of whatever they were doing when Ehsaie appeared and photographed them. This awkwardly constructed attempt at naturalness staged in situ belies the intensely produced nature of these photographs, which is amplified by the curated multi-platform nature of the displays.

The focus on the visuality of the individuals pictured insists on their silence, while the speaking voice of Ehsaie in his endless commentary via captions and explanatory notes for his multi-format installations, curations, and articles gives voice only to his own diasporic subjectivity, which is in search of a mirror. He finds this mirror in the people and place he dubs "Afro-Iran," which he sees as connected to his own status as a hyphenated Iranian-German. The affect being elicited is a diasporic longing and a wonder for the past, which together obfuscate our present understanding in much the same way that Khosronejad's framing of historical photographs obfuscates our understanding of the past. Seeing these photographs helps Iranians in diaspora, like Ehsaie, define themselves against a native Other who nonetheless helps them understand their own diasporic subjectivity.

CROPPING THE PHOTO

In her brief discussion of Khosronejad's work in *Seeing Race* and *The Color Black*, Beeta Baghoolizadeh criticizes Khosronejad for "focus[ing] entirely on enslaved African eunuchs and women, mak[ing] no mention of non-black slaves."[52] As Baghoolizadeh points out, he "goes so far as to crop or ignore the Caucasian slaves out of his selection of photographs,"[53] But the problem that Baghoolizadeh identifies—cropping—is not just about a kind of incorrect focus or insistence on ignoring other forms of enslavement in order to fetishize the enslavement of Africans (though that may also be true). The "cropping" is reflective of a larger set of practices that resists comprehending the whole picture, literally or metaphorically.

While depending on the viewer's sense that the visual offers incontrovertible evidence, Khosronejad's and Ehsaie's exhibitions and presentations of their archives don't just trim images, they also cut out context that would enable us to not just see but possibly *hear*. At an earlier stage in his engagement with the Qajar photographs, Khosronejad seemed able to understand the importance of such listening and even to believe it was a possibility. Yet the displays of these photographs that have been curated/created/archivized by Khosronejad and Ehsaie do not enable us to hear the voices of enslaved Africans or their putative descendants; neither do they allow us to hear the voices of living persons who acknowledge enslaved ancestors, as Kamran Heidari's *Dingomaro* (discussed in the previous chapter) attempts to do. They offer an odd kind of blanket representation that doesn't even seem to go as far as the ventriloquism that Gayatri Spivak calls the "left intellectual's stock-in-trade."[54]

In *Listening to Images*, art historian Tina Campt asks,

> How do we contend with images intended not to figure black subjects, but to delineate instead differential or degraded forms of personhood or subjection—images produced with the purpose of tracking, cataloging, and constraining the movement of blacks in and out of diaspora? What are their technologies of capture and what are the stakes of the forms of accounting that engendered these archives?[55]

Campt's questions point the way to a much richer engagement with these photographs—an engagement that invites us to historicize and deeply question the motivation behind the literal visualization of blackness in both contemporary and Qajar Iran. Khosronejad and Ehsaie's presentations invite us to *see* the enslavement of Africans in Iran and the presence of people who may be their descendants, respectively, but do not offer a way to understand or hear that goes beyond the voice of the savior-scholar/savior-artist who offers to redeem them through representation and exposure. We may experience "wonder" in the sense of amazement the first time we view these photographs, as though they are offering us a link to a history we did not know existed. But the next stage of our contemplation must be to interrogate the assemblages and their circulation, as well as the noise of the diasporic creator-curator who speaks on the behalf of the subjects, however humanely. No ventriloquism, even at its most convincing (or transgressive), can entirely efface the evidence of the person sitting next to the dummy.

Conclusion

TO WHAT ENDS DO WE RECOVER THE VOICES OF THE ENSLAVED?

But I want to say more than this. I want to do more than recount the violence that deposited these traces in the archive. I want to tell a story about *two girls* capable of retrieving what remains dormant—the purchase or claim of their lives on the present—without committing further violence in my own act of narration.[1]

VICTORIA PRINCEWILL'S *IN THE PALACE OF FLOWERS* (2021) IS A NOVEL about an enslaved Ethiopian-born concubine in the Qajar court named Jamila.[2] In Princewill's story, Jamila is what has euphemistically been called a "palace slave" (suggesting a more exalted status) in the household of one of the Shah's minor wives—a woman of lesser birth than the Shah's primary wives and who as yet has no children by the Shah. As such, this minor wife's status at court is low and she takes out her frustrations on Jamila, berating and abusing her.

Princewill's Jamila is based on a letter by an historical person known only as "Jamila Habashi" (Jamila the Ethiopian), of whom Princewill became aware through the work of historian Anthony Lee. Jamila Habashi is, according to Princewill, the only first-person account by an enslaved person in Iran recorded "in their own hand."[3]

A character with a high degree of percipience about the conditions of her life and enslavement, Princewill's fictionalized Jamila anticipates and fears being forgotten by history and endeavors to find ways to be remembered. Princewill takes a good many liberties in her narrative, including transplanting Jamila from the households of merchant enslavers in Shiraz to the court *andaruni* of Nasser al-Din Shah. She also gives Jamila an obsession with the idea of memorialization: for Jamila, to be remembered is to transcend the status of the enslaved as a person erased from history. In Princewill's imagination of the past, to be remembered is to be voiced; to have one's name spoken, and is thus an eradication of the subaltern status of the enslaved.[4]

While *In the Palace of Flowers* takes serious liberties about what little is known about the lives of enslaved persons during this period, it nonetheless attempts to do what few scholars of Iran have done: to imagine the voices (meaning the subjectivity) of enslaved persons in Qajar Iran.[5] Such imagination of "voice"—what is often calling "giving voice to"—is a complex undertaking freighted with critical conceptual questions. To examine its presence/absence in the historiography of Iran is to see what Parisa Vaziri calls "anecdotal antiblackness," meaning that in the scattered but substantial narrative anecdotes about "black" figures or "blackness" that litter the archives of *adab* literature, there is a plethora of attestation—although largely ignored—to enduring attitudes toward blackness in the Persian tradition.[6]

Although Princewill does not mention either Gayatri Spivak's essay "Can the Subaltern Speak?" or Saidiya Hartman's "Venus in Two Acts," it is clear that she has been influenced by both in the writing of *In the Palace of Flowers*, and perhaps particularly by the notion of "critical fabulation"—Hartman's proposal that the way to remediate the problem of the "archive as tomb" is to narratively imagine the lives of the enslaved. Hartman cautions, however, that we must avoid the "fanciful" and "utopian," and that "we too [will] emerge from the encounter with a sense of incompleteness and with the recognition that some part of the self is missing as a consequence of this engagement."[7]

Although she was obviously aware of Gayatri Spivak's famous 1988 reflection on this subject in "Can the Subaltern Speak?", which articulated the anxieties of representation of the colonial subject—particularly the female, classed subject—in the wake of decolonization, Hartman does not name it in "Venus in Two Acts." (Hartman was not only Spivak's student at Wesleyan; she is her colleague at Columbia and is cited in Hartman's first book, *Scenes of Subjection*.) Hartman has been frank in her acknowledgment of a personal connection to the history of enslavement in the US, while Spivak is obviously herself a product of what she calls the "enabling violation" of colonialism in ways that she has perceptively observed and articulated over a long academic career. Spivak has spent a good deal of that career—far beyond the opening overture of "Can the Subaltern Speak?"—in thinking about the ethical problems of representation that the idea of "giving voice to" articulates. She argues, specifically, that "voice" implies that subjectivity is in the gift of the scholar and, as such, can be bestowed (or withheld) by the scholar—thus reaffirming the inability of the subaltern to "speak" or represent herself. At the same time, Spivak has largely abjured acknowledgment of her personal connection to the story of the subaltern, grounding her arguments instead in incisive and often radical readings of continental philosophy.[8]

The fact that Hartman does not name Spivak or the notion of the voice as a source to consider in the elaboration of critical fabulation points to some of the scholarly lacunae in which this book has positioned itself. The critical paradigm of the postcolonial represented by Spivak, which (along with Edward Said's *Orientalism*) has informed so much of the work undertaken in the fields of Middle East and South Asian studies over the past forty years, on the one hand, and that of black feminist thought, represented in its most current (but also most widely adopted) form here by Hartman, on the other, are critically intertwined but also not sufficiently in dialogue. Hartman revises or adapts "giving voice" into "critical fabulation," proposing it as "a mode of close narration" that enables the listener to hear something other than silence in the "scriptural tomb" of the archive.[9] Her approach offers the scholar license to imagine and speak the voices of the enslaved and, it seems, if not to circumvent the ethical problem of ventriloquism altogether, to find a loophole in it, implying that the descendants of the enslaved (however remote) may creatively undertake this project of giving voice, though they are not guaranteed to succeed with it; indeed, Hartman suggests that there can be no "success" with regard to this project, only a less hopeless way to confront the violence of the archive. Still, in the absence of a clearer dialogue between these two scholars (and the realms of scholarship they represent), the question remains: what are the stakes of imagining the voices of the enslaved when they are documentarily absent, and how can or should this project be undertaken? To what ends do we recover the voices of the enslaved, and who is the "we?"

In the context of Indian Ocean world slavery, and in particular with regard to Iran, scholars seem to largely believe this debate does not apply. When black persons are identified as part of Iranian history, scholars such as Khosronejad, Mirzai, Afshar, and others freely claim to characterize their concerns and the quality of their life with little to no critique. When black Iranians are represented in the present, the interest seems to be primarily in documenting them as a novelty for presentation abroad: Heidari is interested in "giving voice" within the scripted confines of the documentary, for example, while Ehsaie offers narration of his subjects through his own diasporic lens and transplants his "Iranian-German" status onto them as "Afro-Iranians." There is no effort akin to that undertaken in the archives of the transatlantic slave trade to retrieve the voices of the enslaved, and, notably, there is no body of scholars from this same heritage who are invested in narrating these lives in scholarly writing. (The efforts of the Collective for Black Iranians, discussed below, may be a notable exception.) The only ostensible self-expression of historical enslaved persons is their muteness in the photographs, which onlookers have felt free to interpret in many ways (e.g., "the faces...confirm their deep sadness and the horror that encapsulated their lives"[10]). Princewill, meanwhile, tries to *recover* a voice in the archive seemingly preserved in a written document and to imagine a character and world on the basis of it. That there are so few such historical documents is part of what her novel mourns, and to critically fabulate seems one way of recovering a life that is all but absent from the archive.

Aside from Princewill's fictional re-casting of Jamila Habashi, there are other written accounts, some quite detailed, of enslaved Africans living with Iranian families. Chapter 5, for example, engaged with several produced by well-known Iranian scholars regarding the black "servants" in their own homes. The issue, however, is that there has not been the same kind of sustained, methodologically grounded approach to reading these texts "against the grain" (as Hartman puts it in *Scenes of Subjection*) in order to draw a more nuanced historical assessment out from between the lines of power, memory, and cultural identity such stories are embedded in. Consider the account of 'Abul Qasim Afnan, a descendant of the original family of Baha'ism—a religion that came into being in the nineteenth century and which positions itself as a fulfillment of Shi'i Islam as well as a distinct religion. In the slim volume *Black Pearls*, Afnan offers the stories of the "beloved servants" ("black pearls") who lived in the household of Sayyed Ali Mohammad Shirazi, better known to history as the "Bab."[11] The Bab (which means "door" or "gate," alluding to his role in ushering in a new theological dispensation) was the founder and first leader of a messianic offshoot of Shi'i Islam called Babism.[12] Afnan's account is an affectionate and, in some ways, even a reverent one, but Afnan refuses these "servants" the only subject status that counts in his world: that of being members of the Babi or Baha'i communities of believers. Instead, the book nostalgically recounts the lives of the slaves who lived with the Bab, as well as those who lived with his maternal relatives and descendants. It is a historicized fabulation, but not a critical one.

The enslaved persons documented in Afnan's account were the "beloved" slaves of a religious group (Babis and Baha'is) that would be relegated to the margins of Iranian society and history before ultimately being driven out of the land where the religion originated. The stories of these enslaved people are resurrected in *Black Pearls* not to preserve their humanity for its own value but rather to attest to the generosity and goodness of the family that enslaved them. As befits a semi-hagiographical account, the family is held up as exemplary in the text. Each chapter of *Black Pearls* is devoted to a different slave: Haji Mubarak, Fiddih, Isfandiyar, Masud, and Salih Aqa. The chapter on Haji Mubarak begins:

> Records indicate that both sides of the family of the Bab (paternal and maternal), in keeping with their social position and customs of the time, owned black slaves. The behavior of both families toward their slaves, however, was reputed to have been exceptional. They were unfailing in their generosity and kindness, and it was often said of them that they treated their servants just as members of their own families.[13]

While one can easily believe that a Shirazi merchant family of means (like the Bab's) were slaveholders, the problem with *Black Pearls* is that it both owns and disowns that history, admitting freely that they owned slaves but refusing to countenance the idea that anything but respect and honor characterized the situation of the enslaved in their households. This chapter goes on to use language that reinforces this ambivalence whenever a choice regarding the acquisition or keeping of slaves is concerned. They owned slaves "as was the custom,"[14] and Afnan describes the education and upbringing Mubarak received from the Bab's brother-in-law, who had purchased him when he was five years old, as "exemplary."[15] He goes on to note, "my grandmother. . .would often recall Mubarak's extreme modesty and politeness,"[16] and later, "She would describe his manners and demeanor as being regal."[17] According to Afnan, Mubarak was never told of the Bab's death because "[t]he family wanted neither to distress them [Mubarak and the other household servants and slaves] nor to allow their servants, who were the only ones of the house who were regularly seen in the marketplace, to become the source of delusive news or rumors."[18] Mubarak, Afnan goes on to say, moved with the Bab's mother to Karbala (in Iraq), where he died at the age of 40.

Although most of the chapters offer similar words of defense and self-justification mingled with fatuous praise of the slaves themselves—they were always, it was noted, "treated. . .just as members of their own families"—this chapter on Mubarak stands out for several reasons. Principal among them is the absence of acknowledgment that Mubarak was almost certainly a eunuch based on contextual details presented by the author.[19] Also importantly, although Mubarak was clearly a witness to the Bab's revelation, he is not considered a "first believer" by the Baha'i community because he was an African slave.

The knowledge that Mubarak was a eunuch would change our understanding of his acquisition, "education," and the trust that was placed in him by the Bab and his family substantially. Orlando Patterson has averred that the eunuch is "the ultimate slave," yet the depiction of him in this work is nostalgic, romantic, and idealized.[20] It suggests that he led a peaceful life of honorable (and voluntary) service. That the violence that creates eunuchs from male children is entirely effaced from this narrative, however, comes as no surprise (see chapter 6). Further, the fact that an enslaved African ("Ethiopian") is not acknowledged as a "first believer" because he was seen by dint of his race to be too childlike or otherwise incompetent to believe (if not to unquestioningly serve) is an issue that created controversy among the Baha'i community when this book was published, particularly in the US.[21] Whereas the original community of Babis (and later Baha'is) was comprised only of Iranians, Baha'ism has in subsequent years become an international faith. It now includes a multiracial, multiethnic community of believers who appeared to chafe at the soft-pedaling of the history of enslavement and the rejection of slaves as among the first believers.[22]

Afnan, however, refuses to countenance the idea that Mubarak should be counted among the first believers; or indeed as a believer at all. According to Anthony Lee, the author of the second edition's prologue, Afnan in fact refused the title *Black Babis*, which was proposed by the publisher. He told Lee that he did not believe that Mubarak and Fiddih could be counted as Babis at all. Lee speculates that Afnan may have believed that they were not capable, as slaves, of making the declaration or fully embracing the faith. Moreover, Lee points out that according to another Baha'i scholar, the affirmation of Mubarak and Fiddih as first believers would mean that their declaration of belief came before the Afnan family's own acceptance of the faith and would thus compromise their own status in the community of believers.[23] However, after offering yet another Baha'i scholar's views on the topic—in this case that Afnan was simply reproducing bureaucratic views on a belief widely held by Bahais in the twentieth century—Lee rejects these perspectives as too charitable. He suggests instead: "I think it more likely that he unconsciously reproduced the views long held within his family—views that were primarily determined by cultural attitudes toward Africans, slaves, and household servants."[24]

The irony of Afnan's refusal is heightened by the fact that the Bab and his Baha'i heirs are credited with being the first religion in world history to take an unequivocally abolitionist position.[25] (Islam is mistakenly credited with being a religion that opposes slavery—a false characterization that effaces the complexity of early Muslim communities' positions on enslavement, which is beyond the scope of this study but is debated elsewhere.[26]) Followers of Baha'ism themselves point to Baha'ullah's tablet to Queen Victoria (ca. 1868) praising her for her commitment to abolition as evidence of the faith's rejection of this practice. Yet, as *Black Pearls* demonstrates, it is also the case that the Bab and his family and descendants (including Baha'ullah) were enslavers for many generations. Oddly, then, this Bahai-produced text, *Black Pearls*, contradicts the idea that their beliefs in abolitionism translated into action in their domestic lives. Instead, it demonstrates that while the faith's core members were aware of and may even have approved of coeval abolitionist movements in other places, they did not practice them at home.

The first edition of *Black Pearls*, published in 1988, has a foreword by Moojan Momen,[27] a member of the Baha'i community and an independent historian, as well as a preface by Afnan. Momen's comments both directly engage but also somehow avoid and obfuscate the very theme/subject of the book: the service of slaves. He looks back to the origins of Islam (from which Baha'ism is derived) to both explain slavery and affirm its radical positions on equality, and he explicitly denies that racism played a role in the treatment of the slaves in the Bab's household. Reflecting common notions about slavery in the Islamic world, he writes:

> The word slave brings to mind, for most people in the West, the evils of the Atlantic slave trade which brought millions of Africans to work on the plantations of the Americas. Slavery in the Islamic world was, however, a very different phenomenon. [...] slaves in many Muslim societies had great opportunities for improving their circumstances and climbing the social ladder. The highest offices of state, even the position of grand vizier, even kingship itself, were not outside their grasp.[28]

Momen goes on to detail the ways in which slavery in Islam was a benevolent institution, collapsing into one all of the various ways in which "slave" soldiers (such as Mamluks) could become rulers and asserting that "the majority of the Abbasid caliphs and Ottoman sultans had slaves as mothers."[29] In short, he proposes, Islam (from which Babism and Baha'ism arise) not only offered a kind of meritocracy-aligned version of slavery in which slaves could "better themselves" but is also not in itself a racist religion. As evidence, he suggests that because "[t]he mothers of several of the Shi'i Imams are recorded as having been African slaves [...] the later Imams must have been dark-skinned."[30] He asserts that they were in no way discriminated against on this basis; in fact, he argues, as imams in the line of Mohammad, they were revered. Significantly, "African" here is interpreted by Momen to mean "black," though only one of the "slave mothers" of these imams is specifically attested to be "black" (*habbashi*; Ethiopian). The others he mentions are "Berber," an indigenous people of northern Africa who frequently assimilate into the other populations of North Africa and do not identify as black. Despite these textual gymnastics, Momen goes on to admit, "in later times, prejudice against blacks increased."[31]

In the second edition, published in 1999, Momen's foreword has been excised and replaced with one by Anthony Lee, who was at that time an editor at Kalimat Press. (Lee would later become a historian of slavery in modern Iran as well as the history of the dissemination of Baha'ism in Africa.) Lee begins his introductory remarks with the blanket assertion that "Few institutions are more repugnant to our modern sensibilities than chattel slavery."[32] While Lee's new foreword is clearly meant as a corrective revelation of the faith to the previous edition's somewhat uncritical stance on the institution of slavery, he still can't quite bring himself to call the people whose lives are chronicled "slaves." He refers to them instead as "servants." He goes on to note, "Nowhere is this feeling of repugnance for slavery stronger than in the United States, where slavery is associated—in a way it is nowhere else—with racist theories and ideas of superiority of white over black."[33] This rhetorical move shifts the most odious ideas associated with "slavery" away from Iran and onto the United States. Yet he does take a more expansive view of their significance in the household and religion than did Afnan, emphasizing their importance to the revelation of the faith to the Bab. Counter to Afnan, Lee suggests that the Bab and his family understood the people they called "Black Pearls" (if only tacitly) to be part of the first cohort of believers—an exalted status within the Bahai community. And he does insist that Baha'ism is the first religion to unequivocally forbid slavery.

Thus, while offering some redress for both Momen and Afnan's less critical assessments, many of the problems remain. The stories narrated in the text both reflect and belie the various frameworks thrust upon them—fabulating to restore or bolster the humanity of Afnan's family but simultaneously diminishing that of the enslaved persons they purport to celebrate. Indeed, *Black Pearls* is a book complicated by the author's, editors', and other associated parties' discomfort with what appears to be a foundational contradiction: the brutality of enslavement, on the one hand, and the desire of the Baha'i community to see these "servants" as voluntary and, in some ways, akin to their own position as servants of God while simultaneously refusing them the status of first believers.³⁴

As the example of *Black Pearls* demonstrates, a group that is itself marginalized and persecuted can still exhibit blindness where tacitly accepted practices of racialized enslavement are concerned. *Black Pearls*, as much as any other cultural project explored in this book, lays bare the way in which elite Iranians of various religious and ethnic backgrounds commonly misunderstand or downplay the history of slavery in Iran, resulting in a self-congratulatory perception of color (or race) blindness that has profound consequences for the way Iranians and diasporic Iranians engage the issue of race in the contemporary world. In the present and especially in the diaspora, questions around such representations have taken on a new poignancy, as chapters 5 and 6 address. The meaning of representing enslavement and race has changed dramatically for Iranian scholars of Iranian heritage, particularly those educated in the US, who find themselves racialized in new ways and struggling to locate themselves in US academic discourses around race. What does it mean now to "give voice," and do we have the capacity to hear it? If Afnan's *Black Pearls* is obviously not the kind of "giving voice" desired by scholars invested in reclaiming the humanity of the enslaved, then what would such a process look like?

Almost twenty years ago, historian Eve Troutt Powell surveyed the state of scholarship on enslavement in the Islamicate world in a piece entitled "Will That Subaltern Ever Speak?" While the critical engagement of blackness in Middle Eastern history has grown exponentially in those twenty years, Powell's comments are nonetheless worth revisiting. Explicitly engaging Spivak's concern, Powell notes some ironies and disappointing aspects of the divide (or perceived divide) between histories of enslavement written outside of the Middle East about the history of slavery in the Islamic world, and the perception that although slavery "stained" Europe and the New World, an appropriate sense of shame in those regions (giving rise to and expressed in the activism surrounding abolition) was thought to redeem it. This sense of shame, according to Western scholars, "had no parallel" in the Islamic world. She notes also the lack of parallel in slaves' narratives, pointing out that whereas in the US, where formerly enslaved persons' own narratives were widely known and canonized, no comparable narratives had been located in the Islamic world. Indeed, she notes scholars' "frustration" at the inability to find them. Powell goes on to ask: "How then can their history be found, much less told? How can we hear them? Or do we, as historians, resign ourselves to the sad statement that the slave, the ultimate subaltern, cannot speak? Or if she ever did, was 'made to unspeak herself posthumously'?"[35]

While Powell endorses the "imperative" to "retrieve" the voices of the enslaved, she repeats Spivak's caution that "it is important to acknowledge our complicity in the muting [of subalterns], in order precisely to be more effective in the long run. Our work cannot succeed if we always have a scapegoat."[36] Thus, she implies that blaming superficial or uncritical scholarship on the idea that there are not adequate archives, for example, indicates a failure of critical reflection and close reading. Powell concludes, "As I read her, *the attribution of blame to explain the silence of the slaves* themselves may well have camouflaged, for many historians, other routes toward information."[37]

Powell also highlights the idea introduced by Spivak of "decipherment" in recovering the voice (or "speech," as Powell puts it) of the enslaved. A false decipherment, however well-meaning, is still, for Spivak, an act of ventriloquism—and I think the word "ventriloquism" is aptly chosen to convey fakery, chicanery, and entertainment. Powell is focused in this piece on Spivak's consideration of the subaltern as she articulated it in "Can the Subaltern Speak?," but Spivak elaborated the idea of "decipherment" between a master and slave more explicitly when she returned to the idea in her Wellek lectures, which were published in 2003 as *Death of a Discipline*. Here, she guides us through the rhetorical staging of power between a master and a slave in J. M. Coetzee's *Waiting for the Barbarians*, in which the master attempts to "decipher" the slave:

> The staging of rhetoricity in the novel is the Magistrate's attempt to *decipher* her. This is quite different from the staging of the logical Magistrate, a capable and experienced senior official who is able to *summarize* the characteristics of empire. A series of dreams may be one account of this deciphering effort. To have sex with the girl is another.
>
> The Magistrate, usually a promiscuous man, is generally unable to perform what would be recognizable as an act of sex with this young barbarian woman. What comes through in his efforts to do so is his repeated generalization that the meaning of his own acts is not clear if he tries to

imagine her perspective: "I feed her, shelter her, use her body, if that is what I am doing, in this foreign way." I cannot forget that

Freud urges us to investigate the uncanny because we are ourselves *Fremdsprächig*, "foreign speakers." What can it mean but seeing the other as placed, native?[38]

This example is most apposite because it simultaneously addresses the sexual contact between master and slave that Princewill places at the center of Jamila's ability in *In the Palace of Flowers* to be treated as human and non-other (as "native," in Spivak's parlance) and recognizes the failure of the "summarizing" approach that Princewill offers here: her novel is full of researched details about life in Qajar Iran, but ultimately does not make it possible to believe in the story of Jamila Habashi. Though *In the Palace of Flowers* is peppered with details about *qalyun*, pomegranates, and other appurtenances of life in that place and space, it is a strangely flat imaginative landscape—articulated by the descriptive imperative to "show, not tell," but otherwise curiously devoid of what Spivak calls "rhetoricity." The question of redress is raised through Jamila and other enslaved characters' preoccupation with remembrance, but ultimately cannot be sufficiently addressed in the genre of realist historical fiction, which values attention to convincing details over speculative imagination of the past.

It is possible that given our contemporary sensibilities around slavery, particularly the enslavement of people originating in Africa, we cannot imagine anything like the understanding that Coetzee allows the Magistrate to develop in his recognition of what he has done and his attempts to make amends for it; nor can we allow for an enslaved person to be unknown to the reader as the "barbarian girl" remains in the logic of that novel. Unlike *In the Palace of Flowers*, *Waiting for the Barbarians* is not an historical novel—it is set in a fictional world, in an unspecified past. Coetzee's refusal to allow the subaltern to speak words that would allow the reader to overtly understand her subjectivity may seem like a failure of the postcolonial project; we are never invited to know *for certain* what the barbarian girl thinks. Yet in contrast, Princewill's well-meaning attempt to enter into the consciousness of an enslaved person through overt narration of exactly what she believes Jamila would think feels like the kind of ventriloquism that Spivak warns us against: the diasporic subject using the subaltern to imagine a place for herself in the present. While the space of fiction *can* provide a site of mediation and redress, it also shows us the limits of certainty that it is the best way to "give voice" to those whose subjectivity has never been considered by historians.

AGAINST "VENTRILOQUISM"

If diasporic identity depends on an articulation of self that uses the home country to claim authenticity in the host country, it is easy to see how the inability to fully understand the existence of slavery in Iran and its legacies has led to profound inconsistencies in attitudes toward race in the Iranian diaspora. If Iranian-Americans and other diasporic Iranians can believe that slavery never existed in Iran—or was benign if it did—and that their ancestors and contemporaries in the home country are "colorblind" and impervious to race and racialization, then the problematic stakes of the ventriloquism they undertake for the newly "discovered" subaltern (who was also black and enslaved) are even higher.

Among those participating in the mediation of the discourse on the history of slavery and blackness in Iran and the diaspora is the Collective for Black Iranians, a group that has sought to create positive content around the intersecting identities of being "black" and "Iranian," and to separate "blackness" from "enslavement." The group was founded in 2020 in the wake of the Black Lives Matter movement amid renewed upheaval over aggregated instances of horrifying police brutality against black Americans. Its members desire to put aside the connection of blackness in Iran with enslavement and to forge an identity around more cosmopolitan, international notions of black diaspora. Highly educated and cosmopolitan themselves, the Collective's members (by self-description on their website) mostly reside now in North America and Europe; only one of them claims to be a descendant of an enslaved person in Iran. The others are, like the Collective's founder Priscillia Konkou-Hoveyda, the children of one non-black Iranian parent and a parent of non-Iranian African descent. For these children of Iranian parentage, the ongoing insistence of Iranian diasporic communities on including the clownish blackface figure Hajji Firuz in Nowruz (New Year) celebrations is a particularly visible example demonstrating that black Iranian humanity is at present either invisible or illegible to most Iranians. For the Collective, the antidote is to exercise creative license and produce new content around more positive ideations of Iranian blackness.

In addition to its curated online content on its website and Instagram, the Collective staged a physical exhibition of art in September 2021 at the Gates Art Gallery in Philadelphia. It was titled "Hasteem: We Are Here." In a piece produced by Maryam Sophia Jahanbin (whose author bio discloses that she is "situated in America, as an immigrant of Kutchi-Iranian heritage, born in the UK"), the exhibition was described as follows:

> *Hasteem* is an exhibition produced by the Collective for Black Iranians to raise awareness on the intersection of being black, African/of African descent and Iranian. An exhibition that powerfully brings together black, non-black, Afro-Iranian, black American and African artists for the first time in the Iranian community, *Hasteem* tells the history and stories of an erased reality.[39]

Jahanbin quotes Konkou-Hoveyda's emphasis that it is "important that the stories of Black and Afro-Iranians around the world are understood not only through a lens of forced migration, but a lens of *chosen* migration'."[40] She adds, "The Collective is a creative and critically conscious initiative proposing an Iranian culture that stands fully at its Black and African intersections."[41]

The Collective's efforts therefore lie at a complicated nexus of histories and motivations: like other diasporic Iranians, the Collective seeks to make positive the image of Iran it promotes. Yet in their attempts to create and present an alternative history and image, they risk supplanting the thinly historicized record of blackness with what Hartman warningly calls the "fanciful" by offering putative histories that are patently ahistorical. The Collective's elaboration of the Zanj Rebellion, which they tacitly posit as an example of a slave rebellion akin to those in the Americas, stands out among these. A short piece of text and an image of a black woman present an imagination of this rebellion as connected to contemporary struggles: the woman's eyes are heavenward, she raises an empty hand to the sky in a gesture of triumph, and she is loosely draped in a veil that appears a fashionable nod to observance of the hejab in contemporary Iran. As such, the image evokes at once several contemporary themes and ideas: the woman as symbol of national struggle, possibly the struggle against compulsory veiling in Iran, but also perhaps against systemic racism in the US.[42] The text accompaniment invites us to see the Zanj Rebellion as an early site of allyship, noting "[t]he Black laborers declared themselves free and took up arms against the ruling powers. They were strengthened by others coming to their cause – including Persians and Arabs who also recognized the corruption and injustices of their society."[43] In doing so, the Collective offers the story as a parable that tends toward the "utopian" that Hartman cautions against[44] and ignores that while the Zanj Rebellion *was* indeed a revolt of enslaved Africans against their own enslavement, the rebels were not opposed to the institution of slavery itself; indeed, the revolt's leader 'Ali bin Mohammad (who is described as the descendant of enslaved Arabs, but not necessarily black Arabs) promised the rebels not only their freedom but also their own slaves as compensation for their participation in the revolt.[45] This latter detail is unsettling even to the casual reader of history, but if used as a touchstone for contemporary affirmations of abolitionist sentiment, rebuttals of anti-blackness, and allyship, it takes on an additional freight that is almost crushing.

Diasporic Iranians, including Konkou-Hoveyda and the Collective, are in the undesirable position of trying to understand a history that is suppressed, poorly documented, and now becoming sensationalized and newly politicized in the wake of renewed interest in race in diasporic sites. At the same time, they are negotiating their own racialization in such sites (especially North America and Europe), where racism is very much alive and, in many cases, has been redirected toward people perceived to be from "Muslim countries" with greater hostility in the wake of the refugee crises of this century. As Vaziri astutely notes, they are in a state of "digital anamnesis" (or perhaps "hypomnesis")—the recovery of a past life never lived through the mechanisms of the internet and the platform (in all senses of the word) of social media.[46]

For the Collective and the collectivity of self-identified black Iranians it represents, the strategies available to many non-black diasporic Iranians are foreclosed to them. Whereas some of the latter have sought in the US to instrumentalize their Otherness—which has assumed the name "brownness"—in order to have access to what we might call the "diversity, equity, and inclusion" regimes of recognition, the idea of brownness (a liminality that enables access to both whiteness and blackness) may not be possible to embrace for persons of African *and* Iranian heritage. They will be and have been racialized in ways that are distinct from Iranians who do not have a black parent. "Brown" cannot account for their struggle.

As the demands of activists for racial and social justice become institutionalized, minorities like Iranians, who are not formally recognized as disprivileged yet feel themselves to be precluded from access to full racial whiteness in the US, have sought to find ways to be understood, and to have access to the privileges that the status of recognized minority can (they believe) bequeath, like preferential hiring and admissions or funding for university education. Thus, in the increasingly institutionalized negotiation of diversity in the US, seeking recognition by conflating microaggressions with the broad systemic racism encountered by black people in the US is a rhetorical move many diasporic Iranians have made. The impulse behind such identifications could be read as self-serving, as the motivation behind such gestures is often expressed as a confusion about their own racial identities in relationship to "blackness" and "brownness" in the racial schemes broadly upheld in the US and Europe. At the same time, the color-based system of multiculturalism that has replaced the ideology of merit in the US seems to invite such moves, however far-fetched.

As early as 2005, Azadeh Moaveni articulated this problem and the beginning of her awareness of it while in college in the late 1990s. As she put it in her memoir, *Lipstick Jihad*:

> All this heightening of consciousness was fascinating to me, but in a detached, impersonal way. To start with, there was no space for Iranians within the multicultural dialogue everyone seemed so bent on having. We were too new, and didn't have a place yet. And then there was the question of race, in the American sense. Was I brown? All the Iranians I knew seemed to consider themselves Europeans with a tan. Was I an immigrant? My family had always insisted we weren't really immigrants as such, but rather a special tribe who had been temporarily displaced. Iranian women like Khaleh [aunt] Farzi lived in daily fear of being mistaken for a Mexican—a pedestrian immigrant rather than a traffic émigré.[47]

She then goes on to relate how she tutored a young Mexican-American student who, although from a much less privileged background than hers, seemed to be getting all the support and attention she wanted for herself:

> As I watched Andy [the young Mexican-American man she tutored] grow into himself, and develop the intellectual confidence to raise his hand in class, I also began to envy him. He was surrounded by brilliant Chicano professors who encouraged and understood him; who plied him with illuminating books that spoke directly to his experience. He saw his anger and confusion mirrored in poetry, and spent hours unraveling it with thoughtful graduate students who had traveled the same path. [. . .] The notion of finding power in your otherness, once I got over the pretentiousness of using those sorts of terms, was incredibly compelling. So was the explosive possibility that I could be confident about who I was, the idea that being Iranian didn't have to be about silly emotional culture clashes with my mother, but a sense of self anchored in history.[48]

Moaveni's memoir pokes fun at herself and the culture of minority that recognizes certain forms of brownness ("Was I brown? All the Iranians I knew seemed to consider themselves Europeans with a tan") as worthy of recognition and support while ignoring other people who didn't fit into the existing schemes for recognizing disprivilege. The culture she observes excludes the latter because they are not visible within the scheme of race in the US, either by choice ("Europeans with a tan") or by assumptions about the wealth of the broader immigrant group that they came from. Given the disparity between the kind of institutional support "Andy" gets as a Latino student and which Moaveni is assumed not to need because of her class privilege and the relative ignorance (or hostility) of Americans regarding Iran, is it any wonder that Iranian-Americans, even those from privileged backgrounds like Moaveni, would seek to be seen and recognized in the way that particular forms of minoritization enable? Is it surprising that she, like others, might begin to self-identify in ways that might help them achieve that recognition?[49]

By the time we arrive at Porochista Khakpour's *The Brown Album*, published in 2020, we find an example of an Iranian-American fully embracing "brownness," using it as her standard adjective for racial self-description and striving fitfully to display her racial marginalization. Yet, at the same time,

Khakpour emphasizes that she is from an elite, affluent, highly educated family displaced by the revolution. As such, neither the idioms of poverty she invokes to describe her college and post-college years nor her self-characterization as being a marginalized "brown" person seem appropriate. She earns a scholarship to attend an elite college but quickly squanders it by becoming involved with drugs and self-harming behaviors that only seem to lift when she embraces her racial liminality and passes, during a trip to Faulkner country in the American South, as white.[50] Whereas fifteen years earlier, Azadeh Moaveni (who is the same age as Khakpour and from a similar class/educational background) could express ambivalence and cultural criticism about the ways she might be racialized ("was I brown?") and her ability to pass as white, Khakpour has fully embraced these ambiguities, opting in and out as she sees fit.

In Khakpour's move to inhabit these sites of racial ambiguity in shifting circumstances, she embodies Neda Maghbouleh's observation that the ability to "pass" as white is a swinging door (or in her terms, *racial hinge*) that can slam in the person's face.[51] She also embodies Frank Wilderson's darker reading in *Afropessimism* of the identity moves embraced by "brown" people: pointing toward "Palestinians, Native Americans, Latinx" as well as "immigrants, White women, [and] the working class," he refers to these various groups as "civil society's junior partners"—unwitting but willing collaborators in white supremacy.[52] From Wilderson's point of view, the ability to pass that Khakpour occasionally embraces is what makes Iranians' ability to form genuine solidarities with black people—nationally or internationally—impossible.

Contemporary identity-based exploration in the US and in the Iranian diaspora more broadly opens up necessary conversations about Iran's relationship to blackness, but at the same time, it invites such conversation in ways that are fraught with self-interest and carry with them the longstanding legacy of Iran's problematic relationship to race. It is in the diasporic space where the issue of Iranian blackness and its relationship to a suppressed history of enslavement has become most charged and acute.

Hartman ends the essay "Venus in Two Acts" by noting that the "task of writing the impossible, (not the fanciful or the utopian but 'histories rendered unreal and fantastic'), has as its prerequisites the embrace of likely failure and the readiness to accept the ongoing, unfinished and provisional character of this effort."[53] The motivations that prompt us—as scholars, diasporic Iranians, or both, or neither—to "write the impossible" and to engage blackness are complex and bedeviled with the politics of past and present, but that does not mean we should *not* attempt it. The bigger problem is, how do we look, listen, and write *without* bringing our own racial hierarchies and baggage to bear on the cultural documents we can find? While the goal of recovering the voices of the enslaved may be impossible to achieve fully, it shouldn't stop us from thoughtfully investigating and deploying a reflexivity that does not simply return us to an affirmation of the non-black Iranian (diasporic) subject's humanity.

Notes

Introduction

1. For a brief overview, see Afshin Matin-Asghar, "EDUCATION xxi. EDUCATION ABROAD," *Encyclopædia Iranica* VIII/3 (1997): 226–30; for a more in-depth history of the motivations behind state encouragement of education abroad, see David Menashri, *Education and the Making of Modern Iran* (The Moshe Dayan Center for Middle Eastern and African Studies [University of Tel Aviv]), 1992).

2. Porochista Khakpour, *The Brown Album* (Penguin Random House, 2020).

3. "Pars" or Persians are only one of many ethnic communities in Iran, albeit the dominant one.

4. Maz Jobrani's stand-up routine "Persian Like the Cat" is the funniest, but not the only, expression of this idea.

5. Countless memoirs by diasporic Iranians in the years since the 1979 Revolution attest to the importance of this way of seeing oneself: Khakpour has already been mentioned, but one can find similar accounts in memoirs like Firoozeh Dumas's *Funny in Farsi* (Villard, 2003) and more recent ones like *Americanized: Rebel Without a Green Card* (Knopf Books for Young Readers, 2018) by Sara Saedi.

6. A Facebook page entitled "Iranian History—the Land of the Original Aryans" is widely "liked" and re-posted by scholars of Iranian history and has over 91,000 followers as of September 27, 2025.https://www.facebook.com/AryanHistory.

7. Reza Zia-Ebrahimi, *The Emergence of Iranian Nationalism: Race and the Politics of Dislocation* (Columbia University Press, 2016).

8. Mohamad Tavakoli-Targhi, *Refashioning Iran: Orientalism, Occidentalism, and Historiography* (Palgrave, 2001).

9. See Ehsan Yarshater's "Communication," *Iranian Studies* 22, no. 1 (1989): 62–65. This is a recurring subject of discussion on the Adabiyat listserv created by the late Franklin Lewis, where scholars of Persian literature exchange ideas.

10. After much consideration, I decided not to capitalize the words "black" or "blackness" in this book except in proper names or titles. The orthographic possibility of capitalization that exists in Latinate alphabets does not exist in Persian, where no words are capitalized, and to capitalize "black" when it is a translation of *siah* seemed to be an imposition of additional and possibly incorrect meanings. Also, inasmuch as this book is about how we see and understand blackness as a racial, social, political, and historical category in Iran and the diaspora, I believe that the position that invites debates and consideration at this moment is *not* to capitalize.

11. The fact that the first Iranian film to win the Academy Award for Best Foreign Film—Asghar Farhadi's *A Separation* (*Jodayi Nader az Simin*)—dramatized the divorce of a husband and wife who were divided over whether or not their daughter's life would be better lived outside of Iran or inside it suggests that this story and the conditions it depicts are legible to audiences both inside and outside of Iran.

12. Neda Maghbouleh, *The Limits of Whiteness: Iranian Americans and the Everyday Politics of Race* (Stanford University Press, 2017).

13. In *This Flame Within: Iranian Revolutionaries in the US* (Duke University Press, 2022), Manijeh Moradian chronicles the story of Iranians in the pre-revolutionary era (roughly the 1960s and 1970s) who became identified and/or allied with the Civil Rights movement in the US during the period of their study abroad and saw it as akin to their struggle to overthrow the Shah. Drawing on personal histories, including that of her father, a "Marxist, working-class Zoroastrian [Iranian]," who taught at Howard University, Moradian uses a framework she calls "revolutionary affects" to describe the kind of identifications Iranian activists in the US felt with black American revolutionary groups like the Black Panthers. (Unfortunately, we do not get to hear if the identification was reciprocated by the black people who they idealized, though the case of Dawud Salahuddin, discussed in chapter 4, may give some insight into such filiations.) Interestingly, one of Moradian's subjects, "Sina," describes the black people he encounters as manifesting a "swagger" he admires: "In their swagger, I see a political figure of emancipation. In their swagger, I see an attitude about capitalism. I see an attitude about the whole arrangement and structure of the world, and I like that. It's not always pleasant when it's addressed at you, but, in and of itself, it's a beautiful thing " (Moradian, *This Flame Within*, 144). Sina also compares the black Americans he meets at protests as similar to the *"lotti"* (by which I believe both Moradian and Sina mean either "luti" or "lati"—see chapter 3 for a discussion of the difference as it applies to the culture of masculinity in Iran)—the

urban vigilante of folklore who persists in the modern era either in the guise of a Robin Hood-esque figure or as a simple and violent thug.

14. See, for example, the work of Steven Salaita (e.g., *Inter/Nationalism Decolonizing Native America and Palestine* [University of Minnesota Press, 2016]) and Nadine Naber (e.g., *Race and Arab Americans* [Syracuse University Press, 2008]) as illustrative of these solidarities.

15. This may in part be attributable to the Islamic Republic's vociferously pro-Palestinian positions, which are part of its larger schema to become a major power in the Middle East. The IRI funds and supports regional actors and groups that oppose Zionism/Israel, and many Iranians believe that this scheme is detrimental to the well-being, both philosophically and materially, of Iranians domestically.

16. The nostalgia these children feel for the "lost radicalism" of their parents' generation remains palpable, with a panel called "Children of Revolutionaries: The Afterlives of the Iranian Left" being staged at a 2019 conference "40 Years and More" at the San Francisco State University Center for Iranian Diaspora Studies.

17. *Better Things*, season 4, episode 8, "Father's Day," written by Patricia Resnick and Robin Ruzan, directed by Pamela Adlon, aired April 16, 2020, on FX.

18. In the concluding chapter of *Racial Blackness and Indian Ocean Slavery* (University of Minnesota Press, 2023), Vaziri engages this concept of "anamnesia" to discuss the way in which a memory of blackness is produced for purposes in the present.

19. Sayeh Dashti, *You Belong: To Our Children Around the World* (Xlibris Corp, 2016). My thanks to Beete Baghoolizadeh for bringing this book to my attention.

20. Dashti, *You Belong*, 47.

21. Dashti, *You Belong*, 48.

22. Dashti, *You Belong*, 47.

23. Ehud R. Toledano, *As If Silent and Absent: Bonds of Enslavement in the Islamic Middle East* (Yale University Press, 2007).

24. Mariam Behnam, *Zelzelah: A Woman before Her Time* (Motivate Publishing, 1994), 33–34. In this citation and throughout the book, I have not corrected the transliteration used by other authors.

25. Beeta Baghoolizadeh, *The Color Black: Enslavement and Erasure in Iran* (Duke University Press, 2024).

26. Afsaneh Najmabadi, *The Story of the Daughters of Quchan: Gender and National Memory in Iranian History* (Syracuse University Press, 1998).

27. Nonetheless, there may be other histories of rural or agrarian enslavement that have not yet been discovered because of the dearth of archival evidence.

28. Taj Al-Saltaneh, *Khaterat-e Taj al-Saltaneh (Memoirs of Taj al-Saltaneh)*, ed. Mansureh Ettahadieh (Tarikh-e Iran, ca. 1983).

29. Jonathan A. C. Brown came under fire for what appeared to many in the local community of Muslims in the DC area (and further afield) to be "glowing" accounts of slavery in the early Islamic communities in *Slavery and Islam* (Oneworld, 2019) and the lectures he gave promoting the book.

30. I address this in greater depth by examining Simin Daneshvar's and Jalal Al-e Ahmad's writings on race in chapter 3.

31. Jalal Al-e Ahmad, *Dorr-e yatim: jazireh-ye Kharg* (*The Orphan Pearl: The Island of Kharg*) (Ketabkhaneh-ye Danesh, 1339/1960), 51.

32. Firoozeh Kashani-Sabet looks at some of the ways that black intellectuals' ideas were engaged in pre-revolutionary Iran in "The Anti-Aryan Moment: Decolonization, Diplomacy, and Race in Late Pahlavi Iran," *International Journal of Middle East Studies* 53 (2021): 691–702.

33. Bernard Lewis, *Race and Slavery in the Middle East: An Historical Enquiry* (Oxford University Press, 1990).

34. Behnaz A. Mirzai, *A History of Slavery and Emancipation in Iran, 1800–1929* (University of Texas Press, 2017).

35. Thomas Ricks, "Slaves and Slave Trading in Shi'i Iran, AD 1500–1900," *Journal of Asian and African Studies (Leiden)* 36, no. 4 (2001): 407–18.

36. Jerzy Zdanowski, *Slavery and Manumission: British Policy in the Red Sea and the Persian Gulf in the First Half of the 20th Century* (Ithaca Press, 2013).

37. Stephanie Cronin, "Islam, Slave Agency and Abolitionism in Iran, the Middle East and North Africa," *Middle Eastern Studies* 52, no. 6 (2016): 953–77; *Social Histories of Iran: Modernism and Marginality in the Middle East* (Cambridge University Press, 2021).

38. Parisa Vaziri, *Racial Blackness and Indian Ocean Slavery* (University of Minnesota Press, 2023).

39. Eve Troutt Powell, *A Different Shade of Colonialism: Egypt, Great Britain, and the Mastery of the Sudan* (University of California Press, 2003).

40. Ehud R. Toledano, *Slavery and Abolition in the Ottoman Middle East* (University of Washington Press, 1998); *As If Silent and Absent: Bonds of Enslavement in the Islamic Middle East* (Yale University Press, 2007).

41. Madeline Zilfi, *Women and Slavery in the Late Ottoman Empire: The Design of Difference* (Cambridge University Press, 2010).

42. Mohammad Ennaji, *Serving the Master: Slavery and Society in 19th Century Morocco* (Palgrave, 1999).

43. Chouri El Hamel, *Black Morocco: A History of Race, Slavery, and Islam* (Cambridge University Press, 2013).

44. M'hamed Oualdi, *A Slave Between Empires: A Transimperial History of North Africa* (Columbia University Press, 2020).

45. Circassians, in this context as in Iran, were often able to successfully obscure or transcend their histories, personal or familial, of enslavement, because of their ability to be assimilated into light-skinned elite populations; or even to be seen by elite natives as offering lightening of skin as a benefit to their progeny.

Chapter 1

1. See Robert Steele's detailed *The Shah's Imperial Celebration of 1971: Nationalism, Culture and Politics in Late Pahlavi Iran* (I.B. Tauris, 2021), for an in-depth history of this event.

2. In "The Anti-Aryan Moment," Firoozeh Kashani-Sabet suggests that the shah's adoption of this title was due to his general inability to listen to the voice/will of the Iranian people, who she believes had already disavowed Aryanism at this historical moment. Although I agree that Mohammad Reza Pahlavi seemed unusually impervious to the social and political currents swirling around him, in this, he was not wrong. The rejection of Aryanism that Kashani-Sabet argues for seems hopeful rather than based on evidence.

3. Pahlavi, Mohammad Reza. "2500-year celebration of the Persian Empire. Persepolis, Iran. October 1971." Persepolis, Iran, October 16, 1971. https://www.youtube.com/watch?v=8VSaqhXuV7Q.

4. I have adopted a modified version (omitting diacritical marks) of the *IJMES* transliteration system for representation of words in Persian. In a book that does not exclusively address literature in Persian, and deals as much with aural and visual texts as much as it does with print, a simplified version of transliteration seems appropriate.

5. Quoted in David Motadel, "Iran and the Aryan Myth," in *Perceptions of Iran: History, Myths and Nationalism from Medieval Persia to the Islamic Republic*, edited by Ali M. Ansari, I. B. Tauris & Company, Limited, 2014. ProQuest Ebook Central, http://ebookcentral.proquest.com/lib/ucdavis/detail.action?docID=5260156 *Perceptions of Iran*, 120.

6. See Edward Polsue, "Being Aryan, a Myth Many Iranians Choose to Believe," IranWire, August 7, 2023, https://iranwire.com/en/society/119259-being-aryan-a-myth-many-iranians-choose-to-believe/.

7. Within the Arabophone Middle East, the slur "Safavid" is sometimes used to describe the contemporary regime to invoke the imperialist Shi'i aspirations of that dynasty.

8. Talinn Grigor, *The Persian Revival: The Imperialism of the Copy in Iranian and Parsi Architecture* (Pennsylvania State University Press, 2021).

9. Fath'ali Akhundzadeh, *Maktubat-e Mirza Fath'ali Akhdunzadeh* (Entesherat-e Mard-e Emruz, 1364/1985).

10. See, for example, David Motadel, "Iran and the Aryan Myth," In *Perceptions of Iran: History, Myths and Nationalism from Medieval Persia to the Islamic Republic*, ed. Ali M. Ansari (I. B. Tauris, 2014), and Zia-Ebrahimi, *The Emergence of Iranian Nationalism*, on this topic.

11. Hamid Algar, "ĀḴŪNDZĀDA," *Encyclopædia Iranica* I/7 (1984): 735–40. The poem was published in 1837.

12. Algar, "ĀḴŪNDZĀDA," n.p.; emphasis added.

13. Hugh Barnes, *The Stolen Prince: Gannibal, Adopted Son of Peter the Great, Great-Grandfather of Alexander Pushkin, and Europe's First Black Intellectual* (Harper Collins, 2006).

14. Catharine Theimer Nepomnyashchy, Nicole Svobodny, and Ludmilla A. Trigos, eds., *Under the Sky of My Africa: Alexander Pushkin and Blackness* (Northwestern University Press, 2006).

15. Dieudonné Gnammankou, ed., *Pouchkine et le Monde Noir* (a special issue of *Présence Africaine*) (Présence Africaine Éditions, 1999).

16. Raquelle Greene, "The African-Aristocrat: Alexander S. Pushkin's Dual Poetic Persona" (PhD diss., Ohio State University, 1999), ii.

17. For example, in one essay, Catherine Theimer Nepomnyashchy reflects on the ways in which Pushkin's own negotiation of his African ancestry played a role in his representations of race in the novel, arguing that the "black baby" that is sent away at the beginning of the novel, as well as the "white baby" that appears at the end, signals anxieties about cuckolding and the dangers of racial impurity that Pushkin himself felt.

18. W. E. B. Du Bois, "Pushkin," *Phylon* 1, no. 3 (1940): 268–69.

19. The webpage on the NYU Jordan Center website was removed during the writing of this book. A summary of the conference and a list of notable participants (including Gatrell) originally featured on the page https://jordanrussiacenter.org/event-recaps/those-crazy-americans-of-course-pushkins-not-black/#.Y-oUHXbMLcc. A screenshot of the page can still be accessed via the Internet Archive's Wayback Machine.

20. Pushkin is not only relevant to a consideration of Akhundzadeh by way of their possible racial link. Although the two men never met, Pushkin visited the Caucasus as it was being brought forcibly under Russian control. He followed his 1822 poem *Prisoner of the Caucasus* with *Journey to Arzrum During the Campaign of 1829*, which documented his visit to the region to visit his brother during the conquest of this Ottoman

city by Russia. (Russia had already extracted the Treaty of Turkmanchay from Iran after defeating the Qajar forces and was bringing the Caucasus under its control.) Pushkin's representations exoticized and romanticized the conquered population.

21. "In a critique written on Mirza Yusef Khan Mostashar od-Dowle's treatise, *Yek Kalameh* (One Word), Akhundzadeh attacked the author for arguing that Islam was compatible with the European ideas of progress, freedom, and constitutionalism. He reminded Mostashar od-Dowle that Islamic law not only stood for inequality between men and women but it also imposed veils on women and supported the institution of 'Harem', *where young men were brutally deprived of their manhood and turned into eunuchs*" (Mehrdad Kia, "Mizra (sic) Fath Ali Akhundzade and the Call for Modernization of the Islamic World," *Middle Eastern Studies* 31, no. 3 [1995]: 439; emphasis added).

22. Janet Afary, *Sexual Politics in Modern Iran* (Cambridge University Press, 2009), 114.

23. Akhundzadeh 1985, 73–74; qtd. in Afary, *Sexual Politics in Modern Iran*, 114–15.

24. Beeta Baghoolizadeh, "Seeing Race and Erasing Slavery" (PhD diss., University of Pennsylvania, 2018), 95; emphasis added. See Vanessa Martin's discussion of this in the scope of her larger and very interesting engagement of the Rokeby case ("The Abyssinian Slave Trade to Iran and the Rokeby Case 1877," *Middle Eastern Studies* 58, no. 1 (2022): 201–13).

25. In *The Color Black*, Baghoolizadeh revises the argument somewhat, acknowledging that Akhundzadeh had an African ancestor, but also, and secondly, sees his representations of eunuchs as less positive.

26. As noted above, Baghoolizadeh acknowledges Akhundzadeh's possible African ancestor in *The Color Black*.

27. Afary, *Sexual Politics in Modern Iran*, 114.

28. Baghoolizadeh, "Seeing Race," 94. Another example of the trouble critics have with defining Akhundzadeh's ethnicity is Mostafa Abedinifard's recent article "Iran's Self-Deprecating Modernity: Toward Decolonizing Self-Criticism," *International Journal of Middle East Studies* 53, no. 3 (2021): 406–23. In it, he describes Akhundzadeh as "the Tbilisi-based Azerbaijani thinker and playwright" (416) and "an Azerbaijani liberal [who] [a]s a pioneer of Iranian nationalism [...] identified mainly as a Persian and Iranian" (417). Abedinifard insists on calling Akhundzadeh an "Azerbaijani" thinker throughout, although there was at that time no entity known as Azerbaijan.

29. "The Adventure of the Lankaran Khanate's Vizier Part 3." Uploaded by Azdrama. https://www.youtube.com/watch?v=lZUXTnrXgJo

30. Tavakoli-Targhi, *Refashioning Iran*.

Chapter 2

1. See Michael Beard, The Blind Owl *as a Western Novel* (Princeton University Press, 1990), and Manoutcher Mohandessi, "Hedayat and Rilke," *Comparative Literature* 23, no. 3 (Summer 1971): 209–16.

2. Iraj Parsinejad, *A History of Literary Criticism in Iran, 1866–1951: Literary Criticism in the Works of Enlightened Thinkers of Iran—Akhundzadeh, Kermani, Malkom, Talebof, Maraghe'i, Kasravi, and Hedayat* (Ibex Publishers, 2003).

3. Sadeq Hedayat, *The Blind Owl*, tr. D. P. Costello (John Calder, 1957).

4. Hedayat's great-great grandfather, Reza Qoli Khan Hedayat, was a Qajar courtier and also affiliated with proto-Aryanist thinkers such as Manekji Limji Hataria, mentioned in chapter 1, who commissioned Reza Qoli Khan Hedayat to write a history of pre-Islamic kings called *Nezhadnameh-ye padshahan-e Iraninezhad* (*The Heritage of Kings of the Iranian Race*, published posthumously in 1879). He also published a dictionary in 1871.

5. Mahmud Katira'i, *Zaban va farhang-e mardom* (*The Language and Culture of the People*), 131.

6. Although this word is used exclusively with regard to the children of enslaved persons who remain in the household of the master in which they were born, this term has been oddly glossed by other critics to mean simply "domestic servant"—a type of gloss that effaces the history and meaning of the word. See, for example, Amirhossein Vafa, "Race and the Aesthetics of Alterity in Mahshid Amirshahi's Dadeh Qadam-Kheyr," *Iranian Studies* 51, no. 1: 141–60).

7. Katira'i, *Zaban va farhang-e mardom*, 132. For such a servant to have been born of a white father in the household, there is at least a strong likelihood that a member of the family would have been the father. Katira'i goes on to describe that Hedayat would ask his friends to send him accounts of folklore, and that "one of Hedayat's companions" recalled accompanying him to "the house of woman to talk" and that Hedayat "took notes" (132).

8. L. P. Elwell-Sutton, "The Influence of Folk-Tale and Legend on Modern Persian Literature," in *Iran and Islam: In Memory of the Late Vladimir Minorsky*, ed. C. E. Bosworth (Edinburgh University Press, 1971), 250.

9. Homa Katouzian, *Sadeq Hedayat: The Life and Literature of an Iranian Writer* (I.B. Tauris, 1991), 86.

10. Nematollah Fazeli, *Politics of Culture in Iran: Anthropology, Politics and Society in the Twentieth Century* (Routledge, 2006), 63.

11. While this looks like a scattered and disorganized list, if one compares it to a work like *The Wild Rue of Persia: Magic, Myth and Folklore in Iran* (1938) by Bess Allen Donaldson, it looks very similar, suggesting a genre. Donaldson was a Presbyterian

missionary and teacher who lived in Iran for thirty years and gathered material for her book during this time.

12. Sadeq Hedayat, *Alaviyeh Khanom va Velengari* (*Alaviyeh Khanom and Tittle-Tattle*) (Amir Kabir, 1963).

13. In this case, the slave's value is signaled through the name given by the enslaver.

14. Omid Azadibougar, *Sadeq Hedayat and World Literature* (Springer, 2020), 36. Azadibougar goes on to suggest that "since his return to Iran he [Hedayat] had been engaged in the study and recording of common language and folk culture and these two books are the products of a different literary and cultural approach to the subjects" (36–37). Azadibougar both acknowledges the effect of European studies of folklore on Hedayat but also attempts to position Hedayat as a native fashioner of folklore studies in Iran, and someone who independently developed the idea of "world literature" through his translations and explorations of foreign literatures. Yet Azadibougar suggests a return to examination of Hedayat's folkloric efforts insofar as such an approach "is another powerful argument against critical readings that insist on the reliance of Hedayat's literary imagination on an exclusively European literary tradition. For him, even modern literature is rooted in older narrative traditions and, therefore, that is why he went to the source of this literary creativity. Second, besides the realistic thrust of the narratives he selected, the Pahlavi language was significant for him because he looked for a universal narrative tradition in the language, presumably pre-national and pre-modern, to bond with the historical human and to go back to a time when the ideological and epistemological atmosphere was not 'contaminated' by modernity" (Azadibougar, *Sadeq Hedayat*, 180).

15. Azadibougar, *Sadeq Hedayat*, 115 (emphasis added).

16. Mohamad Tavakoli-Targhi, "Narrative Identity in the Works of Hedayat and His Contemporaries," in *Sadeq Hedayat: His Work and His Wondrous World*, ed. Homa Katouzian (Routledge, 2008), 107.

17. H. D. G. Law, ed. and tr., "Persian Writers," in *Life and Letters and the London Mercury*, vol. 63, no. 148 (Druid Press, December 1949), 252.

18. Homa Katouzian, "Women in Hedayat's Fiction," in *Sadeq Hedayat: His Work and His Wondrous World*, ed. Homa Katouzian (Routledge, 2008), 89.

19. Hushang Golshiri was famously proud of having come from humble beginnings, and other authors like Ahmad Mahmoud came from lower-class backgrounds and worked as laborers.

20. Hedayat's younger contemporary Ahmad Shamlu allegedly commented that "'there is no obscene word that is not used in it. One only wonders how Hedayat managed to have it published'" (Farzaneh, qtd. in Omid Azadibougar, *Sadeq Hedayat and World Literature* [Springer, 2020], 116). Hedayat reportedly refused to say how he had

learned to "use their [presumably the class of people depicted in the story] language perfectly" and would only disclose that "a friend had given him the idea and he wrote it because the friend could not do it himself" (Farzaneh 129; qtd. in Azadibougar, *Sadeq Hedayat and World Literature*, 116). Azadibougar's somewhat credulous conclusion is that "Given that Hedayat was interested in cataloguing folk culture in all its forms, it is not unlikely that this story was an exercise to give the linguistic cataloguing a narrative form to contextualize the expressions instead of simply giving them a scientific order in a, say, dictionary" (*Sadeq Hedayat and World Literature*, 116).

21. Fazeli, *Politics of Culture*, 3.

22. The other area, besides folklore, identified as essential to Iranian identity was archaeology and architecture—a history that is beyond the scope of this discussion but is explored in Talinn Grigor's fascinating *Persian Revivalism*.

23. Fazeli, *Politics of Culture*, 60.

24. Hedayat, cited in Fazeli, *Politics of Culture*, 60.

25. At the end of his life, he appeared to those around him weary of and frustrated by his efforts, both literary and ethnographic. Although he is largely remembered as a modernist writer, there is some evidence that his peers and friends at the time saw him as equally a folklorist. Among his last visitors was Jean Pierre de Menasce, an Egyptian Jewish convert to Catholicism, as well as a priest and scholar of pre-Islamic Iran. Menasce was interested in Hedayat's folkloric work and attempted to engage him in a conversation about it and prospects for continuing this work in the future, which he tried to convince Hedayat was his primary role/goal in Iranian society (qtd. in Katouzian, *Sadeq Hedayat: Life and Legend of an Iranian Writer*, 170–71).

26. Sistan-Baluchistan is populated by a people whose territorial identity extends across three nations: Iran, Afghanistan, and Pakistan. Baluchis are largely Sunni, not Shia; in this they are distinct from the Arab populations of southern Iran, who are often presumed to be Sunni, since there is often a mistaken assumption, perpetuated by a spate of recent popular writing on the subject, that Arab=Sunni and Iranian=Shia.

27. Al-e Ahmad, *The Orphan Pearl*, 51.

28. Al-e Ahmad, *The Orphan Pearl*.

29. Al-e Ahmad, *The Orphan Pearl*, 51–52.

30. Hamid Dabashi, *The Last Muslim Intellectual* (Edinburgh University Press, 2021), 219.

31. The presence of slavery on Kharg is well-documented: Thomas Ricks reports, "In 1763, the Dutch trading company occupied Kharg Island close to the northern Gulf port of Basra. In order to protect their property and pearl fishing industries, the Dutch settled 100 'caffree slaves' on Kharg Island along with a small contingent of Chinese farmers" (Amin, qtd. in Ricks, "Slaves and Slave Trading in Iran," 412).

32. Gholam-Hossein Sa'edi, *Ahl-e hava (People of the Wind)* (Chapkhaneh-ye Daneshgah, 1966).

33. Gholam-Hossein Sa'edi, *Tars va larz (Fear and Trembling)* (Ketab-e Zaman, 1968).

34. Parisa Vaziri's comments on Sa'edi in "Pneumatics of Blackness" are a notable exception. She has also commented on the difficulties of writing about *zar* in a short but incisive piece entitled "Tracing Absence."

35. Jean Franco, *Decline and Fall of the Lettered City: Latin America in the Cold War* (Harvard University Press, 2002), 159.

36. Franco, *Decline and Fall*, 15.

37. Fatemeh Shams, "Under the Waves: The Many Lives of Moniru Ravanipur's *The Drowned*," *Iranian Studies* 55, no. 1 (2022): 240.

38. Sa'edi, *Ahl-e hava*, 41. Sa'edi does not attribute any of the *zar* as originating in Iran—they have been brought from external sites—India and the Arab world; in other words, sites implicated in the centuries-long traffic in enslaved Africans. These latter *zar* winds that are not from "Zanzibar, Somalia, and Ethiopia" are, according to Sa'edi, from sites characterized by "mysterious mountains and enormous oceans," presumably enabling the movement of the *zar* winds.

39. Sa'edi, *People of the Wind*.

40. Studying and understanding *zar* seems to be one of the enduring mysteries of Middle East studies. Even studies that seek to emphasize its distinctiveness in a particular region tend to see it as the same everywhere—in every case, it is an "African" tradition, tied ambiguously to enslavement.

41. This is sometimes also called *adabiyat-e aqlimi-ye jonub* (literally: "literature of the southern climate").

42. Hassan Mirabedini, *Ṣad sal dastan nevisi-ye Iran (One Hundred Years of Prose in Iran)* (Nashr-e Chashmeh, 1377/1998), 560–61.

43. Yet how can one overlook the obviousness of Iraj Pezeshkzad's *Mashallah Khan in the Court of Haroun al-Rashid* being a riff on Mark Twain's *A Connecticut Yankee in King Arthur's Court*?

44. Interestingly, the translator of this work into English was Minoo Southgate, one of the first scholars to publish a critical article on the deployment of blackness in Persian letters: Minoo Southgate, "The Negative Images of Blacks in Some Medieval Iranian Writings," *Iranian Studies* 17, no. 1 (1984): 3–36, https://doi.org/10.1080/00210868408701620. In the opening paragraph of her essay, Southgate explains: "In 1961, in my last year of high school in Tehran, I wrote two emotional poems inspired by current black liberation movements in Africa and America. Like most Iranians, I did not suspect that the Middle East was as guilty of racism against blacks

as Europe and America were. Ironically, it was in New York, in the late '60s, that I came across medieval Iranian sources showing racism against blacks. I decided then to do a paper on the subject, but resisted the project for a decade. In November 1979, when Khomeini ordered the release of all blacks among the American hostages 'because [blacks] are oppressed by American society' (*New York Times*, November 19, 1979, A:12), I was finally prompted to undertake the present study, to set the record straight" (Southgate, "Negative Images of Blacks," 3). Vaziri uses Southgate's catalogue of blackness in this period to argue persuasively for an "anecdotal antiblackness" in pre-modern Iranian texts that can help inform conceptions of race/blackness in the present. Parisa Vaziri, "On Saidiya: Indian Ocean World Slavery and Blackness beyond Horizon," *Qui Parle* 28, no. 2 (December 2019): 241–80.

45. In a much later work, a play entitled *Otello dar Zamin-e 'Ajayeb* (translated as *Othello in Wonderland*), Sa'edi revisits blackness in a different form, using Shakespeare's play as a platform for critiquing the contradictory morality and race-obsessed politics of the Islamic Republic. Othello's race becomes operative insofar as the IRI officials uncritically believe that "black Muslims" are particularly valiant and "ready to fight," but wonder that the actor playing Othello is not black. The director explains he will be "blackened" (painted with make-up) for the role (and in a 1985 performance in London staged and directed by Nasser Rahmaninejad, the actor playing Othello is already in blackface for the role). The IRI authorities who have come to the theater to censor the play are shocked and see this in terms of the (then-ongoing) US embassy occupation, wondering if the black diplomats they released first were also just wearing blackface. They move from there to connect these "blackened" Americans (and, confusingly, the play being staged) to the "Zionist project." Yet even so, a 2021 article by two Shiraz-based Iranian academics chose to gloss over the racial aspects and the performance of Othello in blackface: Mahdi Javidshad and Alireza Anushiravani, "Setting *Othello* in Tehran from Exile: Metatheatre in Gholām-Hossein Sāedi's *Othello in Wonderland*," *English Studies* 102, no. 3 (2021): 307–21.

46. Mirabedini, *Sad sal dastan nevisi dar Iran*, 563.

47. Jennifer Rae Greeson, *Our South Geographic Fantasy and the Rise of National Literature* (Harvard University Press, 2010), 1.

48. See, for example, Stacey Balkan and Swaralipi Nandi, eds., *Oil Fictions: World Literature and Our Contemporary Petrosphere* (Penn State University Press, 2021).

49. Moniru Ravanipur, *Ahl-e gharq* (*The Drowned*) (Khaneh-ye Aftab, 1990).

50. Shams, "Under the Waves."

51. Houra Yavari, "FICTION ii(b). THE NOVEL," *Encyclopædia Iranica* IX/6 (December 15, 1999): 580–92.

52. Shams, "Under the Waves," 5.

53. Ameneh Shervin Emami, "Persian Magical Realism and the Re-Appropriation of Mythical and Mystical Texts: Rereading Parsipur's Magical Realism and Suhrawardi's Allegories" (PhD diss., University of California–Los Angeles, 2020).

54. Shams, "Under the Waves," 240.

55. Nasrin Rahimieh, "Magical Realism in Moniru Ravanipur's *Ahl-e Gharq*," *Iranian Studies* 23, no. 1–4 (1990): 61–75.

56. Recent criticism in Persian has taken up the theme of "ecology" in the writings of authors from the south, or writings about the south, of Iran.

57. For an anecdotal discussion of Bushehr's history and current Black population, see "A Corner of Africa in Iran," *New African*, November 5, 2018, https://newafricanmagazine.com/17636/. The article does not offer any citations or documentation for its claims, and includes an unattributed photo that is likely not of people living in Bushehr, but is nonetheless interesting insofar as it suggests that there is a population of residents in Bushehr who acknowledge African ancestry and also understand themselves to be descended from their enslavers.

58. Monir Gholamzadeh Bazarbash and Alireza Akbari, "Oil Perturbs Busalmeh: Climate Trauma in *Ahl-e Gharq*," Conference Presentation, https://allameh.academia.edu/MonirGholamzadehBazarbash.

59. For a discussion of one famous case of slave trafficking in Bushehr, see Martin, "The Abyssinian Slave Trade."

60. Moniru Ravanipur, *Afsaneh'ha va bavariha-ye jonub* (*Legends and Beliefs of the South*) (Nashr-e Najva, 2022), 9.

61. Ravanipur, *Folktales of the South*, 13.

62. Franco, *Decline and Fall*, 159.

63. *Seh qatreh khun* (*Three Drops of Blood*) (1933).

64. As Vaziri ("Slavery and the Virtual Archive") observes, the stutter is—along with his title "kaka," which in Shirazi dialects is both a moniker for an older black male slave but can also mean "brother" or "uncle"—part of the evidence that Kaka Rostam's historical antecedent was a black man, and in Mofid's account, the child of Africans enslaved in the Qavvam household.

65. Hamid Naficy, "Iranian Writers, the Iranian Cinema, and the Case of 'Dash Akol,'" *Iranian Studies* 18, no. 2/4, Sociology of the Iranian Writer (Spring–Autumn, 1985): 231–51; A Social History of Iranian Cinema (Duke University Press, 2011).

66. Scholars tend to assume that Hedayat made the cuts from the "original" or folkloric version of the story, but his brother Jahangir told one scholar (Omid Azadibougar) that Hedayat heard the story from people who were "from Shiraz," which leaves open the possibility that the story had already been purged of some of the purportedly "original" elements when he heard it.

67. Naficy, "Iranian Writers," 244.

68. Naficy notes that "in his [Dash Akol's] case, the film's silence about his sexuality misses an important point regarding both Dash Akol's personal story and Iran's national history: the transition from homosocial premodernity to heterosocial modernity. As Afsaneh Najmabadi has noted, 'In a deeply homoerotic culture, falling in love was what a man did with other men, especially with adolescents. Falling with women more often than not was unmanly' (2005:160). The film fails to fully attend to Dash Akol's divided loyalties and pain, which had both heterosexual and homosexual origins. The film highlights the former over the latter in the interest of its compulsion toward modernity, even though it is filled with nostalgia for premodern times" (Naficy, *Social History of Iranian Cinema*, 2:280).

69. Naficy, *Social History of Iranian Cinema*.

70. Naficy, "Iranian Writers."

71. Naficy can't entirely reconcile his impulse to expunge the history of enslavement with the very fact of its presence, and refers to Kaka Rostam's parents in the same sentence as "slave" and "servant": "In researching the film, Kimiai and Mofid, who plays Kaka Rostam, discovered facts they incorporated to give texture and authenticity to the villainous actions of Kaka Rostam. In an extended interview with me, Mofid explained that according to the Shirazi elders they interviewed, Kaka Rostam was a young child in the household of the powerful Qavam family, where his parents, black African *slaves*, were employed as *servants* (Naficy 1984a:12)" (Naficy, *Social History of Iranian Cinema*, vol. 2, 278; emphasis added).

72. In a recent essay on the 1971 film, Parisa Vaziri focuses on the use of blackface for the film's antagonist Kaka Rostam, arguing that this offensive practice actually perversely restores to this legend the elided history of enslavement and blackness to which it is attached. See "Slavery and the Virtual Archive." Oddly, in his recent *Mashya and Mashyana: Myth, Metonym, and the Unknowing Subject* (Edinburgh University Press, 2024), Hamid Dabashi returns to the heteronormative reading of the 1971 Kimiayi film and declines to even mention that the antagonist Kaka Rostam is played in blackface.

73. Arab sets his version of *Dash Akol* in a very specific historical moment (World War I), which both the story and the 1971 film decline to do.

74. Mahmoud Katira'i specifically singles out *'Alaviyeh Khanom* as one of Hedayat's "unique and peerless" (*yekta va bi hamta*) stories in which he embedded fragments of folklore and proverbial/idiomatic language. See pages 135–136 in his chapter "Sadeq Hedayat va Folklor-e Iran" in *Zaban va farhang-e mardom*.

Chapter 3

1. See Firoozeh Kashani-Sabet's work on this subject, particularly her work on Nodushan. See "Colorblind or Blinded by Color? Race, Ethnicity, and Identity in Iran," in Sites of Pluralism: Community Politics in the Middle East, ed. Firat Oruc (Oxford University Press, 2019) and "The Anti-Aryan Moment."

2. There is a famous example of this cited in 'Abbas Milani's *The Persian Sphinx: Amir Abbas Hoveyda and the Riddle of the Iranian Revolution: A Biography* (Mage Publishers, 2000), wherein Al-e Ahmad walked out of a meeting in which he and other intellectuals were being solicited by a representative of the state.

3. Jalal Al-e Ahmad, *Gharbzadegi: Maqaleh* (*Westoxication: The Essay*) (Ravaaq, 1977).

4. Golnar Nikpour, "Revolutionary Journeys, Revolutionary Practice: The Hajj Writings of Jalal Al-e Ahmad and Malcolm X," *Comparative Studies of South Asia, Africa, and the Middle East*, no. 1 (2014): 67–85.

5. Eskandar Sadeghi-Boroujerdi, "Gharbzadegi, Colonial Capitalism and the Racial State in Iran," *Postcolonial Studies*, 24, no. 2 (2021): 173, https://doi.org/10.1080/13688790.2020.1834344.

6. Sadeghi-Boroujerdi, "Gharbzadegi, Colonial Capitalism and the Racial State in Iran," 187.

7. Dabashi, *The Last Muslim Intellectual*, 171–72.

8. Nikpour, "Revolutionary Journeys."

9. In *The Last Muslim Intellectual*, Dabashi rails against what he sees as myriad misunderstandings of Jalal Al-e Ahmad, which only he can put right. Dabashi declaims the "stupidity" (his word) of critics who have ignored Al-e Ahmad's contact with black anti-colonial thought, and, in a confusing and extended meditation, suggests that everyone has overlooked the existence of black thought and its influence on Al-e Ahmad. Although Dabashi himself makes reference to Daneshvar's influence, he neglects to connect the dots between the development of Al-e Ahmad's ideas on the subject and Daneshvar's own time in the US and her contact with US racial thinking. Like those he criticizes, Dabashi assumes that Al-e Ahmad's knowledge of black thought came through his male colleagues, and not through Daneshvar.

10. I am using Willem Floor's expression "clearing center" from his *Encyclopædia Iranica* article "BARDA and BARDA-DARI: From the Mongols to the Abolition of Slavery," *Encyclopædia Iranica* III/7 (1988): 768–74.

11. The Shiraz of Daneshvar's childhood is most extensively memorialized in her first major novel, *Savushun* (1969), which is set in World War II–era Shiraz.

12. See Nasser Hariri, ed. *Honar va adabiyat-e emruz: goft o shenudi ba doktor Simin Daneshvar va Parviz Natel Khanlari (Contemporary Art and Literature: Interviews with Dr. Simin Daneshvar and Dr. Parviz Natel Khanlari)* (Ketabsara-ye Babul, 1366/1987), 33.

13. *Why I Can't Read Wallace Stegner and Other Essays: A Tribal Voice* (University of Wisconsin Press, 1996) by Elizabeth Cook-Lynn is one such work.

14. Shortly after Daneshvar's Fulbright period, Stegner also contracted to work as a propagandist for what was then the Arabian American Oil Company (ARAMCO). The story of Stegner's association with ARAMCO is itself fascinating, as told by Robert Vitalis in "Wallace Stegner's Arabian *Discovery*: Imperial Blind Spots in a Continental Vision," *Pacific Historical Review*, no. 3 (August 2007): 405–38.

15. In *Playing in the Dark*, Toni Morrison suggests the ways in which blackness functions as a foil for white masculinity in American fiction of the late nineteenth and the twentieth centuries. Toni Morrison, *Playing in the Dark: Whiteness and the Literary Imagination* (Vintage, 1993).

16. Daneshvar's letters to Stegner are housed in the Stanford University Library. Daneshvar writes to Stegner while she is at the Harvard Seminar in 1963 to ask for his help in finding work in the United States. She also invites Stegner to visit Iran (which he does) and generally praises the positive influence he has had on her writing. There is also evidence that the choices Daneshvar made in terms of which American works to translate in the period during and following the Fulbright were influenced by Stegner. Her first translation post-Fulbright was *Payk-e marg va zendigi ya komedi-ye ensani (The Messenger of Life and Death, or, The Human Comedy)* by William Saroyan, trans. Simin Daneshvar (Ibn Sina, 1954). Daneshvar would also go on to translate other American works, with Stegner's encouragement, including Nathaniel Hawthorne's *The Scarlet Letter (Dagh-e nang)* (Nil, 1955).

17. See her letters in English to Stegner, which are part of the collection "Wallace Earle Stegner Creative Writing Program: correspondence and manuscripts, 1949–1992," and which are held at the Department of Special Collections, Green Library, Stanford University.

18. Simin Daneshvar, *Shahri chawn behesht (A City Like Paradise)* (Khvarzmi, 2002).

19. In one such example, Daneshvar attempts to explain Quakers to Al-e Ahmad in terms of Sufis.

20. Although Iranians began to go to the United States and Europe for education in large numbers in the 1960s and 1970s, Daneshvar was not part of that wave, by virtue of her age. See, in particular, chapter 3 of Matthew K. Shannon, *Losing Hearts and Minds: Iranian-American Relations and International Education during the Cold*

War (Cornell University Press, 2017), for a fuller discussion of the Iranian student movement in the United States.

21. The words historically used to discuss the practice of enslavement in Iran—*bardegi*; the people who were enslaved, *bardeh, kaniz, gholam*; and black Iranians, *siah*—differ from the translations of terms used in the Iranian press to describe race, racism, or black people when they occur elsewhere (*nezhad, nezhad parasti/ garayi, siah pustan*). The latter terms have the quality of neologisms—they are not deployed in this way in historical documents (including literature) dealing with the trade in enslaved Africans or other peoples in Iran.

22. Simin Daneshvar, *Nameh'ha-ye Simin Daneshvar va Jalal Al-e Ahmad*, (*The Letters of Simin Daneshvar and Jalal Al-e Ahmad*), ed. Masud Jafari-Jazi (Nilufar, 2004), 1:44.

23. See, for example, Daneshvar, *Nameh'ha*, 3:284, 286, 291, 318. See also Judith Butler's reading of Nella Larsen's *Passing* for an interesting comparison: the protagonist of *Passing*, Clare, is married to a racist white man who ostensibly does not know her ancestry, but calls her by the nickname "Nig" (Butler, *Bodies That Matter* [Routledge, 1993], 167–86). When I presented an early version of this work at UC Irvine in 2017, a participant in the seminar took me aside and told me that he had heard that Daneshvar herself had African ancestry, and that this would explain "the way she looked." When I asked for evidence of this, the person promised to send it to me but did not. I mention this to suggest the ways in which Daneshvar has herself been racialized that do not always make it into print.

24. Daneshvar, *Letters*, 1:44.

25. Black students did not matriculate at Stanford until ten years later, in 1962. Although there was not the violent hostility to black matriculation that occurred at southern US universities, one student in this cohort, Sandra Drake, remembers, "Once a girl came up to me and said: 'I've never talked to a Negro.' We were 'Negroes' back then." See Roy Johnson, "What It Was Like to Be an African-American Freshman in 1962," *Stanford Magazine*, September 2017, https://stanfordmag.org/contents/what-it-was-like-to-be-an-african-american-freshman-in-1962.

26. Daneshvar, *Letters*, 1:384–85.

27. Maghbouleh, *Limits of Whiteness*, 10.

28. Ebony Coletu, "A Complicated Embrace," *Transition*, no. 122 (2017): 138–49.

29. *Roots* was published in a Persian translation by Alireza Farahmand in AH 1357/AD 1978 and has never been out of print. Recently, on the occasion of the publication of a new edition of the translation by Amir Kabir Press, Farahmand was interviewed by the newspaper *Hamshahri*. He mentions his own interest in the history of slavery in the United States and how he had the opportunity to meet Alex Haley on two occasions; according to Farahmand, Haley was interested in him as a Muslim,

since Haley had written the *Autobiography of Malcolm X.* "Farahmand: Risheh-ha yeki az hezaran ast," Interview with Alireza Farahmand, *Hamshahri* online AH 18 Azar 1392/December 2013 www.hamshahrionline.ir/news/241770/%D9%81%D8%B1%D9%87%D9%85%D9%86%D8%AF-%D8%B1%DB%8C%D8%B4%D9%87-%D9%87%D8%A7-%DB%8C%DA%A9%DB%8C-%D8%A7%D8%B2-%D9%87%D8%B2%D8%A7%D8%B1%D8%A7%D9%86-%D8%A7%D8%B3%D8%AA.

30. Coletu, "Complicated Embrace," 143.

31. Coletu, "Complicated Embrace," 144.

32. Baghoolizadeh, "Seeing Race and Erasing Slavery."

33. Ira Dworkin, "Radwa Ashour, African American Criticism, and the Production of Modern Arabic Literature," *Cambridge Journal of Postcolonial Literary Inquiry*, no. 1 (2018): 1–19.

34. Dworkin, "Radwa Ashour," 1.

35. Dworkin, "Radwa Ashour," 6.

36. Daneshvar acknowledged in several interviews that Mehrangiz was based on her own nanny. See, for example, p. 11 of her interview with Hariri in *Honar va adabiyat-e emruz* (*Art and Literature of Today*).

37. Daneshvar, *Shahri*, 42.

38. Hajji Firuz, like Zwarte Piet in the Netherlands, is a historically ambiguous and contested aspect of the Nowruz celebration. Explaining the origins of this figure has become part of an apologia related to contemporary Iranian negotiations of race. Several scholars have insisted that Hajji Firuz's blackened face has nothing to do with racial signaling, but is about the fading blackness of winter, since the Iranian New Year is the vernal equinox and many of its rituals have to do with banishing winter and welcoming spring (e.g., *Chaharshanbeh suri*, or "Burning Wednesday," when celebrants jump over bonfires and shout "My yellowness for your redness," meaning my jaundiced [yellow] color for your ruddy [red] color). Scholarship on this topic continues to attempt to distance its racial aspects from the history of enslavement of Africans in Iran; some scholars, indeed, make no note of this possible connection. See, for example, Niayesh Purhassan's "Hajji Firuz: performans: barrassi va mo'arefi-ye 'Hajji Firuz' va negahiye- tatbighi beh namayeshgaran az manzar va didgah-e performans" ("Hajji Firuz: Performance: Research and Introduction to 'Hajji Firuz' and a Comparative Look at the Performers/Actors from a Performance Perspective"), in *Me'mari va honar* (*Architecture and Art*): *Namayesh* (AH 1388/2009), nos. 125–26. In contrast, and for an interesting discussion of the contemporary controversy in the Netherlands over Zwarte Piet and a comparison to the Hajji Nowruz tradition, see Angelita D. Reyes, "Performativity and Representation

in Transnational Blackface: Mammy (USA), Zwarte Piet (Netherlands), and Hajji Firuz (Iran)," *Atlantic Studies*, no. 4 (2018): 521–50.

39. For discussion of this theatrical tradition, see Bahram Beyzai, *Namayesh dar Iran (Drama in Iran)* (Chap-e Kaviyan, 1965); Baghoolizadeh, "Seeing Race"; and Maryam Khakipour's film *Siah Bazi: The Joymakers* (Icarus Films, 2010).

40. Daneshvar, *Letters*, 3:257.

41. Daneshvar, *Letters*, 3:396.

42. Daneshvar, *Letters*, 3:381.

43. Interestingly, Daneshvar never mentions the possibility of translating *Invisible Man* herself, though she did translate several other American novels, and Ellison's novel has still not been translated into Persian in spite of a flourishing translation industry in Iran that is not regulated by international copyright laws (Iran is not a signatory to the Berne Convention).

44. Daneshvar, *Letters*, 3:395.

45. An odd footnote to Daneshvar's and Al-e Ahmad's encounters with Ellison at the Harvard International Seminar is the fact that Ellison later dined with Mohammad Reza Pahlavi at the White House at the invitation of President Johnson. Arnold Rampersad, *Ralph Ellison: A Biography* (Vintage, 2008), 447.

46. In vol. 3 of their letters, Daneshvar tells Al-e Ahmad that she sees Ellison as a "serious" writer (*Letters*, 3:395). She goes on to characterize *Invisible Man* as a work that is focused on the hopelessness and exhaustion of (American) intellectuals, who are worn down by the petty battles of right and left politics, implicitly reading their own situation onto that of the protagonist in *Invisible Man*, and eliding the racial component central to the novel. Al-e Ahmad later wrote a treatise on this theme, *Dar khedmat va khiyanat-e rawshanfekran (On the Service and Treachery of the Intellectuals)* (Ravagh, AH 1343/ 1964).

47. Al-e Ahmad would later meet Ellison when he himself participated in the Harvard International Seminar in 1965. Roy Mottahedeh mentions this meeting in passing in *The Mantle of the Prophet: Religion and Politics in Iran* (Simon & Schuster, 1985), but notably attributes Al-e Ahmad's being chosen to his being one of the obvious intellectual leaders of Iran rather than any advocacy on his wife's part, which is clear to anyone who reads their correspondence. Yet he does not, in my view, read Al-e Ahmad's participation correctly and generally uses this to fit into his own view of Al-e Ahmad. Historical or biographical views of any individual may (indeed must) change over time, but I see Mottahedeh's work as feeding into the hagiographical view of Al-e Ahmad, which sees him as a prefiguring martyr of the revolution.

48. Daneshvar, *Letters*, 3:366. Baldwin's "This Morning, This Evening, So Soon" first appeared in *The Atlantic* in the September 1960 issue.

49. Daneshvar, *Letters*, 3:374. Both Daneshvar and Al-e Ahmad refer to Baldwin as *Jimmy* at times rather than *James*—an informality that, like their use of *mardak* to describe Ellison, may be a linguistic marker of friendly familiarity or an affectation meant to mirror American slang; but in context, reads as a kind of belittling. When I presented this work at the seminar "Roads Not Taken: Literary Translation in Iran" at UC Irvine in December 2018, it was pointed out to me that *mardak* is not always a sign of disregard, and that Al-e Ahmad often used this term much as contemporary American parlance uses *dude*. While I take the point, this is a usage unusual for Daneshvar and remarkable in her letters.

50. Daneshvar, *Letters*, 3:543–44.

51. Daneshvar, *Letters*, 3:385.

52. Daneshvar, *Letters*, 3:428–29.

53. Daneshvar, *Letters*, 3:428–29.

54. See also Beeta Baghoolizadeh, "Seeing Black America in Iran: From Malcolm X to the Hostage Crisis, 1965–1985," *The American Historical Review* 128, no. 4 (2023–12): 1618–42.

55. "Ida Yalzadeh, PhD Candidate, Brown University," posted April 16, 2019, by Iranian Diaspora Network, https://www.youtube.com/watch?v=wTHZ9Q1PU7c.

Chapter 4

1. The attempt to deny the nature and historical connection to enslavement is puzzling and appears contrary to the principles of dispassionate inquiry essential to academic scholarship. See criticisms of this stance in Vaziri, *Racial Blackness*, and Baghoolizadeh, *The Color Black*. Vaziri asserts that the ahistoricity (or a historicity that is shrouded in the mythic past) that scholars insist on is a key feature of the discourse around *siah bazi*.

2. "In Search of the Lost Laleh-Zar and a Screening of the Documentary Film 'Siah Bazi'," Stanford Humanities Center, https://shc.stanford.edu/stanford-humanities-center/events/search-lost-laleh-zar-and-screening-documentary-film-siah-bazi.

3. "Tarabnameh by Bahram Beyzaie," Stanford, https://iranian-studies.stanford.edu/events/stanford-festival-iranian-arts-events/search-lost-laleh-zar-lecture-nasser-rahmaninejad-film.

4. Nasser Rahmaninejad, *A Man of the Theater: Survival as an Artist in Iran* (New Village Press, 2020), 12 (emphasis added). See also Baghoolizadeh's analysis of Afshar's own memoir in *The Color Black*.

5. For an incisive reading and contextualization of Khakipour's films, see Parisa Vaziri, "Antiblack Joy: Transmedial Sīyāh Bāzī and Global Public Spheres," *TDR: The Drama Review* 66, no. 1 (Spring 2022): 62–79.

6. See Vaziri, *Racial Blackness*, for a discussion of the film's sequel *Shadi*.

7. Nasser al-Din Shah's disastrous granting of a generous tobacco concession to an Englishman, Major G. F. Talbot, and the subsequent revolt is a major site of historiographical attention. It is sometimes seen as presaging the revolutionary actions of the twentieth century.

8. Jane Lewisohn, "The Rise and Fall of Lalehzar, Cultural Centre of Tehran in the Mid-Twentieth Century," Tehran Project 1 (UC Irvine, 2015), 1–38. Lewisohn points out that Lalehzar had been declining for many years before the revolution, and cites popular theories as to why this was the case. In the collective diasporic imagination/memory, however, the fall of Lalehzar is intimately connected to the cultural crisis of the revolution.

9. Lewisohn, "Rise and Fall of Lalehzar," 32.

10. In a different genre, Reza Baraheni's 1970 novel *The Infernal Days of Mr. Ayaz* (translated and published in French as *Les Saisons en enfer du jeune Ayyâz* and circulating illegally in unpublished form in Persian as *Ruzegar-e duzakhi-ye Aghaye Ayaz*) uses the formula of black abjection to give shape and "voice" to the metaphorical violation of the (non-black) individual by the Pahlavi state. Set in the distant historical past of the eleventh-century court of Mahmoud of Ghazna, the novel uses a popular trope of Sufi poetry—the lover/beloved relationship between Mahmoud and his favorite male slave Ayyaz—but transforms the love relationship celebrated in classical poetry into one of sexual violation and torture. In *siah bazi*, black abjection is played for humor, whereas in Baraheni's novel, it is deployed for dystopic horror. My thanks to Nasrin Rahimieh and Farshad Sonboldel for bringing this work to my attention.

11. See, for example, Vaziri's chapter on this in *Racial Blackness*.

12. Beyzai, *Namayesh dar Iran*.

13. Critics have speculated, for example, that Milani is the "magician" in Azar Nafisi's best-selling memoir *Reading Lolita in Tehran*: a mysterious and powerful figure who advises her on what to do as she navigates the changed landscape of Iranian culture and education upon returning from the US to revolutionary Iran.

14. Hamid Dabashi, *Masters and Masterpieces of Iranian Cinema* (Mage Publishers, 2007), 262.

15. See Nasrin Rahimieh, "Marking Gender and Difference in the Myth of the Nation," in *The New Iranian Cinema: Politics, Representation and Identity*, ed. Richard Tapper (I.B. Tauris Publishers, 2002).

16. Golestan, qtd. in Naficy, *Social History of Iranian Cinema*, 3:154.

17. Kamran Rastegar, "Treacherous Memory: Bashu the Little Stranger and the Sacred Defense," in *Moments of Silence: Authenticity in the Cultural Expressions of the Iran-Iraq War, 1980–1988*, ed. Arta Khakpour, Mohammad Mehdi Khorrami, and Shouleh Vatanabadi (NYU Press, 2016).

18. Rastegar, "Treacherous Memory," 61.

19. Shouleh Vatanabadi, "Introduction," in *Moments of Silence: Authenticity in the Cultural Expressions of the Iran–Iraq War, 1980–1988*, ed. Arta Khakpour, Mohammad Mehdi Khorrami, and Shouleh Vatanabadi (NYU Press, 2016), 16.

20. See Negar Mottahedeh, "'Le Vent Nous Portera': Of Lovers Possessed, of Times Entangled and Bodies Carried Away," Asian Cinema 27, no. 2 (2016): 177–88, https://doi.org/10.1386/ac.27.2.177_1.

21. Mottahedeh, "Le Vent Nous Portera," 186.

22. See, for example, Maziar Shirazi's op-ed, "Why Are Iranians Laughing at Blackface in 2016?," *AJAM Media Collective*, December 7, 2016, https://ajammc.com/2016/12/07/why-are-iranian-americans-laughing-at-blackface-in-2016/.

23. See Maghbouleh, *Limits of Whiteness*.

24. Naficy, *Social History of Iranian Cinema*, 4:37.

25. Since 2010, Beyzai has held a visiting faculty position at Stanford University created through a contribution from Bita Daryabari. Such positions have the potential to keep alive and preserve particular ideas, practices, and so on through the support of exiled intellectuals and artists like Beyzai, who had fallen from favor in post-revolutionary/contemporary Iran.

26. "Tarabnameh by Bahram Beyzaie."

27. "Tarabnameh: A Modern Interpretation of a Traditional Play," video recording of Bahram Beyzai's lecture on his play *Tarabnameh*, with an introduction by Abbas Milani, posted March 14, 2016, by Stanford Iranian Studies, https://www.youtube.com/watch?v=nPvOYLx5ykE, 00:44:59.

28. Beeta Baghoolizadeh explores another dimension of the Qajar-era engagement of the *Shahnameh* in *The Color Black*, 129–130.

29. The framing of Iranian cultural products in the diaspora—particularly those that are focused on preservation of an art form targeted by the Islamic Republic for elimination or suppression—as vulnerable and in danger of extinction is not unique. A quality of loss and sadness oftentimes accompanies Iranian cultural exhibition in the diaspora, something I discuss in further detail in chapter 6. Although it is the case that many forms of nostalgia for pre-revolutionary art are problematic in the context of the diaspora, where they can easily be mistaken for and conflated with exoticization and exploitation of Iranian culture, bleeding into Islamophobia (since the pre-revolutionary world in Iran is construed as secular), Aryanism (as Iranians attempt to demonstrate that they were the original white people on earth), and, in the case of *siah bazi*, a confluence with an American performative mode that is reviled, if still controversially practiced or invoked.

30. Baghoolizadeh advances a theory of the development of this tradition in *The Color Black*.

31. Shirazi, "Why Are Iranians Laughing at Blackface in 2016?"

32. Shirazi, "Why Are Iranians Laughing at Blackface in 2016?"
33. "Qesmathaye az namayeshnameh Tarab nameh" (Sections of the play Tarab-nameh), posted October 13, 2017, on Tamasha, https://tamasha.com/v/PnK2Z, 4:10.
34. Shirazi, "Why Are Iranians Laughing at Blackface in 2016?"
35. "Abbas Milani: Beyzaie's Singularity in the Labyrinth of Iranian Modernities (Beyzaie Conference)," posted July 9, 2021, by Stanford Iranian Studies, https://www.youtube.com/watch?v=VHhmsoXZg5M, 01:57.
36. Naficy, *Social History of Iranian Cinema*, 3:39.
37. *Iran: A Cinematographic Revolution*, directed by Nader Homayoun. ARTE France, 2006.
38. Dabashi, *Masters and Masterpieces*, 352.
39. *Safar-e Qandahar (Kandahar)*, directed by Mohsen Makhmalbaf (Makhmalbaf Film House/Avatar Films, 2001).
40. Interestingly, Salahuddin was also closely affiliated with Said Ramadan, a leading figure in the Egyptian Muslim Brotherhood from exile until his death in 1995; Ramadan was the son-in-law of the Brotherhood's founder Hassan al-Bana.
41. Naficy, *A Social History*, 4:239.
42. Francis X. Clines, "A Nation Challenged: An Investigation; As Actor's Film Wins Raves, His Identity Attracts Scrutiny," *New York Times*, January 3, 2002, A.14.
43. Mohsen Makhmalbaf, "The Condemned," *Guardian*, January 11, 2002, https://www.theguardian.com/film/2002/jan/11/artsfeatures.
44. Sara Zavaree, "'We Have Our Own Africans': Public Displays of Zār in Iran," in *Language and Tourism in Postcolonial Settings*, ed. Angelika Mietzner and Anne Storch (Channel View Publications, 2019), 49–65.
45. *Ruzi keh zan shodam (The Day I Became a Woman)*, directed by Marziyeh Meshkini (Makhmalbaf Film House/Olive Films, 2000).
46. Makhmalbaf famously boasted, "Five years ago, while I had been the most prolific Iranian filmmaker, with 14 feature films, 3 shorts, 28 books, and 22 editing credits over a 14-year career, I stopped making films and decided to make filmmakers" (Jonathan Rosenbaum, "Under the Chador," *Chicago Reader*, April 6, 2001, https://jonathanrosenbaum.net/2023/06/under-the-chador/).
47. Rosenbaum "Under the Chador" (emphasis added).
48. See Vaziri's chapter on the black maternal in *Racial Blackness*.
49. The presence of Afghans, who are also marked out in discourse and representation as racially different from indigenous Iranians, is another puzzle in the film, which may be clear to Iranian audiences who might know that Kish has been a site of harbor/haven for Afghan refugees during the contemporary conflicts of the past forty years in Afghanistan, and may be invisible to foreign audiences, who cannot distinguish them from other non-black Iranians.

50. Dabashi, *Masters and Masterpieces of Iranian Cinema*, 373.

51. Abu-Lughod borrowed this phrase from Spivak's seminar 1988 essay "Can the Sublatern Speak?" and made it the title of her 2002 essay "Do Muslim Women Really Need Saving? Anthropological Reflections on Cultural Relativism and Its Others," which was written in the wake of the US military invasion of Afghanistan. American Anthropologist, New Series, Vol. 104, No. 3 (Sep., 2002), pp. 783-790.

Chapter 5

1. *Bad-e jinn (Spirit Wind)*, directed by Nasser Taqvai (1969).

2. In addition to the interest in black Iranian culture that he demonstrates through his participation in this film, Shamlu was interested in black American culture, one way he explored this interest was through translation of black poets. Though perhaps well intentioned, his representations of these poems and their authors is disappointing. In *Hamchawn kucheh-ye bi enteha (Like an Alley with No End)* [Moasseh-ye Entesharat-e Negah, (Ahmad Shamlu, tr.,1995)], Shamlu writes in his introduction to the section called "Black American Poets" (which stands out for not being focused on a particular author, like the other sections, but on a racial/national category): "Mario Rospuli, in his very interesting research on black Americans' poetry, says, 'Good Blacks, they're the ones who sing!' And he is right" (*Like an Alley with No End*, 27). Although there is no bibliographic reference for Rospuli in the book, and his interpretation of Rospuli's remarks are somewhat absurd, it seems that Shamlu had access to filmmaker Mario Rospuli's collection *Blues: poésie de l'Amérique noire (Blues, the Poetry of the Black American)* (1947) and translated a collection of poems by Langston Hughes and a few poems by Geraldine Brooks. For a discussion of the Hughes translations, see Levi Thompson's "Vernacular Transactions: Aḥmad Shāmlū's Persian Translations of Langston Hughes's Poetry," *Middle Eastern Literatures* 22, no. 2–3: 128–40. I want to thank Samad Alavi for bringing this body of work to my attention through his presentation of an unpublished paper on the topic at the "Persian Literature Unbound" conference convened by Nasrin Rahimieh at UC Irvine in 2017.

3. Taylor Moore proposes that the practice of *zar* forms its own archive. See her 2023 article "Occult Epidemics," *History of the Present* 13, no. 1 (April 2023): 87–100.

4. Parisa Vaziri's chapters on *zar* and ethnographic film in Iran (particularly, but not exclusively Nasser Taqvai's oeuvre) are attentive to the many ways in which these two categories are deeply enmeshed and commonly constitutive in twentieth-century Iran.

5. Maria Sabaye Moghaddam, "ZAR," *Encyclopædia Iranica*, online edition, 2009. https://www.iranicaonline.org/articles/zar/

6. *The House Is Black*, directed by Forugh Farrokhzad (Golestan Film Co., 1962).

7. Well received at the moment of its creation, Farrokhzad's film has become tangled up in her complicated poetic and proto-feminist legacies, which were compounded by her premature death in a car accident in 1967. Shot at the Babadaghi Leper Colony near Tabriz in northwestern Iran, *The House Is Black* was funded partly by the Society for Assistance to Lepers, with the rest of the support furnished by Farrokhzad's artistic collaborator and lover, filmmaker and writer Ibrahim Golestan, who also narrates the "scientific" portions of the film that document the disease and its treatment.

8. Vincent Barletta, "The House Is Black," Medium, November 14, 2023, https://medium.com/@vincentbarletta/the-house-is-black-23d56c45c085.

9. Many critics have noted Farrokhzad's salutary impulse in making this film and her desire to "humanize" the subjects—Naficy indeed notes that her "empathy, sincerity, and compassion for her subjects" overwhelms the film's "heavy-handedness" (Naficy, *Social History of Iranian Cinema*, 2:84). However, fewer have attended to the way in which the film's structure (including, most prominently, the narrating voices) actually emphasizes her own abjection and makes an appeal for her humanity over and above the humanity of the community documented.

10. Naficy, *Social History of Iranian Cinema*, 2:75.

11. For an American comparandum, see Ross McElwee's *Sherman's March* (First Run Features, 1985), which uncomfortably (but self-consciously) foregrounds McElwee's personal story and his family's connection to enslavement and its legacies in the contemporary American South through the story of anxieties about survivalism and the fear of imminent nuclear holocaust in the South of the early 1980s.

12. In his monograph on the history of anthropology in Iran, Nematollah Fazeli discusses the clear directive from the Pahlavi government's instruments to make ethnographic films about marginalized groups such as the tribes in order to demonstrate their anti-modern and backward qualities, which "should lead scientifically to the conclusion that the nomad tribes must change their life and abandon their primitive culture and social structure. You should know that the Shah is ashamed of the nomad tribes. He wonders why that kind of people is living in such a modern, developed and prosperous country as Iran" (Interview by [Fazeli] of Safinezhad in Tehran July 17, 2000); Fazeli, *Politics of Culture*, 91.

13. See Amy Motlagh, "Autobiography and Authority in the Writings of the Iranian Diaspora," *Comparative Studies of South Asia, Africa, and the Middle East* (*CSSAAME*) 31, no. 2 (2011): 411–24.

14. *Afro-Iranian Lives*, directed by Behnaz A. Mirzai (2008).

15. *The African-Baluchi Trance Dance*, directed by Behnaz A. Mirzai (Social Sciences and Humanities Research Council of Canada, 2012).

16. Mirzai, *History of Slavery and Emancipation in Iran*.

17. The footage is of a memorial in Stone Town, Zanzibar, "home to one of the largest slave markets in the world. Although the slave trade took place all over the island, three major markets saw the bulk of these inhumane transactions. The market in Stone Town was infamous for being the most brutal" ("Slave Market Memorial," Atlas Obscura, October 1, 2020, www.atlasobscura.com/places/slave-market-memorial).

18. *Afro-Iranian Lives*, website, http://www.afroiranianlives.com/ (emphasis added).

19. *Afro-Iranian Lives*, ibid.

20. "Afro-Iranian Lives," Middle East Center, Penn Arts & Sciences, University of Pennsylvania, https://mec.sas.upenn.edu/k-12-resources/media-lending-library/afro-iranian-lives. DOA August 12, 2024.

21. Pedram Khosronejad, "Review of Afro-Iranian Lives, by Behnaz Mirzai; and The African-Baluchi Trance Dance by Behnaz Mirzai," *Canadian Journal of History* 52, no. 2 (2017): 323–25.

22. Khosronejad, "Review," 325.

23. Khosronejad, "Review," 325.

24. Also of note is her insistence that *zar* is (like blackness) essentially African and tied to enslavement. Mianji and Semnani note this: "However, Mirzai Asl (2002) stresses that spirit-possession beliefs and practices such as zar, gowat, and liwa derived from Africa and spread wherever the enslaved settled" (Fahimeh Mianji and Yousef Semnani, "Zār Spirit Possession in Iran and African Countries: Group Distress, Culture-Bound Syndrome or Cultural Concept of Distress?," *Iran Journal of Psychiatry* 10, no. 4 [2015]: 229). In looking at the source they cite, we can see this confirmed: she calls *zar* "the African cultural heritage," and suggests that it came with "Africans." Part of the strange opacity surrounding *zar* is indeed its inability to be located anywhere in particular. While there must have been substantial cultural differences among the enslaved peoples brought to Iran from East Africa (even the scant historical record can confirm that), it is assumed that *zar* comes with all of them—a kind of pan-African tradition that adheres to blackness.

25. For a complementary example of a documentarian working on Indian Ocean Afro-Asian populations who have sought to "help" the communities they document, see Beheroze Shroff's work on the Sidi communities: e.g., *Voices of the Sidis: Two Documentaries* (B.F. Shroff, 2005).

26. *Afro-Iranian Lives*, 00:50–1:21.

27. M. E. Hegland, "Afro-Iranian Lives," *Iranian Studies* 50, no. 1 (2017): 171.

28. This is a problem for research on ethnic and racial groups in Iran. On this topic, see, for example, Rasmus Elling and Kevan Harris, "Difference in Difference: Language, Geography, and Ethno-Racial Identity in Contemporary Iran," *Ethnic and Racial Studies* 44, no. 12 (2021): 2255–81.

29. Motlagh, "Autobiography and Authority."

30. Amy Motlagh, "Toward a Theory of Iranian American Life Writing," *Multi-Ethnic Literatures of the United States (MELUS)* 33, no. 2 (2008): 17–36.

31. See, for example, Abu'l-Qasim Afnan, *Black Pearls: Servants in the Households of the Bab and Bahá'u'lláh* (Kalimat Press, 1988/1999).

32. Haleh Afshar, "Age, Gender and Slavery In and Out of the Persian Harem: A Different Story," *Ethnic and Racial Studies* 23, no. 5 (2000): 905–16.

33. Afshar, "Age, Gender and Slavery," 907.

34. Afshar oddly characterizes Sonbol Baji's role in the household as follows: "It is difficult to translate her 'job' across time and cultures. Sonbol Baji was what might have been called the housekeeper in an equivalent Western household. Alternatively, she could be described as a nanny. But neither term defines her role: she was in charge; there was nothing servile about her position in our family. On the whole we did what she said and did our best to live up to her expectations. We did so because we loved her and owed it to her, not because of any sense of fear of her extensive power and authority. What we respected was very much the moral authority of her central status in the family" ("Age, Gender and Slavery," 912).

35. Afshar, "Age, Gender, and Slavery," 907–908 (emphasis added).

36. In the following chapter, I revisit the story of Sonbol Baji when I discuss Pedram Khosronejad's exhibition and book *Qajar African Nannies*, in which a photo of Sonbol Baji with Haleh and Kamran Afshar is featured.

37. Mirzai, *History of Slavery and Emancipation in Iran*, 23 (emphasis mine).

38. See Fatema Mernissi, *The Forgotten Queens of Islam* (University of Minnesota Press, 1993).

39. Behnam, *Zelzelah*, 34.

40. Behnam, *Zelzelah*, 34.

41. Behnam, *Zelzelah*, 34.

42. Behnam, *Zelzelah*, 35.

43. Behnam, *Zelzelah*, 35.

44. *Afro-Iranian Lives*, 00:08:39. The discussion of eunuchs is also an essential note to sound in recountings of enslaved Africans. Afary (*Sexual Politics in Modern Iran*) and Scheiwiller (*Liminalities of Gender and Sexuality in Nineteenth-Century Iranian Photography: Desirous Bodies* [Routledge, 2017]) both mention eunuchs, as does Mirzai; in all accounts, the violence of castration is downplayed or omitted, and the "protective" role vis-à-vis the female members of the household and "positions of trust" that such men occupied are emphasized, once again stressing the beneficence of Iranian enslavers.

45. Massoumeh Price, "Chaman Andam, Slavery in Early 20th Century Iran," http://www.payvand.com/news/02/oct/1009.html (accessed February 14, 2022;

punctuation altered slightly from original for ease of reading). See also Afary, *Sexual Politics in Modern Iran*, and Scheiwiller, *Liminalities of Gender and Sexuality*.

46. Afary, *Sexual Politics in Modern Iran*.

47. Scheiwiller, *Liminalities*, 184–185.

48. See, for example, Afsaneh's *The Story of the Daughters of Quchan*, which recounts one such significant episode in Iranian constitutional history in which Iranian families protested against their daughters' enslavement in order to pay a municipal debt. It came to the attention of the centralized state and became a pivotal rhetorical device for discussing national sovereignty (which Najmabadi sees as deeply invested in masculine honor and protection of the female body/nation) in constitutional debates of the period.

49. Mirzai, *History of Slavery and Emancipation in Iran*, 130.

50. *Dingomaro*, directed by Kamran Heidari (Autentic Film, 2015).

51. These include *None of Your Business* (2019), the tragic story of Ebrahim Monsefi, a guitar player from southern Iran; *Ali Aqa* (2017), about men who are passionate about pigeon husbandry, and *My Name is Negahdar Ali and I Make Westerns* (2012), a film about an Iranian director who has continued for decades to make American-style Westerns, which have ostensibly been banned in Iran since the Iranian Revolution of 1979.

52. "Dingomaro," Kamran Heidari, http://kamranheidari.com/documentary-films/. DOA February 10, 2023.

53. Bijan Tehran, "Kamran Heidari Films Playing at Spectacle Theater in New York," Cinema Without Borders, April 5, 2019, https://cinemawithoutborders.com/kamran-heidari-films-in-new-york/ (emphasis added). The two stars offer more information about Zanzibar: "** Zanzibar, is a semi-autonomous region of Tanzania. It is composed of the Zanzibar Archipelago in the Indian Ocean, 25–50 kilometres (16–31 mi) off the coast of the mainland and consists of many small islands and two large ones: Unguja (the main island, referred to informally as Zanzibar) and Pemba Island. The capital is Zanzibar City, located on the island of Unguja. Its historic center is Stone Town, which is a World Heritage Site." More to the point, Zanzibar, located on the eastern coast of Africa, was a major site of Indian Ocean slave trafficking.

54. Parisa Vaziri, "Pneumatics of Blackness: Nāṣir Taqvā'ī's Bād-i Jin and Modernity's Anthropological Drive," in *Persian Literature and Modernity: Production and Reception*, ed. Hamid Rezaei Yazdi and Arshavez Mozafari (Routledge, 2018), 218.

55. Vaziri, "Pneumatics of Blackness," 218.

56. Vaziri, "Pneumatics of Blackness," 218.

57. *Dingomaro*, 1:38–1:43.

58. *Dingomaro*, 12:05.

59. *Dingomaro*, 13:45.

60. *Dingomaro*, 05:13–05:50.

61. The clothing is important for two reasons: this kind of attire is associated with Arabness and thus with that which has been excised from a modern Iranian (Persian) nation; it thus appears anti-modern or contrary to modernity men's attire came under the eye of state reform in the late 1920s under Reza Shah Pahlavi, and men were forbidden from wearing traditional clothing. For a more detailed discussion of sartorial reform in Iran, see Houchang Chehabi's "Staging the Emperor's New Clothes: Dress Codes and Nation-Building under Reza Shah," *Iranian Studies* 26, no. 3–4 (1993): 209–33.

62. *Dingomaro*, 00:51–01:07.

63. *Grass: A Nation's Battle for Life*, directed by Merian Cooper and Ernest Schoesdack (Films Sans Frontieres, 1925).

64. In "Reorienting Grass: How a Musical Score Transforms an Orientalist Documentary," *Afterimage* 49, no. 3 (2022): 46–72, Babak Elahi examines the re-scoring of *Grass* in 1992. Elahi sees the original film and score as unabashedly Orientalist, but optimistically believes that the re-scoring is "ethnically appropriate" and achieves a "locative cosmopolitanism." While I disagree with some of the aspects of his argument, I do agree that changing the music/sound in a film can radically change its meaning.

65. Naficy, *Social History of Iranian Cinema*, 1:162.

66. *People of the Wind*, directed by Anthony Howarth (Kino Lorber, 1976). Long before *People of the Wind* but around the same time that *Grass* was made, other forms of romantic documentation of the Bakhtiaris was being undertaken by writers like Vita Sackville-West in *Twelve Days in Persia*.

67. In another seeming full circle, Gholam-Hossein Sa'edi (although not credited in the film) allegedly accompanied Nasser Taqvai when he was filming *Spirit Wind*.

68. See Arash Khazeni's *Tribes and Empire on the Margins of Nineteenth Century Iran* (University of Washington Press, 2010) and Katayoun Shafiee's *Machineries of Oil: An Infrastructural History of BP in Iran* (MIT Press, 2018) for more discussion of the role of the Bakhtiari tribes in this history. Shafiee observes that in early twentieth-century British entrepreneurial documents describing the conditions for exploitation of oil in Iran, "the geographic description was mixed with information outside their domain of interest, namely, the history of power relations between a 'powerful political faction,' known as 'the Bakhtiari Khans,' and 'ourselves,' the author-geologists, and 'Europeans' more generally. Thus, conventions about race relations informed technical explanations of how geological missions in this instance proceeded and encountered success or failure" (Shafiee, *Machineries of Oil*, 70). Shafiee does not explain her usage of "race" in the book, but seems to accept the British distinction between "English" and "Iranian" as a racial one and refers to policies as making distinctions along these lines. Nowhere in the book are specificities of ethnicity or race within the Iranian domain where oil was exploited discussed.

69. Amy Malek, "'If You're Going to Educate 'Em, You've Got to Entertain 'Em Too': An Examination of Representation and Ethnography in *Grass* and *People of the Wind*," *Iranian Studies* 44, no. 3 (2011): 325.

70. Dabashi, *Masters & Masterpieces*.

Chapter 6

1. Anemona Hartocollis, "Images of Slaves Are Property of Harvard, Not a Descendant, Judge Rules," *New York Times*, March 5, 2021, www.nytimes.com/2021/03/04/us/harvard-slave-photos-renty.html.

2. Only this year, Harvard agreed to give up the daguerreotypes but not to surrender them to Lanier, who they claim could not persuasively establish that the persons photographed were her ancestors. Clyde McGrady, "Harvard Relents After Protracted Fight Over Slave Photos," *New York Times*, May 28, 2025, www.nytimes.com/2025/05/28/us/harvard-slavery-daguerreotypes-lawsuit.html.

3. Matthew Fox-Amato, *Exposing Slavery: Photography, Human Bondage, and the Birth of Modern Visual Politics in America* (Oxford University Press, 2019), 67.

4. Beeta Baghoolizadeh devotes a portion of *The Color Black* to this phenomenon—that is, the invisibility of non-black enslaved persons to the modern observer and the problems with conflating "slavery" with "blackness" in the Iranian context.

5. Alan Sekula, "The Body and the Archive," October 39 (Winter 1986): 3–64. We might also usefully consider Allen Feldman's arguments in *Archives of the Insensible: Of War, Photopolitics, and Dead Memory* (University of Chicago Press, 2015). His reading of the manipulation of the Rodney King footage and its afterlives (in the courtroom and—bizarrely—in the home of one of the police officers) offers a compelling way to understand the "appearance" of the photographs of enslaved Africans at this historical moment and some possible directions for theorizing it.

6. See, for example, Britt Rusert, "Disappointment in the Archives of Black Freedom" (*Social Text* 33, no. 4 [125] [2015]: 19–33); Stephen Best, *None Like Us: Blackness, Belonging, Aesthetic Life* (Duke University Press, 2018); Jenny Sharpe, *Immaterial Archives: An African Diaspora Poetics of Loss* (Northwestern University Press, 2020); or Saidiya Hartman's oeuvre, perhaps especially *Beautiful Lives, Wayward Experiments* (W.W. Norton, 2019), wherein she makes choices purposefully intended to discomfit the viewer and to ensure that they must acknowledge the pornographic qualities of the photographs of children.

7. Afsaneh Najmabadi, "Beyond the Americas: Are Gender and Sexuality Useful Categories of Analysis?," *Journal of Women's History* 18, no. 1 (Spring 2006): 11–21.

8. L. Helton, J. Leroy, M. Mishler, S. Seeley, and S. Sweeney, "The Question of Recovery: An Introduction," *Social Text* 33, no. 4 (125) (2016): 1 (emphasis added).

9. Pedram Khosronejad, "Out of Focus," *Anthropology of the Contemporary Middle East and Central Eurasia* 4, no. 1 (2017): 21.

10. I am thinking here not only of Shadi Ghadirian's *Qajar* photos (1998; https://www.shadighadirian.com/qajar), but also of the musical group Abjeez, which dons Qajar-period attire for its performances, and social media evocations of Qajar culture, including the assemblages that Nazli Akhtari discusses, most notably the transposition of a particularly visually complex figure, Ismat al-Dowleh, a daughter of Nasser al-Din Shah, onto a cover of *Playboy* in an Instagram assemblage ("Remixing to Queer the Archives of Diaspora: Qajar Photography and the Persian Carpet," *Camera Obscura* 37, no. 3 [111] [2022]: 1–29).

11. Ali Behdad, *Camera Orientalis: Reflections on Photography of the Middle East* (University of Chicago Press, 2016), 74–75 (emphasis added). See also A.D. Navab, "To Be or Not To Be an Orientalist?: The Ambivalent Art of Antoin Sevruguin." *Iranian Studies*. 2022;35(1–3):113–144.

12. Alan Sekula, "The Body and The Archive" *October* 39 (Winter 1986): 10.

13. Elahe Helbig discusses prisoner photography of this period in "Performing Violence, Displaying Evidence: Photographs of Criminals and Political Inmates in Qajar Iran (1860s–1910s)," *History of Photography* 45, no. 3–4 (2021): 264–77. See Mira Xenia Schwerda's "Death of Display," *Middle East Journal of Culture and Communication* 8, no. 2–3 (2015): 172–91, https://doi.org/10.1163/18739865-00802003, for a discussion of photographs of the assassin of Nasser al-Din Shah by Sevruguin and other photographers.

14. C. E. Dubler, "'Adjā'ib," in *Encyclopaedia of Islam*, 2nd ed., ed. P. Bearman, Th. Bianquis, C. E. Bosworth, E. van Donzel, and W. P. Heinrichs (Brill, 2012), http://dx.doi.org.prext.num.bulac.fr/10.1163/1573-3912_islam_SIM_031.

15. Naghmeh Sohrabi, *Taken for Wonder: Nineteenth-Century Travel Accounts from Iran to Europe* (Oxford University Press, 2012).

16. Mirzai, *History of Slavery and Emancipation in Iran*, 114.

17. Shaun Elizabeth Marmon, *Eunuchs and Sacred Boundaries in Islamic Society* (Oxford University Press, 1995), 90.

18. David Ayalon, *Eunuchs, Caliphs and Sultans: A Study in Power Relationships* (Magnes Press, The Hebrew University, 1999).

19. Jane Hathaway, *The Chief Eunuch of the Ottoman Harem From African Slave to Power-Broker* (Cambridge University Press, 2018).

20. In contrast, Orlando Patterson's characterization of the eunuch in his now-canonical *Slavery and Social Death: A Comparative Study* (Harvard University Press, 1982) is much starker. Calling the eunuch "the ultimate slave," Patterson asserts that the eunuch is a type of slave required by an "absolute ruler" like an emperor (315): a slave entirely cut off from ties to family and kin, unable to generate children and the most thoroughly severed from his past/affective relations to kin.

21. See Rudi Mathee's explanation of the lineage of *quruq* and its practice in the Qajar period ("QOROQ," *Encyclopædia Iranica*, online edition, 2021, http://doi.org/10.1163/2330-4804_EIRO_COM_337731). Also note that the use of eunuchs in many of these settings (in "in-between" spaces) adds another layer to the "vestibular" quality of black life that Hortense Spillers identifies as a consequences of enslavement ("Mama's Baby, Papa's Maybe: An American Grammar Book," in *Feminisms REDUX: An Anthology of Literary Theory and Criticism*, ed. Robyn Warhol-Down and Diane Price Herndl [Rutgers University Press, 2009]).

22. For example, in the Arabic courts of the Normans in Sicily, as described in Jeremy Johns, *Arabic Administration in Norman Sicily: The Royal Dīwān* (Cambridge University Press, 2002); and Jeremy Johns and Nadia Jamil, "Signs of the Times: Arabic Signatures as a Measure of Acculturation in Norman Sicily," *Muqarnas* 21 (2004): 181–92.

23. This is in contrast to a different procedure for making eunuchs, which involved removal only of testicles, a practice used in other societies and in Islamicate societies on non-African boys.

24. In a promising 2024 article in *The American Historical Review* entitled "Gulistan in Black and White: The Racial and Gendered Legacies of Slavery in Nineteenth-Century Qajar Iran," Leila Pourtavaf proposes to address some of the silences around eunuchs pictured in the Golestan Palace archive of photos (Leila Pourtavaf, "Gulistan in Black and White: The Racial and Gendered Legacies of Slavery in Nineteenth-Century Qajar Iran," *The American Historical Review* 129, no. 2 [June 2024]: 395–428, https://doi.org/10.1093/ahr/rhae152). Proposing that race and gender have not been adequately applied as categories of analysis for scrutinizing the fortunes of these eunuchs, she chooses two eunuchs who frequently appear in Nasseri-era photos: one of Georgian origin, Aziz Khan; the other of Ethiopian origin, Agha Bahram.

25. To amplify the understanding of castration as violence (if any is needed), castration was often visited upon political prisoners as a punishment: the founder of the Qajar dynasty, Agha Mohammad Khan Qajar, was himself a eunuch, having been castrated as a young man by the ruling Afsharids in lieu of execution. His successor was therefore his nephew and not a son, and Agha Mohammad himself is portrayed in portraiture as beardless.

26. Bahram Jalali, ed., *Ganj-e payda* (Daftar-i Pizhūhish'hā-yi Farhangī: Bā hamkārī-i Sāzmān-i Mīrās̱-i Farhangī-i Kishvar, 1998).

27. Baghoolizadeh, *Seeing Race*, 83.

28. Baghoolizadeh, *Seeing Race*, 84. Baghoolizadeh's dissertation is remarkable in its scope and for its incisive critique of existing scholarship on the topic of

enslavement in late nineteenth century Iran. However, I disagree with her interpretation of this name. Later in the chapter, Baghoolizadeh suggests that a photograph of another eunuch, Hajji Firuz, is "Victorious Haji" (*Seeing Race*, 190). While *firuz* could be read here as an Arabization of *piruz* (victory), as Baghoolizadeh proposes, since *piruz* continued and continues to be in common usage in contemporary Persian, other interpretations seem equally likely. For example, since many enslaved Africans were given the names of precious stones—for example, *Almas* (diamond), *Yaqut* (ruby)—we might interpret *Firuz* as it is commonly used in Arabic and in a slightly altered form (*firoozeh*) in Persian, to mean turquoise. A second possibility comes from the fact that the name of this character is sometimes written not as Haji but as *Khvajeh* Firuz, which gives a very different connotation to the name since "khvajeh" is the commonly used word for eunuch.

29. Mirzai, *History of Slavery and Emancipation in Iran*.

30. Denise Hassanzade Ajiri for Tehran Bureau, "The Face of African Slavery in Qajar Iran—in Pictures," *Guardian*, January 14, 2016, www.theguardian.com/world/iran-blog/2016/jan/14/african-slavery-in-qajar-iran-in-photos. The *Guardian* describes Tehran Bureau as "an independent news organisation, formerly hosted by the *Guardian*, offering original reporting, comment and analysis on one of the world's most important stories." https://www.theguardian.com/world/series/tehran-bureau.

31. Ajiri, "The Face of African Slavery in Qajar Iran."

32. Ajiri, "The Face of African Slavery in Qajar Iran."

33. Pedram Khosronejad, *Qajar African Nannies* (Visual Studies of Modern Iran, 2017).

34. Wendy DeSouza, following Madeline Zilfi (and perhaps also, inadvertently, Walter Johnson), notes that the enslavement of Africans in the Middle East has been problematically situated and read within an "agency vs victimization" schema that prevents scholars from seeing the brutality of enslavement (Wendy DeSouza, "Race, Slavery and Domesticity in Late Qajar Chronicles," *Iranian Studies* 53, no. 5–6 [2020]: 821–22). She writes, "It is possible to recover agency without minimizing slavery's institutionalized violence, particularly in the way historians have recovered the humanity of African slaves through their surviving testimonies. Of course this approach relies on critical methods and some imagination given the small number of surviving sources" (822). For a reconsideration of the category of "agency" and its importance in studies of enslavement, see Walter Johnson, "On Agency." *Journal of Social History*, Autumn 2003, vol. 37, no.1, pp 113–124.

35. Ayalon, *Eunuchs*, 189.

36. Kathryn Babayan also documents the term's use in the Safavid period: the *"lala-ye ḡolāmān"* was the "guard of the pages" ("EUNUCH iv. THE SAFAVID

PERIOD," *Encyclopædia Iranica* IX/1 [December 15, 1998]: 64–69). "The *lala* of the *golams* trained pages until they attained puberty. According to the manuals, once these pages became bearded they would enter the service (*yuzda*) of the *qullar aqasi* (senior officer of the *golams*). The *Dastur al-moluk* speaks of two *lalas* in the age of Shah Soltan Hosayn (r. 1105–34/1694–1721): one tutored the *golaman-e ḵassa* and the other the *golaman-e anbari*." "Lala" is also used to refer to Taj al-Saltaneh's "tutor" in her memoirs.

37. Khosronejad, *Qajar African Nannies*, vi.

38. The date given in the English caption in *Qajar African Nannies* (numbered 29 in the section titled "Photographs") is 1904 (the Persian date given is 1322, which can't be a *hijri-shamsi* [Islamic solar; used only in Iran] date, but must be a *hijri-qamari* [Islamic lunar] date). (The original Persian gives slightly different information, calling the child "his *own* son" [emphasis added], a distinction that seems somewhat strange, or at least suggestive.)

39. Ajiri, "The Face of African Slavery in Qajar Iran."

40. Patterson, *Slavery and Social Death*, 315.

41. Mahdi Ehsaie, *Afro-Iran* (Berlin Kehrer Verlag, 2015).

42. "Afro-Iran: The Unknown Minority," Kickstarter project, created by Mahdi Ehsaei, last updated June 13, 2015, https://www.kickstarter.com/projects/2023544295/afro-iran-the-unknown-minority.

43. Ali, *Camera Orientalis*, 75.

44. "Afro-Iran: The Unknown Minority."

45. Beeta Baghoolizadeh points out a range of problems associated with Ehsaie's use of the hyphen in her ajam.com long post "Picturing the Other: Race and Afro-Iranians in Documentary Photography,"Ajam Media Collective, July 20, http://ajammc.com/2015/07/20/picturing-them-vs-us-raceand-afro-iranians-in-documentary-photography/. Baghoolizadeh's brief but insightful comments on Ehsaie's work and its "viral" qualities nonetheless reinforce a central tenet of this book: the surprise that spurs such online curations to "go viral" comes from a cognitive dissonance among Iranians and diasporic Iranians about race and the history of slavery that leads them to view such images as fascinating and "wondrous" ("Afro-Iran: The Unknown Minority").

46. Ehsaie endorses the common belief that "abolition" led to immediate freedom and a cessation of enslavement ("Afro-Iran: The Unknown Minority").

47. Reesa Greenberg, Bruce Ferguson, and Sandy Nairne, "Introduction," in *Thinking about Exhibitions*, ed. Reesa Greenberg, Bruce Ferguson, and Sandy Nairne (Routledge, 1996), 1.

48. Joobin Bekhrad, "Untitled Introduction," in Afro-Iran by Mahdi Ehsaei (Kehrer Verlag Heidelberg, 2023), n.p. (emphasis in original).

49. Bekhrad, "Untitled Introduction," n.p.
50. Nahid Mozaffari, "Untitled Introduction," in *Afro-Iran* by Mahdi Ehsaie (Kehrer Verlag Heidelberg, 2023), n.p. (emphasis in original).
51. Mozaffari, "Untitled Introduction," n.p.
52. Baghoolizadeh, *The Color Black*, 13.
53. Baghoolizadeh, *Seeing Race*, 12.
54. Gayatri Chakravorty Spivak, "Can the Subaltern Speak?," in *Marxism and the Interpretation of Culture*, ed. C. Nelson and L. Grossberg (Macmillan, 1988), 27.
55. Tina Campt, *Listening to Images* (Duke University Press, 2017), 3.

Conclusion

1. Saidiya V. Hartman, "Venus in Two Acts," *Small Axe* 26 (2008): 3–4.
2. Victoria Princewill, *In the Palace of Flowers* (Casava Republic Press, 2021).
3. Victoria Princewill, "Postscript," in *In the Palace of Flowers* (Casava Republic Press, 2021), n.p. This is an inaccuracy repeated by reviews and reviewers, who focus upon the idea that this is the "only existing first-person account of an African slave in Iran, written in their own hand." The letter cited by Lee in "Half the Household Was African," which Princewill reproduces as an appendix to her novel, reads as follows:

"My name is Jamila Habashí, my father is Lulá'd-Dín from Sáho, my mother Loshábah, and from the Omarānīah tribe. I was enslaved when I was a child then was brought to Mecca where I was sold to a broker; the broker took me to Basra from the Jabal, and sold me to an Iranian broker named Mullá 'Alí, who shipped me from Basra to Muhammara and from there he took me to the Bushihr port and there he sold me to a merchant called Hájí Mírzá Ahmad Kázirúní who is in Shiraz now, I was his concubine for four years in Bushihr then Hájí took me to Shiraz and kept me there for five years; in total, I was with him for nine years and then he sold me to Nasir Nizám the son of 'Atáu'lláh. After one year, Nasír sold me to Hájí Muhammad 'Alí Khán. Now it has been five years that I have been with him" (Anthony Lee, "Half the Household Was African: Recovering the Histories of Two African Slaves in Iran," *UCLA Historical Journal* 26, no. 1 [2015]: 18–19; Princewill, "Postscript," n.p.).

4. This concern with memorialization/remembrance echoes, or at least accords with, Baghoolizadeh's reading of Nasser al-Din Shah's "memorialization" of his eunuchs in his court photography (see chapter 6).
5. An earlier novel by Anita Amirrezvani, *Equal of the Sun*, features an enslaved non-black person during the Safavid period—but in that case, the person had chosen to become a eunuch, seeing it as a route to advancement that was otherwise foreclosed to him.

6. Vaziri uses this term—"anecdotal blackness"—to describe the catalogue of instances offered by Minoo Southgate in her 1984 article "The Negative Images of Blacks in Some Medieval Iranian Writings." See Vaziri, "On Saidiya."

7. Hartman, "Venus in Two Acts," 14.

8. Spivak is clearly aware of Hartman's work: in a 2011 interview, she implicitly compares her project in "Can the Subaltern Speak?" to that of Hartman's project. "I didn't want the benevolence that people show a Patricia Williams or a Saidiya Hartman," confesses Spivak when she acknowledges that the woman who commits suicide in "Can the Subaltern Speak?" is a "kind of family person"—in fact, her grandmother's sister, or Spivak's own great-aunt (Bulan Lahiri, "In Conversation: Speaking to Spivak," *The Hindu*, February 5, 2011, https://www.thehindu.com/books/In-Conversation-Speaking-to-Spivak/article15130635.ece). Spivak's attitude suggests that she wishes to distance herself from the way in which she sees Hartman as claiming authority to represent based on assertions of kinship to the subaltern(s) she represents.

9. Hartman, "Venus in Two Acts," 5.

10. Khosronejad, *Qajar African Nannies*, vi.

11. Afnan, *Black Pearls*.

12. Babism was immediately controversial and the Shi'i religious establishment and the monarchy tried to suppress it. The Bab was executed in Tabriz in 1850.

13. Afnan, *Black Pearls*, 3.

14. Afnan, *Black Pearls*, 3.

15. Afnan, *Black Pearls*, 5.

16. Afnan, *Black Pearls*, 5.

17. Afnan, *Black Pearls*, 6.

18. Afnan, *Black Pearls*, 17.

19. The information offered by the author includes the fact that Mubarak was purchased by a member of the family at age 5; he was allowed to care for female members of the family in the absence of male members; he died at the age of 40. This is all consistent with practices surrounding eunuchs, who were entrusted with care of female family members in a way a genitally intact male servant or slave would not have been, but suffer shortened lives because of their mutilation.

20. Patterson, *Slavery and Social Death*, 315.

21. The conflict in these efforts, particularly for an American audience, were apparently demonstrated by the community of believers in the US at the time of its publication. Although I was not able to access the online dialogue referenced in Lee's dissertation and monograph based on the dissertation (it appears to be a dead link), it is clear that Baha'is in the US, in particular black American Baha'is, felt uncomfortable with the representation of these "servants in the

household of the Bab." The foreword to the second edition of *Black Pearls* also makes clear that the press and Lee felt there was a need to explain to American readers the impetus for publishing this text and to contextualize the lives of the slaves described (Anthony Lee, "Foreword," in *Black Pearls: Servants in the Households of the Bab and Bah'u'llah*, by Abu'l-Qasim Afnan, 2nd ed. [Kalimat Press, 1999]).

22. Anthony Lee, "The Establishment of the Baha'i Faith in West Africa: The First Decade, 1952–1962" (PhD diss., University of California–Los Angeles, 2007), 19.

23. Lee, "Establishment of the Baha'i Faith," 27–29.

24. Lee, "Establishment of the Baha'i Faith," 29.

25. The desire to see Abdu'l Bah'a as an early abolitionist continues: see, for example, Guy Emerson Mount, "A Troubled Modernity: W. E. B. Du Bois, 'The Black Church,' and the Problem of Causality," in *'Abdu'l-Bahá's Journey West: The Course of Human Solidarity*, ed. Negar Mottahedeh (Palgrave, 2013), and Christopher Buck, "'Abdu'l-Baha's 1912 Howard University Speech: A Civil War Myth for Interracial Emancipation," in *'Abdu'l-Bahá's Journey West: the Course of Human Solidarity*, ed. Negar Mottahedeh (Palgrave, 2013).

26. Consider, for example, Jonathan A.C. Brown's recent *Slavery and Islam* (Oneworld, 2019) and the furor it provoked.

27. Moojan Momen, "Foreword," in *Black Pearls: Servants in the Households of the Bab and Bah'u'llah*, by Abu'l-Qasim Afnan (Kalimat Press, 1988).

28. Momen, "Foreword," ix.

29. Momen, "Foreword," xii.

30. Momen, "Foreword," xv.

31. Momen, "Foreword," xv.

32. Lee, "Foreword," ix.

33. Lee, Introduction, ix.

34. In analyzing Afnan's account, in particular, Beeta Baghoolizadeh points out that when he admits to the existence of slavery at all, he insists that *his* family's slaves were treated like "members of the family" (Baghoolizadeh, *The Color Black*, 142), despite the fact that he documents their purchase price and, in at least one case, sale to another member of the family.

35. Powell, "Will That Subaltern Ever Speak?," 243.

36. Spivak, qtd. in Powell, "Will That Subaltern Ever Speak?," 244.

37. Powell, "Will That Subaltern Ever Speak?," 244 (emphasis added).

38. Spivak, *Death of a Discipline* (Columbia University Press, 2003) (emphasis added), 22.

39. "Hasteem: We Are Here," September 3–24, 2021, Twelve Gates Art, Philadelphia, PA, https://www.twelvegatesarts.org/exhibitions/2021/hasteem.

40. Maryam Sophia Jahanbin, "Hasteem, We Are Here: The Collective for Black Iranians," The Markaz Review, September 15, 2021, https://themarkaz.org/author/maryamsophiajahanbin/ (emphasis added).

41. Jahanbin, "Hasteem, We Are Here."

42. Kounkou Hoveyda, Priscillia, Beeta Baghoolizadeh, and Mina M. Jafari, "Have You Heard of the Zanj Rebellion?," Collective for Black Iranians, https://www.collectiveforblackiranians.org/histories/zanj-rebellion. DOA August 20, 2025.

43. Hoveyda, Baghoolizadeh, and Jafari, "Have You Heard."

44. Hartman, "Venus in Two Acts," 14.

45. The Collective's creative and interpretative work that touches on subjects nearer in time are more persuasive—for example, the juxtaposition of pieces of historical visual culture (such as a painting or photograph that includes, or excludes, or has as its subject, a black Iranian) with new portraiture by Kimia Fatehi of the black person in a manner that critiques or questions the historical work. (https://www.collectiveforblackiranians.org/histories/writing-ourselves).

46. Vaziri, *Racial Blackness*.

47. Azadeh Moaveni, *Lipstick Jihad: A Memoir of Growing Up Iranian in America and American in Iran* (PublicAffairs, 2006), 26.

48. Moaveni, *Lipstick Jihad*, 27.

49. Even Hamid Dabashi, who has written derisively about Moaveni's memoirs (and many others, notably Azar Nafisi's *Reading Lolita in Tehran*), makes a similar rhetorical move in his *Brown Skin, White Masks* (Pluto, 2011), where he attempts to draw parallels between the legacy of slavery in the US (using the model advanced by Malcolm X: a struggle between black Americans who behave like house slaves and those who behave like field slaves) and the contemporary (at the time) struggle for power between comprador intellectuals (the bad guys; house slaves) and exilic intellectuals (the good guys, like himself and Edward Said; the field slaves).

50. Like *The Brown Album*, Khakpour's fictions also evoke popular themes of "Persian" identity (her second novel is about a hero from the Persian epic the *Shahnameh*) while she also self-consciously eschews this identification, seeing it (to some extent) for what it is: a self-aggrandizing but empty claim to a superior racial status that makes her "whiter" than even the whitest of white Americans.

51. Maghbouleh, *Limits of Whiteness*, 5.

52. This is a term Wilderson uses repeatedly and across different publications, including in Frank B. Wilderson, *Afropessimism* (Liveright Publishing Corporation, 2020), 176.

53. Hartman, "Venus in Two Acts," 14.

Bibliography

PRINT

Abu-Lughod, Leila. "Do Muslim Women Really Need Saving? Anthropological Reflections on Cultural Relativism and Its Others." *American Anthropologist,* New Series, Vol. 104, No. 3 (Sep., 2002), pp. 783-790.

Abedinifard, Mostafa. "Iran's Self-Deprecating Modernity: Toward Decolonizing Self-Criticism." *International Journal of Middle East Studies* 53, no. 3 (2021): 406–23.

Adamiyat, Feridun. *Andisheh-ha-ye Mirza Fath'ali Akhundzadeh (The Thought of Mirza Fath'ali Akhundzadeh).* Khvarazmi, 1970.

Afary, Janet. *Sexual Politics in Modern Iran.* Cambridge University Press, 2009.

Afnan, Abu'l-Qasim. *Black Pearls: Servants in the Households of the Bab and Bah'u'llah.* Kalimat Press, 1988.

Afnan, Abu'l-Qasim. *Black Pearls: Servants in the Households of the Bab and Bah'u'llah.* 2nd ed. Kalimat Press, 1999.

Afshar, Haleh. "Age, Gender and Slavery In and Out of the Persian Harem: A Different Story." *Ethnic and Racial Studies* 23, no. 5 (2000): 905–16.

Ajiri, Denise Hassanzade, for Tehran Bureau. "The Face of African Slavery in Qajar Iran—in Pictures." *Guardian,* January 14, 2016. www.theguardian.com/world/iran-blog/2016/jan/14/african-slavery-in-qajar-iran-in-photos.

Akhtari, Nazli. "Remixing to Queer the Archives of Diaspora: Qajar Photography and the Persian Carpet." *Camera Obscura* 37, no. 3 (111) (2022): 1–29.

Akhundzadeh, Fath'ali. *Collected Dramatic Works of Mirza Fath'ali Akhundzadeh and the Story of Yusuf Shah.* Mazda Publishers, 2019.

Akhundzadeh, Fath'ali. *Maktubat-e Mirza Fath'ali Akhdunzadeh*. (*Writings of Mirza Fath'ali Akhundzadeh*). Entesherat-e Mard-e Emruz, 1364/1985.

Akhundzadeh, Fath'ali. *Maqalat (Essays)*. Entesherat-e Ava, 1973.

Akhundzadeh, Fath'ali. *Mirza Fath Ali Akhundzadeh: A Literary Critic*. Jahan Book Co, 1990.

Akhundzadeh, Fath'ali. *Persian Plays: Three Persian Plays with Literal English Translation and Vocabulary*. W.H. Allen, 1890.

Akhundzadeh, Fath'ali. *Sarguzasht-i Mard-i Khasīs*. Sang-e Miil Pablikeshanz, 2009.

Al-e Ahmad, Jalal. *Awrazan: vaz'-e mahal, adab va rusum, folklur* (*Awrazan: an account of the region, its culture and customs, and folklore*), Lahjah. Chap-i 1., Kitab'khanah-i Danish, 1954.

Al-e Ahmad, Jalal. *Dar khedmat va khiyanat-e rawshanfekran* (*On the Service and Treachery of the Intellectuals*). Ravagh, 1343/1964.

Al-e Ahmad, Jalal. *Jazireh-ye Khag: Dorr-e yatim-e khalij* (*The Island of The Orphan Pearl of the Gulf*). Ketabkhaneh-ye Danesh, 1339/1960.

Al-e Ahmad, Jalal. *Gharbzadegi: Maqaleh* (*Westoxication: Essay*). Ravaaq, 1977.

Al-e Ahmad, Jalal. *Karnameh-ye seh saleh* (*The Work of Three Years*). Entesharat-e Ravaq, 1979.

Al-e Ahmad, Jalal. *Panj dastan* (*Five Stories*). Entesharat-e Ravaq, 2013.

Algar, Hamid. "AKUNDZADA." *Encyclopædia Iranica* 1/7 (1984): 735–40.

'Alipur, Narges. *Asnad-i bardah'furushi va man'-i an dar 'asr-i Qajar* (*Records of Slavery and Their Meaning in the Qajar Era*). Muzih va Markaz-i Asnad-i Majlis-i Shura-yi Islami, 2012.

Alsultany, Evelyn, and Ella Shohat, eds. *Between the Middle East and the Americas: The Cultural Politics of Diaspora*. University of Michigan Press, 2013.

Amirshahi, Mahshid. *Madaran va dokhtaran: Dadeh Qadam Khayr* (*Mothers and Daughters: The [Slave] Nanny Qadam Khayr*), vol. 2. Nashr-e Baran, 1999.

Ansari, Ali. "Iranian Nationalism and the Question of Race." In *Constructing Nationalism in Iran*, edited by Meir Litvak. Routledge, 2017.

Atisu, Etsey. "The Little-Known Descendants of Black Iranians Who Are Victims of the Cruel Arabian Slave Trade." *Face2Face Africa*, August 8, 2019. https://face2faceafrica.com/article/the-little-known-descendants-of-black-iranians-who-are-victims-of-the-cruel-arabian-slave-trade.

Ayalon, David. *Eunuchs, Caliphs and Sultans: A Study in Power Relationships*. Magnes Press, The Hebrew University, 1999.

Ayalon, David. *Outsiders in the Lands of Islam: Mamluks, Mongols and Eunuchs*. Variorum Reprints, 1988.

Azadibougar, Omid. *Sadeq Hedayat and World Literature*. Springer, 2020.

'Aẓud al-Dawlah, Sulṭān Aḥmad, and Manoutchehr M. Eskandari. *Life at the Court of the Early Qajar Shahs*. Mage Publishers, 2014.

Babayan, Kathryn. "EUNUCH iv. THE SAFAVID PERIOD." *Encyclopædia Iranica* IX/1 (1998): 64–69.

Baghoolizadeh, Beeta. *The Color Black: Enslavement and Erasure in Iran*. Duke University Press, 2024.

Baghoolizadeh, Beeta. "Seeing Black America in Iran: From Malcolm X to the Hostage Crisis, 1965–1985." *The American Historical Review* 128, no. 4 (2023–12): 1618–42.

Baghoolizadeh, Beeta. "Seeing Race and Erasing Slavery." PhD. diss., University of Pennsylvania, 2018.

Balkan, Stacey, and Swaralipi Nandi, eds. *Oil Fictions: World Literature and Our Contemporary Petrosphere*. Penn State University Press, 2021.

Baraheni, Reza. *Les saisons en enfer du jeune Ayyâz: roman*. Translated by Katayoun Shahpar-Rad. Pauvert, 2000.

Barnes, Hugh. *The Stolen Prince: Gannibal, Adopted Son of Peter the Great, Great-Grandfather of Alexander Pushkin, and Europe's First Black Intellectual*. Harper Collins, 2006.

Barton, Nathalie, and Jean-Daniel Lafond. *American Fugitive: The Truth About Hassan*. InformAction, 2006.

Bazarbash, Monir Gholamzadeh, and Alireza Akbari. "Oil Perturbs Busalmeh: Climate Trauma in *Ahl-e Gharq*." Conference Presentation (as represented by author; no conference cited). https://allameh.academia.edu/MonirGholamzadeh Bazarbash.

Beard, Michael. *The Blind Owl as a Western Novel*. Princeton University Press, 1990.

Behdad, Ali. *Camera Orientalis: Reflections on Photography of the Middle East*. University of Chicago Press, 2016.

Behnam, Mariam. *Zelzelah: A Woman before Her Time*. Motivate Publishing, 1994.

Bekhrad, Joobin. "Untitled Introduction." In *Afro-Iran* by Mahdi Ehsaie. Kehrer Verlag Heidelberg, 2023.

Beyzai, Bahram, dir. *Bashu: Bacheh-ye gharibeh* (*Bashu: The Little Stranger*). Tasvir-e Donya-ye Honar, 2014.

Beyzai, Bahram. *Hezar afsan kojast?* (*Where are the Thousand Legends?*) Entesherat-e Roshangaran va Motala'at-e Zanan, 2023.

Beyzai, Bahram. *Namayesh dar Iran* (*Drama in Iran*). Kaveyan, 1965.

Beyzai, Bahram. *Risheh-yabi-ye derakht-e kuhan* (*In Search of thee Roots of the Ancient Tree*). Entesherat-e Roshangaran va Motala'at-e Zanan, 2004.

Beyzai, Bahram, dir. *Tarabnameh*. Unpublished; performance at De Anza College, March and October 2016.

Birkin, Jane. *Archive, Photography and the Language of Administration*. Amsterdam University Press, 2021.

Bosworth, Clifford Edmund, et al. *Qajar Iran: Political, Social, and Cultural Change, 1800–1925*. Edinburgh University Press, 1983.

Brookshaw, Dominic Parviz, and Seena Fazel. *The Baha'is of Iran: Socio-Historical Studies*. Routledge, 2008.

Brown, Jonathan A. C. *Slavery and Islam*. Oneworld, 2019.

Bryce, Richard. "Islam and the Media: 'Kandahar': Hope and Reason in the Art of Mohsen Makhmalbaf." *Screen Education*, no. 43 (2006): 34–37.

Buck, Christopher. "'Abdu'd-Baha's 1912 Howard University Speech: A Civil War Myth for Interracial Emancipation." In *'Abdu'l-Bahá's Journey West: The Course of Human Solidarity*, edited by Negar Mottahedeh. Palgrave, 2013.

Butler, Judith. *Bodies That Matter*. Routledge, 1993.

Caffee, Naomi Beth. "Russophonia: Towards a Transnational Conception of Russian-Language Literature." PhD diss., University of California–Los Angeles, 2013.

Campbell, Gwyn. *Abolition and Its Aftermath in the Indian Ocean Africa and Asia*. Taylor & Francis, 2005.

Campt, Tina. *Listening to Images*. Duke University Press, 2017.

Chehabi, Houchang. "Staging the Emperor's New Clothes: Dress Codes and Nation-Building under Reza Shah." *Iranian Studies* 26, no. 3–4 (1993): 209–33.

Cheves, Belle. "Untidy Households: Kinship, Service, and Affect in Nineteenth-Century Qajar Iran." PhD diss., Harvard University Graduate School of Arts and Sciences, 2023.

Chi, Jennifer Y., ed. *The Eye of the Shah: Qajar Court Photography and the Persian Past*. Institute for the Study of the Ancient World, New York University / Princeton University Press, 2015.

Clines, Francis X. "A Nation Challenged: AN INVESTIGATION; As Actor's Film Wins Raves, His Identity Attracts Scrutiny." *New York Times*, January 3, 2002, A.14.

Cole, Juan Ricardo. *Modernity and the Millennium: The Genesis of the Baha'i Faith in the Nineteenth-Century Middle East*. Columbia University Press, 1998.

Coletu, Ebony. "A Complicated Embrace." *Transition*, no. 122 (2017): 138–49.

Collective for Black Iranians. *Hasteem* (We Are). September 3–24, 2021. Twelve Gates Arts, Philadelphia.

Conermann, Stephan, et al. *Slaves and Slave Agency in the Ottoman Empire*. Vandenhoeck & Ruprecht, 2020.

Cook-Lynn, Elizabeth. *Why I Can't Read Wallace Stegner and Other Essays: A Tribal Voice*. University of Wisconsin Press, 1996.

Cooper, Merian, and Ernest Schoesdack. *Grass: A Nation's Battle for Life*. Films Sans Frontieres, 1925.

Cronin, Stephanie. "Islam, Slave Agency and Abolitionism in Iran, the Middle East and North Africa." *Middle Eastern Studies* 52, no. 6 (2016): 953–77.

Cronin, Stephanie. *Social Histories of Iran: Modernism and Marginality in the Middle East.* Cambridge University Press, 2021.

Culbertson, Laura, and Indrani Chatterjee, eds. *Slaves and Households in the Near East.* Oriental Institute of the University of Chicago, 2011.

Dabashi, Hamid. *Brown Skin, White Masks.* Pluto, 2011.

Dabashi, Hamid. *The Last Muslim Intellectual.* Edinburgh University Press, 2021.

Dabashi, Hamid. *Mashya and Mashyana Unearthed: Myth, Metonymy and the Unknowing Subject.* Edinburgh University Press, 2024.

Dabashi, Hamid. *Masters & Masterpieces of Iranian Cinema.* Mage Publishers, 2007.

Daneshvar, Simin. *Nameh'ha-ye Simin Daneshvar va Jalal Al-e Ahmad (The Letters of Simin Daneshvar and Jalal Al-e Ahmad).* Edited by Masud Jafari-Jazi. Nilufar, 2004.

Daneshvar, Simin. *Shahri chawn behesht (A City Like Paradise).* Khvarzmi, 2002.

Dashti, Sayeh. *You Belong: To Our Children Around the World.* Xlibris Corp, 2016.

de Silva Jayasuriya, Shihan, et al. *Uncovering the History of Africans in Asia.* Brill, 2008.

DeSouza, Wendy. "Race, Slavery and Domesticity in Late Qajar Chronicles." *Iranian Studies* 53, no. 5–6 (2020): 821–45.

Dubler, C. E. "Adja'ib." In *Encyclopaedia of Islam*, 2nd ed., edited by P. Bearman, Th. Bianquis, C. E. Bosworth, E. van Donzel, and W. P. Heinrichs. Brill, 2012. http://doi.org.prext.num.bulac.fr/10.1163/1573-3912_islam_SIM_031.

DuBois, W. E. B. "Pushkin." *Phylon (1940–1956)* 1, no. 3 (3rd Qtr., 1940): 240–41 + 265–69.

Dumas, Firoozeh. *Funny in Farsi.* Villard, 2003.

Dworkin, Ira. "Radwa Ashour, African American Criticism, and the Production of Modern Arabic Literature." *Cambridge Journal of Postcolonial Literary Inquiry*, no. 1 (2018): 1–19.

Eden, Jeff. *Slavery and Empire in Central Asia.* Cambridge University Press, 2018.

Ehsaie, Mahdi. *Afro-Iran.* Kehrer Verlag Heidelberg, 2023.

Ehsaie, Mahdi. *Afro-Iran.* Berlin Kehrer Verlag, 2015.

El Hamel, Chouri. *Black Morocco: A History of Race, Slavery, and Islam.* Cambridge University Press, 2013.

Elahi, Babak. "Reorienting Grass: How a Musical Score Transforms an Orientalist Documentary." *Afterimage* 49, no. 3 (2022): 46–72.

Elling, Rasmus Christian. *Minorities in Iran: Nationalism and Ethnicity after Khomeini.* Palgrave Macmillan, 2013.

Elling, Rasmus Christian, and Kevan Harris. "Difference in Difference: Language, Geography, and Ethno-Racial Identity in Contemporary Iran." *Ethnic and Racial Studies* 44, no. 12 (Sept. 2021): 2255–81. https://doi.org/10.1080/01419870.2021.1895275.

Elwell-Sutton, L. P. "The Influence of Folk-Tale and Legend on Modern Persian Literature." In *Iran and Islam: In Memory of The Late Vladimir Minorsky*, edited by C. E. Bosworth. Edinburgh, 1971.

Emami, Ameneh Shervin. "Persian Magical Realism and the Re-Appropriation of Mythical and Mystical Texts: Rereading Parsipur's Magical Realism and Suhrawardi's Allegories." PhD diss., University of California–Los Angeles, 2020.

Ennaji, Mohammad. *Serving the Master: Slavery and Society in 19th Century Morocco.* Palgrave, 1999.

Esman, Milton J., et al. *Ethnicity, Pluralism, and the State in the Middle East.* Edited by Milton J. Esman and Itamar Rabinovich. Cornell University Press, 2019.

Farhi, Paul. "In 'Kandahar,' a Political Movie with an Assassination Plot: [FINAL Edition]." *Washington Post*, January 4, 2002, C.1.

Farrokhzad, Forugh, dir. *The House Is Black.* Golestan Film Co., 1962.

Fazeli, Nematollah. *Politics of Culture in Iran: Anthropology, Politics and Society in the Twentieth Century.* Routledge, 2006.

Feldman, Allen. *Archives of the Insensible: Of War, Photopolitics, and Dead Memory.* University of Chicago Press, 2015.

Feldman, Leah. *On the Threshold of Eurasia: Revolutionary Poetics in the Caucasus.* Cornell University Press, 2018.

Fisher, Allan G. B. *Slavery and Muslim Society in Africa: The Institution in Saharan and Sudanic Africa, and the Trans-Saharan Trade.* C. Hurst, 1970.

Floor, Willem M. "BARDA and BARDA-DARI: From the Mongols to the Abolition of Slavery." *Encyclopædia Iranica* III/7 (1988): 768–74. https://www.iranicaonline.org/articles/barda-iv/.

Floor, Willem M. *The Persian Gulf: The Rise of the Gulf Arabs: The Politics of Trade on the Persian Littoral, 1747–1792.* Mage Publishers, 2007.

"The Forgotten Legacy of African-Iranians." *Asia by Africa*. www.asiabyafrica.com/point-a-to-a/afro-iranians-slavery-legacy. Accessed November 5, 2021.

Foucault, Michel. *Archaeology of Knowledge.* Routledge, 2002.

Fox-Amato, Matthew. *Exposing Slavery: Photography, Human Bondage, and the Birth of Modern Visual Politics in America.* Oxford University Press, 2019.

Franco, Jean. *Decline and Fall of the Lettered City: Latin America in the Cold War.* Harvard University Press, 2002.

Georgetown University Center for International and Regional Studies, and Mehran Kamrava. *Gateways to the World: Port Cities in the Persian Gulf.* Oxford University Press, 2016.

Ghanoonparvar, M. R. *Iranian Cities in Persian Fiction*. Mazda, 2022.

Ghanoonparvar, M. R., and John Green. *Iranian Drama: An Anthology*. Mazda, 1989.

Gnammankou, Dieudonné, ed. *Pouchkine et le Monde Noir*. (A special issue of *Présence Africaine*). Présence Africaine Éditions, 1999.

Golestan, Shahrokh. "Sinema-ye Iran Dar Goftogu-ye Bahram Baizai va Shahrokh Golestan" ("Cinema in Iran in Conversation with Bahram Beyzai and Shahrokh Golestan"). *Chesmandaz*, no. 15 (1374/1995): 43–56.

Greenberg, Reesa, Bruce Ferguson, and Sandy Nairne. "Introduction." In *Thinking about Exhibitions*, edited by Reesa Greenberg, Bruce Ferguson, and Sandy Nairne. Routledge, 1996.

Greene, Raquelle. "The African-Aristocrat: Alexander S. Pushkin's Dual Poetic Persona." PhD diss., Ohio State University, 1999.

Greeson, Jennifer Rae. *Our South Geographic Fantasy and the Rise of National Literature*. Harvard University Press, 2010.

Grigor, Talinn. *The Persian Revival: The Imperialism of the Copy in Iranian and Parsi Architecture*. Pennsylvania State University Press, 2021.

Gurney, J. D. "A Qajar Household and Its Estates." *Iranian Studies* 16, no. 3/4 (1983): 137–76. www.jstor.org/stable/4310414.

Hariri, Nasser, ed. *Honar va adabiyat-e emruz: goft o shenudi ba doktor Simin Daneshvar va Parviz Natel Khanlari* (*Contemporary Art and Literature: Interviews with Dr. Simin Daneshvar and Dr. Parviz Natel Khanlari*). Ketabsara-ye Babul, 1366/1987.

Harms, Robert W., et al. *Indian Ocean Slavery in the Age of Abolition*. Yale University Press, 2013.

Hartman, Saidiya V. *Lose Your Mother: A Journey Along the Atlantic Slave Route*. Farrar, Straus and Giroux, 2007.

Hartman, Saidiya V. *Scenes of Subjection: Terror, Slavery, and Self-Making in Nineteenth-Century America*. Oxford University Press, 1997.

Hartman, Saidiya V. "Venus in Two Acts." *Small Axe* 26 (2008): 1–14.

Hartman, Saidiya V. *Wayward Lives, Beautiful Experiments: Intimate Histories of Social Upheaval*. W.W. Norton & Company, 2019.

Hartocollis, Anemona. "Images of Slaves Are Property of Harvard, Not a Descendant, Judge Rules." *New York Times*, March 5, 2021. www.nytimes.com/2021/03/04/us/harvard-slave-photos-renty.html.

Hathaway, Jane. *The Chief Eunuch of the Ottoman Harem from African Slave to Power-Broker*. Cambridge University Press, 2018.

Hathaway, Jane. "Eunuchs." *Encyclopaedia of Islam*, vol. 3. Brill, 2015. https://referenceworks.brillonline.com/entries/encyclopaedia-of-islam-3/eunuchs-COM_27821?s.num=0&s.f.s2_parent=s.f.book.encyclopaedia-of-islam-3&s.q=eunuch.

Hawthorne, Nathaniel. *Dagh-e nang (The Scarlet Letter)*. Translated by Simin Daneshvar. Nil, 1955.

Hedayat, Sadeq. *Alaviyeh Khanom va Velengari (Alaviyeh Khanom and Tittle-Tattle)*. Amir Kabir, 1963.

Hedayat, Sadeq. *The Blind Owl*. Translated by D. P. Costello. John Calder, 1957.

Hedayat, Sadeq. *Buf-e kur (The Blind Owl)*. Mohammad Hassan 'Elmi, 1937.

Hedayat, Sadeq. *Nayrangestan*. Iranzamin, 1986.

———. *Seh qatr-e khun (Three Drops of Blood)*. Tehran: Parastu, 1344 (1965).

Hedayat, Sadeq, and Muḥammad Baharlu. *Majmu'ehyi az asar-e Sadeq Hedayat*. Ṭarḥ-e Naw, 1993.

Hegland, M. E. "Afro-Iranian Lives [Review Essay]." *Iranian Studies* 50, no. 1 (2017): 169–72.

Heidari, Kamran, dir. *Dingomaro*. Autentic Film, 2015.

Heider, Karl G. *Ethnographic Film: Revised Edition*. University of Texas Press, 2006.

Helbig, Elahe. "Performing Violence, Displaying Evidence: Photographs of Criminals and Political Inmates in Qajar Iran (1860s–1910s)." *History of Photography* 45, no. 3–4 (2021): 264–77.

Hobson, Janell. *Body as Evidence: Mediating Race, Globalizing Gender*. State University of New York Press, 2012.

Hopper, Matthew. *Slaves of One Master: Globalization and Slavery in Arabia in the Age of Empire*. Yale University Press, 2015.

Hornback, Robert, ed. *Racism and Early Blackface Comic Traditions: From the Old World to the New*. Springer International Publishing, 2018. https://doi.org/10.1007/978-3-319-78048-1_6.

Howarth, Anthony, dir. *People of the Wind*. Kino Lorber, 1976.

Hughes, Langston. *Siah hamchawn a'maq-e Afriqa-ye khodam (Black Like My Africa)*. Translated by Ahmad Shamlu. Kanun-e Andisheh, 1986.

Jahanbin, Maryam Sophia. "Hasteem, We Are Here: The Collective for Black Iranians." *The Markaz Review*, September 15, 2021. https://themarkaz.org/hasteem-we-are-here-the-collective-for-black-iranians/.

Jalali, Bahram, ed. *Ganj-e payda (Visible Treasure)*. Daftar-e Pazhuhesh'ha-ye Farhangi: Ba hamkari-ye Szman-e Miras-e Fahangi-ye Keshvar, 1998.

Javidshad, Mahdi, and Alireza Anushiravani. "Setting Othello in Tehran from Exile: Metatheatre in Gholām-Hossein Sāedi's Othello in Wonderland." *English Studies* 102, no. 3 (2021): 307–21.

Jerng, Mark C. *Racial Worldmaking: The Power of Popular Fiction*. Fordham University Press, 2017.

Johns, Jeremy. *Arabic Administration in Norman Sicily: The Royal Dīwān*. Cambridge University Press, 2002.

Johns, Jeremy, and Nadia Jamil. "Signs of the Times: Arabic Signatures as a Measure of Acculturation in Norman Sicily." *Muqarnas* 21 (2004): 181–92. www.jstor.org /stable/1523354. Accessed 30 July 2023.

Johnson, Roy. "What It Was Like to Be an African-American Freshman in 1962." *Stanford Magazine*, September 2017. https://stanfordmag.org/contents/what-it -was-like-to-be-an-african-american-freshman-in-1962.

Johnson, Stephen. *Burnt Cork: Traditions and Legacies of Blackface Minstrelsy*. University of Massachusetts Press, 2012.

Johnson, Walter. "On Agency." Special issue, *Journal of Social History* 37, no. 1 (Autumn 2003): 113–24.

Kashani-Sabet, Firoozeh. "The Anti-Aryan Moment: Decolonization, Diplomacy, and Race in Late Pahlavi Iran." *International Journal of Middle East Studies* 53 (2021): 691–702.

Kashani-Sabet, Firoozeh. "Colorblind or Blinded by Color? Race, Ethnicity, and Identity in Iran." In *Sites of Pluralism: Community Politics in the Middle East*, edited by Firat Oruc. Oxford University Press, 2019.

Kashani-Sabet, Firoozeh. *Heroes to Hostages: America and Iran, 1800–1988*. Cambridge University Press, 2023.

Katira'i, Mahmud. *Zaban va Farhang-e Mardom: Naqd*. Entesharat-e Tukaa, 1979.

Katouzian, Homa. *Sadeq Hedayat: His Work and His Wondrous World*. Routledge, 2007.

Katouzian, Homa. *Sadeq Hedayat: The Life and Literature of an Iranian Writer*. I.B. Tauris, 2002.

Khakipour, Maryam, et al. *Siah Bâzi: The Joy Makers; Shadi*. Icarus Films, 2010.

Khakpour, Porochista. *The Brown Album*. Penguin Random House, 2020.

Khosronejad, Pedram. "In the Absence of Fieldwork." *Anthropology of the Contemporary Middle East and Central Eurasia* 4, no. 1 (2017): 56–96.

Khosronejad, Pedram. "Out of Focus." *Anthropology of the Contemporary Middle East and Central Eurasia* 4, no. 1 (2017): 1–31.

Khosronejad, Pedram. *Qajar African Nannies*. Visual Studies of Modern Iran, 2017.

Khosronejad, Pedram. "Review of *Afro-Iranian Lives*, by Behnaz Mirzai; and *The African-Baluchi Trance Dance* by Behnaz Mirzai." *Canadian Journal of History* 52, no. 2 (2017): 323–25.

Khosronejad, Pedram, and Ali Gholipoor. *Untold Stories: The Socio-Cultural Life of Images in Qajar Era Iran*. Lit, 2015.

Kia, Mehrdad. "Mirza (sic) Fath Ali Akhundzade and the Call for Modernization of the Islamic World." *Middle Eastern Studies* 31, no. 3 (1995): 422–48.

Kotwal, Firoze M., Jamsheed K. Choksy, Christopher J. Brunner, and Mahnaz Moazami. "HATARIA, MANEKJI LIMJI." *Encyclopædia Iranica*, online edition, 2016. www.iranicaonline.org/articles/hataria-manekji-limji.

Lahiri, Bulan. "In Conversation: Speaking to Spivak." *The Hindu*, February 5, 2011. https://www.thehindu.com/books/In-Conversation-Speaking-to-Spivak/article15130635.ece.

Law, H. D. G., ed. and tr. "Persian Writers." In *Life and Letters and the London Mercury*, vol. 63, no. 148. Druid Press, December 1949.

Lee, Anthony. "Africans in the Palace: The Testimony of Taj al-Saltana Qajar from the Royal Harem in Iran." In *Slavery in the Islamic World*, edited by M. Fay. Palgrave Macmillan, 2019.

Lee, Anthony. *The Baha'i Faith in Africa: Establishing a New Religious Movement, 1952–1962*. Brill, 2011.

Lee, Anthony. "Half the Household Was African: Recovering the Histories of Two African Slaves in Iran." *UCLA Historical Journal* 26, no. 1 (2015): 17–38. https://escholarship.org/uc/item/okm6m833.

Lenze, Franz. *Der Nativist Ǧalāl-e Āl-e Aḥmad und die Verwestlichung Irans im 20. Jahrhundert: eine Analyse der ethnographischen Monographien Awrāzān, Tāt-nešīnhā-ye bolūk-e Zahrā und Ǧazire-ye Hārg, dorr-e yatīm-e ḫalīǧ unter besonderer Berücksichtigung seiner Programmschrift Ġarbzadegī*. 1. Aufl. Klaus Schwarz, 2008.

Lewis, Bernard. *Race and Slavery in the Middle East: An Historical Enquiry*. Oxford University Press, 1990.

Lewisohn, Jane. "The Rise and Fall of Lalehzar, Cultural Centre of Tehran in the Mid-Twentieth Century." *Tehran Project 1* (UC Irvine, 2015), 1–38.

Lott, Eric, and Greil Marcus. *Love and Theft: Blackface Minstrelsy and the American Working Class*. Oxford University Press, 2013.

Maghbouleh, Neda. *The Limits of Whiteness: Iranian Americans and the Everyday Politics of Race*. Stanford University Press, 2017.

Makhmalbaf, Mohsen. "The Condemned." *Guardian*, January 11, 2002. https://www.theguardian.com/film/2002/jan/11/artsfeatures.

Makhmalbaf, Mohsen. *Nasser al-Din Shah, aktor-e sinema (Once Upon a Time, Cinema)*. Khaneh-ye Cinema, 1992.

Makhmalbaf, Mohsen. *Safar-e Qandahar (Kandahar)*. Makhmalbaf Film House/Avatar Films, 2001.

Malek, Amy. "'If You're Going to Educate 'Em, You've Got to Entertain 'Em Too': An Examination of Representation and Ethnography in *Grass* and *People of the Wind*." *Iranian Studies* 44, no. 3 (2011): 313–25.

Manning, Patrick. *Slavery and African Life: Occidental, Oriental, and African Slave Trades.* Cambridge University Press, 1990.

Marashi, Afshin. "Imagining Hāfez: Rabindranath Tagore in Iran, 1932." *Journal of Persianate Studies* 3, no. 1 (2010): 46–77.

Marmon, Shaun Elizabeth. *Eunuchs and Sacred Boundaries in Islamic Society.* Oxford University Press, 1995.

Marmon, Shaun Elizabeth, ed. *Slavery in the Islamic Middle East.* M. Wiener, 1999.

Martin, Vanessa. "The Abyssinian Slave Trade to Iran and the *Rokeby* Case 1877." *Middle Eastern Studies* 58, no. 1 (2022): 201–13.

Mathee, Rudi. "QOROQ." *Encyclopædia Iranica,* online edition, 2021. http://doi.org/10.1163/2330-4804_EIRO_COM_337731.

McGrady, Clyde. "Harvard Relents After Protracted Fight Over Slave Photos." *New York Times,* May 28, 2025. www.nytimes.com/2025/05/28/us/harvard-slavery-daguerreotypes-lawsuit.html.

Menashri, David. *Education and the Making of Modern Iran.* Merkaz Dayan le-ḥeḳer ha-Mizraḥ ha-Tikhon ṿe-Afriḳah (Universiṭat Tel-Aviv), 1992.

Mernissi, Fatema. *The Forgotten Queens of Islam.* University of Minnesota Press, 1993.

Meshkini, Marziyeh. *Ruzi keh zan shodam (The Day I Became a Woman).* Makhmalbaf Film House/Olive Films, 2000.

Mianji, Fahimeh, and Yousef Semnani. "Zār Spirit Possession in Iran and African Countries: Group Distress, Culture-Bound Syndrome or Cultural Concept of Distress?" *Iran Journal of Psychiatry* 10, no. 4 (2015): 225–32.

Milani, Abbas. *The Persian Sphinx: Amir Abbas Hoveyda and the Riddle of the Iranian Revolution: A Biography.* Mage Publishers, 2000.

Mirabedini, Hassan. *Ṣad sal dastan nevisi-ye Iran.* Nashr-e Chashmeh, 1377/1998.

Mirsepassi, Ali. *The Discovery of Iran: Taghi Arani, a Radical Cosmopolitanism.* Stanford University Press, 2021.

Mirzai, Behnaz A. *The African-Baluchi Trance Dance.* Social Sciences and Humanities Research Council of Canada, 2012.

Mirzai, Behnaz A., dir. *Afro-Iranian Lives.* 2008.

Mirzai, Behnaz A. *A History of Slavery and Emancipation in Iran, 1800–1929.* University of Texas Press, 2017.

Mirzai, Behnaz A., and Mahboob Qirvanian. *The Life of an Enslaved African in the Ottoman Empire and Iran: The Autobiography of Mahboob Qirvanian.* University of Toronto Press, 2025.

Miura, Toru, and John Edward Philips. *Slave Elites in the Middle East and Africa: A Comparative Study.* Kegan Paul International, 2000.

Moaveni, Azadeh. *Lipstick Jihad: A Memoir of Growing up Iranian in America and American in Iran.* PublicAffairs, 2006.

"'Mobarak' in French Annecy Festival." *Financial Tribune*, May 27, 2015. https://financialtribune.com/articles/art-and-culture/17679/mobarak-in-french-annecy-festival.

Moghaddam, Maria Sabaye. "ZAR." *Encyclopædia Iranica*, online edition, 2009. https://www.iranicaonline.org/articles/zar/

Mohandessi, Manoutchehr. "Hedayat and Rilke." *Comparative Literature* 23, no. 3 (Summer 1971): 209–21.

Moore, Taylor. "Occult Epidemics." *History of the Present* 13, no. 1 (April 2023): 87–100.

Moradian, Manijeh. *This Flame Within: Iranian Revolutionaries in the United States*. Duke University Press, 2022.

Morris, Rosalind C., and Gayatri Chakravorty Spivak. *Can the Subaltern Speak?: Reflections on the History of an Idea*. Edited by Rosalind C. Morris. Columbia University Press, 2010.

Morrison, Toni. *Playing in the Dark: Whiteness and the Literary Imagination*. Vintage, 1993.

Motadel, David. "Iran and the Aryan Myth." In *Perceptions of Iran: History, Myths and Nationalism from Medieval Persia to the Islamic Republic*, edited by Ali M. Ansari. I. B. Tauris, 2014.

Motlagh, Amy. "Autobiography and Authority in the Writings of the Iranian Diaspora." *Comparative Studies of South Asia, Africa, and the Middle East (CSSAAME)* 31, no. 2 (2011): 411–24.

Motlagh, Amy. "Toward a Theory of Iranian American Life Writing." *Multi-Ethnic Literatures of the United States (MELUS)* 33, no. 2 (2008): 17–36.

Mottahedeh, Negar, ed. *'Abdu'l-Bahá's Journey West: The Course of Human Solidarity*. Palgrave Macmillan, 2013.

Mottahedeh, Negar. "'Le Vent Nous Portera': Of Lovers Possessed, of Times Entangled and Bodies Carried Away." *Asian Cinema* 27, no. 2 (2016): 177–88. https://doi.org/10.1386/ac.27.2.177_1.

Mottahedeh, Roy P. *The Mantle of the Prophet: Religion and Politics in Iran*. Simon & Schuster, 1985.

Mount, Guy Emerson. "A Troubled Modernity: W. E. B. Du Bois, 'The Black Church,' and the Problem of Causality." In *'Abdu'l-Bahá's Journey West: the Course of Human Solidarity*, edited by Negar Mottahedeh. Palgrave, 2013.

Naber, Nadine. *Race and Arab America*. Syracuse University Press, 2008.

Naficy, Hamid. "Iranian Writers, the Iranian Cinema, and the Case of 'Dash Akol.'" *Iranian Studies* 18, no. 2/4, Sociology of the Iranian Writer (Spring–Autumn 1985): 231–51.

Naficy, Hamid. "Nonfiction Fiction: Documentaries on Iran." *Iranian Studies* 12, no. 3/4 (1979): 217–38.

Naficy, Hamid. *A Social History of Iranian Cinema*. Duke University Press, 2011.

Naghibi, Nima. *Rethinking Global Sisterhood: Western Feminism and Iran*. University of Minnesota Press, 2007.

Najmabadi, Afsaneh. "Beyond the Americas: Are Gender and Sexuality Useful Categories of Analysis?" *Journal of Women's History* 18, no. 1 (Spring 2006): 11–21.

Najmabadi, Afsaneh. *The Story of the Daughters of Quchan: Gender and National Memory in Iranian History*. Syracuse University Press, 1998.

Nepomnyashchy, Catharine Theimer, Nicole Svobodny, and Ludmilla A. Trigos, eds. *Under the Sky of My Africa: Alexander Pushkin and Blackness*. Northwestern University Press, 2006.

Nikpour, Golnar. "Revolutionary Journeys, Revolutionary Practice: The Hajj Writings of Jalal Al-e Ahmad and Malcolm X." *Comparative Studies of South Asia, Africa, and the Middle East*, no. 1 (2014): 67–85.

Nyong'o, Tavia. *Afro-Fabulations: The Queer Drama of Black Life*. New York University Press, 2018.

Omidsalar, Mahmoud. "Dar pich o khamha-ye Ketab-e kucheh." In *Man bamdadam saranjam: yadnameh-ye Ahmad-e Shamlu (And So I Am the Dawn: In Memory of Ahmad Shamlu)*. Entesherat-e Hermes, 2017.

Oualdi, M'hamed. *A Slave Between Empires: A Transimperial History of North Africa*. Columbia University Press, 2020.

Paradiz, Valerie. *Clever Maids: The Secret History of the Grimm Fairy Tales*. Basic Books, 2005.

Parsinejad, Iraj. *A History of Literary Criticism in Iran, 1866–1951: Literary Criticism in the Works of Enlightened Thinkers of Iran—Akhundzadeh, Kermani, Malkom, Talebof, Maraghe'i, Kasravi, and Hedayat*. Ibex Publishers, 2003.

Patterson, Orlando. *Slavery and Social Death: A Comparative Study*. Harvard University Press, 1982.

Polsue, Edward. "Being Aryan, a Myth Many Iranians Choose to Believe." *IranWire*, August 7, 2023. https://iranwire.com/en/society/119259-being-aryan-a-myth-many-iranians-choose-to-believe/.

Pourazimi, Saeid. "ŠĀMLU, AḤMAD." *Encyclopædia Iranica*, online edition, 2018. https://referenceworks.brillonline.com/entries/encyclopaedia-iranica-online/samlu-ahmad-COM_363927

Pourtavaf, Leila. "Gulistan in Black and White: The Racial and Gendered Legacies of Slavery in Nineteenth-Century Qajar Iran." *The American Historical Review* 129, no. 2 (June 2024): 395–428. https://doi.org/10.1093/ahr/rhae152.

Powell, Eve Troutt. *A Different Shade of Colonialism: Egypt, Great Britain, and the Mastery of the Sudan*. University of California Press, 2003.

Powell, Eve Troutt. "The Empire and Its Other Servants." *Journal of Women's History* 21, no. 3 (2009): 144–48.

Powell, Eve Troutt. "History, Slavery, and Liberation." *International Journal of Middle East Studies* 44, no. 2 (2012): 330–31. https://doi.org/10.1017/S0020743812000104.

Powell, Eve Troutt. "Ignore the Poets at Your Peril: A Reflection on Neither Settler nor Native; The Making and Unmaking of Permanent Minorities." *Journal of Palestine Studies* 51, no. 1 (2022): 78–84. https://doi.org/10.1080/0377919X.2021.2010498.

Powell, Eve Troutt. *Tell This in My Memory: Stories of Enslavement from Egypt, Sudan, and the Ottoman Empire*. Stanford University Press, 2012.

Powell, Eve Troutt. "Will That Subaltern Ever Speak? Finding African Slaves in the Historiography of the Middle East." In *Middle East Historiographies: Narrating the Twentieth Century*, edited by Israel Gershoni. University of Washington Press, 2006.

Price, Massoumeh. "Chaman Andam, Slavery in Early 20th Century Iran." www.payvand.com/news/02/oct/1009.html. Accessed February 14, 2022.

Princewill, Victoria. *In the Palace of Flowers*. Casava Republic Press, 2021.

Purhassan. Niayesh. "Hajji Firuz: performans: barrassi va mo'arefi-ye 'Hajji Firuz' va negahiye- tatbighi beh namayeshgaran az manzar va didgah-e performans" (Hajji Firuz: Performance: Research and Introduction to "Hajji Firuz" and a Comparative Look at the Performers/Actors from a Performance Perspective). *Me'mari va honar (Architecture and Art): Namayesh*, nos. 125–26 (1388/2009): 42–47.

Rahimieh, Nasrin. "Magical Realism in Moniru Ravanipur's *Ahl-e Gharg*." *Iranian Studies* 23, no. 1–4 (1990): 61–75.

Rahimieh, Nasrin. "Marking Gender and Difference in the Myth of the Nation." In *The New Iranian Cinema: Politics, Representation and Identity*, edited by Richard Tapper. I.B. Tauris Publishers, 2002.

Rahmaninejad, Nasser. *A Man of the Theater: Survival as an Artist in Iran*. New Village Press, 2020.

Rajabi, Ayyub. "Magical Realism: The Magic of Realism." *Rupkatha Journal on Interdisciplinary Studies in Humanities* 12, no. 1 (January–March 2020): 1–13.

Rampersad, Arnold. *Ralph Ellison: A Biography*. Vintage, 2008.

Rastegar, Kamran. "Treacherous Memory: Bashu the Little Stranger and the Sacred Defense." In *Moments of Silence: Authenticity in the Cultural Expressions of the*

Iran-Iraq War, 1980–1988, edited by Arta Khakpour, Mohammad Mehdi Khorrami, and Shouleh Vatanabadi. NYU Press, 2016.

Ravanipur, Moniru. *Afsaneh'ha va bavarha-ye jonub (Folktales of the South)*. Nashr-e Najva, 2022.

Ravanipur, Moniru. *Ahl-e gharq (The Drowned)*. Khaneh-ye Aftab, 1990.

Reyes, Angelita D. "Performativity and Representation in Transnational Blackface: Mammy (USA), Zwarte Piet (Netherlands), and Hajji Firuz (Iran)." *Atlantic Studies*, no. 4 (2018): 521–50.

Ricks, Thomas. "Slaves and Slave Traders in the Persian Gulf, 18th and 19th Centuries: An Assessment." *Slavery and Abolition: A Journal of Slave and Post-Slave Studies* 9, no. 3 (1988): 60–70.

Ricks, Thomas. "Slaves and Slave Trading in Shi'i Iran, AD 1500–1900." *Journal of Asian and African Studies* (Leiden) 36, no. 4 (2001): 407–18.

Rosenbaum, Jonathan. "Under the Chador." *Chicago Reader*, April 6, 2001. https://jonathanrosenbaum.net/2023/06/under-the-chador/.

Rushdy, Ashraf H. A. *Neo-Slave Narratives: Studies in the Social Logic of a Literary Form*. Oxford University Press 1999.

Sadeghi-Boroujerdi, Eskandar. "Gharbzadegi, Colonial Capitalism and the Racial State in Iran." *Postcolonial Studies* 24, no. 2 (2021): 173–94. https://doi.org/10.1080/13688790.2020.1834344.

Sa'edi, Gholam-Hossein. *Ahl-e hava (People of the Wind)*. Chapkhaneh-ye Daneshgah, 1966.

Sa'edi, Gholam-Hossein. "Otello dar Sarzamin-e Ajayeb" ("Othello in Wonderland"). In *Pardehdaran-e Ayineh-afruz va Oyello dar Sarzamin-e Ajayeb: Do Namayeshnameh az Gholam-Hossein Sa'edi*. Ketab-e Alefba, 1985.

Sa'edi, Gholam-Hossein. *Tars va larz (Fear and Trembling)*. Ketab-e Zaman, 1968.

Saedi, Sara. *Americanized: Rebel Without a Green Card*. Knopf Books for Young Readers, 2018.

Salaita, Steven. *Inter/Nationalism: Decolonizing Native America and Palestine*. University of Minnesota Press, 2016.

Al-Saltaneh, Taj. *Khaterat-e Taj al-Saltaneh (Memoirs of Taj al-Saltaneh)*. Edited by Mansureh Ettahadieh. Tarikh-e Iran, ca. 1983.

Salzman, Philip Carl. *Black Tents of Baluchistan*. Smithsonian Institution Press, 2000.

Saroyan, William. *Payk-e marg va zendigi ya komedi-ye ensani (The Messenger of Life and Death, or, The Human Comedy)*. Translated by Simin Daneshvar. Ebn-e Sina, 1954.

Scheiwiller, Staci. *Liminalities of Gender and Sexuality in Nineteenth-Century Iranian Photography: Desirous Bodies*. Routledge, 2017.

Schwerda, Mira Xenia. "Death on Display." *Middle East Journal of Culture and Communication* 8, no. 2–3 (2015): 172–91. https://doi.org/10.1163/18739865-00802003.

Scott, Darieck. *Extravagant Abjection: Blackness, Power, and Sexuality in the African American Literary Imagination*. Vol. 17. NYU Press, 2010.

Segal, Ronald. *Islam's Black Slaves: The Other Black Diaspora*. Farrar, Straus & Giroux, 2001.

Sekula, Alan. "The Body and the Archive." *October* 39 (Winter 1986): 3–64.

Shamlu, Ahmad, tr. *Hamchawn kucheh-ye bi enteha (Like an Alley with No End)*. Moasseh-ye Entesharat-e Negah, 1995.

Shamlu, Ahmad. *Ketab-e kucheh*. Entesharat-e Maziyar, 1978.

Shams, Fatemeh. "Under the Waves: The Many Lives of Moniru Ravanipur's *The Drowned*." *Iranian Studies* 55, no. 1 (2022): 237–49.

Shannon, Matthew K. *Losing Hearts and Minds: Iranian–American Relations and International Education during the Cold War*. Cornell University Press, 2017.

Shirazi, Maziar. "Why Are Iranians Laughing at Blackface in 2016?" *AJAM Media Collective*, December 7, 2016. https://ajammc.com/2016/12/07/why-are-iranian-americans-laughing-at-blackface-in-2016/.

Shohat, Ella, and Robert Stam, eds. *Race in Translation Culture Wars around the Postcolonial Atlantic*. NYU Press, 2012.

Shroff, Beheroze. "My Filmic Journey to Sidis: Indians of African Descent." *Journal of Global Slavery* 5, no. 1 (2020): 45–61.

Shroff, Beheroze. *Voices of the Sidis: Two Documentaries*. B. F. Shroff, 2005.

Siraji, Mohsen. *Nazzariyeh-ye namayesh-e siah bazi*. Nashr-e Qatreh, 2018.

Sohrabi, Naghmeh. *Taken for Wonder: Nineteenth-Century Travel Accounts from Iran to Europe*. Oxford University Press, 2012.

Southgate, Minoo. "The Negative Images of Blacks in Some Medieval Iranian Writings." *Iranian Studies* 17, no. 1 (1984): 3–36. https://doi.org/10.1080/00210868408701620.

Spillers, Hortense. "Mama's Baby, Papa's Maybe: An American Grammar Book." In *Feminisms REDUX: An Anthology of Literary Theory and Criticism*, edited by Robyn Warhol-Down and Diane Price Herndl. Rutgers University Press, 2009.

Spivak, Gayatri Chakravorty. "Can the Subaltern Speak?" In *Marxism and the Interpretation of Culture*, edited by C. Nelson and L. Grossberg. Macmillan, 1988.

Spivak, Gayatri Chakravorty. *Death of a Discipline*. Columbia University Press, 2003.

Spivak, Gayatri Chakravorty. "Righting Wrongs." *The South Atlantic Quarterly* 103, no. 2 (2004): 523–81. http://muse.jhu.edu/journals/south_atlantic_quarterly/v103/103.2spivak.html.

Spooner, Brian. "BALUCHISTAN i. Geography, History and Ethnography (cont.)." *Encyclopædia Iranica* III/6 (1988): 598–632.

Stanford Iranian Studies. "Abbas Milani: Beyzaie's Singularity in the Labyrinth of Iranian Modernities (Beyzaie Conference)." July 9, 2021. https://www.youtube.com/watch?v=VHhmsoXZg5M.

Steele, Robert. *Pahlavi Iran's Relations with Africa Cultural and Political Connections in the Cold War*. Cambridge University Press, 2024.

Steele, Robert. *The Shah's Imperial Celebrations of 1971: Nationalism, Culture and Politics in Late Pahlavi Iran*. I.B. Tauris, 2021.

Stone, Lucian. *Iranian Identity and Cosmopolitanism: Spheres of Belonging*. Bloomsbury, 2016.

Taqvai, Nasser. *Bad-e jinn (Spirit Wind)*. 1969.

Tavakoli-Targhi, Mohamad. "Narrative Identity in the Works of Hedayat and His Contemporaries." In *Hedayat and His Wondrous World*, edited by Homa Katouzian. Routledge, 2008.

Tavakoli-Targhi, Mohamad. *Refashioning Iran: Orientalism, Occidentalism, and Historiography*. Palgrave, 2001.

Thompson, Levi. "Vernacular Transactions: Aḥmad Shāmlū's Persian Translations of Langston Hughes's Poetry." *Middle Eastern Literatures* 22, no. 2–3 (2019): 128–40.

Toledano, Ehud R. *As If Silent and Absent: Bonds of Enslavement in the Islamic Middle East*. Yale University Press, 2007.

Toledano, Ehud R. *Slavery and Abolition in the Ottoman Middle East*. University of Washington Press, 1998.

Toledano, Ehud R. "Women and Slavery in the Late Ottoman Empire: The Design of Difference." *Insight Turkey*, July 2011. www.insightturkey.com/book-reviews/women-and-slavery-in-the-late-ottoman-empire-the-design-of-difference.

Vafa, Amirhossein. "Race and the Aesthetics of Alterity in Mahshid Amirshahi's Dadeh Qadam-Kheyr." *Iranian Studies* 51, no. 1 (2018): 141–60.

Vaziri, Parisa. "Antiblack Joy: Transmedial Sīyāh Bāzī and Global Public Spheres." *TDR: The Drama Review* 66, no. 1 (Spring 2022): 62–79.

Vaziri, Parisa. "No One's Memory: Blackness at the Limits of Comparative Slavery." *POMEPS Studies* 44 (2021): 14–19.

Vaziri, Parisa. "On Saidiya: Indian Ocean World Slavery and Blackness beyond Horizon." *Qui Parle* 28, no. 2 (December 2019): 241–80.

Vaziri, Parisa. "Pneumatics of Blackness: Nāṣir Taqvā'ī's Bād-i Jin and Modernity's Anthropological Drive." In *Persian Literature and Modernity: Production and Reception*, edited by Hamid Rezaei Yazdi and Arshavez Mozafari. Routledge, 2018.

Vaziri, Parisa. *Racial Blackness and Indian Ocean Slavery*. University of Minnesota Press, 2023.

Vaziri, Parisa. "Slavery and the Virtual Archive: On Iran's Dāsh Ākul." In *The Cambridge Companion to Global Literature and Slavery*, edited by L. Murphy. Cambridge Companions to Literature. Cambridge University Press, 2022.

Vaziri, Parisa. "Tracing Absence." *Historical Studies in the Natural Sciences* 53, no. 1 (2023): 106–108.

Vick, Karl. "An Assassin for Iran Says He'd Never Be Spy for U.S., Says Robert Levinson Didn't Explain He Was Working for the CIA." *Time*, December 16, 2013. https://world.time.com/2013/12/16/american-born-assassin-in-iran-robert-levinson-never-said-he-was-working-for-the-cia/.

Vitalis, Robert. "Wallace Stegner's Arabian *Discovery*: Imperial Blind Spots in a Continental Vision." *Pacific Historical Review*, no. 3 (August 2007): 405–38.

Wagknenekt, Maria D. *Constructing Identity in Iranian-American Self-Narrative*. Palgrave Macmillan, 2015.

"Wallace Earle Stegner Creative Writing Program: Correspondence and Manuscripts, 1949–1992." Stanford University Library.

Walz, Terence, and Kenneth M. Cuno. *Race and Slavery in the Middle East: Histories of Trans-Saharan Africans in Nineteenth-Century Egypt, Sudan, and the Ottoman Mediterranean*. The American University in Cairo Press, 2010.

Wexler, Laura. *Tender Violence: Domestic Visions in an Age of U.S. Imperialism*. University of North Carolina Press, 2000.

Wilderson, Frank B. *Afropessimism*. Liveright Publishing Corporation, 2020.

Woodson, C. G. "Review of La Poblacion Negra de Mexico, 1510–1810, Estudio Etnohistorico." *The Journal of Negro History* 31, no. 4 (1946): 491–94. https://doi.org/10.2307/2715225.

Yarshater, Ehsan. "Communication." *Iranian Studies* 22, no. 1 (1989): 62–65.

Yavari, Houra. "FICTION ii(b). THE NOVEL." *Encyclopædia Iranica* IX/6 (December 15, 1999): 580–92.

Yavari, Houra. "Nahamzamani-e ensan o dastan." *Iran Nameh* 9/4 (Autumn 1991): 635–43.

Zavaree, Sara. "'We Have Our Own Africans': Public Displays of Zār in Iran." In *Language and Tourism in Postcolonial Settings*, edited by Angelika Mietzner and Anne Storch. Channel View Publications, 2019.

Zdanowski, Jerzy. *Slavery and Manumission: British Policy in the Red Sea and the Persian Gulf in the First Half of the 20th Century*. Ithaca Press, 2013.

Zia-Ebrahimi, Reza. *The Emergence of Iranian Nationalism: Race and the Politics of Dislocation*. Columbia University Press, 2016.

Zilfi, Madeline. *Women and Slavery in the Late Ottoman Empire: The Design of Difference*. Cambridge University Press, 2010.

NON-PRINT

AFRO-IRAN (@afro_iran) · *Instagram Photos and Videos.* Unpublished photos from the #afroiran series. The first photobook on Iranians of African descent by German-Iranian @mahdiehsaei. https://www.instagram.com/afro_iran/?hl=en. Accessed 28 June 2022.

"Hasteem: We Are Here." Description and dates of exhibition at Twelve Gates Arts Gallery in Philadelphia, PA. www.twelvegatesarts.org/exhibitions/2021/hasteem.

"In Search of the Lost Laleh-Zar and a Screening of the Documentary Film 'Siah Bazi'." Recording of lecture by Nasser Rahmaninejad, Iranian Studies Program, Stanford University, June 13, 2014. https://shc.stanford.edu/stanford-humanities-center/events/search-lost-laleh-zar-and-screening-documentary-film-siah-bazi.

"In Search of the Lost Lalehzar: A Lecture by Nasser Rahmaninejad." Podcast of lecture by Rahmaninejad at Stanford University Iranian Studies Program, June 13, 2014. https://soundcloud.com/stanford-iranian-studies-program/in-search-of-the-lost-laleh-zar-a-lecture-by-nasser-rahmaninejad-a-film-screening-of-siah-bazi.

Mahdi Ehsaei (@mahdiehsaei) · *Instagram Photos and Videos.* www.instagram.com/mahdiehsaei/?hl=en. Accessed 28 June 2022.

"Qesmathaye az namayeshnameh Tarab nameh" (Sections of the play *Tarabnameh*). Tamasha, October 13, 2017. https://tamasha.com/v/PnK2Z.

"A Rare Look Inside Tehran's Nasr Theater: A Photo Essay." Entry by "Pontia" on her blog "My Persian Corner." https://www.mypersiancorner.com/a-rare-look-inside-tehrans-nasr-theater-a-photo-essay/.

"Tarabnameh: A Modern Interpretation of a Traditional Play." Video recording of Bahram Beyzai's lecture on his play Tarabnameh, with an introduction by Abbas Milani. https://www.youtube.com/watch?v=nPvOYLx5ykE.

"Tarabnameh by Bahram Beyzai." Description of Beyzai's play, produced by the Iranian Studies Program at Stanford University. https://iranian-studies.stanford.edu/events-mediamedia-collectionphoto-galleries/tarabnameh-bahram-beyzaie.

Index

Abedinifard, Mostafa, 199n28
Abjeez, 223n10
abolitionism, 180–81
Academy Awards, 194n11
accents, 143
'Adjaib al-Makhlukat (al-Qazvini), 158, 210n38
Adlon, Pamela, 7–8
Afary, Janet, 37, 136
Afghanistan/Iraq invasions, 4–5, 119
Afnan, 'Abul Qasim, 178–83, 229n21, 229n34
Africa, 35–36
The African Presence in Asia (Harris), 22
African rituals. See *zar*
"The African-Aristocrat" (Greene), 35
The African-Baluchi Trance Dance (film), 125, 126–28, 141
Afriqayi music. See *Dingomaro*
"Afro-Iran" (Ehsaie), 167–72
Afro-Iran (Ehsaie), 169–71

Afro-Iranian Lives (film), 125–26, 127–29, 135–36, 141
Afropessimism, 23, 153, 191
Afsaneh'ha va bavarha-ye jonub (Ravanipur), 63–64
Afshar, Haleh, 131–34, 147, 219n34
Afshar, Sa'di, 92
Agassiz, Louis, 148
"Age, Gender and Slavery In and Out of the Persian Harem" (Afhsar), 131–34, 219n34
agency/victimization, 225n34
agha. See eunuchs
Agha Mohammad Khan Qajar, 224n25
Ahl-e gharq (Ravanipur), 61–63
Ahl-e hava (Sa'edi), 56, 58, 203n28
'*ajab*. See wonder/surprise
'*ajab/'ajaib* literature, 152
Ajam Media Collective, 105
Akbari, Alireza, 63
Akhundzadeh, Mirza Fath'ali, 32–34, 36–40, 198n20, 199, 199n28

251

'*Alaviyeh Khanom* (Hedayat), 48–49
Al-e Ahmad, Jalal: overview, 70–71; and Baldwin, 212n49; and Daneshvar, 74, 75, 79, 89, 207n9, 211n47; and Ellison, 211n47; and Kharg, 53, 54–55; and race, 72–75, 79, 88; and US experience, 76
Algar, Hamid, 34
Ali Aqa (film), 220n51
Allen, Bess, 200–201n11
Alone in the Crowd (Al-e Ahmad), 73
"The American Husband" (Al-e Ahmad), 88
American-Iraq war, 4–5, 119
Amirrezvani, Anita, 227
amnesia, 9, 11–15, 125, 141–42. *See also* enslavement; "good treatment" thesis; wonder/surprise
ancient Iran, 3, 4
anecdotal antiblackness, 175
anthropology, 50–51, 55
"The Anti-Aryan Moment" (Kashani-Sabet), 197n45
Arab, Mohammad, 66–67
Arab countries/culture (other): vs. African heritage, 53; and Akhundzadeh, 33; and geopolitical designation, 5; and Hedayat, 48–49, 51; and Iran distancing from, 3, 4 (*see also* Aryans/Aryan exceptionalism); and kinship, 30; and *1,001 Nights*, 107–8; vs. realism, 40. *See also individual countries*
Arab-Americans, 6
Arabian American Oil Company (ARAMCO), 208n14
archaeology, 202n22

archival photographs. *See* photography (general)
archives: overview, 151, 152–53; loss of, 153; and photographs as degrading, 172; recovery, 154; and revolution, 153; shadow archives, 157. *See also* Khosronejad, Pedram
Archives of the Insensible (Feldman), 222n5
'*Arusi-ye khuban* (film), 109
Aryamehr, 27–28
Aryanism/Aryan exceptionalism: overview, 31–32; and ancient Iran, 3, 4; and Beyzai, 108; and Darius the Great, 28; and Hedayat, 43; and S. Hedayat, 45–51; and R.Q.K Hedayat, 200n4; Iranian vs. Nazi conceptualization, 28–29; and IRI, 30; and Kermani, 32, 33; and Mohammad Rezi Pahlavi, 27, 29–30, 197n45; and neo-imperialism, 30; and Pahlavi language, 27; and race understanding, 18; and realism, 41; rejection of, 197n45; and scholarship, 20, 30–32, 33. *See also* Persian exceptionalism
Ashour, Radwa, 81–82
Ashraf Pahlavi, 29
assimilation: black Iranians, 170; and diaspora, 2, 90, 130; former enslaved people, 14, 24, 132, 170, 197n45; immigrant children, 2; white families, 100
Atash-e khamush (Daneshvar), 77
Atlantic slave trade: overview, 15; in Afshar's writings, 132–33; as benchmark for cruelty, 16; denying Iranian connection to, 138–39;

histories written, 183–84; and Iranian racial thinking, 22–23; in Lee's writings, 182; in Mizari's works, 132–33; in Mozaffari's writings, 170
autobiography, 130
The Autobiography of Malcom X (Malcolm X), 73
axis of evil, 5
Ayalon, David, 163
"'Ayd-e iraniha" (Daneshvar), 78
Azadibougar, Omid, 49, 201n14, 202n20

Bab, 178–79, 180–81, 182
Babayan, Kathryn, 163–64, 225–26n36
Bad-e jin (film), 121–22
Baghoolizadeh, Beeta, 21–22, 37, 81, 160–61, 172, 224–25n28, 226n45, 229n34
Baha'ism, 178–81, 182–83, 228–29n21
Bahari, Mazyar, 162
Bakhtiari tribes, 146–47, 221n68
Baldwin, James, 87, 212n49
Baraheni,' Reza, 213n10
Bashu (film), 99–102
Baskerville, Howard, 69
Bazarbash, Monir Gholamzadeh, 63
Behdad, Ali, 156
Behnam, Mariam, 12, 134–35
Bekhrad, Joobin, 169–70
Belfield, Teddy, 111–14
Better Things (TV show), 7–8
Beyzai, Bahram, 66–67, 98–108, 214n25
bin Mohammad, 'Ali, 188
black Americans: Arab-American identification with, 6; and Baha'ism, 228–29n21; behaviors and slavery, 230n49; and Daneshvar, 79–81, 85–88, 91; Iranian identification with, 6–7, 17; and Iranian-Americans, 114, 142–43, 194–95n13; in *One Nation*, 78; and Shamlu, 216n2; at Stanford, 209n25. *See also* black radical thought
black Iranians: overview, 125; and abolishment of slavery, 14–15; and African heritage, 53; "Afro-Iran," 167–72; Akhundzadeh's heritage, 34; and Al-e Ahmad, 54; as "Arabs," 53; and Aryanism, 32; in *Bashu*, 99–102; vs. black Americans, 114; Collective for Black Iranians, 13, 22, 186–88, 230n45; and Daneshvar's nanny, 91; as descendants of enslaved people, 145; in *Dingomaro*, 139–45; documenting, 149; in *Fear and Trembling*, 59; and historical amnesia, 9, 11–15, 125 (*see also* enslavement; "good treatment" thesis); Kharg Island, 17, 53, 54–55, 202n31; and Mirzai, 125–30; in Persian families, 10–13; in southern Iran, 52–56, 121–22 (see also *Dingomaro*; Iranian South; Southern Style/School); and written testimonies, 130, 132. *See also* enslavement
Black Lives Matter movement, 186
Black Morocco (El Hamel), 24
Black Pearls (Afnan), 178–83, 229n21
black radical thought, 72–76, 81–82, 86–88, 194–95n13, 203–4n44, 230n49. *See also* Civil Rights movement
blackface, 65, 66, 105, 204n45. *See also* Hajji Firuz; *siah/siah bazi*

INDEX

blackness: and Akhundzadeh, 36, 37, 39; and Al-e Ahmad, 54; anecdotal antiblackness, 175; and black Iranians, 145; in *Book of Kings*, 104; vs. brown people, 191; and capitalization, 194n10; and the coup, 70; and Daneshvar, 80–81, 82–85, 91; in *Dash Akol*, 65, 66, 67; in Egypt, 81; and Hedayat critics, 49–50; and Iranian-Americans, 23, 90; and IRI, 17; as joke, 110, 112 (see also *siah/siah bazi*); and Makhmalbaf, 109–10, 112; as metaphor, 76, 82, 89, 94, 114–20, 204n45; of oil, 60–61; and Pushkin, 34–35, 198n17; and Russia, 35–36; and scholarship, 20–21, 23–24; and white masculinity, 208n15; and *zar*, 58, 142. *See also* Iranian South
The Blind Owl (Hedayat), 44, 45
Blues (Rospuli), 216n2
Bodies That Matter (Butler), 209n23
Book of Kings (Ferdowsi), 104, 107–8
book overview, 8–9, 18, 25
Britain, 14, 69
Brown, Jonathan A. C., 196n29
The Brown Album (Khakpour), 2, 190–91
Brown Skin, White Masks (Dabashi), 230n49
brownness, 189–90
Bu Salma (sprit), 61
Buf-e Kur (Hedayat), 44, 45
Bush, George W., 5
Bushehr, 205n57
Butler, Judith, 209n23

"Can the Subaltern Speak?" (Spivak), 175–76, 184, 228n8
Carter, Jimmy, 2

castration, 159–60, 164, 224n25. *See also* eunuchs
censorship, 82, 95, 104, 115
The Chair (film), 86
Chaman Andam, 136–38
chasticy, 138, 220n48
Christianity, 27–28
cinema (general), 98, 123. *See also* individual films
Circassians, 24, 197n45
"A City Like Paradise" (Daneshvar), 78, 83
A City Like Paradise (Daneshvar), 78, 83–84, 86
"A City Like Paradise" (Daneshvar), 78
Civil Rights movement: and Al-e Ahmad, 75, 76–77; and Daneshvar, 76–77, 79–80, 86; and Iranian slavery, 17; and Iranian-Americans, 90; March on Washington, 88–89; Moradian on, 194n13. *See also* black radical thought
class: Daneshvar, 83–84; eunuchs, 227; Hedayat, 48–49; Khakpour, 191; Moaveni, 190; Persian as term, 3; vs. race, 133; writers, 201n19. *See also* common people; elites
clothing, 144, 221n61
clowns, 37–38
Coetzee, J. M., 184–85
Collective for Black Iranians, 13, 22, 186–88, 230n45
collective memory, 94–95
colonization, 6, 24, 82, 84, 155–56, 175, 176. *See also* decolonization; imperialism
The Color Black (Baghoolizadeh), 21, 160–61, 172

INDEX 255

colorblindness: overview, 16–17, 64; in *Dash Akol*, 67; defined, 18; of Islam, 111; and scholarship, 60, 100. *See also* historical amnesia; surprise/wonder
comedy, 37–38
common people, 46–50, 53–56, 201–2n20. *See also* class
"A Complicated Embrace" (Coletu), 81
concubinage, 134
coup, 69–70, 84
critical fabulation, 175, 176
Cronin, Stephanie, 22–23
Culture Institute for the Iranian Language, 51
Cyrus Cylinder, 29
Cyrus the Great, 27, 28, 29

Dabashi, Hamid, 55, 73–74, 98, 118, 206n72, 207n9, 230n49
Daneshvar, Simin: about, 77; and Al-e Ahmad, 74, 75, 79, 89, 207n9, 211n47; and Baldwin, 212n49; and blackness, 80–81, 82–85, 91; and Civil Rights movement, 76; and class, 83; and Ellison, 211n43, 211nn46–47, 212n49; and enslavement, 82, 83, 91; nanny of, 91; and race, 75, 78–81, 82–83, 86–87, 89; racialized, 79, 209n23; and Stegner, 208n16; and United States, 77–81, 82–88, 91
Darius the Great, 28, 29
Dash Akol (film) (1971), 65, 66, 205n66, 206n68, 206nn71–2
Dash Akol (film) (2018), 66–67
Dash Akol (Hedayat), 64–65, 205n64
Dash Akol (play), 66–67
Dashti, Sayeh, 9–10

The Daughters of Quchan (Najmabadi), 14
The Day I Became a Woman (*TDBW*) (film), 115–19
Death of a Discipline (Spivak), 184–85
decipherment, 184–85
Decline and Fall of the Lettered City (Franco), 56
decolonization, 69
Derrida, Jacques, 152
DeSouza, Wendy, 163, 225n34
diaspora: and assimilation, 2, 90, 130; and *Bashu*, 100, 101–2; foreign education, 1; and Iranian new wave, 123–24; and loss of culture, 214n29; and migration, 187; and model minorities, 1; and passports, 98–99; and racism, 105; recognizing, 4; and returning, 5–6; and Sevruguin's work, 155–56; as term, 5–6; and trauma, 150. *See also* exile; Iranian-Americans; United States; *individual people*
A Different Shade of Colonialism (Powell), 24, 81
digital anamnesis, 188
Dingomaro (film), 139–45, 147, 168
diversity, 129
Drake, Sandra, 209n25
Drama in Iran (Beyzai), 98
The Drowned (Ravanipur), 61–63
Du Bois, Shirley Graham, 82
Du Bois, W. E. B., 35, 73
dubbing, 143, 146
Dubler, C. E., 158
Dworkin, Ira, 82

"Eastern Poem" (Akhundzadeh), 34
education, 1

Egypt, 24, 81
Ehsaie, Mahdi, 149–50, 167–72, 173, 226n45
El Hamel, Chouki, 24
Elahi, Babak, 221n64
elites, 4, 5, 15–16, 191, 197n45. *See also* Aryans/Aryan exceptionalism; Pahlavi era; Persian exceptionalism; Qajar era; *individual people*
Ellison, Ralph, 86–87, 211n43, 211nn45–47, 212n49
Emami, Shervin, 62
Encyclopædia Iranica (Algar), 34
Encyclopedia Africana (Du Bois), 35
Encyclopedia of Islam (Dubler), 158
Ennaji, Mohammad, 24
enslavement: abolishment of, 14–15, 55, 128; agency/victimization schema, 225n34; Akhundzadeh on, 36–37; and Baha'ism, 179–80, 228–29n21; in *Better Things*, 9–10; Black Iranians and Black Americans, 17; in *Black Pearls*, 178–83, 229n34; and Bushehr, 205n57; and castration (*see* eunuchs); Chaman Andam's story, 136–38; in "A City Like Paradise," 78; in *A City Like Paradise*, 83; and Daneshvar, 83; and Daneshvar's work, 82, 91; in *Dash Akol*, 66; "discovery" of (*see* wonder/surprise); in documentaries (general), 130–31; domestic vs. plantation, 136; in *The Drowned*, 63; and Ehsaie's work, 168; and elites, 15–16; erasing violence from, 134–36 (*see also* "good treatment" thesis); fetishization of, 172; in *Folktales of the South*, 63–64; and Hajji Firuz, 210n38 (*see also* Hajji Firuz); and Heidari's work, 144–45; hierarchy, 230n49; and historical amnesia overview, 9, 11–15, 125, 141–42 (*see also* wonder/surprise); history in Iran, 14–16, 17, 21–22; images of, 148; Iranians enslaved, 14–15; and IRI, 151; and Islam, 180, 181–82, 183–84; Jamila Habashi's story, 174–75, 185–86; Kharg Island, 17, 53, 54–55, 202n31; language in Iran, 209n21; and Makhmalbaf, 109–10; as metaphor, 81, 82, 101, 213n10; and Mirzai's work, 125–26, 127, 135–36; and mixed race people, 62; and oil industry, 60–61, 62–63; in *In the Palace of Flowers*, 174–75, 185–86; and photographs (*see* eunuchs; Khosronejad, Pedram); population in Tehran, 20; Pushkin's grandfather, 34; and race, 18, 60; rebellion, 187–88; recovery/impossibility of recovery, 154; *Roots* in Egypt, 81; and scholarship (overview), 21–23, 24, 60, 125, 138–39, 177–78, 183–85 (*see also individual scholars*); and shame, 183; in *Slavery and Islam*, 196n29; Sonbol Baji's story, 131–34, 219n34; and southern Iran, 52, 53, 55–56, 63, 64; in *Tarabnameh*, 103, 104; in United States, 148 (*see also* Atlantic slave trade); voices of enslaved people, 154, 175–78, 183–86; in *Waiting for the Barbarians*, 184–85; and written testimonies, 16, 130, 132; and *zar*, 218n24; in *Zelzelah*, 134–35. *See also* black Iranians; eunuchs; "good treatment" thesis; racism; *siah/siah bazi*
Equal of the Sun (Amirrezvani), 227

ethnic diversity, 129
ethnography, 124–25, 217n12. *See also* photography (general); *individual ethnographers*
eunuchs: overview, 133, 152, 157–58, 159–60, 228n19; Agha Mohammad Khan Qajar, 224n25; in Akhundzadeh's works, 36–37; Baghoolizadeh's interpretations, 225n28; in *Black Pearls*, 179; and class, 227; as fragile, 161; and Khosronejad, 162–67; in Mizari's works, 133; as nannies, 162–67; and Nasser al-Din Shah, 161; photographs of, 157; in Pourtavaf's works, 224n24; romanticized, 160, 179; as "ultimate slave," 223n20; and wealth, 166; and wonder, 158–59. See also *siah/siah bazi*
Eunuchs and Sacred Boundaries in Islamic Society (Marmon), 158–59
exile, 1, 4, 5. *See also* diaspora
exploitation, 131–32, 165. *See also* enslavement
Extinguished Fire (Daneshvar), 77

Fanon, Franz, 17
fantastical, 59, 60
Faqir al-Ghameh, 160
Farahmand, Alireza, 209–10n29
Farhadi, Asghar, 194n11
Farhangestan-e zaban-e Iran, 51
Farrokhzad, Forugh, 122–23, 216–17n7, 217n9
Farsi shekar ast (Jamalzadeh), 41
Fatehi, Kimia, 230n45
Fazeli, Nematollah, 47, 50–51, 217n12
Fear and Trembling (Sa'edi), 56, 57, 59
Feldman, Allen, 222n5

feminism, 115–20, 132, 135, 216–17n7
film scores, 221n64
folklore, 40–41, 43–44, 63. *See also* Hedayat, Sadeq; Southern Style/School
Folktales of the South (Ravanipur), 63–64
"Forty Years After" conference, 90
Foucault, Michel, 152
Franco, Jean, 56

Ganj-e payda (Jalali), 160
Gav (film), 58
Gharbzadegi (Al-e Ahamd), 71–72
giving voice, 154, 175–78, 183–86, 228n8
Golestan, Ibrahim, 123, 217n7
Golshiri, Hushang, 201n19
"good treatment" thesis: overview, 15–16; and Afnan, 178–79, 182–83; and Afshar, 219n34; and Dashti, 10; in Iranian-American writer's family story, 11; and Mirzai, 138–39, 161–62; and Mozaffari, 170; and saviors, 80–81, 130, 138
Grass: A Nation's Battle for Life (film), 145–46
Greene, Raquelle, 35
Greeson, Jennifer, 60
Grimms' folktales, 47
"Gulistan in Black and White" (Pourtavaf), 224n24
Guppy, Shusha, 146

Hajji (Haji) Firuz, 78, 83–84, 94, 186–87, 210n38, 225n28
Haley, Alex, 81, 209–10n29
Hamchawn kucheh-ye bi enteha (Shamlu), 216n2

Hansen's disease, 122–23, 216–17n7, 217n9
harems, 131–32, 135. *See also* enslavement
Harris, Joseph E., 22
Hartman, Saidiya, 175–77, 191–92, 228n8
"Hasteem: We Are Here" (exhibition), 187
Hatami, Ali, 97
Hedayat, Jahangir, 205n66
Hedayat, Reza Qoli Khan, 200n4
Hedayat, Sadeq: overview, 43, 44–45; Azadibougar on, 201n14; and class, 48–49; and common people, 46–52; and folklore overview, 45–46, 201n14; language used, 201–2n20; and Menasce, 202n25; and Omm-e Layla, 67–68; research, 200n7, 205n66. *See also Dash Akol*
Heidari, Kamran, 139–45, 147, 220n48
heterosexual romance, 66–67
historical amnesia, 9, 11–15, 125, 141–42. *See also* enslavement; "good treatment" thesis; wonder/surprise
The History of Literary Criticism in Iran (Parsinejad), 44
A History of Slavery and Emancipation in Iran (Mirzai), 21, 133, 158
Homayoun, Nader, 109
homoeroticism, 65–66, 117, 206n68
hostages, 1, 204nn44–45
The House Is Black (film), 122–23, 216–17n7, 217n9
human rights, 29–30
Husayn, General, 24
hybridity, 155–56
hypomnesis, 144

imams, 181–82
immigration/immigrants. *See* diaspora; exile; Iranian-Americans
imperialism, 17, 31, 62–63, 69–70, 146. *See also* colonization; decolonization
Indo-Aryanism. *See* Aryans/Aryan exceptionalism
The Infernal Days of Mr. Ayaz (Baraheni), 213n10
intellectuals. *See* scholarship; *individual people*
Invisible Man (Ellison), 86–87, 211n43, 211n46
Iran: A Cinematographic Revolution (film), 109
Iran Hostage Crisis, 1, 204nn44–45
Iranian New Wave, 58
Iranian South, 52–56, 63, 64, 121–22, 125–26. *See also Dingomaro*; Southern Style/School
Iranian-Americans: and blackness, 23; and Civil Rights movement, 90, 194–95n13; population in California, 101; and race, 90; and racism, 2; stereotypes, 2
"The Iranians' New Year" (Daneshvar), 78, 83
Iran-Iraq war, 100, 109
"Iran's Self-Deprecating Modernity" (Abedinifard), 199n28
Iraq invasion, 4–5, 119
Islam: and Akhundzadeh, 32–33; and enslavement, 36–37, 180, 181–82, 183–84; and Iran distancing from, 3, 28, 51 (*see also* Aryans/Aryan exceptionalism); and Iranian-ness, 4; Mostashar od-Dowle and Akhundzadeh, 199n21; and racism,

181–82; and revolution, 72; and Salahuddin, 111; and unity, 30; and wonder, 158

Islamic Republic of Iran (IRI): overview, 30; black American hostages, 204nn44–5; censorship, 95; discourse on blackness, 17; and enslavement, 151; and Makhmalbaf, 109; and Mirzai, 128; and Palestine, 195n15; and Salahuddin, 112, 114. *See also* revolution

Islamophobia, 4, 150–51, 188

Ismat al-Dowleh, 223n10

Jahanbin, Maryam Sophia, 187
Jalali, Bahman, 160
Jamalzadeh, Mohammad Ali, 41
Jamila Habashi, 174, 185–86, 227n3
Jazireh-ye Kharg (Al-e Ahmad), 53, 54
Jesus, 27–28
Jewish people, 95
Jodayi Nader az Simin (film), 194n11
Johnson, Lyndon B., 211n45
Journal of Music (Hedayat), 51
Judeo-Christianity, 27–28

Kandahar (film), 110–11, 112–14
Kashani-Sabet, Firoozeh, 197n45
Katira'i, Mahmud, 46
Katouzian, Homa, 50
Kermani, Mirza Abdol Hossein Agha Khan, 32, 33
Kermani, Reza, 156
Khakipour, Maryam, 93, 95–96, 230n50
Khakpour, Porochista, 2, 190–91
khanehzad, 46, 200n4
Kharg Island, 17, 53, 54–55, 202n31

Khasi dar miqat (Al-e Ahmad), 73
Khayyam, Omar, 44
Khosronejad, Pedram, 127, 149–50, 153–54, 162–63, 164–67, 172, 173
khvajeh. *See* eunuchs
Kimiai, Masoud, 66, 206n71
King, Rodney, 222n5
Konkou-Hoveyda, Priscillia, 186, 187

Lafond, Jacques, 111–12
laleh, 163–64, 225–26n36. *See also* eunuchs
Lalehzar area, 93, 95–97, 213n8
language: and Al-e Ahmad's writings, 53–54; Arabic word replacement, 51; in *Dingomaro*, 143–44; and ethnic/racial conflict, 100; and Hedayat's writings, 49–50, 201–2n20; and non "Persians," 30; Pahlavi language, 27; and realism in reform, 41; and Sa'edi's writings, 56; translations, 39, 44, 77, 208n16, 211n43. *See also* Persian language
The Language and Culture of the People (Katira'i), 46
Lanier, Tamara, 148, 222n2
Larsen, Nella, 209n23
The Last Muslim Intellectual (Dabashi), 73–74, 207n9
Law, Henry D.G., 50
Layla, Omm-e, 46–47
Leacock, Richard, 86
Lee, Anthony, 21, 22, 174–75, 180, 182, 228–29n21
Legend (Hedayat), 48, 50–51
lepers, 122–23, 216–17n7, 217n9
Lewis, Bernard, 20, 22
Lewisohn, Jane, 96, 213n8

Like an Alley with No End (Shamlu), 216n2
The Limits of Whiteness (Maghbouleh), 6, 23, 90
Lipstick Jihad (Moaveni), 189–90
Listening to Images (Campt), 172
literary writing, 39–41, 43–44. *See also* Southern Style/School; *individual authors*
literature of wonder, 152, 158. *See also* wonder/surprise
Ludwig, Jack, 87
luti, 65–66, 194–95n13, 205n64
luxury, 3

Machineries of Oil (Shafiee), 221n68
Maghbouleh, Neda, 6, 23, 80, 90, 101, 191
Maghreb, 24
magic, 158–59
magical realism, 56–60, 61–64
Mahmoud, Ahmad, 201n19
Majaleh-ye Musiqi (Hedayat), 51
Makhmalbaf, Mohsen, 109, 112–14, 215n45
Malcolm X, 73
A Man of the Theater (Rahmaninejad), 93–94
The Mantle of the Prophet (Mottahedeh), 211n47
March on Washington, 88–89
mardak, 212n49
mardom, 40, 46
Marmon, Shaun, 158–59
Marriage of the Blessed (film), 109
Marvels of Creation (al-Qazvini), 158, 210n38
Mason, James, 146

Masters and Masterpieces of Iranian Cinema (Dabashi), 118
Maziyar (Hedayat), 48
McElwee, Ross, 217n11
memoirs, 130
Menasce, Jean Pierre de, 202n25
Mernissi, Fatemeh, 134, 135
Meshkini, Marzieh, 115–19
Middle East as category, 5
migration, 187. *See also* diaspora
Milani, Abbas, 98, 102, 107, 213n13
military defeat, 39
Mirabedini, Hassan, 58, 60
Mirzai, Behnaz: *The African-Baluchi Trance Dance*, 125, 126–28, 141, 218n24; *Afro-Iranian Lives*, 125–26, 127–29, 135–36, 141; enslavement as disappeared, 162; and eunuchs, 161; *A History of Slavery and Emancipation in Iran*, 21, 132–33, 138, 158
mixed race people, 34–35, 46, 62
Moaveni, Azadeh, 189–90, 230n49
model minorities, 1
modernization: overview, 18–19; clothing, 221n61; film dubbing, 146; foreign education, 1; human rights, 29; and Islam, 33, 51; and oil industry, 60–61; Pahlavi's ethnographic films, 217n12; and Persian-ness, 3; and saviors of enslavement, 138; and United States, 76; and *zar*, 141–42. *See also* Akhundzadeh, Mirza Fath'ali; Aryans/Aryan exceptionalism; folklore; Hedayat, Sadeq; Southern Style/School
Mofid, Bahman, 65, 66, 206n71

Mohammad, Khvajeh, 160
Mohammad Reza Shah Pahlavi: and Aryanism, 27–28, 29–30; coronation, 27; and human rights, 29–30; and Johnson, 211n45; monarchy celebration, 26–27; restoring power to, 69; and soil in exile, 2; and torture, 29
Momen, Moojan, 181–82
Moments of Silence (Kakpour, Vatanabadi and Khorrami, eds.), 100–101
monarchy celebration (1971), 26–27
Moradian, Manijeh, 194n13
Morocco, 24
Morrison, Toni, 208n15
Mossadeq, Mohammad, 69–70, 84
Mostashar od-Dowle, Mirza Yusef Khan, 199n20
Mottahedeh, Negar, 101
Mottahedeh, Roy, 211n47
Mozaffar al-Din Shah, 160
Mozaffari, Nahid, 170
Mubarak, Haji, 178–81, 228n8
multiculturalism, 189
music, 221n64
Muslim Brotherhood, 215n40
My Name is Negahdar Ali and I Make Westerns (film), 220n51

Naficy, Hamid, 65–66, 101, 113, 123, 206n68, 206n71, 217n9
Nafisi, Azar, 213n13
Naghibi, Nima, 118–19
Najmabadi, Afsaneh, 14, 19, 153, 220n48
Namayesh dar Iran (Beyzai), 98
Nasser al-Din Shah Qajar, 39, 96, 155, 156, 160–61, 213n7

nationalism. *See* Aryans/Aryan exceptionalism; folklore
Native Americans, 6
nativism, 72, 73
Nazism, 28–29
"The Negative Images of Blacks in Some Medieval Iranian Writings" (Southgate), 203–4n44
Nepomnyashchy, Catherine Theimer, 198n17
networks, 1
New Orleans, 142–43
new wave cinema, 123–24
Neyrangestan (Hedayat), 47–48, 51–52, 67–68
Nikpour, Golnar, 73
9/11 attacks, 4–5, 6
1979 revolution. *See* revolution
nomad tribes, 217n12
None of Your Business (film), 220n51
nostalgia: and Aryanism, 30; and Beyzai, 104; and Daneshvar, 214n29; and diaspora, 150; and exoticization/exploitation, 214n29; lost radicalism, 195n16; and Mirzai's, 127; Qajar era, 96–98, 155, 223n10 (see also *siah/siah bazi*)
nudity, 165, 166, 170–71

oil industry, 52–53, 55, 60–61, 62–63, 69, 208n14, 221n68
Omm-e Layla, 67–68
Once Upon a Time, Cinema (film), 110
One Nation (Stegner), 78
One Word (Mostashar od-Dowle), 199n20
1,001 Nights (various), 107

Otello dar Zamin-e 'Ajayeb (Sa'edi), 204n45
Othello in Wonderland (Sa'edi), 204n45
otherness: in *Bashu*, 99; and Daneshvar's works, 82–83, 85; and Ehsaie, 171; in film overview, 124; in *People of the Wind*, 146; power in, 190, 191; and recognition, 188–90, 191; and Sa'edi's works, 60. *See also* black Iranians
Oualdi, M'hamed, 24
Owsaneh (Hedayat), 48, 50–51

Pahlavi era, 1, 51, 72, 217n12. *See also* Ashraf Pahlavi; Mohammad Reza Shah Pahlavi; Reza Shah Pahlavi
Pahlavi language, 27
In the Palace of Flowers (Princewill), 174–75, 185–86
Palestine, 6, 195n15
parabolic realism, 118
Parsinejad, Iraj, 44
Passing (Larsen), 209n23
Patterson, Orlando, 167, 223n20
pearl diving, 55
People of the Wind (film), 146
People of the Wind (Sa'edi), 56, 58
Persian exceptionalism, 1, 2–4, 7–8, 25, 30. *See also* Aryans/Aryan exceptionalism
Persian Is Sweet (Jamalzadeh), 41
Persian language, 30, 32, 34, 51
photography (general): overview, 148–50; cropping, 172; as degradation, 172; of eunuchs, 160–67; and IRI, 151–52; and King footage, 222n5; and Qajar era, 155; Sevruguin's work, 155–56; as tool, 150, 222n5. *See also* archives;

Ehsaie, Mahdi; Khosronejad, Pedram
"The Playhouse" (Daneshvar), 78, 84–85
Playing in the Dark (Morrison), 208n15
Polsue, Edward, 28
Pouchkine et le Monde Noir (Gnammankou), 35
Pourtavaf, Leila, 224n24
Powell, Eve Troutt, 24, 81, 183–84
Price, Massoumeh, 136–38
Princewill, Victoria, 174–75, 185–86, 227n3
Pushkin, Alexander, 34–35, 198n17, 198–99n20
Pushkin and the Black World (Gnammankou), 35

Qajar African Nannies (Khosronejad), 162–67
Qajar era: enslavement in archives (*see* archives); military defeats, 39; nostalgia, 155, 223n10; photographs of Africans, 149; photography of king, 155; scholarship, 154–55; and ties to ancients, 3; women in archives, 153. *See also* Aryans/Aryan exceptionalism; enslavement; eunuchs; Nasser al-Din Shah Qajar
Qajar Women's Worlds, 153

race: and Al-e Ahmad, 72, 79, 207n9; and ancient Iran, 3; and *Book of Kings*, 108; and Daneshvar, 75, 78–81, 82–83, 85–87, 89; disavowing (*see* colorblindness); and Ehsaie, 170; and enslavement, 18, 60; and enslavement in Iran, 133; and European Americans, 3; and exile,

4; and magical realism, 56–57, 64; and 9/11 attacks, 5; and "passing," 191, 197n45; and Pushkin, 34–35, 198n17; scholarship, 19–22, 183; and Shafiee, 221n58; in *TDBW*, 115–20; in United States, 188–91 (*see also* Civil Rights movement); and younger generations, 90. *See also* Aryans/Aryan exceptionalism; black Iranians; blackface; blackness; Islamophobia; mixed race people; whiteness

Race and Slavery in the Middle East (Lewis), 20, 22

Racial Blackness and Indian Ocean Slavery (Vaziri), 23

racism: and Al-e Ahmad, 89; anti-black racism, 6; Baha'ism and enslaved persons, 179–80, 181, 228–29n21; in *Bashu*, 99; and black family members, 10–11; and Daneshvar, 79, 87–88; and diaspora, 105; diasporic sites (general), 188; in Egypt, 82; in *Fear and Trembling*, 56, 59; and folklore, 46–47, 49–50; and Iranian-Americans, 2; and Islam, 181–82; as metaphor, 82, 101; and 9/11 attacks, 6; and Persian-ness, 2–3; in United States, 189 (*see also* Atlantic slave trade; black radical thought; Civil Rights movement)

Rahimieh, Nasrin, 62
Rahmaninejad, Nasser, 93–94, 96, 100
Ramadan, Said, 215n40
rape, 135, 137
Rastegar, Kamran, 100
Ravanipur, Moniru, 61–64

Reading Lolita in Tehran (Nafisi), 213n13
Reagan, Ronald, 2
realism, 40–43, 56–57, 59–60, 61–64, 118. *See also* common people
reflexivity, 124
reform, 40
"Reorienting Grass" (Elahi), 221n64
research. *See* archives
Rethinking Global Sisterhood (Naghibi), 118–19
revolution: and archives, 153; and exile, 1; "Forty Years After" conference, 90; and Islam, 72; and loss of culture, 214n29; and monarchy celebrations, 26; and musicians, 140; and scholarship, 72, 125; and *Westoxication*, 72. *See also* Islamic Republic of Iran
Reza Shah Pahlavi: abolishing slavery, 14, 83, 128; choosing Pahlavi name, 27; and Hedayat, 51; modernization through clothing, 221n61
Ricks, Thomas, 22, 202n31
"The Rise and Fall of Lalehzar" (Lewisohn), 213n8
rituals, 126–28, 142–43. *See also zar*
Roots (Haley), 81, 209–10n29
Rosenbaum, Jonathan, 115–16
Rospuli, Mario, 216n2
Russia, 33–35, 39
Ruzi keh zan shodam (film), 115–19

sabk-e jonubi. *See* Southern Style/School
Sadeghi-Boroujerdi, Eskandar, 73
Sadeq Hedayat and World Literature (Azadibougar), 49, 201n14

Sa'edi, Gholam-Hossein, 56, 57–58, 203n38, 204n45
Safar-e Qandahar (film), 110–11, 112–14
Said, Edward, 153
Sa'id, Hamid, 139
Salahuddin, Dawud, 111–14, 215n40
Saleha (enslaved person), 134–35
saviors, 80–81, 130, 138. *See also* "good treatment" thesis
Savushun (Daneshvar), 82–83
Scheiwiller, Staci Gem, 136
scholarship: overview, 18–25; and Afghanistan/Iraq invasions, 119; Aryanism and diaspora, 30–32, 33; on *Bashu*, 100; censorship, 82; and colorblindness overview, 60, 71; and the coup, 70; Egypt rejecting blackness, 81; and enslavement, 60, 138–39, 161–62, 183–84 (*see also* *individual scholars*); and faculty positions, 214n25; and folklore, 40–41; and Hedayat, 49–50; photographs of Africans, 149; Qajar era, 154–55; and race in US, 183; and realism, 40–42; and research (*see* archives); and revolution, 72, 125
secret police, 29
Seeing Race (Baghoolizadeh), 37, 160–61, 172, 224–25n28
Seh qatreh khun (Hedayat), 64–65, 205n64
Sekula, Alan, 157
A Separation (film), 194n11
Serving the Master (Ennaji), 24
settler colonialism, 6
Sevruguin, Antoin, 155–56, 167, 169
sexuality, 87–88, 105, 206n68, 206n72. *See also* homoeroticism

Shadi (film), 95
Shafiee, Katayoun, 221n68
Shahanshah, 27
Shahnameh (Ferdowsi), 104, 107–8
Shahri chawn behesht (Daneshvar), 78, 83–84, 86
"Shahri chawn behest" (Daneshvar), 78
shame, 183
Shamlu, Ahmad, 121, 201–2n20, 216n2
Shams, Fatemeh, 61–62
Sherman's March (film), 217n11
Shirazi, Maziar, 105–6
Siah Bazi: The Joymakers (film), 93, 95–96, 105
siah/siah bazi, 37–38, 84–85, 92–98, 103–5. *See also Bashu*; blackface; *Tarabnameh*
Siraaj (Ashour), 82
Sistan-Baluchistan, 202n25
Under the Sky of My Africa (Nepomnyashchy, Trigos and Svobodny), 34–35
A Slave Between Empires (Oualdi), 24
Slavery and Islam (Brown), 196n29
Slavery and Social Death (Patterson), 223n20
soccer, 28–29
Social Histories of Iran: Modernism and Marginality in the Middle East (Cronin), 22–23
A Social History of Iranian Cinema (Naficy), 65–66
Social Text (journal), 154
Sohrabi, Naghmeh, 158
Sonbol Baji, 131–34, 219n34
The Souls of Black Folk (Du Bois), 73
Southern Style/School, 44, 57–64, 66. *See also* Iranian South

Southgate, Minoo, 203–4n44
Spirit Wind (film), 121–22
Spivak, Gayatri, 175–76, 184–85, 228n8
Stanford University, 209n25, 214n25
Stegner, Wallace, 77–78, 208n14, 208n16
stereotypes: *Afro-Iran* exhibition book, 169; of black Americans, 11, 143; Daneshvar's works, 87–88; Hedayat's works, 49; Iranians in America, 2; and nostalgia, 150–51; Pahlavi's ethnographic films, 217n12
The Story of the Daughters of Quchan (Afsaneh), 220n48
strangers, 60
supernatural, 56, 59, 64. *See also* fantastical; magical realism
"Suratkhaneh" (Daneshvar), 78, 84–85
surprise/wonder. *See* wonder/surprise
surveillance, 151

Tabataba'i, Ali Akbar, 111
Taj al-Saltaneh, 15–16
Taken for Wonder (Sohrabi), 158
Talbot, G. F., 213n7
Tarabnameh (Beyzai), 102–7
Tars va larz (Sa'edi), 56, 57, 59
Tavakoli-Targhi, Mohamad, 41, 49
theatre, 93, 95, 97. *See also siah/siah bazi*
This Flame Within (Moradian), 194n13
Three Drops of Blood (Hedayat), 64–65, 205n64
Toledano, Ehud, 11
torture, 29
transatlantic slave trade. *See* Atlantic slave trade
translations, 39, 44, 77, 208n16, 211n43
trauma, 150
"Treacherous Memory" (Rastegar), 100
The Trouble with Hassan (film), 111–12
Tsvetaeva, Marina, 35
Turkiya, Maleka, 134–35

ummah, 30
United Kingdom, 14, 69
United States: blackface minstrelsy, 105; in *A City Like Paradise*, 83–84; enslavement in, 148, 182, 183–84, 230n49 (*see also* Atlantic slave trade); idealism about, 69–70; imperialism, 17; and IRI, 104; New Orleans, 142–43; race in, 148, 188–91; race scholarship, 183; Salahuddin in, 111. *See also* black radical thought; Civil Rights movement; Daneshvar, Simin; Iranian-Americans

Vatanabadi, Shouleh, 101
Vaziri, Parisa, 23, 141–42, 188, 204n44, 206n72
veiling, 116, 119, 199n21
ventriloquism, 184, 185–87
"Venus in Two Acts" (Hartman), 175–76, 191–92, 228n8
vernacular speech, 41
videos, 90
The Vizier of Lankaran (Akhundzadeh), 38
voice, 154, 175–78, 182–86, 228n8
voyeurism, 123

Waiting for the Barbarians (Coetzee), 184–85
war, 39
Westoxication (Al-e Ahmad), 71–72
White Revolution, 29
white saviors, 80–81

white supremacy, 191
whiteness: and assimilation, 2; and Daneshvar, 80–81; and feminism, 118–19; and Iranian-Americans, 90; and Khakpour, 230n50; "passing," 191, 197n45, 209n23; Persian-ness as, 4; saviors, 80–81; and surprise of slavery, 157–58
The Wild Rue of Persia (Donaldson), 200–201n11
Wilderson, Frank, 191
"Will That Subaltern Ever Speak?" (Powell), 183–84
women, 19, 153
wonder/surprise: overview, 19–20, 152, 157–58; and "naturalness," 171; and ownership, 150; and stereotypes, 169; as suppressing analysis, 166; and "viral" qualities, 226n45. *See also* "good treatment" thesis; historical amnesia
writing, 39–41, 43–44. *See also* Southern Style/School; *individual authors*

X, Malcolm, 73

Yalzadeh, Ida, 90
Yaqut Khan, 164–65
Yek Kalameh (Mostashar od-Dowle), 199n20
You Belong (Dashti), 9–10
younger generations, 7–8, 90

Zaban va farhang-e mardom (Katira'i), 46
Zanj Rebellion, 187–88
Zanzibar, 54, 55, 126, 203n38, 217–18n17, 220n53
zar: overview, 58, 203n40; and Beyzai's works, 101; in *Dingomaro*, 140–41; in *Spirit Wind*, 121–22; and Mirzai's works, 126, 218n24; in *People of the Wind*, 56, 58, 203n38
Zarei, Gholam, 141, 168
Zdanowski, Jerzy, 22
Zell-e Soltan, 164–65
Zelzelah (Behnam), 12, 134–35
Zia-Ebrahimi, Reza, 4
Zoroastrian uprising, 48–49
Zwarte Piet (character), 210n38

Stanford Studies in Middle Eastern and
Islamic Societies and Cultures

Lara Deeb and Sherene Seikaly, editors

The State of Lebanon: Popular Politics and Institution Building in the Wake of Independence   2026
ZIAD M. ABU-RISH

Plots and Deeds: Agrarian Annihilation and the Fight for Land Justice in Palestine   2026
PAUL KOHLBRY

Race and the Question of Palestine   2025
LANA TATOUR AND RONIT LENTIN, EDITORS

Dust That Never Settles: Literary Afterlives of the Iran-Iraq War   2025
AMIR MOOSAVI

The Revolution Within: Islamic Media and the Struggle for a New Egypt   2025
YASMIN MOLL

Unruly Labor: A History of Oil in the Arabian Sea   2024
ANDREA WRIGHT

The Incarcerated Modern: Prisons and Public Life in Iran   2024
GOLNAR NIKPOUR

Elastic Empire: Refashioning War Through Aid in Palestine   2023
LISA BHUNGALIA

Colonizing Palestine: The Zionist Left and the Making of the Palestinian Nakba   2023
AREEJ SABBAGH-KHOURY

On Salafism: Concepts and Contexts   2023
AZMI BISHARA

Revolutions Aesthetic: A Cultural History of Ba'thist Syria   2022
MAX WEISS

Street-Level Governing: Negotiating the State in Urban Turkey 2022
ELISE MASSICARD

Protesting Jordan: Geographies of Power and Dissent 2022
JILLIAN SCHWEDLER

Media of the Masses: Cassette Culture in Modern Egypt 2022
ANDREW SIMON

States of Subsistence: The Politics of Bread in Contemporary Jordan 2022
JOSÉ CIRO MARTÍNEZ

Between Dreams and Ghosts: Indian Migration and Middle Eastern Oil 2021
ANDREA WRIGHT

Bread and Freedom: Egypt's Revolutionary Situation 2021
MONA EL-GHOBASHY

Paradoxes of Care: Children and Global Medical Aid in Egypt 2021
RANIA KASSAB SWEIS

The Politics of Art: Dissent and Cultural Diplomacy in Lebanon, Palestine, and Jordan 2021
HANAN TOUKAN

The Paranoid Style in American Diplomacy: Oil and Arab Nationalism in Iraq 2021
BRANDON WOLFE-HUNNICUTT

Screen Shots: State Violence on Camera in Israel and Palestine 2021
REBECCA L. STEIN

Dear Palestine: A Social History of the 1948 War 2021
SHAY HAZKANI

A Critical Political Economy of the Middle East and North Africa 2020
JOEL BEININ, BASSAM HADDAD, AND SHERENE SEIKALY, EDITORS

Showpiece City: How Architecture Made Dubai 2020
TODD REISZ

Archive Wars: The Politics of History in Saudi Arabia 2020
ROSIE BSHEER

For a complete listing of titles in this series, visit the Stanford University Press website, www.sup.org.

www.ingramcontent.com/pod-product-compliance
Ingram Content Group UK Ltd.
Pitfield, Milton Keynes, MK11 3LW, UK
UKHW040902220126
467228UK00005B/326